THE COMPLETE
THÉRÈSE OF LISIEUX

Sister Thérèse of the Child Jesus

PARACLETE
GIANTS

The COMPLETE

OF LISIEUX

Translated and Edited by
Robert J. Edmonson, CJ

 PARACLETE PRESS BREWSTER, MASSACHUSETTS

The Complete Thérèse of Lisieux

2009 First Printing

Part One and Appendix 2, Copyright © 2009 by Paraclete Press, Inc.
Introduction, Parts Two through Five, and Appendix 1, Copyright © 2009
by Robert J. Edmonson

ISBN 978-1-55725-670-6

Library of Congress Cataloging-in-Publication Data

Thérèse, de Lisieux, Saint, 1873-1897.
  [Histoire d'une âme. English]
  The complete Thérèse of Lisieux / translated and edited by Robert J. Edmonson.
    p. cm.
  ISBN 978-1-55725-670-6
  1. Thérèse, de Lisieux, Saint, 1873-1897. 2. Christian saints--France--Lisieux--Biography.
3. Lisieux (France)--Biography. I. Edmonson, Robert J. II. Title.
  BX4700.T5A3 2009
  282.092--dc22
  [B]
                              2009021239

10 9 8 7 6 5 4 3 2 1

Published by Paraclete Press
Brewster, Massachusetts
www.paracletepress.com
Printed in the United States of America

CONTENTS

INTRODUCTION TO
The Complete Thérèse of Lisieux

When in 1997 Pope John Paul II declared Thérèse of Lisieux a Doctor of the Church, the number of saints with this title rose to thirty-three, of whom only three are women: Catherine of Siena, Teresa of Avila, and the humble saint whose story is told in these pages.

Thérèse would probably be surprised to find herself designated a Doctor, even though her life's aim was, as she told her father at an early age, to be "a great saint." Was she extraordinary? To be sure. But she taught us that ordinary people can have an extraordinary love for God *if* our hearts are turned to God as hers was.

No better explanation of Thérèse's contribution to all of Christendom can be given than that of Pope John Paul II, in his homily of October 19, 1997:

> Thérèse of the Child Jesus and the Holy Face is the youngest of all the "doctors of the Church," but her ardent spiritual journey shows such maturity, and the insights of faith expressed in her writings are so vast and profound that they deserve a place among the great spiritual masters. . . .
>
> Thérèse of Lisieux did not only grasp and describe the profound truth of Love as the centre and heart of the Church, but in her short life she lived it intensely. It is precisely this convergence of doctrine and concrete experience, of truth and life, of teaching and practice, which shines with particular brightness in this saint, and which makes her an attractive model especially for young people and for those who are seeking true meaning for their life.
>
> Before the emptiness of so many words, Thérèse offers another solution, the one Word of salvation which, understood and lived in silence, becomes a source of renewed life. She counters a rational culture, so often overcome by practical materialism, with the disarming simplicity of the "little way" which, by returning to the essentials, leads to the secret of all life: the divine Love that surrounds and penetrates every human venture.

In a time like ours, so frequently marked by an ephemeral and hedonistic culture, this new doctor of the Church proves to be remarkably effective in enlightening the mind and heart of those who hunger and thirst for truth and love.

THE HISTORICAL SETTING

St. Thérèse of Lisieux was born on January 2, 1873, and baptized two days later as Marie-Françoise-Thérèse Martin. This was just two years after the Franco-Prussian War had ended with the collapse of the French armed forces, the ending of France's Second Empire, and the creation of the Third Republic. The nineteenth-century Church into which Thérèse was baptized had fallen greatly from its former glory. The leaders of the French Revolution ravaged the Church during the latter part of the eighteenth century, and even after the restoration of the French monarchy in 1814, other revolutions broke out in 1830 and 1848, creating conditions that would prevent the Church from ever regaining its pre-Revolutionary power. And yet, in 1815 the Carmelite order was reintroduced into France, and by 1880 there were 113 convents of Discalced Carmelite nuns.

The Carmelites take their name from Mount Carmel, a group of mountains in the Holy Land. Inspired by the prophet Elijah, who had defeated the prophets of Baal on these same mountains, a thirteenth-century group of men comprised of former Crusaders and pilgrims settled on Mount Carmel and took the name of the Brothers of the Blessed Virgin Mary. In 1206, Saint Albert of Jerusalem gave these hermits a Rule of Life, and the Church officially recognized them as an Order. In 1452, Blessed John Soreth, then Prior General of the Order, added a Second Order of Carmelites, comprised of women religious, and a Third Order of Carmelites, also called the Carmelite Order Secular, or Tertiaries, consisting of lay persons who felt called to live in harmony with Carmelite spirituality outside of convents or monasteries.

In the sixteenth century, the great Spanish Carmelite mystic St. Teresa of Avila was inspired to renew the fervor of the order and return it to its spiritual beginnings. Aided by St. John of the Cross, she began a reform movement that spread to the friars as well. After her death, convents and monasteries of her reform were established in France and Belgium, and from these two countries daughter houses were founded in England, Scotland, and Wales. Today Carmelite convents and monasteries can be found in almost every country of the world.

Founded in 1838, the Carmel of Lisieux was based on the reformed rule of St. Teresa of Avila. Five nuns from the Carmel of Poitiers established the new Carmel, including two senior nuns, Mother Elizabeth of St. Louis, the Prioress; and Mother Geneviève of St. Teresa, the Sub-Prioress and Novice Mistress, who died in 1891, soon after Thérèse entered the convent.

In the mid-1890s, the Carmel of Lisieux was comprised of twenty-six nuns—twenty-two choir nuns and four lay Sisters. Its superior at the time of Thérèse's entrance, Mother Marie de Gonzague, was an educated woman, a refined member of the nobility. In 1893, Thérèse's elder sister Pauline, who had entered the community before Thérèse and had taken the name of Sister Agnes of Jesus, was elected prioress. Mother Marie and Mother Agnes were to alternate as prioress for a number of years.

THE MARTIN FAMILY

Thérèse's father, Louis Martin (1823–94), was a successful watchmaker and the manager of his wife's lace-making business. Born into a military family, Louis spent his early years at various French army posts, where he was attracted to the military sense of order and discipline. Feeling drawn to the religious life, at the age of twenty-two Louis attempted to enter the monastery of the Augustinian Canons of the Great St. Bernard Hospice in the Alps. However, disappointed at finding himself unable to master the required Latin courses, Louis left the monastery and took up watchmaking, settling in Alençon.

Thérèse's mother, Zélie Guérin (1831–77), was also from a military family and was also drawn to the religious life. After an attempt to enter the order of Sisters of the Hôtel-Dieu was denied because of her delicate health, she took up the lace-making trade that had made Alençon lace famous throughout France. Talented and creative, she started her own business and soon became extremely successful.

When Louis and Zélie met in Alençon, they found they had much in common. Their similar backgrounds, their love of order and discipline, and their good business sense alone would have made them a good match for each other, but it was their common love of God that drew them into a union of spirit with spirit. They were married on July 13, 1858.

Over the next fifteen years, Louis and Zélie were to have nine children—seven girls and two boys. But as was all too common in the era before modern medicine, both of their boys and two of their girls died at a young age.

When the youngest Martin child was born, there were four surviving sisters: Marie, age twelve; Pauline, age eleven; Léonie, age nine; and Céline, age three. Thérèse was born weak and frail, and the doctors warned the family to prepare for yet another loss. Because Zélie was suffering from breast cancer, Thérèse was sent to a wet nurse, who fed and cared for her. The child survived her illness and grew strong.

THÉRÈSE'S FIRST YEARS

The future saint had a nature that her mother found challenging. Zélie wrote this about her: "As for the little imp, it's hard to know how she'll turn out, she's so little, so scatterbrained! She has more intelligence than Céline, but she's not as sweet, and her hardheadedness is practically unshakable. When she says 'no' nothing can make her give it up. You could put her in the cellar for a whole day and she'd go to sleep there rather than to say 'yes.' Yet she has a heart of gold. She's full of hugs and says exactly what she thinks."

Despite her hardheadedness, from her earliest years the "little imp" had a heart turned toward God. "She would never lie for all the gold in the world," wrote Zélie. "All she talks about is God; she wouldn't miss saying her prayers for anything."

Not only did Thérèse talk about God, but also she displayed keen discernment about Him. Zélie wrote, "She comes up with answers that are quite unusual at her age; she shows up Céline, who's twice as old as she is. The other day Céline was saying, 'How is it that God can be in such a little Communion host?' Little Thérèse said, 'That's not so surprising since God is all-powerful.' 'What does that mean, "all-powerful"?' 'Well, it means He can do what He wants! . . .' "

Thérèse recalled one childhood event that revealed much about her character: "One day Léonie, thinking she was now too big to play with dolls, came and found us both with a basket full of dresses and pretty little pieces of cloth intended to make others; on top was sitting her doll. 'Here, little sisters,' she said, 'you *choose*, I'm giving you all this.' Céline stuck out her hand and took a little ball of yarn that she liked. After thinking about it for a moment, I in turn stuck out my hand and said, '*I choose all!*' And I took the basket without further ceremony."

THE DEATH OF THÉRÈSE'S MOTHER

In August of 1877, after a long illness with breast cancer, Zélie Martin lay dying. Thérèse later wrote, "I was going to have to pass through the crucible of trials and to suffer, beginning in my childhood, in order to be able to be offered sooner to Jesus."

Years later, after Thérèse had entered Carmel, she recounted an event that followed her mother's funeral. Writing to her sister Pauline, who as Mother Agnes of Jesus was now superior of the convent, she recalled, "All five of us were together, looking at each other sadly. Louise [our maid] was there, too, and upon seeing Céline and me, she said, 'Poor little girls, you don't have a mother any more! . . .' Then Céline jumped into Marie's arms and said, 'Well! You will be Mama now.' Now, I was accustomed to doing just as she did, but this time I turned toward you, Mother, and, as if the veil over the future had already been torn open, I threw myself into your arms and cried out, 'Well, for me, Pauline will be Mama!' "

Thérèse found that her character had changed: "I, who had been so lively, so expansive, became timid and mild, sensitive to excess. . . . I couldn't stand the company of strangers, and I resumed my accustomed high spirits only when I was with the intimate family."

PRESCHOOL

Shortly after Zélie's death, Louis moved his family to Lisieux, where they would live close to relatives. Louis took special care of his youngest daughter, who had been deprived so early of her mother. "Every afternoon I would go on a little walk with Papa. We would go visit the Blessed Sacrament, visiting a different church each day, and that's how I entered the chapel of the Carmelite convent for the first time. Papa showed me the grille in the choir and told me that there were nuns behind it. I certainly didn't suspect that nine years later I would be one of them! . . ."

Louis had a special nickname for each of his daughters: For Thérèse it was "my little queen"—and she in turn affectionately called him "my dear king." Thérèse blossomed under her father's care: "Oh! How could I tell you all the tenderness that Papa showered on his little queen? There are things that the heart feels, but that words and even thoughts can't manage to express."

Every winter Thérèse would fall sick: "When little Thérèse was sick, something that happened every winter, it's impossible to say with what motherly tenderness she was taken care of." Pauline would care for her and serve as her teacher and confidante, just as she would, years later, at Carmel.

Sundays were special days in the Martin family, and Thérèse loved going to church services and sitting with her father. She learned as much from him as from the services themselves: "I used to look at Papa more often than at the preacher; his beautiful face told me so many things! . . . Sometimes his eyes used to fill with *tears* that he would try in vain to hold back. He seemed already not to hold on to earth, so much did his soul love to plunge into eternal truths. . . ." As Sundays were ending, she would grow sad: "I used to think how the day of *rest* was going to end . . . and the next day I'd have to go back to life, work, and learning lessons, and my heart would feel the *exile* of the world. . . . I would long for the eternal rest of heaven, the *Sunday* where the sun never sets in the *Homeland!*"

School Years

When Thérèse was eight and a half, Louis sent her to join Céline as a day boarder at Lisieux's Benedictine Abbey school of Notre-Dame du Pré. Thérèse was unhappy to be away from home: "I've often heard that time spent at school is the best and the sweetest time of life. That's not how it was for me; the five years I spent there were the saddest of my life. If I hadn't had my dear Céline with me, I wouldn't have been able to stay a single month without falling sick. . . ."

The homeschooling that Thérèse had received from Marie and Pauline had prepared her well: "You had taught me so well, dear Mother [Pauline], that upon arriving at the school I was the most advanced of the children my age. I was placed in a class of pupils who were all bigger than I was." But being with older children was a trial for Thérèse. "Fortunately, each night I would go home to my father, and there my heart would expand. I would jump into my king's lap, telling him about the grades that had been given to me, and his kiss would make me forget all my troubles. . . ."

The years settled into a routine, with Céline watching out for her little sister at the Abbey boarding school, especially concerning her ever-precarious health.

The routine was shattered, however, when Thérèse learned of Pauline's upcoming departure for Carmel. "I didn't know what 'Carmel' was, but I understood that Pauline was going to leave me to enter into a convent. . . . I felt as if a sword had been thrust into my heart."

This was the moment when Thérèse became aware of her own vocation: "I will always remember, beloved Mother, with what tenderness you comforted me. . . . Then you explained to me about the life at Carmel that seemed so beautiful to me. As I was going over in my mind everything that you had told me, I felt that Carmel was *the desert* where God wanted me as well to go and hide. . . . I felt it with so much strength that there wasn't the slightest doubt in my heart. This was not the dream of a child who lets herself be carried away, but the *certainty* of a Divine call. I wanted to go to Carmel, not for *Pauline*, but for *Jesus alone*."

After Pauline's entry into Carmel, once a week Louis and the other girls would go visit her at the convent. "Every Thursday we would go as a *family* to the convent, and I, who was used to speaking at length, heart to heart, with *Pauline*, obtained with great difficulty two or three minutes at the end of the meeting. Of course I spent them crying, and I went away with my heart broken. . . . [I]t didn't take me long to fall sick."

MYSTERIOUS ILLNESS AND OUR LADY'S SMILE

Around Easter 1883, Thérèse was struck with an undiagnosed illness. The family called in a doctor, who concurred that Thérèse was seriously ill. Later, Thérèse wrote, "for a long time after I got well I thought that I had become sick on purpose, and that was a *true martyrdom* for my soul."

As the family lavished care on their littlest member, April gave way to Mary's month—May—and it was to Mary that Thérèse turned for comfort: "All of nature was adorning itself with flowers and breathing gaiety. Only the 'little flower' was languishing and seemed to be forever wilted. . . . However, she had one Sun near her, and that Sun was the *miraculous Statue* of the Blessed Virgin that had spoken twice to Mama. And often, quite often, the little flower turned its petals toward that blessed Star. . . .

"Finding no help on earth, poor little Thérèse had turned toward her Heavenly Mother. . . . Suddenly the Blessed Virgin seemed *beautiful* to me, *so beautiful* that I had never seen anything so beautiful. Her face was breathing inexpressible goodness and tenderness, but what penetrated right to the depths of my soul was the 'lovely smile of the Blessed Virgin.' Then all my sufferings melted away, and two big tears burst from my eyelids and streaked silently down my cheeks—but these were tears of an unadulterated joy. . . . Oh! I thought, the Blessed Virgin smiled at me, how happy I am. . . ."

From that moment on, Thérèse began to get well.

FIRST COMMUNION

Thérèse now immersed herself in preparations for receiving her first Communion. "The 'beautiful day of days' arrived at last. What indescribable memories have left in my soul the *slightest details* of this day from heaven! . . . The joyous waking at first light, the *respectful* and tender hugs of the teachers and the older classmates. . . . The big room filled with *snow-white garments* that each child in turn saw herself clothed with. Above all the entrance into the chapel and the *morning* singing of the beautiful hymn, 'O holy Altar surrounded by Angels!' "

And then Thérèse received her first Communion. "Oh! How sweet was the first kiss of Jesus on my soul! . . . It was a kiss of *love*. . . . For a long time Jesus and poor little Thérèse had been *looking at* each other and understanding each other. . . . That day it was no longer a *look*, but *a fusion*. They were no longer *two*; Thérèse had disappeared, like a drop of water that disappears into the ocean. . . . After that Communion, my desire to receive God became greater and greater, and I obtained permission to receive it on all the principal feast days."

CONFIRMATION

"A short time after my first Communion, I went on retreat again for my Confirmation. I had prepared myself with great care to receive the visit of the Holy Spirit. . . . Ordinarily only one day of retreat was spent in preparation for Confirmation, but since the Bishop wasn't able to come on the appointed day, I had the consolation of having two days of solitude. . . . Oh! How joyful my soul was. . . . Finally the happy moment came. I didn't feel a violent wind at the moment of the coming down of the Holy Spirit, but rather that *gentle breeze* the murmur of which Elijah heard on Mount Horeb. . . ."

ILLNESS OF SCRUPLES

After the mountaintop experiences of First Communion and Confirmation, Thérèse's life returned to its normal rhythm: "I had to go back to the life of a boarding schoolgirl that was so painful to me."

Unable to make earthly friends, Thérèse now found herself afraid of losing God's favor as well. "It was during my retreat before my second Communion that I saw myself assailed by the terrible illness of scruples [excessive fear of having sinned]. . . . You would have to pass through that martyrdom in order to understand it well. It would be impossible for me to say what I suffered for *a year and a half*. . . ."

At the end of the school year Céline, having finished her studies, returned home. "Thérèse, who had to go back by herself, wasn't long in getting sick. The only charm that had kept her in school was to live with her inseparable Céline. Without her, 'her little daughter' could never stay there. . . ." So Thérèse left the abbey school at the age of thirteen and continued her education through private lessons.

No longer physically ill, but still suffering from her excessive fear of having sinned, Thérèse confided continually in her godmother, Marie. But Thérèse was to receive one more blow: Marie announced her intention to follow Pauline into the Carmel of Lisieux.

Shortly after Marie's announcement, Léonie left precipitously to try out in the order of Poor Clares. When Marie entered Carmel in October, only Céline and Thérèse remained at home.

Deprived of her one earthly confidante, Thérèse now turned to her departed brothers and sisters for consolation: "When Marie entered Carmel, I was still excessively scrupulous. No longer being able to confide in her, I turned toward heaven. It was to the four little angels who had gone up there before me that I spoke. . . . The answer wasn't long in coming. Soon peace came and flooded my soul with its delicious waves, and I understood that if I was loved on earth, I also was loved in heaven. . . ."

By the time Léonie returned home after a two-month trial with the Poor Clares, Thérèse had been largely freed from her illness of scruples.

CHRISTMAS CONVERSION

A little over two months after Marie's entrance into Carmel, a seemingly innocuous occurrence at Christmas brought about a turning point in Thérèse's life. "It was on December 25, 1886, that I received the grace to leave my childhood—in a word, the grace of my complete conversion."

The Martin family followed the French tradition of placing, in the children's shoes, presents for them to find after Midnight Mass. Thérèse described what happened on this special Christmas: "This traditional practice had caused us so much joy during our childhood that Céline wanted to continue to treat me like a baby, since I was the youngest in the family. . . . But Jesus, who wanted to show me that I needed to undo these childish shortcomings, also took away these innocent joys from me. He allowed Papa, who was tired from the Midnight Mass, to feel annoyed at seeing my shoes on the fireplace, and for him to say these words that pierced me to the heart: 'Well, fortunately this is the last year.' I then ran up the stairs to take off my hat.

"Céline, who knew how sensitive I was, saw the tears shining in my eyes; she also felt like crying, because she loved me a lot and understood my grief. 'Oh, Thérèse,' she said, 'don't go back down. It will hurt you too much to look in your shoes right away.'

"But Thérèse wasn't the same any longer; Jesus had changed her heart! Forcing back my tears, I ran quickly back down the stairs, and, restraining my pounding heart, I took my shoes, and, placing them in front of Papa, *joyously* I took out all the objects, looking happy as a queen. Papa was laughing. He had also become joyful again. . . . Little Thérèse had regained the strength of soul that she had lost at the age of four and a half, and she was to keep it forever! . . .

"On that *night of light* the third period of my life began, the most beautiful of them all, the most filled with graces from heaven. . . . In an instant, the work that I hadn't been able to do in ten years—Jesus did it, being content with the *good will* that I had no shortage of. . . . I felt *charity* enter into my heart, the need to forget myself in order to please others, and ever afterward I was happy! . . ."

THIRST FOR SOULS

Thérèse set out immediately to pray for the conversion of sinners. "I felt myself consumed with *thirst* for *souls*. . . . I *was burning* with the desire to snatch them from the everlasting flames. . . ."

Not content to pray for *ordinary* sinners, Thérèse learned about an unrepentant criminal, Henri Pranzini, who had been condemned to death for murder. Enlisting Céline's help, Thérèse stormed heaven for Pranzini's soul. "I told God that I was quite sure that He would forgive poor miserable Pranzini, and that I would believe this even if he *did not confess* and showed *no sign of repentance*, so much did I have confidence in Jesus' infinite mercy, but that I asked Him only for '*a sign*' of repentance simply for my consolation. . . .

"My prayer was granted to the letter! . . . The day after his execution I put my hand on the newspaper. . . . Pranzini had not confessed; he had climbed up onto the scaffold . . . when suddenly, gripped with a sudden inspiration, he turned back, grabbed a *Crucifix* that the priest was holding up to him, and *kissed its sacred wounds three times!* . . . Then his soul went to receive the *merciful* judgment of the One who declares that in heaven there will be more joy for a single sinner who repents than for ninety-nine righteous persons who have no need for repentance!" Thérèse had gained her first soul for heaven.

That same year, Léonie applied for admission to the Visitation convent in Caen, and this time, she was accepted. A subsequent health crisis caused Léonie to return home, but for now there were three Martin daughters in religious orders. Then, at fourteen and a half, Thérèse found the courage to speak to her father about becoming the fourth.

THÉRÈSE'S QUEST TO ENTER CARMEL

Thérèse struggled with how best to approach her father. "I found the opportunity to talk to my dear father. . . . Through my tears I confided in him my desire to enter Carmel. Then his tears began mingling with my own, but he didn't say a word to turn me away from my vocation, being simply content to point out that I was still quite young to make such a serious determination. But I defended my cause so well, that with Papa's simple and upright nature, he was soon convinced that my desire was that of God Himself, and in his deep faith he cried out that God was giving him a great honor to ask him for his children in this way."

Having received her father's permission, Thérèse thought her path to Carmel would be smooth. But she did not anticipate her Uncle Isidore's firm refusal. However, seeing Thérèse's determination, and recognizing that she truly had a vocation, her uncle relented.

Thérèse later recalled the next hurdles: "A few days after I obtained my uncle's consent, I went to see you, beloved Mother [Pauline], and I told you about my joy that now my trials had passed. But how surprised and disappointed I was at hearing you tell me that the Superior would not consent to my entrance before the age of twenty-one. No one had thought about that opposition, the most invincible of all."

However, the little flower was determined. Thérèse went immediately with her father and Céline to visit their priest, who coldly refused to hear of such a young girl's entrance into an austere religious order. "Finally he ended by adding that he was only the *bishop's delegate,* and that if the bishop wanted to let me enter Carmel, he himself would have nothing more to say. . . ."

No sooner said than done! Thérèse and her father made their way to Bayeux for an appointment with Bishop Hugonin and his grand vicar, Fr. Révérony. "His Excellency, thinking that he was being kind to Papa, tried to make me stay a few more years with him. So he was not a little *surprised* and *edified* to see him stand up for me, interceding for me to obtain the permission to leave the nest at the age of fifteen. However, it was all of no use. He said that before he made a decision a meeting with *the Superior of Carmel* was absolutely necessary. I couldn't have heard anything that would have given me greater suffering, because I knew about the total opposition of our rector."

One last recourse remained open to Thérèse, and that was to ask permission from the Holy Father, Pope Leo XIII himself.

APPEAL TO THE POPE

One week after the meeting with the bishop, Thérèse, Céline, and Louis Martin boarded a train for Rome in the company of a group of pilgrims who were journeying to the Eternal City to celebrate Pope Leo XIII's Golden Jubilee as a priest.

The long-awaited audience with Pope Leo XIII came on November 20, 1887. "Leo XIII was seated on a great chair. . . . I was quite resolved *to speak,* but I felt my courage weaken when I saw, at the Holy Father's right hand, Fr. *Révérony!* . . . Almost at the same moment we were told on *his behalf* that he *forbade us to speak to* Leo XIII, since the audience was going on too long. . . .

"I turned toward . . . Céline, in order to learn her opinion. 'Speak,' she told me. A moment later I was at the Holy Father's feet and had kissed his slipper, and he was extending his hand out to me. But instead of kissing it, I joined my hands together and, lifting toward his face my eyes bathed in tears, I cried out, 'Most Holy Father, I have a great grace to ask of you! . . . Most Holy Father,' I said to him, 'in honor of your jubilee, allow me to enter Carmel at the age of fifteen! . . .'

"Emotion had without a doubt made my voice tremble, so, turning around toward Fr. Révérony, who was looking at me with surprise and discontent, the Holy Father said, 'I don't understand very well.' . . . 'Most Holy Father,' replied the Grand Vicar, 'this is *a child* who wants to enter Carmel *at the age* of fifteen, but the superiors are examining the question right now.' 'Well, my child,' the Holy Father continued as he looked at me kindly, 'do what the superiors tell you.' Then, placing my hands on his knees, I attempted one last effort, and I told him with a pleading voice, 'Oh! Most Holy Father, if you were to say yes, everyone would be willing! . . .' He looked at me fixedly and pronounced these words, emphasizing each syllable: 'All right. . . . All right. . . . *You will enter if it is God's will.*'

"The Holy Father's kindness was so encouraging that I wanted to speak to him some more, but the two gentlemen of the Papal Guard *touched me politely* to make me stand. . . . The two Papal Guards carried me so to speak as far as the door."

Thérèse had pleaded her case before the highest authority in the Church, and now the audience was over. The remainder of the pilgrimage passed in a blur, and the three Martins returned home.

ENTRANCE INTO CARMEL

Immediately Thérèse went to visit Pauline at Carmel and told her every detail of the trip. Pauline told her to write His Excellency the bishop to remind him about his promise. Thérèse did so, and then waited. But Christmas came, and there was no response.

On the day before her fifteenth birthday, Thérèse received the news that her desire had been granted—but she would have to wait: "The first day of the year 1888 . . . a *letter from Pauline* [now Sr. Agnes of Jesus] arrived, letting me know that His Excellency the bishop's reply had arrived on December 28, the feast day of the *Holy Innocents*, but that she hadn't let me know about it, having decided that my entrance would not take place *until after Lent.*"

April 9, 1888, was chosen for Thérèse's entrance. "After embracing all the members of my beloved family, I knelt before my incomparable father, asking for his blessing. In order to give it to me he *knelt as well* and blessed me while weeping. . . . A few moments later, the doors of the blessed ark [Carmel] closed on me, and there I received the welcoming embraces of the *dear Sisters.* . . . Finally my desires had been accomplished, and my soul felt such sweet and such deep PEACE that it would be impossible for me to express it."

LIFE AT CARMEL

Despite her youth, Thérèse understood the sacrifice that was now required of her: "With what deep joy did I repeat these words, 'It's forever, forever that I'm here!' This happiness wasn't fleeting. It wasn't to fly away with 'the illusions of the first days.' As for the *illusions*, God gave me the grace *not to have* ANY as I entered Carmel. I found the religious life to be as I had conceived it. No sacrifice surprised me, despite the fact that, as you know, my dear Mother, my first steps met with more thorns than roses! . . . Yes, suffering held out its arms to me, and I threw myself into those arms with love. . . ."

Thérèse's life at Carmel was much more demanding than the picture she paints in her writing. Daily life was rigorous, from rising at 4:45 AM until bedtime at 11 PM. Prayer, occupying about seven hours, was the nuns' most important duty. Work, occupying about five hours, was performed in solitude; it consisted of such tasks as doing laundry, washing dishes, baking, gardening, and caring for the sick. The nuns slept for six hours in the summer and seven in the winter.

Thérèse followed a time-honored path in becoming a nun: Her postulancy of nine months ended with her taking the Carmelite habit on January 10, 1889. The next stage was her period as a Novice, lasting until she made her religious vows on the Blessed Virgin Mary's birthday, September 8, 1890, and took the veil on September 24.

A year later, Thérèse had the blessing of being present at the death of Mother Geneviève, the revered cofoundress of the convent. Soon afterward, Thérèse had a vivid dream: "One night after Mother Geneviève's death . . . I dreamed that she was making her testament, giving to each Sister one thing that had belonged to her. When my turn came, I thought I wouldn't receive anything, because she had nothing left. But standing up, she said three times with a penetrating accent, "To you, I leave my *heart*.""

Mother Geneviève's saintly heart was evident in Thérèse's behavior during the epidemic of influenza that attacked the convent in the winter of 1890–91. "The day of my nineteenth birthday was celebrated by a death, followed soon by two others. At that time I was the only one in the sacristy. The head Sister for this duty being gravely ill, I was the one who had to prepare the burials, open the grilles of the choir at the time of Mass, etc. God had given me many graces of strength at that time. . . . Death was the rule everywhere. The sickest ones were cared for by those who could hardly walk. As soon as one Sister had given up her last breath, we were obliged to leave her alone."

When the surviving members of the community recovered, Thérèse had gained acceptance. Most of the members of the Carmel community saw Thérèse as a simple little girl who became a good nun, but nothing more. In her nine years in the convent, Sr. Thérèse worked in the sacristy, cleaned the refectory, painted pictures, wrote short plays with religious themes for the Sisters, and composed poems.

THÉRÈSE'S LITTLE WAY

In a letter to her sister Marie, Thérèse described one of her best-known legacies—her "little way":

"I want to seek the means of going to heaven by a little way that is very straight, very short, a completely new little way.

"We're in an age of inventions. Now there's no more need to climb the steps of a staircase. In rich homes there are elevators that replace stairs to great advantage. I would also like to find an elevator to lift me up to Jesus, because I'm too little to climb the rough staircase of perfection. So I sought in the holy books the indication of the elevator that is the object of my desire, and I read these words that come from the mouth of Eternal Wisdom: 'Let all who are *simple* come to my house.' So I came, suspecting that I had found what I was looking for, and wanting to know, God, what You would do with the simple little one who would respond to Your call.

"I've continued my search, and here is what I've found: 'As a mother comforts her child, so I will comfort you. . . . [Y]ou will nurse and be carried on her arm and dandled on her knees.' Oh! Never have words more tender, more melodious, come to rejoice my soul. The elevator that must lift me up to heaven is Your arms, Jesus! For that I do not need to become big. On the contrary, I have to stay little—may I become little, more and more."

WRITING DOWN HER STORY

Were it not for the Holy Spirit's leading her sister Pauline, who in 1893 was elected prioress of Carmel, Sr. Thérèse of the Child Jesus of the Holy Face might have passed into obscurity. But in the winter of 1894, Pauline asked Thérèse to write the memoirs of her childhood. Over a period of time, Thérèse wrote the charming recollections that have come down to us as "Manuscript A," comprising chapters one through eight of the traditional editions of *The Story of a Soul*, including this edition.

In September, 1896, a few months after Thérèse showed the first symptoms of tuberculosis, her sister Marie asked her to write a memoir of a retreat she had taken. Thérèse wrote some of her loftiest words in this treatise that she called "My Vocation: Love," which has come down to us as "Manuscript B," comprising chapter nine of *The Story of a Soul*.

As Thérèse's illness worsened, she was finally confined to the infirmary. There, at Mother Marie de Gonzague's direction, less than three months before her death, she penned her last writings, known as "Manuscript C," comprising chapters ten and eleven of *The Story of a Soul*.

Sensing Thérèse's impending death, her sister Marie told her she would be very sorry when Thérèse died. "Oh! No, you will see," replied Thérèse. "It will be like a shower of roses. After my death, you will go to the mailbox, and you will find many consolations." The advancing tuberculosis ravaged Thérèse's frail body, and on September 30, 1897, her exile came to an end. At the young age of twenty-four, she had found what she so longed for as a child: "the eternal rest of heaven, the *Sunday* where the sun never sets in the *Homeland*!"

Yes, heaven would be a place of rest. But in another well-known passage, Thérèse presented a concept of eternity that shows the thinking of her mature years. She no longer saw heaven as a time of rest, but of action: "I will spend my heaven doing good on earth." Millions bear testimony that Thérèse is continuing her mission to do good, to this day.

PUBLISHING *The Story of a Soul*

Sensing the importance of the writings Thérèse had left behind, her sister Pauline, now Mother Agnes of Jesus, proposed to Mother Marie de Gonzague, who in 1896 had been reelected prioress, to publish them in place of the obituary that it was customary to send around to other Carmelite houses when a Sister died. Mother Marie agreed, and Mother Agnes set about organizing and editing the lengthy manuscripts. In March, 1898, Mother Marie sent the revised copy to

Dom Godefroid Madelaine, a longtime friend of the community who had preached retreats there. Dom Madelaine suggested a few changes, including dividing the work into chapters and giving it the title *The Story of a Soul*.

The original printing of two thousand copies of the book was completed in time for the anniversary of Thérèse's death on September 30, 1898. It was an instant success, and reprint after reprint was made. In 1901 the book was translated into English, and by 1906 it had been published in six languages. By the time Thérèse was canonized in 1925, over twenty million copies had been sold in France alone.

Widespread interest in the original, unedited text brought about the publication of a facsimile edition of Thérèse's manuscripts in 1956. The Centenary Edition—a critical edition of Thérèse's complete works—was published in 1988. Further research brought the publication in 1992 of the New Centenary Edition, a copy of which was presented to Pope John Paul II on February 18, 1993.

Much discussion has been conducted about Mother Agnes's contribution to the original text. Did she make excessive changes or edits to the original text? But when the edited book is compared to the unedited manuscripts, it becomes clear that it is Thérèse who speaks in *The Story of a Soul*, not Mother Agnes.

> Cardinal Pizzardo, secretary of the Congregation of the Consistory, wrote on 18th June, 1956, to the Prioress of the Lisieux Carmel: "I am convinced that Mother Agnes was guided, not only by the authorized directives of the Congregation of Rites, but also by a clear inspiration from on high."
>
> A study of the unedited manuscripts makes it clear that the value of her edition lies in its clarity and simplicity; it reveals Thérèse as she really was and makes her teaching available to all. Pope Saint Pius X did not hesitate to declare that "in this account of her life, which has now achieved a world-wide distribution, the virtues of the Maid of Lisieux shine so brightly that it is her very soul, as it were, that one breathes therein."[1]

---

[1] *The Story of a Soul*, tr. Michael Day (Wheathampstead, Hertfordshire, UK: Anthony Clarke Books, 1973), back cover.

Still, the proof of the value of Mother Agnes's work lies in the millions of lives that have been touched by the book that resulted.

ABOUT PART ONE OF THIS EDITION

Many editions of the original French version of *The Story of a Soul* are in the public domain. For the original Paraclete Press edition, I obtained two of them. One was closer to Mother Agnes's edited version in that it did not contain Dom Madelaine's chapter divisions. The other contained the chapter divisions and subheadings that characterize most French editions. I compared the two editions word for word and found them nearly identical. In the very few cases where there were variants, I chose the variant that most closely followed the spirit of the rest of the text.

Out of respect for the writings of this Doctor of the Church, I have given the complete and unabridged text. Every word that appeared in Mother Agnes's edited version appears in this edition, including obscure references that many editions leave out. I retained the author's use of italics and her use of capitalization in places where current usage might call for lower case. I kept her frequent use of ellipsis points, an important aspect of her personal writing style that represents a transition in thought, not an omission from the text. I also retained the author's style of referring to herself in the first person and in the third person, often within the same paragraph. As much as is possible in a translation, I wanted this edition to retain the same feel as the original French version.

To make the text more understandable and pleasing to the eye, I retained Dom Madelaine's chapter divisions and the traditional subheadings. One area in which I exercised editorial discretion was in dividing very long paragraphs and very long sentences into shorter ones.

Since in manuscripts A (chapters one through eight) and C (chapters ten and eleven), Thérèse wrote in conversational style, I used the

English conversational convention of contracting words such as "I'm" and "can't" instead of using the more formal "I am" and "cannot." For manuscript B (chapter nine), which is written in a more formal style of French, I used a more formal style of English.

To avoid confusion between religious persons and Thérèse's natural relatives, I used initial lower case when referring to her sisters, her mother, and her father. The convention in this edition is therefore that nuns and priests are Sisters, Mothers, and Fathers, with initial capitals. When "Sister" and "Father" are followed by a name, their titles are abbreviated as "Sr." and "Fr."—for example, "Sr. Marie," "Fr. Pichon."

Following the practice of many editions, the French sources contained numerous Scripture references, most of which I incorporated into the text within brackets. In many cases, I added additional references suggested by the text.

Thérèse knew the Bible intimately and made constant allusions to Scripture. The Bible she read was based on the Latin Vulgate text by St. Jerome. In most cases, modern Bible versions, translated from the original languages, read much the same as the Vulgate. In keeping with the flowing style of Thérèse's writing, I have used *Today's New International Version* to render most Scriptures into English, and the *New Revised Standard Version* (NRSV) to render a few others. In a few cases, the Vulgate read differently enough from modern versions that to accurately convey the point Thérèse was making, I used the Douay-Rheims version (D-R), which was translated into English using the Vulgate.

Thérèse's words were written to persons who would know the people she described, the events that occurred on dates she mentioned, and the religious terminology she used. To clarify passages that might not easily be understandable to today's reader, I have added brief explanations in brackets within the text itself, rather than using footnotes or endnotes, with the exception of a few footnotes where longer notes within brackets would have interrupted the flow of the text.

ABOUT PARTS TWO THROUGH FIVE
OF THIS EDITION

In the years that followed Thérèse's death, the nuns of the Lisieux
Carmel gathered stories of her final days and published them as
chapter twelve of *The Story of a Soul*. The editor is privileged to
make this final chapter available to English-speaking readers. The
nuns also gathered memories of her words of saintly counsel to
them. Part two of this edition consists of chapter twelve and the
Sisters' remembrances of Thérèse's words of advice and counsel,
both of them unabridged.

In addition to the notebooks that have been published as *The
Story of a Soul*, a number of prayers written by Thérèse have been
preserved. Part three of this volume gives the complete prayers of
Thérèse from the 1920 edition of Thérèse's writings.

While it is the aim of *The Complete Thérèse of Lisieux* to tell the
story of the "Little Flower" through her words and the words of
those who knew her personally, our story would not be complete
without the prayers in part three and the selection of numerous
letters and poems written by Thérèse that comprise parts four and
five of this volume.

ABOUT THE PHOTOGRAPHS AND
ENGRAVINGS THAT APPEAR IN THIS EDITION

In 1920, the Carmel of Lisieux published a comprehensive edition
of Thérèse's writings that included many photographs and engravings.
Through an antiquarian book dealer, this editor obtained a copy of
that edition, in such pristine condition that the bound pages had not
been cut. We are now able to share many of the book's photographs
and engravings with today's readers, nearly a century after the book
was printed.

A Shower of Roses

For well over a hundred years, St. Thérèse of Lisieux's words have brought a spiritual shower of roses to all who have read them. It is to that aim that *The Complete Thérèse of Lisieux* is offered.

—Robert J. Edmonson, cj

PART
ONE
The Story of a Soul

"I have come to bring fire on the earth,
and how I wish it were already kindled!" —Luke 12:49

Remember that this most gentle flame
That You desired to kindle in hearts,
That fire from heaven, You placed it in my soul;
I also want to spread its warmth.
A little spark, O mystery of life!
Is enough to light an immense fire.
How I desire, O dear God,
To carry Your fire far and wide,
Remember!

1
ALENÇON
1873–1877

The song of the mercies of the Lord / Surrounded by love
Trip to Le Mans / My character / I choose all

Springtime story of a little white Flower
written by herself and dedicated to
the Reverend Mother Agnes of Jesus

[my sister Pauline, the current Prioress of the
Carmelite Convent at Lisieux]

I t is to you, beloved Mother,
to you who are twice my
Mother, that I am coming to
entrust the story of my soul. . . .

The day you asked me to do this, it seemed to me that it would consume my heart needlessly by causing it to be engrossed with itself. But afterward Jesus made me feel that by simply obeying I would be pleasing to Him. Besides, I'm going to only do one thing: begin to sing of what I ought to repeat forever: "*The mercies of the Lord!!!*" [see Ps. 89:1] . . .

Before taking my pen in hand, I knelt before the statue of Mary (the one that gave us so many proofs of the Queen of Heaven's motherly partiality for our family), and I begged her to guide my hand so that I might not write a single line that would not be pleasing to her. Then, opening the Gospels, my eyes fell on these words: "Jesus went up on a mountainside and called to him those he wanted, and they came to him" [Mk. 3:13]. Now this is the mystery of my calling, of my whole life, and above all the mystery of Jesus' privileges over my soul. He doesn't call those who are worthy, but those He wants, or, as St. Paul puts it: "'I will have mercy on whom I have mercy, and I will have compassion on whom I have compassion.' It does not, therefore, depend on human desire or effort, but on God's mercy" [Rom. 9:15–16].

For a long time I wondered why God showed partiality, why all souls don't receive the same amount of graces. I was astounded to see Him lavish extraordinary favors on the Saints who had offended Him, such as St. Paul and St. Augustine, and whom He so to speak forced to receive His graces. Or when I read the life of Saints whom Our Lord was pleased to embrace from the cradle to the grave, without leaving in their path any obstacles that might hinder them from rising toward Him, and granting these souls such favors that they were unable to tarnish the immaculate brightness of their baptismal robes, I wondered why poor primitive people, for example, were dying in great numbers without even having heard the name of God pronounced. . . .

Jesus consented to teach me this mystery. He placed before my eyes the book of nature; I understood that all the flowers that He created are beautiful. The brilliance of the rose and the whiteness of the lily don't take away the perfume of the lowly violet or the delightful simplicity of the daisy. . . . I understood that if all the little flowers wanted to be roses, nature would lose its springtime adornment, and the fields would no longer be sprinkled with little flowers. . . .

So it is in the world of souls, which is Jesus' garden. He wanted to create great Saints who could be compared to lilies and roses. But He also created little ones, and these ought to be content to be daisies or violets destined to gladden God's eyes when He glances down at His feet. Perfection consists in doing His will, in being what He wants us to be. . . .

I understood that Our Lord's love is revealed as well in the simplest soul who doesn't resist His grace in anything, as in the most sublime of souls. In fact, since the essence of love is to bring oneself low, if every soul were like the souls of the holy Doctors who have shed light on the Church through the clarity of their doctrine, it seems that God wouldn't come down low enough by coming only as far as their great hearts. But He created the child who doesn't know anything and only cries weakly, He created poor primitive persons who only have natural law as a guide—and it is to their hearts that He consents to come down: Here are wildflowers whose simplicity delights Him. . . .

By bringing Himself low in this way, God shows His infinite greatness. Just as the sun shines at the same time on the tall cedars and on each little flower as if it were the only one on earth, in the same way Our Lord is concerned particularly for every soul as if there were none other like it. And just as in nature all the seasons are arranged in such a way as to cause the humblest daisy to open on the appointed day, in the same way all things correspond to the good of each soul.

———·•·———

Doubtless, dear Mother, you're wondering with surprise where I'm going with all this, because until now I haven't said anything that looks like the story of my life. Yet you've asked me to write without holding back anything that might come to my thoughts. But it isn't about my life, properly speaking, that I'm going to write; it's about my thoughts concerning the graces that God has consented to grant me. I find myself at a point in my life when I can take a look back at the past. My soul has matured in the crucible of outward and inward trials. Now, like a flower strengthened by the storm, I lift my head, and I see that the words of the twenty-third psalm are coming true in me. ("The LORD is my shepherd, I lack nothing. He makes me lie down in green pastures, he leads me beside quiet waters, he refreshes my soul. . . . Even though I walk through the darkest valley, I will fear no evil, for you are with me; your rod and your staff, they comfort me.") Always the Lord has been for me "compassionate and gracious, slow to anger, abounding in love" [Ps. 103:8].

So, Mother, it is with happiness that I come to sing near you of the mercies of the Lord. . . . It is for you alone that I'm going to write the story of the *little flower* picked by Jesus. So I'm going to talk without restraint, without worrying about the style or the many digressions that I'm going to make. A mother's heart always understands her child, even when the child doesn't know how to do anything but stammer, so I'm sure that I'll be understood and read by you who formed my heart and offered it to Jesus! . . .

It seems to me that if a little flower could talk, it would tell simply what God has done for it, without trying to hide its blessings. Under the pretext of a false humility it wouldn't say that it is unsightly and lacking in perfume, that the sun has taken away its beauty and its stem has been broken, while it recognizes just the opposite in itself.

The flower that is going to tell its story rejoices in having to publish abroad the completely undeserved kindness of Jesus. It recognizes that nothing in itself was capable of attracting His divine glance, and that His mercy alone has made everything that there is of good in it. . . . It is He who caused it to be born on holy ground and, as it were, completely imbued with a *virginal perfume*. It is He who caused it to be preceded by eight dazzlingly white Lilies [my older sisters and brothers]. In His love, He wanted to preserve His little flower from the poisoned breath of the world. Hardly had its petals begun to open when the divine Savior transplanted it onto the mountain of Carmel, where already the two Lilies who had surrounded it and gently rocked it in the springtime of its life [my sisters Pauline and Marie] were spreading forth their sweet perfume. . . .

Seven years have passed since the little flower took root in the garden of the Bridegroom of virgins, and now *three* Lilies wave their scented petals around her [now that my sister Céline has also entered Carmel]. A little farther away one more lily [my sister Léonie] is blossoming under Jesus' gaze, and now the two blessed stalks who produced these flowers [Papa and Mama] are reunited for eternity in the heavenly Homeland. . . . There they have found once again the four lilies [my two brothers and two sisters who died at an early age] whom the earth did not see in bloom. . . . Oh! May Jesus consent not to leave long on the far shore the flowers who remain in exile; may the branch of lilies be soon complete in heaven!

Mother, I have just summarized in a few words what the Good Lord has done for me. Now I'm going to enter into the details of my life as a child. I know that where another would only see a boring tale, your *motherly heart* will find charms. . . .

And then the memories that I'm going to bring up are also yours, since it is by your side that my childhood flowed, and I have the happiness of belonging to the incomparable parents who surrounded us with the same care and the same tenderness. Oh! May they consent to bless the littlest of their children and help her sing of the mercies of the Lord! . . .

In the story of my soul up to my entrance into Carmel I distinguish three very different periods. The first, in spite of its shortness, is not the least fruitful in memories: It extends from the awakening of my reason, up to the departure of our dear mother for the Homeland of heaven. God gave me the grace to open my intelligence quite early and to engrave so deeply in my memory the remembrances of my childhood that it seems to me that the things that I'm going to tell about happened yesterday. Without a doubt, Jesus wanted, in His love, to make me know the incomparable mother that He gave me, but whom His divine hand was hastening to crown in heaven! . . .

All my life it pleased the Good Lord to surround me with *love*. My earliest memories are imprinted with smiles and the most tender of embraces! . . . But if He had placed much *love* near me, He had also placed love into my little heart, creating it to be loving and sensitive. So I loved Papa and Mama very much, and showed them my tenderness in a thousand ways, because I was very expansive. Only the means that I used were sometimes strange, as a passage from a letter from Mama shows:

> The baby is an unparalleled imp; she comes and gives me a hug and tells me she wants me to die: "Oh! How I wish that you would die, my poor little mother! . . ." She's scolded, and she says, "But it's so that you will go to heaven, since you say that you have to die to go there." In the same way she wishes death for her father when she's in the midst of her excesses of love.

On the twenty-fifth of June, 1874, when I was barely eighteen months old, here is what Mama said about me:

> Your father has just installed a swing. Céline [three and a half years older than Thérèse] is an unparalleled joy, but you ought to see the little one swing—it makes me laugh. She holds herself like a big girl; there's no danger that she'll let go of the rope, but when it doesn't go high enough, she cries out. We attach another rope onto her in front, but in spite of that I'm uneasy when I see her perched up there.
>
> A funny adventure happened to me recently with the little one. I'm in the habit of going to Mass at 5:30 AM. In the early days I didn't dare to leave her alone, but when I saw that she never woke up, I wound up deciding to leave her. I put her to bed in my own bed, and I pulled the cradle so close that it was impossible for her to fall out. One day I forgot to push the cradle into place. When I got home the little one wasn't in my bed. At the same time I heard a cry, so I looked around, and I saw her sitting on a chair across from the head of my bed. Her little head was lying

on the cross bar, and she was asleep there—sleeping badly, because she was uncomfortable. I couldn't understand how she had fallen into that chair in a sitting position, because she'd been lying in bed. I thanked God that nothing had happened to her. This was really providential—she ought to have rolled off onto the floor. Her guardian Angel watched over her, and the souls in purgatory to whom I pray every day for the little one protected her. That's how I figure this . . . go figure it out for yourself! . . .

At the end of the letter, Mama added, "The little baby has just passed her little hand over my face and kissed me. This poor little one doesn't want to leave me, she's with me continually. She loves to go out in the garden, but if I'm not there she doesn't want to stay and cries until she's brought back to me. . . ." Here's a passage from another letter:

Little Thérèse was asking me the other day if she would go to heaven. I told her yes, if she was very good; she replied, "Yes, but if I weren't cute, I'd go to hell. . . . But I know what I'd do, I'd fly up to be with you who would be in heaven. How would God do to take me? . . . You would be holding me tight in your arms?" I saw in her eyes that she positively believed that God couldn't do anything to her if she were in her mother's arms. . . .

Marie [twelve years older than Thérèse] loves her little sister a lot—she finds her very cute. It would be very difficult for her not to, since the poor little one is very afraid of hurting her. Yesterday I wanted to give her a rose, knowing that that would make her happy, but she started begging me not to cut it, because Marie had told her not to. She was red in the face with emotion, but in spite of that, I gave her two of them. She didn't dare to appear in the house. It didn't matter that I told her the roses belonged to me. "No, no," she said, "they're Marie's."

She's a child who easily gets emotional. As soon as some little bad thing happens to her, the whole world has to know about it. Yesterday after she unwittingly dropped a little corner of the tapestry, she was in a pitiful state, and then her father had to be told right away. He came home four hours later. Nobody was thinking about it any more, but very quickly she went to Marie and told her, "Tell Papa that I tore the paper." She was like a criminal awaiting the judge's sentence, but she has in her little head that she's going to be forgiven more easily if she accuses herself.

I loved my dear *godmother* [my oldest sister, Marie] very much. Without looking like it, I paid a lot of attention to everything that was being done and said around me. It seems to me that I had as much discernment about things as I do now. I used to listen attentively to what Marie was teaching Céline so I could do as she did. After she left the Visitation school, in order to be granted the favor of being allowed in her room during the lessons that she was teaching Céline, I was very good and I did everything she asked. So she showered me with presents, which, in spite of their being of little value, gave me a great deal of pleasure.

I was quite proud of my two big sisters [Marie and Pauline], but the one who was my *ideal* as a child was Pauline. . . . When I started to talk and Mama asked me, "What are you thinking about?" the answer was an invariable, "Pauline! . . ." Another time, I was tracing my little finger over the floor tiles, and I said, "I'm writing 'Pauline'! . . ." Often I used to hear that of course Pauline was going to be a *nun*. So, without knowing too much about what that was, I thought, *I'm going to be a nun, too.* That's one of my earliest memories, and ever since, I've never changed my resolve! . . .

You were the one, dear Mother [Pauline], whom Jesus chose to engage me in marriage to Himself. You weren't at my side then, but a link had already been formed between our souls. . . . You were my *ideal*, I wanted to be like you; and it was your example that, from the age of two, drew me to the Bridegroom of virgins. . . . Oh! What sweet thoughts I would like to confide in you! But I need to pursue the story of the little flower, its complete and general story, because if I wanted to talk in detail about my relationship with "Pauline," I'd have to leave everything else out! . . .

Dear little Léonie [my middle sister, nine years older than I] also held a big place in my heart. She loved me a lot. In the evening she was the one who watched me when the whole family used to go for a walk. . . . It seems as if I can still hear the gentle songs that she used to sing in order to help me go to sleep. . . . In everything she looked for a way to please me, so I would have been very upset if I gave her trouble.

I remember her first Communion very well, especially the moment when she carried me in her arm to take me with her into the rectory. It seemed so beautiful to be carried by a big sister dressed all in white like me! . . . That night I was put to bed early because I was too little to stay at the big dinner, but I can still see Papa coming in, bringing his little darling some pieces of the dessert. . . .

The next day, or a few days later, we went with Mama to Léonie's little girlfriend's house. I think that that was the day our dear Mother took us behind a wall to give us some wine to drink after the dinner (that poor Mrs. Dagorau had served), because she didn't want to hurt the good woman, but she also didn't want us to miss out on anything. . . . Ah! How delicate is the heart of a mother! How it translates its tenderness into a thousand watchful caring acts that no one would think about!

Now it remains to me to talk about my dear Céline, my little childhood friend, but I have such an abundance of memories that I don't know which ones to choose. I'm going to excerpt a few passages from letters that Mama wrote you at the Visitation school, but I'm not going to copy everything—that would take too long. . . . On July 10th, 1873 (the year I was born), here is what she told you: "The wet nurse brought back little Thérèse on Thursday. All she does is laugh. She especially liked little Céline, and she burst into laughter with her. You might say that she already wants to play; that will come soon. She holds herself up on her little legs, stiff as a little post. I think she's going to walk early and that she will have a good character. She seems very intelligent and gives the appearance of having a good future. . . ."

But it was especially after I came home from the wet nurse's that I showed my affection for dear little Céline. We got along very well, only I was livelier and more naïve than she was. Although I was three and a half years younger, it seemed to me that we were the same age.

Here's a passage from one of Mama's letters that will show you how sweet Céline was and how naughty I was:

My little Céline is completely given over to virtue—it's the innermost feeling of her being; she has a truthful soul and hates evil. As for the little imp, it's hard to know how she'll turn out, she's so little, so scatterbrained! She has more intelligence than Céline, but she's not as sweet, and her hardheadedness is practically unshakable. When she says "no" nothing can make her give it up. You could put her in the cellar for a whole day and she'd go to sleep there rather than to say "yes."

Yet she has a heart of gold. She's full of hugs and says exactly what she thinks. It's curious to see her run after me and confess, "Mama, I pushed Céline just once, I hit her once, but I won't do it again." (It's like that for everything she does.)

Thursday evening we were taking a walk near the train station when she absolutely wanted to enter the waiting room to look for Pauline. She ran ahead with a joy that pleased me, but when she saw that we had to go back home without getting on board the train to go get Pauline, she cried all the way home.

This last part of the letter reminds me of the happiness that I felt when I saw you come back from the Visitation school. You, Mother, took me in your arms, and Marie took Céline. Then I gave you lots of hugs and I bent over backward in order to admire your big pigtail. . . . Then you gave me a chocolate bar that you had been keeping for three months. You can imagine what a treasure this was for me! . . .

I also remember the trip that I took to Le Mans; this was the first time that I went on a train. What a joy it was to be traveling alone with Mama! . . . However, I don't know why anymore, but I began to cry, and all our dear Mother could present to my aunt in Le Mans was a little *ugly duckling*, all red with the tears that she had shed on the way. . . .

I don't remember anything about that visit, but only the moment when my aunt passed me a little white mouse and a little cardboard basket full of candies on which were *enthroned* two little sugar rings, just about the thickness of my finger. Immediately I cried out, "Such happiness! There will be a ring for Céline!"

But, such sadness! I took my basket by the handle, gave my other hand to Mama, and we left. After a few steps I looked at my basket and saw that my candies were almost all strewn on the street, like Tom Thumb's stones. . . . I looked closer and saw that one of the precious rings had suffered the deadly fate of the candies . . . I didn't have one to give to Céline! . . . Then my sorrow burst out, and I asked to go back; Mama didn't seem to be paying attention to me. It was all too much—my *tears* were followed by my *cries*. . . . I couldn't understand why she didn't share my pain, and that very much increased my suffering. . . .

Now I'll come back to the letters in which Mama talked to you about Céline and me. They're the best means I can use to let you know my character. Here's a passage in which my faults stick out like a sore thumb: "There's Céline, who plays a dice game with the little one. They argue from time to time, and Céline gives in, in order to have a pearl in her crown. I'm obliged to correct the little baby, who flies into terrible rages. When things don't go the way she wants them to, she rolls on the ground like a madwoman who thinks all is lost. There are times when it gets so strong that she loses her breath. She's quite a nervous child, but she's cute and very intelligent—she remembers everything." You see, Mother, how far I was from being a little girl with no faults!

Nobody could even say about me that "I was good when I was asleep," because at night I was even more wiggly than during the day. I would send the covers flying, and then (asleep all the while) I would crash against the wood of my little bed. The pain would wake me up, and I would say, "Mama, I've been *bumped*." My poor dear mother had to get up and establish that I did in fact have knots on my forehead, and that I had been *bumped*. She would cover me up securely and go back to bed. But after a short time I started *being bumped* again, so that they had to *tie me in* my bed. Every night, little Céline would come and tie the several cords that were intended to keep the little imp from getting *bumped* and waking up her mama. This method finally worked, so from then on I was *good* while I was *asleep*. . . .

Another fault I had (when I was awake) and which Mama didn't talk about in her letters, is that I was very conceited. I'm only going to give

Thérèse as a Child and Her Mother

I remember Mama's smile;
Her deep gaze seemed to say,
"Eternity delights me and draws me . . .
I'm going to go into the blue heavens
To see God!"

you two examples so as not to make my story too long. One day Mama told me, "Dear little Thérèse, if you want to kiss the ground, I'm going to give you a penny." A penny was quite a lot of money for me. In order to get it I didn't have to lower my *great* height, because my *little* height didn't put a big distance between me and the ground. However, my pride revolted at the thought of *kissing the ground*, so, standing up very straight, I told Mama, "Oh! No, Mother, I'd rather not have a penny! . . ."

Another time we were supposed to go to Grogny to Mrs. Monnier's. Mama told Marie to dress me in my pretty, sky-blue, lace-trimmed dress, but not to leave my arms bare so the sun wouldn't burn them. I let myself be dressed with the indifference that children my age should have, but inside I was thinking that I would have been much nicer if my little arms were bare.

With a nature like mine, if I had been brought up by parents who lacked virtue, or even if like Céline I had been spoiled by Louise [our maid], I would have become bad and perhaps would have become lost. . . . But Jesus was watching over His little bride-to-be. He wanted everything to turn out for her good, even her faults, which, curbed early on, have been used for her growth in perfection. . . . Since I was full of *self-love* and also *love* of *good*, as soon as I began to think seriously (which I did when I was quite little) it was enough for someone to tell me that something wasn't good, for me not to want to repeat it twice. . . .

I'm pleased to see in Mama's letters that as I grew up I gave her more consolation. Since all I had around me were good examples, I naturally wanted to follow them. Here's what Mama wrote in 1876: "Even Thérèse sometimes wants to get involved in religious practices. . . . She's a charming child, fine as a shadow, very quick, but her heart is sensitive. Céline and she love each other a lot. They're all each other needs to keep from getting bored. Every day right after dinner Céline goes and gets her little rooster doll. She suddenly catches Thérèse's hen doll—I can't get over it!—but she's so quick that she grabs it on the first jump. Then they both take their animals and sit beside the fire and play nicely together for a long time." (It was little Rose who had given me the hen and the rooster as a present, and I had given the rooster to Céline.)

The other day Céline was sleeping with me, and Thérèse was sleeping on the second floor in Céline's bed. She had begged Louise [our maid] to take her downstairs so they could dress her. Louise went up to look for her and found the bed empty. Thérèse had heard Céline and had gone down to be with her. Louise said to her, "So you don't want to go down and get dressed?" "Oh no, poor Louise, we're like the two little chickens, we can't be separated!" And when she said that, the two girls kissed and hugged each other. . . . Then that evening, Louise, Céline, and Léonie left for the Catholic circle and left poor Thérèse, who understood very well that she was too little to go. So she said, "If only they wanted to put me to bed in Céline's bed! . . ." But no, they didn't want to. . . . She didn't say anything and stayed alone with her little lamp, and fifteen minutes later she was fast asleep. . . .

Another day Mama wrote again: "Céline and Thérèse are inseparable; you can't imagine two children loving each other more. When Marie comes to get Céline to teach her her lesson, poor Thérèse dissolves into tears. Alas, what is going to become of her? Her little friend is going to go away! . . . Marie feels sorry for her, she takes her along, too, and the poor little one sits on a chair for two or three hours. They give her pearls to string or a rag to sew. She doesn't dare budge and often heaves great sighs. When her needle loses its thread she tries to rethread it. It's curious to see her, not managing to get it threaded and not daring to disturb Marie; soon you can see two big tears running down her cheeks. . . . Marie quickly comforts her, rethreads the needle, and the little angel smiles through her tears. . . ."

In fact I can remember that I couldn't be separated from Céline. I would rather leave the table before finishing my dessert than not follow her as soon as she got up to leave. I would turn in my high chair and ask to be put down, and then we would go play together. Sometimes we went with a little friend, which pleased me to no end because of the park and all the beautiful toys that she used to show us, but it was really to please Céline that I would go.

What I really preferred was to stay in our little yard to *scratch the walls*, because we would pull off all the little shiny flakes of stone that we would find there, and then we would go *sell them* to Papa, who would buy them, looking very serious.

On Sundays, since I was too little to go to services, Mama stayed to watch me. I was very good, and I would only walk on tiptoe during the Mass. But as soon as I saw the door open, there was an unparalleled explosion of joy. I would rush in front of my *pretty* little sister, who was then *decked out like a chapel* . . . and I would say, "Oh, dear Céline, quick, give me some blessed bread!" Sometimes she didn't have any, since she had arrived there too late. . . . What could I do now? It was impossible for me to go without it; it was *my Mass*. The answer was quick in coming: "You don't have any blessed bread? Well, make some!" No sooner said than done. Céline would take a chair, open the cupboard, take out some bread, cut a mouthful, and very *seriously* recite a *Hail Mary* over it, then present it to me. And I, after making the sign of the Cross with it, would eat it with *great devotion*, claiming that it *tasted* exactly like *blessed bread*.

Often we would do *spiritual teachings*. Here's one example that I'm borrowing from Mama's letters: "Our two dear little ones, Céline and Thérèse, are angels of blessing, two little angelic natures. Thérèse is Marie's joy, happiness, and glory; it's unbelievable how proud she is of her. It's true that she comes up with answers that are quite unusual at her age; she shows up Céline, who's twice as old as she is. The other day Céline was saying, 'How is it that God can be in such a little Communion host?' Little Thérèse said, 'That's not so surprising since God is all-powerful.' 'What does that mean, "all-powerful"?' 'Well, it means He can do what He wants! . . .' "

One day Léonie, thinking she was now too big to play with dolls, came and found us both with a basket full of dresses and pretty little pieces of cloth intended to make others; on top was sitting her doll. "Here, little sisters," she said, "you *choose*, I'm giving you all this." Céline stuck out her hand and took a little ball of yarn that she liked. After thinking about it for a moment, I in turn stuck out my hand and said, "*I choose all!*" And I took the basket without further ceremony. Those who were watching the scene thought it was quite fair—Céline herself didn't think to complain. (Besides, she had no lack of toys; her godfather showered her with presents, and Louise found a way to get her anything she wanted.)

This childhood trait sums up my whole life. Later, when perfection made its appearance to me, I understood that in order to become *a Saint* you have to suffer a lot, always be in search of what is the most perfect, and forget yourself. I understood that there are many degrees of perfection, and that each soul is free to respond to Our Lord's advances, to do little or much for Him—in a word, to *choose* among the sacrifices that He requires. Then, just as in the days of my childhood, I cried out, "Dear God, *I choose all*. I don't want to be a *halfway Saint*. It doesn't scare me to suffer for You; I'm afraid of only one thing, and that is to hold onto my *will*. Take it, because '*I choose all*,' all that You want! . . ."

I have to stop here. I shouldn't talk yet about the time of my youth, but about the little four-year-old imp. I remember a dream that I must have had around that age and that is deeply engraved in my imagination. One night I dreamed that I was going out to take a walk alone in the garden. Arriving at the foot of the steps that I had to go up to get there, I stopped, paralyzed with fear. In front of me, near the arbor, stood a barrel of lime, and on that barrel two *horrible* little *devils* were dancing with surprising agility in spite of the clothing irons they had on their feet. Suddenly they cast their flaming eyes on me, but just at the same time, looking more scared than I was, they jumped off the barrel and went and hid in the laundry that was just across the way. When I saw how unbrave they were, I wanted to know what they were going to do, and I went up to the window. The poor little devils were there, running on the tables, not knowing what to do to escape my looks. Sometimes they would go up to the window, looking out with a troubled expression to see if I were still there. When they saw me still there, they started running around again like madmen.

No doubt this dream is nothing out of the ordinary, but nonetheless I think that God allowed me to remember it in order to prove to me that a soul in the state of grace has nothing to fear from demons, who are cowards, capable of running away from a child's glance. . . .

Here's another passage that I found in Mama's letters: Poor Mother was already sensing that the end of her earthly exile was coming:

> The two little ones don't worry me, they both get along so well. They are chosen natures; certainly they will be good. Marie and you will be perfectly able to raise them. Céline never commits the slightest voluntary fault. The little one will be good, too. She would never lie for all the gold in the world. She has a mind and a spirit like I've never seen in the rest of you.
>
> The other day she was at the grocer's with Céline and Louise, and she was talking about her religious practices and was discussing this strongly with Céline. The lady said to Louise, "What does she mean, when she plays in the garden and all she hears about is religious practices? Mrs. Gaucherin sticks her head out her window to try to understand what this debate about religious practices is all about." . . .
>
> This poor little one is our happiness, she will be good, you can already see it coming. All she talks about is God; she wouldn't miss saying her prayers for anything. I wish you could see her reciting little fables; I've never seen anything so nice. All by herself she finds the expression that she needs to give, and the tone, but it's especially when she says, "Little blond-haired child, where do you think God is?" When she comes to "He's up there in the blue sky," she turns her face upward with an angelic expression. We never get tired of having her do it, it's so beautiful. There's something so heavenly in her look that we're quite taken by it! . . .

Oh, Mother! How happy I was at that age. Already I was beginning to enjoy life. Virtue had its charms for me, and I was, it seems to me, already disposed in the same way I am now, already having great control over my actions. Ah! How quickly they passed by, those sunny years of my early childhood, but what a sweet imprint they left on my soul!

I remember with happiness the days when Papa took us to the *cottage* [Papa's little property at the entrance to the city]; the slightest details are engraved on my heart. . . . I especially remember the Sunday walks when Mama always went with us. . . . I can still feel the deep and *poetic* impressions that were born in my soul at the sight of the wheat fields spangled with *cornflowers* and wildflowers. Already I loved *faraway places.* . . . The spaces and the giant pine trees with branches touching the ground left in my heart an impression like the one I still feel today at the sight of nature. . . .

Often during these long walks we used to meet poor people, and it was always little Thérèse whose duty it was to give them alms, and she was happy to do so. But also, Papa often would find that the route was too long for his little queen, so he would take her home earlier than the others (much to her great displeasure). So, to comfort her, Céline would fill her pretty little basket with daisies and give them to her when she got back home. But alas! The poor "granny" would find that her "granddaughter" had too many of them, so she would take a good part of them to [place in front of the statue of] the Blessed Virgin. . . . Little Thérèse didn't like that, but she was careful not to say anything about it, having adopted the good habit of never complaining, even when something that belonged to her was taken away, or when she was unjustly accused. She preferred to hold her tongue and not excuse herself. This wasn't merit on her part, but natural virtue. . . .

What a shame that this good disposition vanished! . . . Oh! truly, everything on earth was smiling at me: I found flowers under every one of my steps, and my happy character also contributed to making my life pleasant. But a new period was going to begin for my soul. I was going to have to pass through the crucible of trials and to suffer, beginning in my childhood, in order to be able to be offered sooner to Jesus. In the same way as the springtime flowers begin to germinate under the snow and begin to open at the first rays of the Sun, even so the little flower whose memories I'm writing about had to pass through the winter of trial. . . .

2

AT "LES BUISSONNETS"
1877–1881

Mama's death / Lisieux / Papa's tenderness / First confession
Family holidays and Sundays / Prophetic vision / Trouville

All the details of our dear mother's illness are still present in my heart. I especially remember the last weeks that she spent on earth. Céline and I were like little exiles. Every morning Mrs. Leriche would come and get us, and we would spend the day at her place. One day we hadn't had the time to say our prayers before leaving, and as we went, Céline whispered to me, "Should we tell her that we haven't said our prayers? . . ."

"Oh, yes," I answered. So, timidly, she told Mrs. Leriche, who replied, "Well, little girls, you're going to say them." And then, putting us both in a big room, she left. . . . Then Céline looked at me, and we said, "Oh, that's not like Mama. . . . She always had us say our prayers with her! . . ."

When we played with other children, the thought of our dear mother always stayed with us. Once Céline was given a beautiful apricot. She leaned over and whispered to me, "We aren't going to eat it; I'm going to give it to Mama." Alas, our dear little mother was already too sick to eat the fruits of the earth. She was no longer able to have her hunger *satisfied* except in heaven, filled with the *glory* of God, and her thirst assuaged except by *drinking* with Jesus *the mysterious wine* that He talked about in His Last Supper, when He said that He would share it with us in His Father's kingdom [Mt. 26:29].

The touching ceremony of Last Rites is also imprinted on my soul. I can still see the place where I stood beside Céline. All five of us stood, from oldest to youngest, and our dear father was also there, sobbing. . . .

The day after Mama left us, or perhaps the next, he took me in his arms and said, "Let's go kiss your poor little mother one last time." And without saying anything, I reached my lips to my dear mother's forehead. . . . I don't remember crying a lot; I didn't talk to anyone about the deep feelings I was experiencing. . . . I watched and listened in silence. . . . Nobody had the time to be concerned with me, so I saw lots of things that they might have wanted to keep hidden from me. Once, I found myself standing in front of the coffin lid. . . . I stopped and considered it for a long time. I had never seen anything like it, but nevertheless I understood. . . . I was so little that despite Mama's short stature, I was obliged to *raise* my head to see the top, and it seemed very *big* . . . very *vast* to me. . . .

Fifteen years later I found myself in front of another coffin, that of Mother Geneviève [the cofoundress of the Carmel at Lisieux]; it was the same size as Mama's, and I thought I was back in the days of my childhood. . . . All my memories crowded in. It really was the same little Thérèse who was watching, but she had *grown up* and the coffin looked little to her. She didn't have to *raise* her head to see it; she no longer *raised* it except to contemplate *heaven*, which seemed *quite joyful* to her, because all her trials had come to an end and the winter of her soul had passed away forever [Song 2:10–11]. . . .

The day when the Church blessed the mortal remains of our dear mother, who was now in heaven, it was God's will to give me another mother on earth, and He wanted me to choose her freely. All five of us were together, looking at each other sadly. Louise [our maid] was there, too, and upon seeing Céline and me, she said, "Poor little girls, you don't have a mother any more! . . ." Then Céline jumped into Marie's arms and said, "Well! You will be Mama now." Now, I was accustomed to doing just as she did, but this time I turned toward you, Mother, and, as if the veil over the future had already been torn open, I threw myself into your arms and cried out, "Well, for me, Pauline will be Mama!"

As I said before, beginning with this time in my life I had to enter the second period of my existence, the most painful of the three, especially after the entrance into the Carmelite convent of the one whom I had chosen to be my second "Mama." This period stretches from the age of four and a half until my fourteenth year, the period when I found my character as a *child* again, while yet entering into the seriousness of life.

I have to tell you, Mother, that starting with Mama's death, my happy character changed completely. I, who had been so lively, so expansive, became timid and mild, sensitive to excess. One look was enough to make me burst into tears. I was happy only when nobody was bothering with me. I couldn't stand the company of strangers, and I resumed my customary high spirits only when I was with the intimate family. . . .

Nonetheless, I continued to be surrounded by the most delicate *tenderness*. Papa's heart, which was so *tender*, had joined a truly motherly love to the love that he already had! . . . Weren't you, Mother, and Marie the *most tender*, the most impartial of mothers to me? . . . Oh! If God hadn't lavished His kindly *rays* on His little flower, she would never have been able to become acclimated to the earth. She was still too weak to endure rain and storms; she needed warmth, gentle dew, and springtime breezes. She never went without these blessings; Jesus caused her to find them, even underneath the snows of trials!

———·—·———

I wasn't upset at leaving Alençon. Children like change, and I was pleased to go to Lisieux. I remember the trip and arriving in the evening at my aunt's. I can still see Jeanne and Marie [my cousins] who were waiting for us at the door. . . . I was so happy to have such nice little cousins. I loved them a lot, as well as my aunt [Céline Guérin] and especially my uncle [Isidore Guérin, Mama's brother]—only I was afraid of him, and I didn't feel at ease in his home as I did at "Les Buissonnets" ["The Hedges," our family's rented house]—it was there that my life was truly happy. . . .

In the morning you would come see me and ask me if I had given my heart to God. Then you would dress me while talking about Him, and then, at your side, I would say my prayers. After that came my reading lesson. The first word I could read by myself was this: "Heaven." My dear godmother [my sister Marie] was in charge of the writing lessons, and you, Mother, were in charge of all the others. I didn't find it very easy to learn, but I had a good memory. Catechism and sacred history were my favorites. I used to study them with joy, but grammar often brought me to tears. . . . "Remember which French nouns are masculine and which are feminine!"

As soon as my class was over, I would climb up on the belvedere [a small, roofed pavilion] carrying my little red chalk and my note for Papa. How happy I was when I could tell him, "I got a five without any *exceptions*. *Pauline* was the one who said it *first*! . . ." That's because when I asked you if I got a five without any exceptions and you said yes, in my eyes it was one point less. You also used to give me points for being good. When I had accumulated a certain number of them, I got a reward and a day off. I remember that those days seemed much longer to me than the others, and that pleased you, since that showed that I didn't like to sit around doing nothing.

Every afternoon I would go on a little walk with Papa. We would go visit the Blessed Sacrament, visiting a different church each day, and that's how I entered the chapel of the Carmelite convent for the first time. Papa showed me the grille in the choir and told me that there were nuns behind it. I certainly didn't suspect that nine years later I would be one of them! . . .

After our walk, during which Papa always used to buy me a little gift for a small coin or two, I would go back home. Then I would do my homework, and then all the rest of the time I would stay to go skipping in the garden around Papa, because I didn't *know how* to play with dolls.

It was a great joy to me to prepare "herb teas" using little grains from tree bark that I would find on the ground. I would then take them to Papa in a pretty little cup. Poor Papa would leave his work and then, smiling, pretend to drink it. Before giving me back the cup he would ask me (sort of on the sly) if he should toss the contents. Sometimes I would say yes, but more often I would take away my precious herb tea, wanting to serve it several times. . . .

I used to love to cultivate my little flowers in the garden that Papa had given me. I would have a good time making little altars in the hollow that was in the middle of the wall. When I had finished, I would run to Papa, and, leading him along, I would tell him to shut his eyes tight and open them only when I told him to. He did everything I wanted, and let himself be led to my little garden. Then I would cry out, "Papa, open your eyes!" He would open them and gush in order to give me pleasure, admiring what I thought was a masterpiece! . . .

I'd never stop if I told you the thousand little stories like that one that come crowding into my memory. . . . Oh! How could I tell you all the tenderness that Papa showered on his little queen? There are things that the heart feels, but that words and even thoughts can't manage to express. . . .

Those were beautiful days for me, days when my "dear king" used to take me fishing with him. I used to love the country, the flowers, and the birds so much! Sometimes I would try to fish with my little fishing pole, but I preferred to go sit *alone* on the flower-covered ground. Then my thoughts were very deep, and without knowing what it meant to meditate, my soul would plunge into real prayer. . . . I would hear distant noises. . . . The murmur of the wind and even the distant, indistinct music of soldiers whose sounds came to my ears would bring a sweet melancholy to my heart. . . . The earth seemed to me a place of exile, and I would dream of heaven. . . .

The afternoon would pass by quickly, and soon we would have to go back to "Les Buissonnets." But before leaving I would take out the snack that I had brought in my little basket. The *beautiful* bread and jam that you had prepared for me had changed in appearance: Instead of its bright color I saw only a light rose tint, old and worn out. . . . Then the world seemed still sadder, and I understood that only in heaven would joy be without clouds. . . .

Speaking of clouds, I remember that one day the beautiful blue sky of the countryside covered over and soon a storm began to rumble. Lightning streaked across the dark clouds, and I saw thunderbolts strike. Not at all frightened, I was thrilled. It seemed that God was so close to me! . . . Papa was not at all as happy as his little queen; it was not that the storm made him afraid, but the grass and the big daisies (which were as tall as I was) shimmered with raindrops like precious stones. We had to cross several meadows before finding our way, and my dear father, fearing that the diamonds would get his little girl wet, picked her up, despite his baggage of fishing poles, and carried her on his back.

During the walks that I used to take with Papa, he liked to have me give alms to the poor people we met. One day we saw a man who was hobbling along painfully on crutches. I approached him and offered him a small coin, but, not finding himself poor enough to receive charity, he looked at me, smiling sadly, and refused to take what I was offering him. I can't say what happened in my heart; I would have liked to give him some comfort, some relief. Instead of that I thought I had hurt him. No doubt the poor invalid guessed what I was thinking, because I saw him turn around and smile at me.

Papa had just bought me a cake. I really wanted to give it to the man, but I didn't dare. But I wanted to give him something that he couldn't refuse, because I felt great sympathy for him. So I remembered hearing that on the day of your first Communion you get whatever you ask for. This thought comforted me, and even though I was only six years old, I told myself, "I'll pray for *my poor person* on the day of my first Communion." I kept my promise five years later, and I hope that God heard and granted the prayer that He had inspired me to direct toward Him for one of His suffering children. . . .

I loved God very much, and I often gave Him my heart using the little formula that my mama had taught me. One day, however, or rather one evening in the beautiful month of May, I committed a fault that's well worth the trouble of being reported. It gave me quite an opportunity to be humbled, and I believe that I've made perfect contrition for it.

Since I was too little to go to the special devotions for Mary's month [the month of May], I stayed with our maid, Victoire, and with her I made my devotions in front of *my little Mary's month*, which I arranged in my own way. Everything was so little: candleholders and pots of flowers, which two wax "Vesta" matches illumined perfectly. Sometimes Victoire would surprise me with two little wax tapers, but that was rare.

One night everything was ready for us to begin our prayers, when I said, "Victoire, would you please start the 'Memorare' ["Remember"—a prayer asking for the Virgin Mary's protection]? I'm going to light the matches." She pretended to begin, but she didn't say anything and looked at me, laughing. As I watched my *precious matches* burning quickly down, I begged her to start the prayer, but she continued to keep quiet. Then, getting up, I started telling her that she was very naughty, and, departing from my usual mildness, I stamped my feet as hard as I could. . . . Poor Victoire didn't feel like laughing any more; she looked at me with surprise and showed me the wax tapers that she had brought me. . . . After having shed tears of anger, I now cried tears of sincere repentance and made a firm resolve not to do that ever again!

Another time I had an adventure with Victoire, but I didn't have any cause for repentance that time, because I stayed perfectly calm. I wanted to have an inkwell that was kept on the mantel in the kitchen. Since I was too little to get it, I asked Victoire very *nicely* to give it to me, but she refused, telling me to get up on a chair. I pulled out a chair without saying anything, but I was thinking that she wasn't very kind. Wanting to make her feel that, I searched in my little head for what was the most offensive thing to me, which was that when she was annoyed with me she often called me a "little brat," and that humiliated me a lot. So, before *jumping off* my *chair*, I turned with *dignity* and told her, "Victoire, you're a *brat!*" Then I ran off, leaving her to meditate on the profound word that I had just spoken to her. . . .

The result was unexpected: Soon I heard her crying out, "Miss Marie . . . Thérèse just told me that I'm a *brat!*" Marie came and made me apologize, but I did it without being sorry, finding that since Victoire hadn't wanted to extend *her big arm* to do me a *little favor*, she deserved the title of *brat*. . . .

Nonetheless, she liked me a lot, and I liked her a lot too. One day she pulled me out of a *grave danger* that I had fallen into through my own fault. Victoire was ironing, having next to her a bucket with water in it. I was watching her while swinging (as was my custom) on a chair. Suddenly the chair gave way and I fell, not on the floor, but into the *bottom* of the *bucket!* . . . My feet touched my head and I filled the *bucket* like a little chick fills an egg! . . . Poor Victoire looked at me with extreme surprise, never having seen such a thing. I really wanted to get out of my *bucket* immediately, but it was impossible. My prison was so tight that I couldn't move an inch. With a little bit of trouble she saved me from my *great danger*. Not so with my dress and all the rest of my clothing, which she was obliged to change, because I was soaked.

Another time I fell into the fireplace, but fortunately the fire wasn't lit. Victoire's only misfortune was to pick me up and shake off the ashes that I was covered with. It was on Wednesdays, when you were off at chant with Marie, that all these adventures used to happen to me.

It was also on a Wednesday that Fr. Ducellier [archpriest of the Cathedral of Saint Peter of Lisieux] came to pay a visit. When Victoire told him that nobody was home except little Thérèse, he came into the kitchen to see me and look at my homework. I was very proud to welcome *my confessor*, because a short time before that I had gone to confession for the first time. What a delightful memory that was for me! . . . Oh, dear Mother! With such care you prepared me! Telling me that it wasn't to a man, but to God, that I was going to tell my sins. I was really quite convinced of that, so I made my confession with a great spirit of faith, and I even asked you if I should tell Fr. Ducellier that I loved him with all my heart because I was going to talk to God through him. . . .

Well instructed in what I should say and do, I went into the confessional and knelt down, but when he opened the grille Fr. Ducellier didn't see anyone. I was so little that my head was below the little shelf on which people fold their hands. So he told me to stand up. Obeying immediately, I stood up and, turning directly toward him so I could see him well, I made my confession like a *big girl*, and I received his blessing with *great devotion*, because you had told me that at that moment the *tears* of the *Baby Jesus* were going to purify my soul. I remember that the first exhortation that was addressed to me invited me especially to devotion to the Blessed Virgin, and I promised to redouble my tenderness toward her.

When I left the confessional I was so happy and so light that I've never felt so much joy in my soul. Afterward I returned to confess at every important holiday, and it was a true celebration for me each time I went.

———·‒·———

Holidays! . . . Oh! how this word brings back memories! . . . *Holidays!* How I loved them so much! . . . You knew how to explain to me, dear Mother, all the mysteries hidden underneath each one of them so that they were truly, for me, days from heaven. I especially loved the processions of the Blessed Sacrament. What a joy it was to cast flowers under God's feet! . . . But before letting them fall there I would throw them as high as I could, and I was never so happy as when I saw my leafless roses *touch* the sacred monstrance [a receptacle in which the consecrated host was placed in an opening through which it could be viewed]. . . .

Holidays! Oh! If the big ones are rare, each week brings one that's quite dear to my heart: "Sunday!" What a day it is, this day called *Sunday*! . . . It was God's holiday, the day of *rest*. First of all I stayed *in bed* longer than on other days. And then Mama Pauline would spoil her little daughter, bringing her hot chocolate as she lay in bed. And then she would dress her up like a little queen. . . . The godmother [Marie] curled the hair of her *goddaughter*, who wasn't always nice when her hair was pulled. But then she was quite happy to go take the hand of her king who, on that day, kissed her even more tenderly than usual. And then the whole family would leave to go to Mass.

All along the way and even in church, little "Papa's queen" would give him her hand. Her place was at his side, and when we were obliged to go down for the sermon he had to find another two chairs side by side. This wasn't hard to do; everybody looked as if they found it so nice to see such a *handsome* elderly man with *such a little girl* that people moved aside to give up their places. My uncle, who used to sit in the church-wardens' pew, was delighted to see us arrive. He used to say that I was his little ray of sunshine. . . .

I hardly worried about being looked at, and I listened quite attentively to the sermons, even though I could hardly understand anything about them. The first one that I *understood* and that *touched me deeply* was a sermon on the Passion preached by Fr. Ducellier, and after that I understood all the other sermons.

When the preacher would talk about St. Teresa, Papa used to bend over and whisper to me, "Listen, my little queen, they're talking about your Patron Saint." In fact I was listening, but I used to look at Papa more often than at the preacher; his beautiful face told me so many things! . . . Sometimes his eyes used to fill with tears that he would try in vain to hold back. He seemed already not to hold on to earth, so much did his soul love to plunge into eternal truths. . . . However, his course was far from being finished; long years were to pass before beautiful heaven was to open to his delighted eyes and the Lord was to wipe away the *tears* of his good and faithful servant! . . . [see Rev. 21:4, Mt. 25:21].

———·––·———

But I'll come back to my day on Sundays. This *joyful* day, which passed so quickly, had its own tinge of *melancholy*. I remember that my happiness was unmixed until Compline [the evening service]. During that service I used to think how the day of *rest* was going to end . . . and the next day I'd have to go back to life, work, and learning lessons, and my heart would feel the *exile* of the world. . . . I would long for the eternal rest of heaven, the *Sunday* where the sun never sets in the *Homeland*! . . .

It wasn't until the walks that we used to take before going back to "Les Buissonnets" that a feeling of sadness would enter my soul, since the family wasn't complete anymore. That's because to please my uncle, every Sunday evening Papa would leave Marie *or Pauline* with him. Only I was quite happy when I stayed, too. I liked that better than being invited all alone, because they paid less attention to me. My greatest pleasure was to listen to everything my uncle used to say, but I didn't like it when he would ask me questions, and I was quite scared when he would put me on *only one* of his knees and sing "Bluebeard" with gusto.

It was with pleasure that I would see Papa come back to get us. On my way home I would look at the *stars* that were twinkling gently, and that sight would fill me with delight. . . . There was especially one group of *golden pearls* that I noticed joyfully, finding that it had the shape of a T (well, that's about what its shape was . . .). I would show it to Papa and tell him that my name was written in the heavens [Lk. 10:20], and then, not wanting to see anything on the horrid old earth, I would ask him to guide me while, without watching where I was stepping, I would thrust my little head into the air, never growing tired of contemplating the starry sky! . . .

---·—·—·---

What can I say about winter evenings, especially Sunday evenings? Oh! How sweet it was after the *checkers game* to sit with Céline on Papa's lap. . . . With his beautiful voice, he would sing songs that filled the soul with deep thoughts. . . . Or sometimes, rocking us gently, he would recite poems full of eternal truths. . . . Then we would go up to say our prayers together, and the little queen would be alone with her king, having only to watch him to know how the Saints pray. . . .

At the end we would all come in order of age to say good night to Papa and get a kiss. Naturally, the *queen* was last, and to give her a hug the *king* would take her by the *elbows* and she would cry out, "Good night, Papa, have a good night, sleep well." That's the way it was every night. . . .

Then my dear mama would take me into her arms and carry me to Céline's bed, and I would say, "Pauline, have I been cute today? . . . Are the *little Angels going to fly around me?*" The answer was always yes—otherwise I would have spent the whole night crying. . . . After giving me a hug, as well as my dear godmother, *Pauline* would go back downstairs, and poor little Thérèse would be all alone in the dark. It was in vain that she would try to imagine the *little Angels flying around her.* Soon dread would overtake her; the shadows would make her afraid, since from her bed she couldn't see the stars that were gently twinkling. . . .

I see it as a true grace to have become accustomed by you, dear Mother, to overcoming my fears. Sometimes you would send me alone at night to get an object from a distant room. If I hadn't been so well trained, I would have become quite fearful, but instead now it's really hard to scare me. . . . I sometimes wonder how you could have raised me with so much *love* and sensitivity without spoiling me, because it's true that you never let me get away with a single imperfection. You never reproached me without a cause, but you never took back anything that you had decided on. I knew this so well that I would have neither been able to nor wanted to take a single step if you had told me not to.

Papa himself was obliged to conform to your will. Without *Pauline's* consent I wouldn't go out for walks, and when Papa would tell me to come, I would answer, "Pauline doesn't want me to." Then he would come and ask for me to go, and sometimes to please him *Pauline* would say yes. But little Thérèse could see by the look on her face that it wasn't willingly that she said yes, so little Thérèse would start crying inconsolably until *Pauline would say yes and give her a big hug!*

When little Thérèse was sick, something that happened every winter, it's impossible to say with what motherly tenderness she was taken care of. Pauline would put her in her own bed (an incomparable favor), and then she would give her everything she wanted.

One day Pauline pulled out from underneath the bolster a *pretty little knife of hers*, and, giving it to her little girl, left her plunged into indescribable delight. "Oh! Pauline," she cried out, "so you love me so much that for me you're depriving yourself of your pretty little knife that has a *mother of pearl star*? . . . But since you love me so much, would you sacrifice your *watch* in order to keep me from *dying*? . . ." "Not only to keep you from dying would I give you my watch, but just to see you get well soon, I'd make that sacrifice in an instant." When I heard those words of *Pauline's*, my great surprise and my thankfulness were so great that I can't begin to express them. . . .

In the summer I sometimes used to have a stomach ache. Again, Pauline would take care of me tenderly. In order to cheer me up, which was the best of remedies, she would *wheel me in a wheelbarrow* all around the garden, and then, helping me down, she would put in my place a pretty little head of daisies that she would *wheel* very *carefully* up to my garden, where it was placed with great ceremony. . . .

Pauline was the one who heard my most intimate confidences, who enlightened all my doubts. . . . One time I was expressing surprise that God should not give equal glory in heaven to all His elect, and I was

Alençon

The house where Thérèse
was born

Our Lady of Alençon

The church where Thérèse
was baptized

Les Buissonnets (Lisieux)

The window marked with a cross shows Thérèse's room.

afraid that everyone would not be happy. Then Pauline told me to go get Papa's big glass and to put it next to my little dice cup, and to fill them with water. Then she asked me which one was the most full. I told her that one was as full as the other and that it was impossible to put in more water than they could hold. Then my dear mother helped me understand that in heaven, God would give to His elect as much glory as they could hold, and so the last would have nothing to envy about the first. This is how, by placing within my grasp the most sublime of secrets, you knew, Mother how to give my soul the nourishment that it needed. . . .

———·—·———

With what joy I came every year to the end-of-school-year distribution of prizes! There, as always, *justice* was respected; I would receive only the rewards that I had earned. Standing *all alone* in the midst of the *noble assembly*, I would hear my sentence, read by the king of France and Navarre [as I called Papa]. My heart would beat fast as I received the prize and the crown. . . . For me this was like an image of the Last Judgment! . . . Right after the distribution of prizes, the little queen would take off her white dress, and then they would hurry to disguise her so she could take part in *the big play*! . . .

Oh! How joyful were these family celebrations. . . . How far I was then, when I saw my dear king so radiant, from foreseeing the trials that were to visit him! . . . One day, however, God showed me in a really extraordinary *vision*, the *living* image of the trial that it was His will to prepare us for in advance, since His cup of suffering was already filling up.

Papa had been away on a trip for several days, and he wasn't supposed to come home for two more days. It could have been two or three o'clock in the afternoon. The sun was shining brightly, and all of nature seemed to be celebrating. I was alone in the window of a dormer overlooking the big garden. I was looking ahead of me, my mind filled with cheerful thoughts, when I saw, in front of the wash-house just across the way, a man dressed absolutely like Papa, with the same height and the same walk, only he was *much more hunched over.* . . . His *head* was covered with a sort of apron of an indistinct color in such a way that I couldn't see his face. He wore a hat that looked like the ones Papa wore. I saw him approach with measured steps, walking through my little garden.

Suddenly a feeling of supernatural dread invaded my soul, but in an instant I decided that no doubt Papa had come back home and that he was hiding in order to surprise me. So I called out loudly, my voice trembling with emotion, "Papa, Papa! . . ." But the mysterious person didn't seem to hear me, and continued his measured steps without even turning around. Following him with my eyes, I saw him heading toward the woods that cut the big driveway in two. I expected to see him reappear on the other side of the big trees, but the prophetic vision had vanished! . . . All of this lasted only an instant, but it was engraved so deeply on my heart that today, after fifteen years, the memory is still as present as if the vision were still before my eyes. . . .

Marie was with you, Mother, in a room adjoining the one where I was. When she heard me calling Papa, she felt an impression of dread, feeling, she told me later, that something extraordinary must have happened. Without letting me see her emotion she ran to me and asked what had come over me to make me call Papa, who was in Alençon. So I told her what I had just seen. To reassure me, Marie told me that no doubt it was Victoire who, to scare me, had hidden her head under her apron. But when she was asked, Victoire assured us that she hadn't left her kitchen. Besides, I was quite sure that I saw a man, and that this man had Papa's appearance. Then all three of us went behind the stand of trees, but when we didn't find any sign indicating that someone had passed by, you told me not to think about this anymore. . . .

Not to think about it wasn't in my power. Quite often my imagination would bring back the mysterious scene that I had seen. . . . Quite often I would try to lift the veil that hid its meaning, because deep in my heart I had the inner conviction that this vision had a *meaning* that was going to be revealed someday. . . .

That day was a long time in coming, but after fourteen years God Himself tore open the mysterious veil. I was on leave with Sr. Marie of the Sacred Heart [my sister Marie], and we were talking as always about things of the other life and our childhood memories, when I recounted the vision that I had had at the age of six or seven. Suddenly as we recalled the details of that strange scene, we both understood at the same time what it meant.... It really was *Papa* that I had seen, trudging forward, hunched over by age. . . . It really was Papa, bearing on his venerable face, on his head white with age, the sign of his *glorious* trial [of suffering from dementia]. . . . Like Jesus' adorable face, which was veiled during His Passion [Lk. 22:64], the face of His faithful servant was to be veiled during the days of his suffering, in order to shine in the heavenly Country with his Lord, the Eternal Word! . . .

It was in the midst of that indescribable glory, when he was reigning in heaven, that our dear Papa obtained for us the grace to understand the vision that his little queen had had at an age when there's no need to be afraid of illusion! It's from the midst of that glory that he obtained for us that sweet comfort of understanding that ten years before our great trial, God was already showing it to us, as a Father who sets before His children the glorious future that He's preparing for them and is pleased to consider in advance the priceless riches that are to be their lot. . . .

Oh! Why was I the one to whom God showed this light? Why did He show such a little child something that she was unable to understand, something that, if she had understood it, would have caused her to die with suffering—why? . . . Herein lies one of the mysteries that no doubt we will understand in heaven and that will be the source of our unending admiration. . . .

How good God is! . . . How He apportions out trials according to the strength that He gives us. Never, as I have just said, would I have been able to stand even the thought of the bitter pains that the future held in store for me. . . . I couldn't even think without shuddering that Papa *was going to die*. . . . Once he had climbed up on a ladder, and as I was standing just under him he called out, "Step away, little dearie—if I fall I'm going to land on top of you." When I heard that I felt an inner revolt; instead of stepping away, I clung to the ladder, thinking, "At least if Papa falls, I'm not going to have the suffering of watching him die, since I'm going to die with him!"

I can't say how much I loved Papa. Everything about him caused me admiration. When he would explain his thoughts to me (as if I had been a big girl), I would tell him naïvely that of course if he said all that to the great men of the government, they would take him and make him king, and then France would be happy as it had never been. . . . But in my heart I was happy (and I reproached myself for thinking this out of selfishness) that I was the only one who *knew Papa well*, because if he had become the king *of France* and *Navarre* I knew that he would have been unhappy, since that's the fate of all monarchs, and especially because he would no longer have been my king and mine alone!

———————

I was six or seven years old when Papa took us to Trouville. I'll never forget the impression that the sea made on me. I couldn't keep myself from looking at it without stopping. Its majesty, the roaring of its waves, everything spoke to my soul about the Greatness and the Power of God. I remember that during the walk that we were taking on the beach, a gentleman and a lady watched me playing joyfully around Papa. Approaching, they asked him if *I were his*, and they said that I was a very nice little girl. Papa told them yes, but I became aware that he was making signs to them not to pay me compliments. . . .

This was the first time that I heard that I was nice, and that gave me a lot of pleasure, because I didn't believe it. You gave a lot of attention, dear Mother, not to let me near anything that might tarnish my innocence, especially not to let me hear a single word that might be capable of letting vanity slip into my heart. Since I paid attention only to your words and Marie's, and you had never addressed a single compliment toward me, I didn't attach much importance to the lady's words and admiring glances.

That evening, at the time when the sun seems to swim in the immensity of the waves, leaving before it a *luminous wake*, I went to sit on a rock all alone with *Pauline*. Then I remembered the touching story of "The Golden Wake." I contemplated that shiny wake for a long time, the image of grace lighting the path that the little vessel with the gracious white sail was to take. . . . Near Pauline, I made a resolution never to distance my soul from Jesus' gaze, so that my soul might sail in peace to its heavenly Homeland!

My life flowed along, tranquil and happy. The affection with which I was surrounded at "Les Buissonnets" made me, so to speak, grow up. But I was no doubt big enough to begin to struggle, to begin to become familiar with the world and the distresses that fill it. . . .

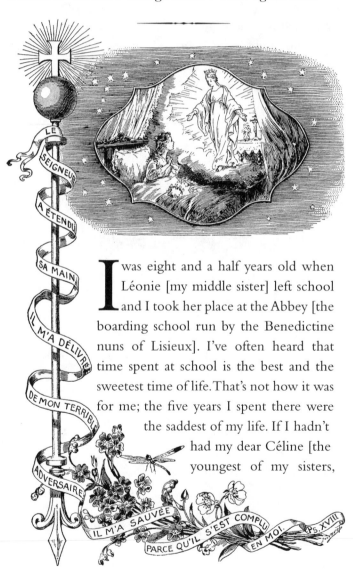

3
SORROWFUL YEARS
1881–1883

Pupil at the abbey / Free days / Céline's First Communion
Pauline at Carmel / Strange illness / The Virgin's smile

I was eight and a half years old when Léonie [my middle sister] left school and I took her place at the Abbey [the boarding school run by the Benedictine nuns of Lisieux]. I've often heard that time spent at school is the best and the sweetest time of life. That's not how it was for me; the five years I spent there were the saddest of my life. If I hadn't had my dear Céline [the youngest of my sisters, three and a half years older than I] with me, I wouldn't have been able to stay a single month without falling sick. . . . The poor little flower had been accustomed to plunging her fragile roots into *chosen ground*, made especially for her, so it seemed to her that it was very hard to see herself among flowers with all kinds of roots that were often not very delicate, and to be obliged to find in *common ground* the sap that was necessary to her subsistence! . . .

You had taught me so well, dear Mother, that upon arriving at the school I was the most advanced of the children my age. I was placed in a class of pupils who were all bigger than I was. One of them, aged thirteen or fourteen, was not so intelligent, but she knew how to impress the students and even the teachers. Seeing that I was so young, almost always the first in my class, and beloved by all the nuns, she no doubt felt a jealousy that was quite forgivable for a schoolgirl, and she made me pay for my little successes in a thousand ways. . . .

With my timid and delicate nature, I didn't know how to defend myself, and I was content to weep without saying anything, not complaining *even to you* about what I was suffering. But I didn't have enough virtue to rise above these griefs that life brings, and my poor little heart suffered a great deal. . . .

Fortunately, each night I would go home to my father, and there my heart would expand. I would jump into my king's lap, telling him about the grades that had been given to me, and his kiss would make me forget all my troubles. . . . With what joy I announced the results of my *first composition* (a composition on sacred history). *A single point* was all I needed to get a perfect paper—I didn't know the name of Moses' father. So I was first in the class, and I had brought home a beautiful silver decoration.

As a reward Papa gave me a *pretty little coin* worth four pennies, and I placed it in a box that was destined to receive, nearly every Thursday, a new coin always of the same *size*. . . . (I used to go into that box on certain important feast days when I wanted to give an offering from my purse, either for the propagation of the Faith or for other similar works.) *Pauline*, delighted with the success of her little pupil, made her a gift of a pretty hoop to encourage her to continue to study hard. The poor little one had a real need for these joys in the family. Without them, life in school would have been too hard.

Thursday afternoons were time off from school, but these were not like *Pauline's times off*; I wasn't in the belvedere with Papa. . . . I had to play, not with my *Céline*, which I liked when I was *all alone with her*, but with my little cousins and the little girls from the Maudelonde family.

For me this was truly painful, not knowing how to play like the other children. I wasn't pleasant company, but nonetheless I did my best to be like the others, but without success, and I was bored a lot, especially when I had to spend a whole afternoon *dancing the quadrille*. The only thing I liked was to go to the *star garden*. Then I was the first one everywhere, picking flowers in profusion. Since I knew how to find the prettiest ones, I excited the envy of my little classmates. . . .

What pleased me still more was when by chance I was alone with little Marie [Marie Guérin, my cousin]. Not having Céline Maudelonde with her any more to drag her into her *ordinary games*, she would leave me free to choose, and I would choose a completely new game. Marie and Thérèse became two *hermits*, having only a little hut, a little wheat field, and a few vegetables to cultivate. Their life was spent in continual contemplation, that is, one of the *hermits* replaced the other in prayer when it became necessary to be concerned with the active life. Everything was done with understanding, silence, and such religious etiquette that it was perfect.

When my aunt would come and get us for our walk, our game would continue even on the road. The two hermits would recite the Rosary together, using their fingers so as not to show their devotion to an indiscreet public. One day, however, the youngest hermit forgot herself, and having received a piece of cake at snack time, before eating it she made a great sign of the Cross over it, which made all the irreverent folks of this age laugh. . . .

[My cousin] Marie and I were always of the same opinion. We even had the same tastes, and one day our *union of wills* passed all limits. On the way back from the Abbey one evening, I told Marie, "Guide me,

I'm going to close my eyes." "I want to close mine, too," she replied. No sooner said than done; *without discussing it*, each one did *her will*. . . . We were on a sidewalk, so there was no need to be afraid of carriages, so after a pleasant walk lasting several minutes, having savored the delights of walking without seeing where they were going, the two little scatterbrains fell *together* on some boxes outside the door of a store. Or rather, they made the *boxes fall*. The shopkeeper came out quite angrily to pick up his merchandise. The two voluntarily blind girls had gotten back up and started walking, taking *big steps*, eyes *wide* open, while listening to the just reproaches of Jeanne [my other cousin], who was as angry as the shopkeeper! . . . So, to punish us she resolved to separate us, and from that day on Marie and Céline would go together while I would go with Jeanne. This put an end to our great *union of wills*, and this wasn't a bad thing for the older girls, who on the contrary were never of the same opinion and used to argue all along the way. So the peace was complete.

———

I haven't said anything yet about my close relationship with Céline. Oh! If had to tell it all, I wouldn't be able to finish. . . .

At Lisieux, the roles had changed. It was Céline who had become a clever little imp, and Thérèse was no longer anything more than a sweet little girl who was a *big cry-baby*. . . . That didn't prevent Céline and Thérèse from loving each other more and more. Sometimes there were little spats, but it was nothing serious, and in their hearts they were always of the same mind. I can say that my dear little sister *never* gave me any *trouble*, but that she was for me like a ray of sunshine, giving me joy and always comforting me. . . . Who can say with what fearlessness she defended me at the Abbey when I was accused of something? . . . She took such good care of my health that it bothered me sometimes.

What didn't bother me was to *watch her playing*. She would put the whole group of our dolls in rows and would teach them a class like a gifted schoolmistress, only she would take care that her girls were always well behaved, while mine were often sent out the door because of their bad behavior. . . . She would tell me all the new things that she had just learned in her class, which amused me a lot, and I looked at her as a fountain of knowledge.

I had received the title of "Céline's little girl," so when she was angry with me, her biggest sign of discontent was to say to me, "You aren't my little girl any more, it's over, I'll *always remember what you did!*" Then all I had to do was cry like a baby, begging her to treat me like her little girl again. Soon she would hug me and promised *not to remember anything* again! . . . To comfort me she would take one of her dolls and would say to her, "My dear, hug your aunt." One time the doll was in such a hurry to hug me tenderly that she put her two little arms around *my nose*. . . . Céline, who hadn't done it on purpose, looked at me totally shocked, with the doll hanging off my nose. *The aunt* didn't take long to push away the too-tender embrace of her *niece* and start laughing with all her heart at such a remarkable adventure.

The funniest thing was to see us buy our New Year's gifts, together at the bazaar; we would carefully hide from each another. Having ten small coins to spend we needed five or six different objects, so it was up to us to buy the most *beautiful things*. Delighted with our purchases, we would wait impatiently for New Year's Day in order to offer our *magnificent presents* to each other. The one who woke up before the other would hurry to wish her a Happy New Year. Then we would give each other our *New Year's gifts*, and each would be in ecstasy over the *treasures* given for ten small coins! . . . These little gifts gave us almost as much pleasure as the *beautiful New Year's gifts* given by my *uncle*. However, this was only the beginning of the joyous times. That day we would get dressed quickly and each one would lie in wait to jump on Papa's neck, as soon as he came out of his room. There would be shouts of joy in the whole house, and poor dear father would seem happy to see us so content. . . .

The New Year's gifts that Marie and Pauline used to give to their little girls weren't worth a lot, but they gave them *great joy*. . . . Oh! It was just that at that age we weren't blasé. Our souls in all their freshness were opening like flowers that are happy to receive the morning dew. . . . The same breeze caused our petals to flutter, and what gave joy or sorrow to one did the same thing at the same time to the other. Yes, our joys were shared.

I was keenly aware of this on that beautiful day of my beloved Céline's first Communion. I wasn't attending school at the Abbey yet, since I was only seven, but I've preserved in my heart the sweet memory of the preparation that you, beloved Mother, had given Céline. Each night you used to take her on your lap and speak to her about the important act that she was going to do. I used to listen, keen to prepare myself as well. But often you would tell me to go away because I was too little. Then my heart would be quite heavy, and I used to think that four years were not too long to prepare oneself to receive God. . . .

One night I heard you say that beginning with first Communion, we must begin a new life. Immediately I resolved not to wait for that day but to begin a new life at the same time as Céline. . . . I had never felt so much that I loved her as I did during her three-day retreat. For the first time in my life, I was far from her, I wasn't going to sleep in her bed. . . .

The first day, forgetting that she wasn't going to come back, I kept a little sprig of cherries that Papa had bought for me, intending to eat them with her. When I didn't see her arrive I was quite upset. Papa comforted me by saying that he would take me to the Abbey the next day to see my Céline, and that I would give her another sprig of cherries! . . .

The day of Céline's first Communion left an impression on me like the day of my own. Waking in the morning all alone in the big bed, I felt myself *overcome with joy.* "It's today! . . . The big day has arrived. . . ." I never got tired of repeating those words. It seemed to me that I was the one who was going to take my first Communion. I think that I received great graces that day, and I consider it to be one of the most *beautiful* of my life. . . .

I've gone back in time a bit in order to recall that delicious, sweet memory. Now I have to speak about the painful trial that came and broke little Thérèse's heart, when Jesus took away from her, her dear *Mama*: her so tenderly beloved *Pauline*! . . .

One day, I had told Pauline that I would like to be a hermit and go away with her to a faraway deserted place. She answered that my desire was hers as well, and that she *would wait* until I was big enough to leave. No doubt this wasn't said seriously, but little Thérèse took it seriously, so what suffering it was one day to hear her dear Pauline talking with Marie about her upcoming entry into Carmel. . . . I didn't know what "Carmel" was, but I understood that Pauline was going to leave me and enter a convent. I understood that she *wouldn't wait for me*, and that I was going to lose my second *mother*. . . . Oh! How can I tell you of the anguish in my heart? . . .

In an instant I understood what life was. Until then I hadn't seen it as so sad, but it appeared to me in all its reality, and I saw that it was only suffering and continual separation. I shed the most bitter tears, because I didn't understand yet the *joy* of sacrifice. I was *weak, so weak* that I see it as a great grace to have been able to endure a trial that seemed well beyond my strength! . . . If I had learned in a gentle way about my beloved Pauline's departure, perhaps I wouldn't have suffered so much, but since I learned it by surprise, I felt as if a sword had been thrust into my heart [Lk. 2:35].

I will always remember, beloved Mother, with what tenderness you comforted me. . . . Then you explained to me about the life at Carmel that seemed so beautiful to me. As I was going over in my mind everything that you had told me, I felt that Carmel was *the desert* where God wanted me as well to go and hide. . . . I felt it with so much strength that there wasn't the slightest doubt in my heart. This was not the dream of a child who lets herself be carried away, but the *certainty* of a Divine call. I wanted to go to Carmel, not for *Pauline*, but for *Jesus alone*. . . . I thought *many* things that words can't express, but which left a great peace in my soul.

The next day I confided my secret to Pauline, who, viewing my desires as the will of heaven, told me that soon I would go with her to see the Prioress of the Carmelite convent, and that I would need to tell her what God was making me feel. . . . One Sunday was chosen for this solemn visit. My perplexity was great when I learned that Marie Guérin [my cousin] was to stay with me, since I was still little enough to see the Carmelite Sisters.

Nonetheless, I had to find a way to be alone, so here is what came to my mind: I told Marie that since we had the privilege of seeing the Prioress, we had to be very nice and very polite. For that we had to confide *secrets* to her, so each one of us had to go out for a moment and leave the other one all alone. Marie took me at my word, and in spite of her dislike of having to confide *secrets that she didn't have*, we stayed alone, one after the other, with Mother Marie de Gonzague.

Having heard my *great confidences*, this good Mother believed in my vocation, but she told me that they didn't receive *nine-year-old* postulants, and that I would have to wait until I was sixteen. . . . I resigned myself to this, in spite of my strong desire to enter as soon as possible and to make my first Communion on the day that Pauline was to take the nun's habit. . . .

That was the day that I received compliments for the second time. Sr. Thérèse of St. Augustine came to see me and never got tired of saying that I was nice. But I wasn't counting on coming to the convent to receive praise. So after that time in the parlor, I never stopped repeating to God that it was for Him alone that I wanted to be a Carmelite nun.

I tried to take full advantage of my beloved Pauline during the few weeks that still remained to her in the world. Each day Céline and I would buy her a cake and some candies, thinking that soon she would no longer be eating any such thing. We were always at her side, not leaving her a minute's rest. Finally the *second of October* came, a day of tears and blessings, when Jesus gathered the first of His flowers, who was to be the *mother* of the ones who would be coming to join her a few short years later.

I can still see the place where I received *Pauline's* last kiss. Then my aunt took us all to Mass while Papa was going up on the mountain of Carmel to offer his *first sacrifice* [like Abraham as he was preparing to offer his son Isaac on Mount Moriah, Gen. 22:1–19]. . . . The whole family was in tears, so that when people saw us entering the church they looked at us with great surprise. But I paid no attention, and I couldn't keep myself from crying. I think that if everything had crumbled around me I wouldn't have paid any attention. I was watching the beautiful blue sky, and I was astounded that the sun could shine with so much brilliance, while my soul was flooded with sadness! . . .

Perhaps, beloved Mother, you might find that I'm exaggerating the pain that I felt. . . . I'm quite aware that it shouldn't have been so great since I held the hope of finding you at Carmel later, but my soul was FAR from being *matured*; I had to pass through many crucibles before attaining the end that I desired so much. . . .

———·—·———

October 2nd was the day appointed for going back to school at the Abbey. So I had to go in spite of my sorrow. . . . In the afternoon my aunt came and got us so we could go to the Carmelite convent, and I saw my *beloved Pauline* behind the *grille*. . . . Oh! How I suffered at that *meeting* at the convent! Since I'm writing the story of my soul, I ought to tell everything to my dear Mother, and I admit that the sufferings that had preceded her entrance into the convent were nothing compared to the ones that followed it. . . .

Every Thursday we would go as a *family* to the convent, and I, who was used to speaking at length, heart to heart, with *Pauline*, obtained with great difficulty two or three minutes at the end of the meeting. Of course I spent them crying, and I went away with my heart broken. . . . I didn't understand that it was out of tactfulness toward my aunt that you preferred to address the conversation toward Jeanne and Marie [my cousins] instead of speaking to your little girls [your sisters]. . . . I didn't understand, and I would say deep in my heart, "Pauline is lost to me!!!" It's surprising to see how much my mind developed in the midst of suffering. It developed to such a point that it didn't take me long to fall sick.

The illness that struck me came most certainly from the devil, who was furious at your entry into Carmel. He wanted to take revenge on me for the wrong that our family was to do to him in the future. But he didn't know that the gentle Queen of Heaven was watching over her fragile little flower, and that she was *smiling* at her from her throne on high, and was getting ready to make the storm cease at the very moment when her flower was about to become crushed beyond return. . . .

Toward the end of the year I was taken with a headache that, though continual, almost didn't make me suffer. I was able to pursue my studies, and no one was worried about me. This lasted until Easter, 1883. Papa had gone to Paris with Marie and Léonie, so my aunt took me to her house, with Céline. One night my uncle, who had taken me with him, talked to me about Mama, about past memories, with a goodness that touched me deeply and made me cry. Then he told me that I was too tenderhearted, and that I needed to be distracted. So he resolved with my aunt to bring us some pleasure during the Easter vacation. That night we were to go to the Catholic circle, but finding that I was too tired, my aunt put me to bed. As I was getting undressed I was taken with a strange trembling. Thinking that I was cold, my aunt covered me with blankets and hot water bottles, but nothing could lessen my agitation, which lasted almost all night. When my uncle came back from the Catholic circle with my cousins and Céline, he was quite surprised to find me in a state that he deemed to be serious, but he didn't want to say so in order not to frighten my aunt.

The next day he went to find Dr. Notta, who concluded, like my uncle, that I had a very serious illness that had never struck such a young child. Everybody was quite dismayed. My aunt was obliged to keep me at her place and took care of me with truly *motherly* solicitude. When Papa came back from Paris with my big sisters, Aimée greeted them with such a sad face that Marie thought I was dead. . . .

But this illness was not so that I would die. It was rather like the one Lazarus had, so that God might be glorified [Jn. 11:4]. . . . And in fact He was, through the admirable resignation of my poor dear *father*, who thought "his little girl was going to go mad or that she was going to die." God was also glorified by *Marie's* resignation as well! . . . Oh! How she suffered because of me. . . . How grateful I am for the care that she poured out on me with so much unselfishness. . . . Her heart dictated to her what was necessary for me, and truly, a *mother's heart* is much more *knowledgeable* than a doctor's heart—it knows how to *guess* what is suited to its child's illness. . . .

Poor Marie was obliged to come live at my uncle's, because it was impossible to transport me to Les Buissonnets at that time. However, Pauline's taking of the habit was approaching. They avoided talking about it in front of me, knowing the pain that I felt at not being able to go. But I talked about it often, saying that I would be well enough to go see my beloved Pauline. And in fact God didn't want to refuse me that comfort, or rather, He wanted to comfort His beloved *Betrothed* [Pauline] who had suffered so much from the illness of her little girl [Thérèse]. . . .

I've noticed that Jesus doesn't want to send trials to His children on the day of their betrothal. That holiday should be cloudless, a foretaste of the joys of heaven. Hasn't He shown this five times already? So I was able to *kiss* my beloved mother [Pauline], *sit* on her *lap* and flood her with hugs. . . . I was able to contemplate her being so attractive, under the white garment of Bride [her Carmelite habit]. . . . Oh! That was a *beautiful day*, in the midst of my dark trial, but that day went by quickly. . . .

Soon I had to climb into the carriage that took me so far from Pauline . . . far from my beloved Carmel. Arriving at Les Buissonnets, they put me to bed. In spite of myself I assured them that I was perfectly well and no longer needed to be taken care of. Alas, I was still only at the beginning of my ordeal. . . . The next day I was stricken again like I had been before, and the illness became so serious that I wasn't supposed to survive it according to human calculation. . . . I don't know how to describe such a strange illness. I'm persuaded now that it was the work of the devil, but for a long time after I got well I thought that I had become sick on purpose, and that was a *true martyrdom* for my soul.

I told this to Marie, who reassured me as best she could, with her ordinary *goodness*. I told it at Confession, and there again my confessor tried to calm me down, saying that it wasn't possible to pretend to be sick to the point where I had been. God, who no doubt wanted to purify me and especially to *humble* me, left me with this *inner martyrdom* right up to my entrance into Carmel. There, the *Father* of our souls took away all my doubts as if it were with His own hand, and since then I have been perfectly peaceful.

It isn't surprising that I was afraid that I looked sick without in fact being sick, because I would say and do things that I wasn't thinking. I almost always seemed to be delirious, saying words that had no meaning, and nevertheless I'm *sure* that I wasn't *deprived for a single instant of the use of my reason*. . . . Often I appeared to have fainted, not making the slightest movement.

At that time I would have let be done to me anything anyone might have wanted, even kill me. Nonetheless I was hearing everything that was being said around me, and I still remember everything. It happened to me once that I stayed for a long time without being able to open my eyes, and yet I opened them for an instant while I was alone.

I think that the devil had received an *outward* power over me, but he couldn't approach my soul or my mind, unless it was to inspire in me *great fear* of certain things, for example, fears of the very simple remedies that people tried in vain to make me accept.

But if God was allowing the devil to come near me, He was also sending me visible angels. . . . Marie was always at my bedside, taking care of me and comforting me with the tenderness of a mother. She never showed the slightest irritation, despite the fact that I gave her a lot of trouble by not allowing her to leave me. Nonetheless she had to go to meals with Papa, but I wouldn't stop calling her the whole time she was away. Victoire, who was taking care of me, sometimes was obliged to go get my dear "Mama" since I was calling for her. . . . When Marie wanted to go out it had to be in order to go to Mass or to see *Pauline*, and then I didn't say anything. . . .

My uncle and aunt [Isidore and Céline Guérin] were also very good to me. My dear aunt came *every day* to see me and spoiled me a lot. Other people who were friends of the family also came to visit me, but I begged Marie to tell them that I didn't want any visits. I didn't like "seeing people sitting around my bed *all squashed together*, looking at me like some strange animal."

The only visitors I liked were my uncle and my aunt. Since that illness I couldn't tell you how much my affection for them increased. I understood better than ever that they were not ordinary relatives to us.

Oh! Poor dear father was quite right when he repeated so often the words that I have just written. Later he experienced the fact that he hadn't been wrong, and now [that he's in heaven] he must protect and bless those who poured out such devoted care on him. . . . But as for me, I am still in exile, and since I don't know how to show my gratefulness, I have only one means to relieve my heart: Pray for the relatives that I love, who were and still are so good to me!

Léonie was also quite good to me. She tried to entertain me as best she could. But sometimes I hurt her because she could see quite clearly that nobody could take Marie's place at my side.

And my dear Céline, what did she not do for her Thérèse? On Sunday, instead of taking a walk she would stay indoors for hours on end with a poor little girl who looked like an idiot. Truly, it would have taken love not to run away from me. . . . Oh! Dear sisters, how I made you suffer! No one had given you so much *trouble* as I, and no one had received so much *love* as you poured out on me. . . . Fortunately, I will have heaven to pay you back. My Bridegroom is very rich, and I will dig into His treasures of *love* in order to give you back a hundred times as much as all that you suffered because of me.

My greatest comfort while I was sick was to receive a letter from *Pauline*. . . . I read it and reread it until I knew it by heart. . . . One time, dear Mother, you sent me an hourglass and one of my dolls dressed up as a Carmelite nun. To say how much joy I felt would be impossible. . . . My uncle wasn't happy. He said that instead of making me think about Carmel I ought to put it out of my mind, but I felt on the contrary that it was the hope of being a Carmelite nun someday that kept me alive. . . .

My pleasure was to work for Pauline. I made her little objects of Bristol-board paper, and my greatest occupation was to made crowns of daisies and forget-me-nots for the Blessed Virgin. We were now in the beautiful month of May [Mary's month]. All of nature was adorning itself with flowers and breathing gaiety. Only the "little flower" was languishing and seemed to be forever wilted. . . .

However, she had one Sun near her, and that Sun was the *miraculous statue* of the Blessed Virgin that had spoken twice to Mama. And often, quite often, the little flower turned its petals toward that blessed Star. . . . One day I saw Papa go into Marie's room, where I was lying in bed. And giving her several gold coins with an expression of great sadness, he told her to write to Paris and have Masses said to Our Lady of Victories so that she would heal his poor little daughter. Oh! How touched I was at seeing the faith and love of my beloved king. I would have liked to be able to tell him that I was well, but I had already given him enough false joys. It was not my desires that could make a *miracle*, because it was going to take one to heal me. . . .

A *miracle* was needed, and it was Our Lady of Victories who did it. One Sunday during the novena [nine days of Masses], Marie went out into the garden, leaving me with Léonie, who was reading near the window. After a few minutes I started calling almost silently, "Mama . . . Mama." Léonie, who had become accustomed to hearing me call out like that, didn't pay attention to me. This went on for a long time, so I called out louder, and finally Marie came back in. I saw her clearly when she entered, but I couldn't say that I recognized her, and I continued to call out ever louder, "Mama."

I was suffering a lot from this strong and inexplicable struggle, and Marie was suffering from it perhaps even more than I. After vain efforts to show me that she was beside me, she got down on her knees beside my bed with Léonie and Céline, and then, turning toward the Blessed Virgin, and praying with the fervor of a mother who was asking for the life of her child, *Marie* obtained what she desired. . . .

Finding no help on earth, poor little Thérèse had turned toward her Heavenly Mother. She was praying to her with all her heart to finally have pity on her. . . . Suddenly the Blessed Virgin seemed *beautiful* to me, so *beautiful* that I had never seen anything so beautiful. Her face was breathing inexpressible goodness and tenderness, but what penetrated right to the depths of my soul was the "lovely smile of the Blessed Virgin." Then all my sufferings melted away, and two big tears burst from my eyelids and streaked silently down my cheeks—but these were tears of an unadulterated joy. . . . Oh! I thought, the Blessed Virgin smiled at me, how happy I am. . . . Yes, but I will never tell anyone about it, because then my *happiness would disappear.*

Without any effort I lowered my eyes and saw Marie, who was watching me with love. She seemed moved, and seemed to suspect the favor that the Blessed Virgin had granted to me. . . . Oh! It was to her, to her touching prayers, that I owed the grace of the *smile* of the Queen of Heaven. When she saw my gaze fixed on the Blessed Virgin, she had said to herself, "Thérèse has been healed!" Yes, the little flower was going to be born anew to life. The glowing *Ray* that had warmed her was not going to stop its blessings. It doesn't act suddenly, but sweetly, gently, it picked its flower back up and strengthened it in such a way that five years later it opened up on the fertile mount of Carmel.

As I said, Marie had guessed that the Blessed Virgin had granted me some hidden grace, so when I was alone with her and she asked me what I had seen, I couldn't resist her questions that were so tender and pressing. Surprised to see that my secret had been discovered without my having revealed it, I confided the whole story to my dear Marie. . . . Alas! Just as I had felt, my happiness was to disappear and change into bitterness. For four years the memory of the inexpressible grace that I had received was for me a true *suffering of the soul.* I was to find my happiness again only at the feet of Our Lady of Victories, but then it was given back to me in *all its fullness.* . . .

I will talk again later about this second grace of the Blessed Virgin. Now I have to tell you, dear Mother, how my joy changed into sadness. After hearing me tell my naïve and sincere story about "my grace," Marie asked me for permission to tell it to the Carmelite nuns—and I couldn't say no. On my first visit to this beloved convent, I was full of joy at seeing my *Pauline* with the habit of the Blessed Virgin [the

The Healing of Thérèse by the Most Blessed Virgin
May 10th, 1883

nuns' habit, which was like the garments worn by the Blessed Virgin Mary]. This was a very sweet moment for us both. . . . There were so many things to say that I couldn't say anything at all, my heart was too full. . . .

The good Mother Marie de Gonzague [the prioress] was there as well, giving me many signs of affection. I saw still other Sisters, and in front of them I was questioned about the grace that I had received. Marie asked me if the Blessed Virgin was carrying the baby Jesus, or if there was a lot of light, etc. All these questions troubled me and gave me a lot of distress. I could say only one thing: "The Blessed Virgin seemed to me to be *very beautiful* . . . and I saw her *smile at me.*" It was her *face alone* that had struck me, so when I saw that the nuns were imagining something completely different (the sufferings of my soul were already beginning concerning my illness), I figured that I *had lied.* . . .

No doubt, if I had kept my secret, I would have kept my happiness. But the Blessed Virgin allowed this torment for the good of my soul. Perhaps without it I would have had some thought of vanity. Instead, *humiliation* became my lot. I couldn't look at myself without a feeling of *deep horror.* . . . Oh! What I suffered, I will be able to tell only in heaven!

4

FIRST COMMUNION—
BOARDING SCHOOL
1883–1886

Pictures and reading / First Communion / Confirmation
Illness of scruples / Mrs. Papinau / Child of Mary
New separations

Speaking of visits to the Carmelites, I remember my first one, which took place a short time after *Pauline's* entrance. I forgot to mention it earlier, but it's a detail that I shouldn't leave out. The morning of the day when I was to go to the parlor, reflecting all alone in my bed (because it was there that I prayed my deepest prayers and, contrary to the bride in the Song of Songs, I always found my Beloved there [Song 3:1–4]), I wondered what name I would have at Carmel. I knew that there was a Sr. Thérèse of Jesus. However, my beautiful name of Thérèse couldn't be taken away from me. Suddenly I thought about the *Little* Jesus whom I loved so much, and I told myself, "Oh, how happy I would be to be called Thérèse of the Child Jesus!" I *didn't say anything* in the parlor about the dream that I'd had while completely awake, but when dear Mother *Marie de Gonzague* asked the Sisters what name should be given to me, it came to her to call me by the name that I had dreamed about. . . . Great was my joy, and that happy meeting of thoughts seemed to me to be a gentle touch from my Beloved Little Jesus.

I've forgotten a few more details of my childhood before your entrance into Carmel. I haven't talked to you about my love of pictures and books. . . . And yet, beloved Mother, I owe to the beautiful pictures that you used to show me as a reward, one of the sweetest joys and the strongest impressions that have excited me in the practice of virtue. . . . I used to forget the time as I was looking at them; for example, *The Divine Prisoner's Little Flower* [a poem made into a picture book] told me so many things that I was completely immersed in it. When I saw that the name of *Pauline* was written at the bottom of the little flower, I would have liked for Thérèse's to be there, too, and I used to offer myself to Jesus to be His *little flower*. . . .[1]

If I didn't know how to play games, I loved reading a lot, and I would have spent my life doing it. Fortunately, I had as my guides earthly *angels* who chose books for me that, while entertaining me, nourished my heart and my mind. And then I was supposed to spend only a certain amount of time reading, and that was for me the subject of great sacrifices, since my reading was often interrupted in the middle of the most fascinating passage. . . .

[1] The text of *The Divine Prisoner's Little Flower* is given in appendix one.

This attraction to reading lasted until my entrance into Carmel. It would be impossible for me to say how many books passed through my hands, but God never allowed me to read a single one that was capable of harming me. It's true that as I read certain tales about knights, I didn't always feel at first glance the *truth* about *life*; but soon God let me feel that true glory is the one that will last forever, and that to obtain it, it isn't necessary to do outstanding works, but to remain hidden and to practice virtue in such a way that the right hand doesn't know what the left hand is doing [Mt. 6:3]. . . .

So, when I was reading the tales of the patriotic actions of French heroines, in particular those of the *Venerable* Joan of Arc,[1] I had a great desire to imitate them. It seemed to me that I felt within me the same burning desire that stirred them, the same heavenly inspiration. Then I received a grace that I have always regarded as one of the greatest of my life, because at that age I wasn't receiving *enlightenment* like that with which I'm flooded now. I thought that I was born for glory, and in my search for the means of obtaining it, God inspired in me the feelings that I've just written about.

He also gave me to understand that my own glory wouldn't be apparent to mortal eyes, that it would consist in becoming a great *Saint*!!! . . . This desire might seem foolhardy if one were to consider how weak and imperfect I was, and how much I still am after seven years spent in the religious life, but nonetheless I still feel the same audacious confidence that I'll become a great Saint. That's because I'm not counting on my merits, since I have *none*, but I hope in the One who is Virtue and Holiness Itself. It is He alone who, being content with my feeble efforts, will raise me up to Himself and, covering me with His infinite merits, will make me a *Saint*. I wasn't thinking then that one has to suffer a great deal to arrive at sainthood, but God wasn't long in showing me this by sending me the trials that I told about earlier. . . .

[1] Joan of Arc was declared a saint in 1920, twenty-five years after these words were written.

———•+•———

Now I need to pick up my story at the point where I left off: Three months after I was healed, Papa took us on a trip to Alençon. This was the first time I had gone back there, and great was my joy when I saw once again the places where I had spent my early childhood, especially to be able to pray over Mama's grave and to ask her to protect me always. . . .

God gave me the grace to know the *world* only enough to hold it in contempt and to remove myself from it. I could say that it was during my stay at Alençon that I had my *first entrance* into the *world.* Everything was joy and happiness around me. I was received with open arms, fussed over, admired—in a word, my life for two weeks was just strewn with flowers. . . . I admit that this life had charms for me. Wisdom was right to say, "the bewitching of the trifles of the world seduces even the spirit that is far from evil" [see Wis. 4:12]. At the age of ten the heart can easily let itself be dazzled, so I see it as a great grace not to have stayed in Alençon. The friends that we had there were too worldly. They knew too well how to mix the joys of the world with God's service. They didn't think about *death* enough, and yet *death* has come to visit a great number of persons whom I have known, young, rich, and happy! . . .

I love to return in my thoughts to the *enchanting* places where they lived, to wonder where they are, what use they now have of the castles and parks where I saw them enjoying the commodities of life. . . . And I see that all is a meaningless chasing after the wind under the Sun [Eccl. 2:11] . . . and that *the only good* is to love God with our whole heart and here below to be *poor* in spirit [Mt. 5:3]. . . .

Perhaps Jesus wanted to show me the world before the *first visit* that He was to pay me so that I might freely choose the path that I was to promise Him that I would follow.

My First Communion remains engraved on my heart, like a cloudless memory. It seems to me that I couldn't have been better disposed than I was, and then the troubles of my soul left me for nearly a year. Jesus wanted to cause me to taste as perfect a joy as is possible in this valley of tears. . . .

Do you remember, beloved Mother, the delightful little book that you gave me three months before my First Communion? . . . This is what helped me to prepare my heart in an unwavering and rapid manner, for if I had already been preparing it for a long time, I had to give it a new forward impulse, fill it with *new flowers* so that Jesus could find rest there with pleasure. . . . Each day I did a great number of practices that yielded as *many flowers*. I fulfilled a still greater number of objectives that you had written in my little book for each day, and these acts of love formed the flower *buds*. . . .

Each week you wrote me a lovely little letter that filled my soul with deep thoughts and helped me practice virtue. This was a comfort for your poor little daughter, who was making such a *great sacrifice* in accepting not being *prepared* by sitting on your lap every night as her dear Céline had been. . . .

It was Marie who took Pauline's place for me. I would sit on her lap, and there I would listen *avidly* to what she was telling me. It seemed to me that her whole heart, so *big*, so *generous*, was passing into me. Like those illustrious warriors who teach their children the craft of weaponry, that is how she spoke to me about the *combats* of life, about the palm that is given to those who are victorious. . . . Marie talked to me still more about the everlasting riches that it's easy to store up each day, about how unfortunate it is to pass by without wanting to take the trouble to reach out our hand to take them. Then she indicated to me the way to be *holy* through faithfulness in the smallest of things. She gave me the little booklet "On Renouncing Oneself," and I meditated on it with delight. . . .

Oh! How *eloquent* was my dear godmother! I would have wanted not to be the only one to hear her profound teachings. I felt myself so *touched* that in my naïveté I believed that the greatest sinners would have been touched as I was, and that leaving right there their perishable riches, they would no longer have wanted to gain anything but the riches of heaven. . . .

At that time no one had taught me yet how to pray at length. I certainly wanted to, but Marie thought I was pious enough, so she let me say only my set prayers.

One day one of my teachers at the Abbey school asked me what I did on my days off when I was alone. I replied that I would go behind my bed into an empty space that was there and that was easy for me to shut off with the curtain, and there, "*I would think.*" "But what do you think about?" she said. "I think about God, about life . . . about ETERNITY, I just *think*! . . ." The good nun laughed a lot at me. Later she liked to remind me of the time *when I used to think*, and asked me if I was still *thinking*. . . . I understand now that I was praying at length without knowing it, and that already God was teaching me in secret.

———·•·———

The three months of preparation went by quickly. Soon I was to go on retreat, and for that I was to become a full boarder at the Abbey and sleep there. I cannot tell the sweet memory that this retreat left me. Truly, if I suffered a lot by staying full time in the Abbey, I was amply repaid by the inexpressible happiness of those few days spent awaiting Jesus. . . . I don't believe that one can taste that joy elsewhere than in religious communities. Since the number of children is small, it's easy to be concerned with each one in particular, and truly our teachers poured out motherly care on us at that time. They were concerned with me even more than the others. Each night the head teacher came with her little lantern to kiss me good night as I went to my bed, showing me great affection. One night, touched by her goodness, I told her that I was going to confide in her a *secret*. Taking my *precious little book* that was under my pillow, I showed it to her, my eyes shining with joy. . . .

In the morning, I found it very nice to see all the pupils getting out of bed as soon as they had been awakened and to do as they did. But I wasn't used to getting myself ready all alone. *Marie* wasn't there to *curl my hair*, so I found myself obliged to go and timidly present my comb to the mistress of the dressing room. She laughed when she saw a big girl, eleven years old, who didn't know how to take care of herself. However, she combed my hair, but not as *gently* as Marie. Nonetheless, I didn't dare to *cry out*, something that I used to do every day under the *gentle* hand of my *godmother*. . . .

I had the experience during my retreat of being a child who was fussed over and watched over like few people on earth, especially among children who have been deprived of their mother. . . . Every day Marie and Léonie used to come to see me with Papa, who spoiled me a great deal, so I didn't suffer the privation of being away from the family, and nothing came to obscure the beautiful heaven of my retreat.

I listened with a great deal of attention to the instructions that Fr. Domin gave us, and I even wrote down a summary of them. As far as my *thoughts* were concerned, I didn't want to write any of them down, saying that I would remember them well, which was true. . . .

For me it was a great happiness to go with the nuns to all the services. I made myself noticed among my classmates due to a *big Crucifix* that Léonie had given me and that I would place on my belt the way missionaries do. This Crucifix was the envy of the nuns, who thought that by wearing it I wanted to imitate my *Carmelite sister*. . . . Oh! It really was toward her that my thoughts would go. I knew that *my Pauline* was on retreat like me, not so that Jesus would give Himself to her, but to give herself to Jesus. So this solitude spent waiting was doubly precious to me. . . .

I remember that one morning they had me go to the infirmary because I was coughing a lot. (Since my illness the teachers used to pay a lot of attention to me. For a slight headache, or if they saw that I was more pale than usual, they would send me to get some air or to rest in the infirmary.) I saw my *beloved Céline* come in. She had obtained permission to come see me in spite of the retreat, in order to offer me a picture that gave me a lot of pleasure. It was "*The Divine Prisoner's Little*

Flower." Oh! how sweet it was to receive this memento from the hand of *Céline*! . . . How many thoughts of love I had because of her! . . .

The day before the big day I received absolution for the second time. My general confession left me with great peace in my soul, and God didn't allow the slightest cloud to come and trouble it. In the afternoon I asked for forgiveness of *the whole family* who came to see me, but I could speak only by my tears—I was too moved. . . . Pauline wasn't there, but I nonetheless felt that she was near me in heart. She had sent me a *beautiful picture* through Marie. I never got tired of admiring it and having everyone else admire it, too! . . .

I had written to the good Fr. Pichon to commend myself to his prayers, telling him that soon I would be a Carmelite nun and then he would be my spiritual director. (That is in fact what happened four years later, since it was at Carmel that I opened my soul to him. . . .) Marie gave me a *letter from him*, and truly I was too happy! . . . All this happiness came to me at once. What pleased me the most in his letter was this sentence: "Tomorrow I will go up to the Holy Altar for you and your Pauline!" Pauline and Thérèse became more and more united on the eighth of May, since Jesus seemed to mingle them together by flooding them with His graces. . . .

The "beautiful day of days" arrived at last. What indescribable memories have left in my soul the *slightest details* of this day from heaven! . . . The joyous waking at first light, the *respectful* and tender hugs of the teachers and the older classmates. . . . The big room filled with *snow-white garments* that each child in turn saw herself clothed with. Above all the entrance into the chapel and the *morning* singing of the beautiful hymn "O Holy Altar surrounded by Angels!"

But I don't want to enter into the details. Just as there are things that lose their sweet scent as soon as they are exposed to the air, there are also *thoughts of the soul* that cannot be interpreted in the language of the earth without losing their intimate and heavenly feeling. They are like that white stone that will be given to those who are victorious and on which is written a new name that no one *knows other than the one* who receives it [cf. Rev. 2:17].

Oh! How sweet was the first kiss of Jesus on my soul! . . . It was a kiss of *love*. I *felt myself loved*, and I also said, "I love You, I give myself to You forever." There were no demands, no struggles, no sacrifices. For a long time Jesus and poor little Thérèse had been *looking at* each other and understanding each other. . . . That day it was no longer a *look*, but a *fusion*. They were no longer two; Thérèse had disappeared, like a drop of water that disappears into the ocean. Jesus alone remained; He was the master, the King. Hadn't Thérèse asked Him to take away her *freedom, for her freedom* made her afraid? She felt herself to be so weak, so fragile, that forever she wanted to unite herself with the Divine Strength! . . .

Her joy was too great, too deep for her to be able to contain it. Delicious tears soon flooded her, to the great surprise of her friends, who later said to one another, "So, why did she cry? Wasn't there something that was bothering her? . . ." "No, it was rather that she wasn't able to have her mother near her, or her sister that she loves so much, the one who is a Carmelite nun." They didn't understand that when the joy of heaven comes into a heart, that exiled heart can't bear it without shedding tears. . . .

Oh, no, Mama's absence didn't cause me pain on the day of my First Communion. Wasn't heaven in my soul, and hadn't Mama taken her place there [in heaven] a long time ago? So on receiving Jesus' visit, I was also receiving that of my beloved mother, who was blessing me and rejoicing at my happiness. . . .

I wasn't grieving over Pauline's not being there; no doubt I would have been happy to see her at my side, but for a long time my sacrifice had been accepted. That day, joy alone filled my heart. I was uniting myself with Pauline, who was giving herself irrevocably to the One who was giving Himself so lovingly to me! . . .

In the afternoon I was the one who pronounced the act of consecration to the Blessed Virgin. It was quite just that I should *speak* in the name of my classmates to the Mother in heaven, I who had been deprived so young of my earthly mother. I put my whole heart into *speaking to her*, to consecrating myself to her, like a child who throws herself into her mother's arms and asks her to watch over her. It seems to me that the Blessed Virgin must have gazed at her little flower and *smiled* at her. Wasn't she the one whom she had cured with a *visible smile?* . . . Hadn't she placed, into the blossom of her little flower, her Jesus, the Flower of the Fields, the Lily of the Valley? . . .

On the evening of that beautiful day, I joined my earthly family again. Already the morning after the Mass, I had hugged *Papa* and all my dear relatives, but then it was the real reunion, with Papa taking the hand of his little queen and heading toward the *Carmelite convent.* Then I saw my *Pauline,* who had become Jesus' bride [by taking the nun's veil]; I saw her with her white veil like mine, and her crown of roses. . . . Oh! My joy knew no bitterness: I hoped to join her soon and with her to await *heaven*!

I was not insensitive to the family celebration that took place on the evening of my First Communion. The beautiful watch that my king gave me, gave me great pleasure. But my joy was tranquil, and nothing came to trouble my inner peace.

Marie took me with her the night that followed that beautiful day, for the most radiant days are followed by the shadows of night. Only the day of the first, the only, the eternal Communion in heaven will be without a sunset! . . .

The day after my First Communion was again a beautiful day, but it was stamped with melancholy. The beautiful outfit that Marie had bought me, all the presents that I had received, these were not filling my heart. It was only Jesus who could satisfy me. I longed for the moment when I could receive Him a second time.

About a month after my First Communion I went to confession for Ascension, and I dared to ask permission to receive Holy Communion. Against all hope, the priest allowed me to do so, and I had the happiness of going to kneel at the Holy Table between Papa and Marie. What a sweet memory I retained of that second visit of Jesus! My tears flowed again with an inexpressible sweetness. I kept repeating unceasingly to myself the words of St. Paul, "I no longer live, but Christ lives in me" [Gal. 2:20]. . . .

After that Communion, my desire to receive God became greater and greater, and I obtained permission to receive it on all the principal feast days. The day before those happy days Marie would take me in the evening on her lap and prepare me as she had done for my First Communion. I remember that once she talked to me about suffering, telling me that I would probably not walk on that path, but that God would always carry me like a child. . . .

The day after my Communion, Marie's words came back to my thoughts. I felt arising in my heart a great *desire* for *suffering* and at the same time the intimate assurance that Jesus was reserving for me a great number of crosses. I felt myself flooded with such great *consolations* that I see them as one of the *greatest* graces of my life. Suffering became my attraction; it had charms that delighted me without my being really familiar with them. Until then I had suffered without *loving* suffering. Since that day I've felt a veritable love of it. I also felt the desire to love only God, to find joy only in Him.

Often during my Communions, I would repeat these words from the *Imitation of Christ*: "O Jesus, inexpressible *sweetness*, change for me into *bitterness*, all the consolations of the earth. . . ." This prayer came out of my lips without effort, without constraint. It seemed to me that I was repeating it, not by my will, but like a child who repeats the words that a friend inspires in her. . . . Later I will tell you, beloved Mother, how Jesus was pleased to make my desire come true, how He was always, He alone, my inexpressible *sweetness*. If I were to talk to you about this right away I would be obliged to anticipate the time of my life as an adolescent, yet I still have many details to give you about my life as a child.

A short time after my First Communion, I went on retreat again for my Confirmation. I had prepared myself with great care to receive the visit of the Holy Spirit. I didn't understand why great attention wasn't paid to receiving this sacrament of Love. Ordinarily only one day of retreat was spent in preparation for Confirmation, but since the Bishop wasn't able to come on the appointed day, I had the consolation of having two days

Thérèse at Boarding School   *Thérèse at 13*

Thérèse on the Day of Her First Communion

Inner Chapel of the Benedictines of Lisieux
Where Thérèse Received Her First Communion

of solitude. To keep us occupied our teacher took us to Mount Cassin, and there I picked handfuls of big daisies for Corpus Christi [the Feast Day on the Thursday after Trinity Sunday, celebrating the institution of the Eucharist]. Oh! How joyful my soul was. Like the apostles, I was happily awaiting the visit of the Holy Spirit [Acts 2:1–4]. . . . I was full of joy at the thought that soon I would be a complete Christian, and especially at the thought that forever I would have on my forehead the mysterious cross that the Bishop would mark there when he bestowed the sacrament. . . .

Finally the happy moment came. I didn't feel a violent wind at the moment of the coming down of the Holy Spirit, but rather that *gentle breeze* the murmur of which Elijah heard on Mount Horeb [1 Kings 19:11–12]. . . . On that day I received the strength to *suffer*, for soon afterward the martyrdom of my soul was to begin. . . . It was dear Léonie who served as my sponsor [just as Marie had been my sponsor at my baptism]. She was so moved that she couldn't stop her tears from flowing the whole time of the ceremony. With me she received Holy Communion, for once again I had the happiness of uniting myself to Jesus on that beautiful day.

After these delightful and unforgettable festivities, my life went back to being *ordinary.* That is, I had to go back to the life of a boarding schoolgirl that was so painful to me. At the time of my First Communion I loved that existence with children of my age, all full of good will, having made, like me, the resolution to practice virtue seriously. But I had to get back into contact with very different students, self-indulgent, not wanting to follow the rules, and that made me very unhappy. I was of a cheerful nature, but I didn't know how to give myself over to the games of my age.

Often during recess I would lean against a tree, and there I would contemplate the *evil eye,* giving myself over to serious reflections! I had invented a game I liked. It consisted in burying the poor little birds that we used to find dead under the trees. Lots of students wanted to help me, so our cemetery became very pretty, planted with trees and flowers proportionate to the size of our little feathered friends.

Furthermore, I liked to tell stories that I made up as they came to my mind. My classmates would surround me eagerly, and sometimes older students would mix with the listeners. The same story lasted for several days, because I liked to make it more and more interesting according to how I saw the impressions that it produced and that manifested themselves on the faces of my classmates. But soon the teacher forbade me to continue my career as an orator, preferring to see us play and *run* rather than to *make speeches*.

I would easily retain the meaning of the things that I learned, but I had trouble learning word for word. So for the catechism, almost every day during the year that preceded my First Communion, I asked for permission to learn it during recess. My efforts were always crowned with success, and I was always at the head of the class. If by chance, due to a *single forgotten word*, I lost my place, my sorrow manifested itself by bitter tears that Fr. Domin didn't know how to soothe. He was quite happy with me (not because I used to cry) and used to call me his *little doctor*, because of my name of Thérèse [since Thérèse is the French version of the Spanish "Teresa," referring to St. Teresa of Avila, a Doctor of the Church].

One time the student who came after me didn't know how to ask her classmate the question about the catechism. Father went around to all the students in turn before coming back to me and saying that he was going to see if I was worthy of my place at the head of the class. In my *profound humility*, that's all I was waiting for. Standing up with assurance, I said what was asked of me without making a single mistake, to the great surprise of everybody. . . . After my First Communion, my enthusiasm for the catechism continued until I left school.

I had great success with my studies—I was nearly always first in the class. My greatest successes were history and writing. All my teachers regarded me as a very intelligent student. It wasn't the same at my uncle's, where I was considered to be a little know-nothing, good and sweet, with upright judgment, but incapable and awkward. . . . I'm not surprised at this opinion that my aunt and uncle had and no doubt still have of me. Since I was very timid, I almost never talked, and when I wrote, my *cat's scrawl* and my spelling, which is nothing less than natural, were not too *attractive*. . . .

In the little jobs of sewing, embroidery, and so forth, I was a success, it's true, in the opinion of my teachers, but the *gauche* and awkward manner in which I *held my work* justified the rather poor opinion that they had of me. I look at that as a grace. Since God wanted my heart for Himself alone, He granted my prayer by "changing into bitterness the consolations of this world." I needed this much more than I would have if I hadn't been sensitive to praise. Often in front of me people would brag about the intelligence of others, but never about mine. So I concluded that I didn't have any, and I resigned myself to seeing myself as being deprived of it. . . .

My sensitive and loving heart would have easily given itself away if it had found another heart capable of understanding it. . . . I tried to link up with other little girls my age, especially with two of them. I loved them, and for their part they loved me as much as they were *capable* of loving. But alas! How *narrow and flighty* is the heart of created beings!!! . . . Soon I saw that my love wasn't understood.

One of my girlfriends, who had been obliged to go back home to her family, came back several months later. During her absence I had *thought about her*, carefully guarding a little ring that she had given me. My joy was great when I saw my friend again, but alas! All I got was an indifferent look. . . .

When I saw that Céline *loved* one of our teachers, I wanted to do as she did, but since I didn't *know* how to gain the good graces of others, I was unable to succeed. Oh, happy ignorance! How many great ills it caused me to avoid! . . . How I thank Jesus for making me find only "bitterness in the friendships of this world." With a heart like mine, I would have let myself be taken and my wings clipped, and then how would I have been able to "fly away and find rest"? How can a heart that is given over to the affection of created beings be intimately united with God? . . . I feel that that is not possible. Without having drunk from the poisoned cup of the too-ardent love of created things, I *feel* that I cannot be deceived.

I have seen so many souls, seduced by that *false light*, flying like poor butterflies and burning their wings, then coming back toward the true, the sweet light of love that gave them new wings, more brilliant and light, so that they might fly toward Jesus, that Divine Fire "who burns without consuming." Oh! I feel it: Jesus knew I was too weak to be exposed to temptation. Perhaps I would have let myself be burned up completely by the *deceitful light* if I had seen it shining before my eyes. . . .

But that is not how it was. I encountered only bitterness where stronger souls encounter joy and detach themselves from it out of faithfulness. So I have no merit in not having given myself over to the love of created things, since I was preserved from this only by God's great mercy! . . . I recognize that without Him, I would have fallen as low as Mary Magdalene did, and the profound words of Our Lord to Simon echo with great sweetness in my soul. . . . I know, "Whoever has been forgiven little, loves little" [Lk. 7:47], but I also know that Jesus has *forgiven me more* than He did for *Mary Magdalene*, since He forgave me *in advance*, keeping me from falling. Oh! How I would like to be able to explain what I'm feeling! . . .

Here's an example that will interpret my thoughts a little: Suppose that the son of a capable doctor encounters on the road a rock that makes him fall, and that as a result of this fall he breaks a limb. Immediately his father comes to him, picks him up lovingly, takes care of his wounds, and in so doing uses all the resources of his art, and soon his son, now completely healed, bears witness to his gratitude. Without any doubt, this son is quite right to love his father! But I'm going to make still another supposition. The father, knowing that on the road his son was taking there was a rock, hurries to go before him and removes it (without anybody seeing him). Certainly, this son, the object of the father's prevenient tenderness, not KNOWING the misfortune from which he's been delivered by his father, won't bear witness of his gratitude, and will *love him less* than if he had been cured by him. . . . But if he comes to know the danger that he has just escaped, *will he not love him more?*

Well, I am this child who is the object of the anticipatory love of a Father who sent His Word not to redeem the *righteous* but *sinners*. He wants me to *love Him* because He has *forgiven* me, not much, but *everything*. He didn't wait for me to *love Him* much like Mary Magdalene, but He wanted ME TO KNOW how much He loved me with an inexpressible anticipation, so that now I might love Him *to distraction!* . . . I've heard it said that there is no pure soul that can be found who loves more than a repentant soul. Oh! How I would like to belie that saying! . . .

————•————

I perceive that I've strayed far from my subject, so I'll hasten to come back to it. The year that followed my First Communion was spent almost entirely without any interior trials for my soul. But it was during my retreat before my second Communion that I saw myself assailed by the terrible illness of scruples [excessive fear of having sinned]. . . . You would have to pass through that martyrdom in order to understand it well. It would be impossible for me to say what I suffered for *a year and a half.* . . .

All my thoughts and my simplest actions became a subject of trouble for me. I had no rest except when I told them to Marie, and that cost me a lot, because I thought I was obliged to tell her the extravagant thoughts that I had about her. Immediately after my burden was laid down, I enjoyed an instant of peace, but that peace passed like a flash of lightning, and soon my martyrdom started up again.

What patience didn't my dear Marie have to have, to listen to me without ever showing annoyance! . . . Scarcely had I come back from the Abbey when she began to curl my hair for the next day (because every day in order to please Papa the little queen had her hair curled, to the great surprise of her classmates and, above all, of her teachers, who never saw students who were made so much of by their family). While my hair was being curled I couldn't stop crying as I told all my scruples.

At the end of the year Céline, who had finished her studies, came back home, and poor Thérèse, who had to go back by herself, wasn't long in getting sick. The only charm that had kept her in school was to live with her inseparable Céline. Without her, "her little girl" could never stay there. . . .

So I left the abbey school at the age of thirteen, and I continued my education by taking several lessons each week at "Mrs. Papinau's." She was a very good person who was *well educated*, and who had somewhat the ways of the spinster. She lived with her mother. It was charming to see the little home that the *three* of them had together (because her *cat* was a member of the *family*, and I had to put up with her purring over my notebooks and even admire her pretty coat). I had the advantage of living intimately with the family: Since Les Buissonnets was too far for the somewhat elderly legs of my teacher, she asked me to come to my lessons in her home. When I arrived, all I would usually find was the elderly Mrs. Cochain, who would look at me "with her big, bright eyes," and then she would call out with her calm and sententious voice, "*Mrs. Pa-apinau* . . . Miz Thé . . . rèse is here! . . ." Her daughter would promptly reply with a *childish* voice, "Here I am, *Mother.*" And soon the lesson would begin.

These lessons had the advantage (besides the instruction that I received) of making me familiar with the world. . . . Who would have believed it! In that room furnished in antique style, surrounded by books and notebooks, I often witnessed visits of all types—priests, ladies, girls, and so forth. Mrs. Cochain carried on the conversation as much as possible in order to let her daughter teach me my lesson, but on those days I didn't learn much.

With my nose in a book, I heard everything that was being said, and even what it would have been better for me not to hear: Vanity slips so easily into the heart! . . . One lady said that I had beautiful hair. . . . As another was leaving, thinking that I couldn't hear her, she asked who this girl was who was so pretty, and these words, which were so much more flattering because they weren't said in front of me, left on my soul an impression of pleasure that showed me clearly how full of self-love I was.

Oh! How much compassion I feel for souls who are becoming lost! . . . It's so easy to wander off onto the flowery paths of the world. . . . No doubt, for a soul that's a bit haughty, the sweetness that it offers is mixed with bitterness and the *immense emptiness of the desires* could never be filled by the praises of a moment. . . . But if my heart hadn't been *lifted toward God beginning with its awakening*, if the world had smiled on me beginning with my entrance into life, what would have become of me? . . .

Oh, beloved Mother, with what gratitude do I sing of the mercies of the Lord! . . . Wasn't I, according to these words of Wisdom, "taken away, lest wickedness should alter my understanding, or deceit beguile my soul" [cf. Wis. 4:11]? . . . The Blessed Virgin also was watching over her little flower, and not wanting her to be faded by contact with the things of the earth, she drew her away onto *her mountain* before she had fully opened. . . . While awaiting that happy moment, little Thérèse was growing in the love of her Heavenly Mother. To prove her love for her, she did *an act* that *cost her a great deal* and that I'm going to tell in a few words, despite its *length*. . . .

Almost immediately after my entrance into the Abbey school, I had been received into the Association of the Holy Angels. I very much liked the devotional practices that it required, having a most particular attraction for praying to the Blessed Spirits from heaven, and particularly to the one [my guardian angel] whom God had given me to be my companion in my exile on earth.

A short time after my First Communion, the ribbon of the candidate for the Children of Mary replaced the one for the Holy Angels, but I left the Abbey without having been received into the Association of the Blessed Virgin. Having left before finishing my studies, I didn't have permission to enter the Association as a graduate. I admit that this privilege didn't excite my desire, but thinking that all my sisters had been "Children of Mary," I was afraid of being less the child of my Heavenly Mother than they were. So I went very humbly (in spite of what it cost me to do so) to ask for permission to be received into the Association of the Blessed Virgin at the Abbey. The head teacher didn't want to refuse, but she placed on me the condition that I would have to come back for two afternoons a week so I could show that I was worthy of being admitted.

Far from bringing me pleasure, this permission was extremely costly for me. I didn't have, like the other former students, a *teacher friend* with whom I could go spend several hours. So I had to content myself with going and greeting the teacher, and then I would work in silence until the end of the lesson. Nobody paid attention to me, so I went up to the gallery of the chapel and I remained before the Blessed Sacrament until the time when Papa would come get me. This was my only comfort: Wasn't Jesus my *only friend*? . . . I knew how to speak to Him alone. Conversations with created beings, even pious conversations, tired out my soul. . . . I felt that it was better to talk to God rather than to talk about God, because so much pride gets mixed into spiritual conversations! . . . Oh! It really was for the Blessed Virgin alone that I was coming to the Abbey. . . .

Sometimes I felt that I was *alone*, quite alone. As during the days of my life as a resident in the boarding school, when I would walk, sad and ill, in the big courtyard, I would repeat these words that always brought peace again and strength in my heart: "Life is your ship and not your dwelling! . . ." Even when I was quite little these words used to give me courage. And still, now, in spite of the years that have caused so many impressions of childish piety to disappear, the picture of the ship still charms my soul and helps it endure exile. . . .

Doesn't Wisdom also say that "Life is like a vessel that ploughs through the troubled waves and leaves after it no trace of its rapid passage" [see Wis. 5:10]? When I think about these things, my soul plunges into infinity and seems to me already to touch the everlasting shore. . . . It seems to me to receive Jesus' embraces. . . . I think I see my Heavenly Mother coming to meet me with Papa . . . Mama . . . the four little angels. . . . I think I'm finally enjoying forever the true, the everlasting life with my family. . . .

Before seeing the family reunited in the *Father's home* in heaven, I would still have to go through many separations. The year when I was received as a Child of the Blessed Virgin, she took away my dear Marie, the only support of my soul. . . . Marie it was who guided me, comforted me, helped me practice virtue: She was my sole oracle.

Without a doubt, Pauline had remained right in the forefront of my heart, but Pauline was far, very far from me! . . . I had suffered martyrdom in order to become accustomed to living without her, in order to see between her and me walls that could not be scaled, but finally I had wound up recognizing the sad reality: Pauline was lost for me, almost in the same way as if she had died. She still loved me and prayed for me, but in my eyes, *my beloved Pauline* had become a Saint who must no longer understand the things of earth, and, if she had known them, the miseries of her poor Thérèse would have surprised her and prevented her from loving her so much. . . . Besides, even though I would have liked to confide my thoughts to her, as at Les Buissonnets, I wouldn't have been able to; the meetings at the convent parlor were only for Marie. Céline and I didn't have permission to go to them until the end, just in order to have the time to have our hearts wrung. . . .

So in reality I had only Marie. For me she was, so to speak, indispensable. She was the only one to whom I told my scruples, and I was so obedient that my confessor never knew my wretched illness. All I told him was the number of sins that Marie allowed me to confess to him, not one more, so I would have passed for being the least scrupulous soul on earth, in spite of the fact that I was one to the nth degree. . . . So Marie knew everything that was going on in my soul. She also knew my desire to enter Carmel, and I loved her so much that I couldn't live without her. My aunt used to invite us every year to come one after the other to her home in Trouville. I would have liked to go there, only with Marie. When I didn't have her I was bored to death. However, one time I experienced pleasure in Trouville. This was the year of Papa's trip to Constantinople. In order to take our minds off of it a little (because we were quite distressed that Papa was so far away), Marie sent Céline and me to spend two weeks by the sea. I had a great time there because I had my Céline. My aunt secured every possible pleasure for us: donkey rides, fishing for eels, and the like. I was still a child in spite of being twelve and a half. I remember what joy I felt when I put on pretty sky-blue ribbons that my aunt gave me for my hair. And I also remember going to confession at Trouville to confess even that childish pleasure that seemed to me to be a sin. . . .

One night I had an experience that surprised me a lot. Marie Guérin [my cousin], who was always sick, often used to *whimper like a baby*. So my aunt would sweet-talk her and call her by the most tender of names, and my dear little cousin would continue nonetheless to bawl that she had a headache. I also had a headache nearly every day and didn't complain about it, but one night I tried to copy Marie. So I took it upon myself to start sniveling in an armchair in a corner of the living room. Soon Jeanne [my other cousin] and my aunt rushed around me and asked what was wrong. I replied, like Marie, "I have a headache." It seems that it wasn't befitting for me to complain. I never was able to convince them that the headache made me cry.

Instead of sweet-talking me, they spoke to me like a grownup, and Jeanne scolded me for my lack of trust in my aunt, because she thought that I had something troubling my conscience. . . .

In the end I was no better off for all my trouble and was quite resolved not to copy others. And I understood the fable of "The donkey and the little dog." *I was the donkey* who, seeing how *the little dog* was petted, came and put his heavy hoof on the table so he could receive his share of the petting. But alas! If I wasn't beaten like that poor animal, I received my just desserts, and those desserts cured me for life of the desire to attract attention. The only time I tried to do that it cost me too much! . . .

———————

The next year was the one when my dear godmother [Marie] left [for Carmel]. My aunt invited me to come again, but alone this time, and I was so out of my element that after two or three days I fell sick and they had to take me back to Lisieux. My sickness, which they were afraid was serious, was only homesickness for Les Buissonnets. Hardly had I set foot there when my health returned. . . . And it was from that very child that God was going to tear away the only support that attached her to life! . . . As soon as I learned about Marie's determination, I resolved no longer to take any pleasure on earth. . . .

Since I had left school, I had moved into *Pauline's* former painting room, and I had arranged it according to my taste. It was a real hodge-podge, an assemblage of piety and curios, a garden and an aviary. . . . Accordingly, at the end there stood out from the wall a *big cross* made of black wood, without a Christ figure, along with a few drawings that I liked.

On another wall, there was a hamper decorated with muslin and pink ribbons with herbs and flowers. Finally, on the last wall a portrait of *Pauline* at the age of ten was enthroned alone. Underneath that portrait I had a table on which was placed a *big cage*, housing a *great* number of birds whose melodious chirping deafened the ears of my visitors, but not those of their little mistress, who appreciated them very much. . . .

In addition there was yet the "little white piece of furniture" full of my school books, notebooks, etc. On that piece of furniture was placed a statue of the Blessed Virgin, with vases always full of natural flowers and candles. All around them there were a large number of little statues of Saints, little baskets decorated with shells, boxes made of Bristol board, and so on! Finally, my garden was *suspended* in front of the window. In it I raised pots of flowers (the rarest that I could find).

I had one more plant stand in the inner part of "my museum," and there I put my most privileged plant. . . . In front of the window stood my table, covered with a green rug, and on that rug I had placed, in the center, an *hourglass*, a little statue of St. Joseph, a watch stand, baskets of flowers, an inkwell, and a few other things. . . . A few *rickety* chairs and *Pauline's* delightful doll bed completed my furnishings. This poor little attic room was truly a world for me, and, like Mr. de Maistre, I could compose a book entitled *A Journey Around My Room*. [A book by this name, by Xavier de Maistre, was published in 1795.] It was in this room that I loved to stay by myself for hours on end to study and meditate before the beautiful view that stretched out before my eyes. . . .

When I learned about Marie's leaving, my *room* lost all its charms for me. I didn't want to leave, even for a single moment, the beloved sister who was to fly away soon. . . . How many acts of patience I caused her to practice! *Each time* I passed in front of her bedroom door, I knocked until she opened the door for me, and I hugged her with my whole heart. I wanted to store up hugs for all the time that I would be without them.

A month before she entered Carmel, Papa took us to Alençon, but that trip was far from being like the first one, because everything there for me was sadness and bitterness. I couldn't say how many tears I shed over Mama's grave, because I had forgotten to bring a bouquet of cornflowers that I had picked for her. I really had trouble over *everything*. It was the opposite of now, because God has given me the grace not to be downhearted over any passing thing.

When I remember the past, my soul overflows with gratitude on seeing the favors that I've received from heaven. Such a change has come over me that I'm not recognizable. . . . It's true that I desired the grace "to have absolute control over my actions, to be the master and not the slave." These words from the *Imitation of Christ* touched me deeply, but I had, so to speak, to purchase, by my desires, that inestimable grace. I was still only a child who seemed to have no other will than that of other people, which made people at Alençon say that I had a weak character. . . .

It was during that trip that Léonie tried out at the order of St. Clare. I was quite put out at her *extraordinary* entrance into that order, because I loved her a lot and I hadn't been able to give her a hug and a kiss before she left.

I'll never forget the goodness and the perplexity of that poor dear priest when he came to announce to us that Léonie had already taken the habit of a nun of the Poor Clares. . . . Like us, he found that quite odd, but he didn't want to say anything when he saw how unhappy

Marie was. He took us to the convent, and there I felt *heart pangs* as I have never felt at the sight of a convent. It produced on me the opposite effect of Carmel, where everything gladdened my soul. . . . Neither did the sight of the nuns enchant me, and I wasn't tempted to remain with them. Poor Léonie was nonetheless quite nice in her new outfit. She told us to look deeply into her eyes, because we were to see them no longer (since the Poor Clares always lower their eyes when they are seen). But God was content with two months of sacrifice, and Léonie came back to show us her blue eyes that were often wet with tears. . . .

When we left Alençon, I thought she would stay with the Poor Clares, so it was with a very heavy heart that I went away from the sad street of the half moon. Now there were only three of us, and soon our dear Marie was to leave us. . . .

The fifteenth of October was the separation day! Of the joyful, large family that lived at Les Buissonnets, only the last two children were left. . . . The doves had flown away from the father's nest. Those who remained would have liked to fly away and follow the others, but their wings were still too weak for them to be able to take flight. . . .

God, who wanted to call to Himself the littlest and weakest of all, hastened to develop her wings. He who is pleased to show His goodness and His power by using the least worthy instruments, wanted to call me before Céline, who without a doubt was the one rather than I who was worthy of that favor. But Jesus knew how weak I was, and it was for that reason that He hid me first in the cleft in the rock [Ex. 33:22; see also Song 2:14 and 1 Cor. 1:26–29].

When Marie entered Carmel, I was still excessively scrupulous [concerned with whether I had sinned]. No longer being able to confide in her, I turned toward heaven. It was to the four little angels who had gone up there before me that I spoke, because I thought that those innocent souls who had never known trouble or fear must surely have pity on their poor little sister, who was suffering on earth. I talked to them with the simplicity of a child, pointing out to them that since I was the last child in the family, I had always been the most loved, the most showered with tenderness by my sisters, and that if they had remained on earth, they would no doubt also have given me proofs of their affection. . . . Their leaving for heaven didn't seem to me to be a reason for them to forget me. On the contrary, now that they were where they could make withdrawals straight from the Divine treasure house, they ought to withdraw *peace* for me and show me, as well as heaven, that they still know how to love! . . .

The answer wasn't long in coming. Soon peace came and flooded my soul with its delicious waves, and I understood that if I was loved on earth, I also was loved in heaven. . . . Since that moment my devotion has grown for my little brothers and sisters, and I love to talk often with them, to speak to them about the sadnesses of exile . . . and about my desire to go soon to be with them in the Homeland! . . .

5
AFTER THE GRACE
OF CHRISTMAS
1886–1887

The blood of Jesus / Pranzini, my first child
The Imitation of Christ *and Arminjon / Desire to enter Carmel*
Confiding in my father / Sudden change in my uncle
Opposition by the Superior / Visit to Bayeux

If heaven was pouring out graces on me, it wasn't because I deserved them. I was still quite imperfect. It's true that I had a great desire to practice virtue, but I undertook it in a funny way. Here's one example: Since I was the youngest, I wasn't used to taking care of myself. Céline cleaned the room where we slept together, and I never did any housework. After Marie entered Carmel, it happened to me sometimes to please God by trying to make the bed, or, in Pauline's absence, to bring in her pots of flowers at night. As I said, it was *for God alone* that I did these things. So I shouldn't have been waiting for a *thank you* from created beings. Alas! It was completely otherwise. If Céline had the misfortune not to look happy and surprised at my little services, I wasn't happy, and I proved it by my tears. . . .

I was really unbearable due to my overly great sensitivity. So if it happened that I involuntarily gave a slight amount of trouble to a person I loved, instead of taking the high road and *not crying*, I increased my fault, instead of reducing it, by *crying* like a baby. And when I started to become comforted by the thing itself, I *cried because I had cried.* . . . All this reasoning was useless, and I couldn't manage to correct this wicked fault. I don't know how I could soothe myself with the sweet thought of entering Carmel, seeing that I was still in *baby diapers!* . . .

It was necessary for God to do a small miracle in order to make me *grow up* in one moment, and He did that miracle on the unforgettable day of Christmas. On that radiant night that sheds light on the delights of the Holy Trinity, Jesus the sweet *little* Child, just one hour old, changed the night of my soul into torrents of light [Ps. 139:12]. . . . On that *night when* He made Himself *weak* and suffering out of love for me, He made me *strong* and courageous. He put his armor on me [Eph. 6:11], and since that blessed night I was never defeated in combat. On the contrary, I marched from victory to victory, and I began, so to speak, to run a champion's course [Ps. 19:5]. The fount of my tears was dried up, and since that time it opened only rarely and with difficulty, justifying this word that had been said to me: "You cry so much in your childhood that later you won't have any more tears to shed!"

It was on December 25th, 1886, that I received the grace to leave my childhood—in a word, the grace of my complete conversion: We were coming back from Midnight Mass, where I'd had the happiness of receiving the *strong* and *powerful* God [Ps. 24:8]. Upon arriving at Les Buissonnets, I was rejoicing at going to get my shoes [on which my

Christmas presents had been placed] from the fireplace. This traditional practice had caused us so much joy during our childhood that Céline wanted to continue to treat me like a baby, since I was the youngest in the family. . . . Papa loved to see how happy I was, to hear my shouts of joy as I took out each surprise from my *magic shoes*, and the gaiety of my dear king increased my happiness even more.

But Jesus, who wanted to show me that I needed to undo these childish shortcomings, also took away these innocent joys from me. He allowed Papa, who was tired from the Midnight Mass, to feel annoyed at seeing my shoes on the fireplace, and for him to say these words that pierced me to the heart: "Well, fortunately this is the last year." I then ran up the stairs to take off my hat. Céline, who knew how sensitive I was, saw the tears shining in my eyes; she also felt like crying, because she loved me a lot and understood my grief. "Oh, Thérèse," she said, "don't go back down. It will hurt you too much to look in your shoes right away."

But Thérèse wasn't the same any longer; Jesus had changed her heart! Forcing back my tears, I ran quickly back down the stairs, and, restraining my pounding heart, I took my shoes, and, placing them in front of Papa, *joyously* I took out all the objects, looking happy as a queen. Papa was laughing. He had also become joyful again, and Céline thought she was dreaming! . . . Fortunately, it was a sweet reality. Little Thérèse had regained the strength of soul that she had lost at the age of four and a half, and she was to keep it forever! . . .

On that *night of light* the third period of my life began, the most beautiful of them all, the most filled with graces from heaven. . . . In an instant, the work that I hadn't been able to do in ten years—Jesus did it, being content with the *good will* that I had no shortage of. Like His apostles, I could say, "Lord, I fished all night without catching anything" [see Lk. 5:5–10]. Then, more merciful toward me than He was toward His disciples, Jesus *Himself took* the net, threw it out, and brought it back in, full of fish. . . . He made me into a fisher *of souls* [Mk. 1:17]. I felt a great desire to work for the conversion of sinners, a desire that I had never felt so strongly. . . . In a word, I felt *charity* enter into my heart, the need to forget myself in order to please others, and ever afterward I was happy! . . .

———·—·———

One Sunday, as I was looking at a picture showing Our Lord on the Cross, I was struck by the blood that was falling from one of His divine hands. I felt great pain at the thought that this blood was falling to the ground without anyone hurrying to collect it, and I resolved to keep myself in spirit at the foot of the Cross in order to receive the divine dew that was flowing down from it, understanding that I must then spread it over souls. . . . Jesus' cry on the Cross also resounded continually in my heart: "*I am thirsty!*" [Jn. 19:28]. These words set on fire within me a keen fervor that I hadn't known before. . . . I wanted to give something to drink to my Beloved, and I felt myself consumed with *thirst* for *souls*. . . . It was no longer the souls of priests that attracted me, but those of *great sinners*. I *was burning* with the desire to snatch them from the everlasting flames. . . .

In order to stir up my fervor, God showed me that my desires were pleasing to Him. I heard about a terrible criminal who had just been condemned to death for some horrible crimes. Everything would lead one to believe that he would die without repenting. I wanted at all cost to prevent him from going to hell. In order to do that I used every imaginable means: Sensing that in myself I could do nothing, I offered to God all the infinite merits of Our Lord and the treasures of the Holy Church. Finally I begged Céline to have a Mass said for my intentions, not daring to ask myself, for fear that I would be obliged to admit that it was for Pranzini, the terrible criminal. I didn't want to tell Céline, either, but she put such tender and such pressing questions to me that I confided my secret in her.

Far from making fun of me, she asked to help me convert *my sinner*. I accepted with gratitude, because I would have wanted every creature to unite with me in imploring for grace for the guilty one. Deep in my heart I felt *certainty* that our desires would be granted, but in order to give myself courage to continue to pray for sinners, I told God that I was quite sure that He would forgive poor miserable Pranzini, and that I would believe this even if he *did not confess* and showed *no sign of repentance,* so much did I have confidence in Jesus' infinite mercy, but I asked Him only for "*a sign*" of repentance simply for my consolation. . . .

My prayer was granted to the letter! Despite Papa's having forbidden us to read any newspaper, I didn't believe that I was disobeying him by reading the articles that talked about Pranzini. The day after his execution [on September 1st, 1887] I put my hand on the newspaper *La Croix.* I opened it hurriedly, and what did I see? . . . Oh! My tears betrayed my emotion, and I was obliged to go hide. . . . Pranzini had not confessed; he had climbed up onto the scaffold and was getting ready to put his head into the ominous opening in the guillotine, when suddenly, gripped with a sudden inspiration, he turned back, grabbed a *Crucifix* that the priest was holding up to him, and *kissed its sacred wounds three times!* . . . Then his soul went to receive the *merciful* judgment of the One who declares that in heaven there will be more joy for a single sinner who repents than for ninety-nine righteous persons who have no need for repentance [Lk. 15:7]! . . .

I had obtained "the sign" that I had asked for, and that sign was the faithful reproduction of the graces that Jesus had granted in order to draw me to pray for sinners. Wasn't it when I was facing *Jesus' wounds,* seeing His Divine *blood* flow, that the thirst for souls had entered into my heart? I wanted to give them to drink this *immaculate blood* that must cleanse them from their stains, and the lips of "*my first child*" were pressed upon the sacred wounds!!! . . . What an expressibly sweet reply! . . .

Oh! Since that unique grace, my desire to save souls has been growing every day. It seems to me that I can hear Jesus tell me, as He did to the Samaritan woman, "Give me a drink!" [see Jn. 4:6–15]. This was a true exchange of love: To souls I gave the *blood* of Jesus; to Jesus I offered these same souls, refreshed by His *Divine dew.* In that way it seemed to me that I was quenching His thirst, and the more I gave Him to drink, the more my poor little soul's thirst increased. And it was this burning thirst that He gave me as the most delicious beverage of His love. . . .

———•••———

In a short time God had managed to pull me out of the narrow circle in which I was spinning without knowing how to get out. When I see the road that He had me travel, my gratitude is great. But I must admit that if the biggest step was taken, I still had many things to get rid of. Freed from its scruples and its excessive sensitivity, my spirit developed.

I had always loved great and beautiful things, but at that time I was seized with an extreme desire *for knowledge.* Not content with the lessons and homework that my teacher gave me, I applied myself all alone to special studies of *history* and *science.* The other studies left me indifferent, but these two subjects attracted my entire attention. The result was that in a few months I acquired more knowledge than during my years of study. Oh! That was nothing but a meaningless chasing after the wind [Eccl. 2:11]. . . .

The chapter in the *Imitation of Christ* that talks about *knowledge* would often come to my thoughts, but I found the means to continue anyway, telling myself that since I was of school age, there was no harm in doing it. I don't think I offended God (although I recognize that I spent some useless time in doing this) because I spent only a certain number of hours studying and didn't want to go beyond that amount of time in order to mortify my overly keen desire for knowledge. . . .

I was at the most dangerous age for girls, but God did for me what Ezekiel reports in his prophecies: Passing close to me, Jesus saw that the time had come for me to be *loved* [see Ezek. 16:8–14]. So He made an alliance with me and I became *His.* . . . He spread His mantle over me, He washed me with precious perfume, clothed me with embroidered garments, giving me priceless necklaces and jewelry. . . . He nourished me with the finest of wheat, honey, and oil *in abundance.* . . . Then I became beautiful in His sight, and He made me into a powerful queen! . . .

Yes, Jesus did all that for me. I could go back over each word that I've just written and prove that it became real in my favor, but the graces that I wrote about earlier are proof enough of that. So I'm only going to talk about the food that He poured out on me "*in abundance.*" For a long time I had been nourishing myself on the "finest of wheat" contained in the *Imitation of Christ.* This was the only book that did me good, because I hadn't yet found the treasures hidden in the Gospels [Is. 45:3]. I knew by heart almost all the chapters of my dear *Imitation.* This little book never left me: In summer, I carried it in my pocket, in winter, in my muff, so it had become traditional. At my aunt's they found this quite amusing, and opening it at random they had me recite the chapter that they found before their eyes.

At the age of fourteen, with my desire for knowledge, God found that it was necessary to join "to the finest wheat," "honey and oil in abundance." This honey and this oil, He had me find in Fr. Arminjon's teachings about the present world and the mysteries of the future life. This book had been lent to Papa by my dear Carmelites, so, contrary to my usual habit (because I didn't read Papa's books), I asked to read it. This reading was again one of the great graces of my life. I read it at the window of my study room, and the impression that I felt from it is too intimate and too sweet for me to be able to tell you about it. . . .

All the great truths of religion, the mysteries of eternity, plunged my soul into a happiness that was not of earth [1 Cor. 2:9]. . . . I was already feeling what God reserves for those who love Him (not with the human eye, but with that of the heart), and seeing that eternal rewards have no proportion to the slight sacrifices of life [2 Cor. 4:17], I wanted to *love, love* Jesus with *passion*, give Him a thousand signs of love while I could still do it. . . . I copied several passages about perfect love and about the reception that God will give to His elect at the time when He *Himself* will become their great and eternal reward. I repeated unceasingly these words of love that had inflamed my heart. . . .

Céline had become the intimate confidante of my thoughts. Since Christmas we had been able to understand each other. The difference in age no longer existed, since I had grown big in size and especially in grace [2 Pet. 3:18]. . . . Before that time I often used to complain about not knowing Céline's secrets. She used to tell me that I was too little, that I would have to grow "to the height of a stool" in order for her to be able to trust me. . . . I used to love to climb up on that precious stool when I was at her side, and I used to tell her to speak intimately to me, but my industriousness was useless—a distance still separated us! . . .

Jesus, who wanted us to go forward together, formed in our hearts links that are stronger than those of blood. He made us become *soul sisters*. These words of St. John of the Cross, in his *Spiritual Canticle*, became a reality in us (speaking to the Bridegroom, the bride cries out): "Following your traces, the girls crossed the path lightly. The touching of the spark, the spiced wine, caused them to produce aspirations that were divinely perfumed." Yes, it was quite *lightly* that we followed Jesus' traces. The sparks of love that He sowed bountifully into our souls, the delicious and strong wine that He gave us to drink, caused passing things to disappear before our eyes, and from our lips there came out aspirations of love inspired by Him.

How sweet were the conversations that we used to have each evening in the belvedere! Our gaze fixed on faraway things, we would consider the white moon that was gently rising behind the big trees. . . . The silvery reflections that it would spread over sleeping nature, the brilliant stars shimmering in the infinite heavens . . . the light puff of the evening breeze making the snow-laden clouds float in the sky—all these things would lift our souls toward heaven, that beautiful heaven of which we were still contemplating only "the translucent *reverse* side." ["Sky" and "heaven" are the same word in French, thus the metaphor: the sky is the reverse side of heaven.]

I don't know if I'm wrong, but it seems to me that the outpouring of our souls was like that of St. Monica with her son [St. Augustine], when at the port of Ostia they remained lost in ecstasy at the sight of the marvels of the Creator! . . . It seems to me that we were receiving graces on as high an order as those granted to the great Saints. As the *Imitation* says, God sometimes communicates Himself amidst great splendor, and sometimes "gently veiled, in the form of shadows and figures." It was in this manner that He stooped down to manifest

Himself to our souls. But how *transparent* and *light* was the veil that hid Jesus from our eyes! . . . Doubt was impossible; already Faith and Hope were no longer necessary; *love* made us find on earth the One that we were seeking [1 Cor. 13]. "Having found Him alone, He had given us His kiss, to the end that henceforth no one might be able to deride us."

Graces as great as these must not remain fruitless, therefore their fruits were abundant. The practice of virtue became sweet and natural to us. At the beginning my face often betrayed the struggle, but little by little that impression disappeared, and renouncement became easy for me, even at the start. Jesus said, "For those who have will be given more, and they will have an abundance" [Mt. 25:29]. For one grace faithfully received He granted me a multitude of others. . . .

He gave Himself to me in Holy Communion more often than I would have dared to hope. I had taken as a rule of conduct to receive, without missing a single one, the Communions that my confessor would give me, but to let him set the number of them without ever asking him to do so. In those days I didn't have the *audacity* that I now possess. Without that I would have behaved differently, because I'm quite sure that a soul ought to tell her confessor the attraction that she feels toward receiving her God. It isn't just to remain in the golden ciborium [the covered receptacle that holds the consecrated Communion wafers] that He comes down *every day* from heaven. It's to find another heaven that is infinitely dearer to Him than the first one, the heaven of our soul, made in His image, the living temple of the adorable Trinity [1 Cor. 3:16]! . . .

Jesus, seeing my desire and the uprightness of my heart, permitted that during the month of May, my confessor told me to receive Holy Communion four times per week, and once that beautiful month had passed, he added a fifth time each time there was a feast day. The sweetest tears fell down my cheeks when I left the confessional. It seemed to me that it was Jesus Himself who wanted to give Himself to me, because I spent only a short time in the confessional. I would never say a word about my inner feelings. The road on which I was marching was so straight, so shining, that no other guide was needed for me than Jesus. . . . I used to compare spiritual directors to faithful mirrors who reflected Jesus into souls, and I used to say that for me God didn't use an intermediary, but He would act directly! . . .

When a gardener pours out attention on a fruit that he wants to mature before its season, it's never to leave it hanging from the tree, but in order to serve it on a brilliantly set table. It was with such an intention that Jesus poured out His graces on His little flower. . . . The One who cried out during the days of His mortal life, transported by joy, "I praise you, Father, . . . because you have hidden these things from the wise and learned, and revealed them to little children" [Lk. 10:21], wanted to make His mercy blaze within me. Because I was small and weak, He bent down to me and instructed me in secret about the *things* of His *love*. Oh! If the wise who have spent their lives studying had come to ask me, no doubt they would have been astonished to see a child of fourteen understand the secrets of perfection, secrets that all their knowledge could not reveal to them, since to possess it you have to be poor in spirit [Mt. 5:3]! . . .

As St. John of the Cross put it in his canticle, "I had neither guide, nor light, except the one that was shining in my heart. That light guided me more surely than that of noonday to the place where the One was waiting for me who knows me perfectly." That place was Carmel. Before resting in the shade of the One whom I desired [Song 2:3], I was to pass through many trials, but the Divine call was so pressing that even if I had had to *pass through flames*, I would have done so in order to be faithful to Jesus. . . .

To encourage me in my vocation, I found only one *single soul*, and that was that of my *dear Mother* [my sister Pauline]. . . . My heart found in hers a faithful echo, and without her I would no doubt not have arrived at the blessed shore that had received her five years earlier on its ground imbued with the heavenly dew. . . . Yes, for five years I had been separated from you, *dear Mother*. I had thought that I had lost you, but at the time of trial it was your hand that showed me the road that I needed to follow. . . .

I needed this relief, because my times at the parlor at Carmel had become more and more painful for me. I couldn't talk about my desire to enter the Convent without feeling myself being pushed away. Marie, who thought that I was too young, did everything in her power to prevent me from entering. You yourself, Mother, in order to test me, tried sometimes to slow down my enthusiasm. In short, if I hadn't truly had the vocation, I would have stopped at the beginning, because I encountered obstacles as soon as I began to respond to Jesus' call.

I didn't want to tell Céline about my desire to enter Carmel so young, and that made me suffer more, because it was very hard for me to hide anything from her. . . . That suffering didn't last long. Soon my dear sister [Céline] learned about my determination, and far from trying to turn me away from it, she accepted with admirable courage the sacrifice that God was asking of her.

To understand how great that sacrifice was, you would have to know how united we were. . . . It was so to speak the same soul that made us live. For a few months we had been enjoying together the sweetest life that girls could dream of. Everything around us responded to our desires, the greatest freedom was given to us, to the point where I used to say that our life on earth was the *ideal* of *happiness*. . . .

Hardly had we had the time to enjoy this *ideal* of *happiness* when we had to turn away from it freely, and my dear Céline didn't rebel for an instant. However, she wasn't the one whom Jesus called first, therefore she could have complained. . . . Having the same vocation as I, it was up to her to depart! . . . But in the time of the martyrs, those who remained in prison joyously gave the kiss of peace to their brothers who were the first to leave for the combat in the arena, comforting themselves with the thought that perhaps they were reserved for even greater combats: That's how *Céline* let her Thérèse go away, and she remained alone for the glorious and bloody combat [the lonely task of caring for Papa during his long illness] to which Jesus destined her as the *privileged one* of His *love*. . . .

So Céline became the confidante of my struggles and my sufferings. She took the same part in it as if it had been a question of her own vocation. From her I had no fear of opposition, but I didn't know what means to take to announce it to Papa. . . . How was I to talk to him about letting go of his queen, he who had just sacrificed his three oldest ones? . . . Oh! What inner struggles I suffered before feeling the courage to talk about it! . . . However, I had to come to a decision.

I was about to turn fourteen and a half. Only six months still separated me from that beautiful *Christmas night* when I had resolved to enter [Carmel], at the very time when the year before I had received "my grace." In order to make my great revelation I chose the day of *Pentecost*. All day long I pleaded with the Holy Apostles to pray for me, to inspire in me the words that I was going to have to say. . . . Weren't they the ones in fact who had to help the timid child that God was destining to become the apostle of apostles through prayer and sacrifice?[1]

It was only in the afternoon when, coming back from Vespers [the late afternoon church service], I found the opportunity to talk to my dear father. He had gone to sit at the edge of the cistern, and there, with hands clasped together, he was contemplating the marvels of nature. The sun, whose fiery rays had lost their ardor, was tingeing with gold the tops of the tall trees, in which the little birds were joyfully singing their evening prayer. Papa's beautiful face had a heavenly expression. I was feeling that peace was flooding his heart. Without saying a single word I went and sat beside him, with my eyes already wet with tears. He looked at me tenderly, and, taking my head, he pressed it against his heart, and said, "What's the matter, my little queen? . . . Tell me all about it. . . ." Then, standing up, as if to hide his own emotion, he walked slowly, still holding my head against his heart.

Through my tears I confided in him my desire to enter Carmel. Then his tears began mingling with my own, but he didn't say a word to turn me away from my vocation, being simply content to point out that I was still quite young to make such a serious determination. But I

---

[1] Carmelites have a special mission to pray for priests, and thus are "apostles" to the "apostles" (priests).

Thérèse at 15 and Her Father

"What's the matter, my little queen? . . . Tell me all about it. . . ."
Through my tears I confided in him my desire to enter Carmel.

defended my cause so well, that with Papa's simple and upright nature, he was soon convinced that my desire was that of God Himself, and in his deep faith he cried out that God was giving him a great honor to ask him for his children in this way.

We continued our walk for a long time. My heart, relieved by the goodness with which my incomparable father had greeted these confidences, poured itself out gently into his. Papa seemed to enjoy the tranquil joy that sacrifice, once accomplished, brings. He talked to me like a Saint, and I would like to remember his words in order to write them here, but I have retained only a memory that is too sweet to be able to write it down. What I do remember perfectly was the *symbolic* act that my beloved king accomplished without knowing it. Approaching a low wall, he showed me some *little white flowers* that looked like miniature lilies, and taking one of those flowers, he gave it to me, explaining to me with what care God had caused it to grow and had preserved it until that day. And hearing him talk, I thought I was listening to my story, so much resemblance there was between what Jesus had done for the *little flower* and *little Thérèse*. . . .

I received that little flower as if it were a Saint's relic, and I saw that by trying to pick it Papa had pulled up all its *roots* without breaking them. It seemed destined to live on in another piece of ground, more fertile than the tender moss in which its first mornings had been spent. . . . It was truly that same action that Papa had just done for me a few moments earlier, by allowing me to climb the mountain of Carmel and to leave the sweet valley that had witnessed my first steps in life.

I placed my little white flower in my copy of the *Imitation*, in the chapter entitled "On loving Jesus above all things." It's still there, only the stem has broken near the root, and God seems to be saying to me by that that He will soon break His little flower's bonds and will not leave her to fade on earth!

After I obtained Papa's consent, I thought I would be able to fly without fear to Carmel. But many sorrowful trials were still to test my vocation. It was only with trembling that I confided to my uncle [Isidore Guérin, Mama's brother] the resolve that I had taken. He showered upon me every sign of tenderness possible, but nonetheless, he didn't give me permission to leave. On the contrary, he forbade me from talking about my vocation before the age of seventeen. It was contrary to human prudence, he said, to allow the entrance into Carmel of a fifteen-year-old child. Since this life of a Carmelite nun was, in the eyes of the world, the life of a philosopher, it would be doing a great wrong to the religious life to let an inexperienced child embrace it. . . . Everybody would be talking about it. . . . etc. . . . etc. . . . He even said that to make him decide to let me leave, it would take a *miracle*.

I saw clearly that all reasoning would be useless. So I withdrew, my heart plunged into the deepest bitterness. My only comfort was prayer. I begged Jesus to do the *miracle* my uncle was requiring, since only at that cost would I be able to respond to His call.

A rather long time passed before I dared to talk about this again to my uncle. It cost me dearly to go see him. For his part, he no longer seemed to be thinking about my vocation, but I found out later that my great sadness influenced him a great deal in my favor. Before shining a ray of hope on my soul, God wanted to send me a most sorrowful martyrdom that lasted for *three days*. Oh! I have never understood so well as during that time of trial, the sorrow of the Blessed Virgin and St. Joseph as they were searching for the divine Child Jesus [Lk. 2:41–50]. . . .

I was in a sad desert, or rather my soul was like a fragile skiff with no pilot at the mercy of the storm-tossed waves. . . . I know, Jesus was there, asleep on my dinghy [Mk. 4:35–41], but the night was so dark that it was impossible for me to see Him. Nothing gave me light; not a single flash of lightning came to pierce the dark clouds. . . . Doubtless, lightning gives off quite a sad glimmer, but at least, if the storm had burst into the open, I would have been able to catch sight of Jesus for an instant. . . . It was *night*, the deep night of the soul. . . . Like Jesus in the agony in the garden [Lk. 22:39–46] I felt *alone*, finding comfort neither on earth nor on behalf of heaven. God seemed to have forsaken me [Mt. 27:46]!!! . . .

Nature seemed to have taken part in my bitter sadness. During those three days, the sun didn't shine a single one of its rays, and rain fell in torrents. (I've noticed that during the serious circumstances of my life, nature was the image of my soul. On days of tears, the sky wept with me; on days of joy, the sun sent its gleeful rays in profusion, and not one single cloud obscured the sky. . . .)

Finally, the fourth day arrived. It was a *Saturday*, the day dedicated to the sweet Queen of Heaven, when I went to see my uncle. What was my surprise when I saw him look at me and invite me into his office, without my having shown the desire to do so! . . . He began by reproaching me gently for seeming to be afraid of him, and then he told me that it wasn't necessary to ask for a *miracle*. He had only prayed to God to give him a "simple inclination of heart," and it had been granted. . . .

Oh! I wasn't tempted to plead for a miracle, because for me the *miracle had been granted*. My uncle was no longer the same. Without making any illusion to "human prudence," he told me that I was a little flower that God wanted to pick, and he would no longer be opposed to it! . . .

That definitive answer was truly worthy of him. For the third time that Christian from another age allowed one of the daughters whom his heart had adopted to go bury herself far from the world. My aunt [Céline Guérin] as well was admirable for her tenderness and prudence. I don't remember that during my trial she said a word to me that might have increased it. I saw that she had great pity upon her poor little Thérèse. So when I obtained my dear uncle's consent, she gave me hers, but not without proving to me in a thousand ways that my leaving would cause her pain. . . .

Alas! At that moment our dear relatives were far from expecting that they would have to renew the same sacrifice two more times. . . . But by holding out His *hand* to continue to ask, God didn't present it *empty*. His dearest friends were able to draw from it, in abundance, the strength and courage that they needed so much. . . . [Their own daughter Marie would enter Carmel as well.] But my heart carries me quite far from my subject. I return to it almost regretfully.

After my uncle's response, you understand, Mother, with what happiness I took the road back to Les Buissonnets, under *"the beautiful sky*, whose clouds had completely dissipated"! . . . In my soul as well, the night had ended. Jesus, upon waking, had given joy back to me. The roar of the waves had subsided. Instead of the wind of the trial, a light breeze filled my sail, and I thought I would soon arrive on the blessed shore that I was seeing so close to me. It was in fact quite close to my dinghy, but *more than one storm* was still to crop up, and, concealing the sight of its bright beacon light, cause it to fear being tossed, without any return, far away from the shore that it so fervently desired to reach. . . .

A few days after I obtained my uncle's consent, I went to see you, beloved Mother [Pauline], and I told you about my joy that now my trials had passed. But how surprised and disappointed I was at hearing you tell me that the Superior would not consent to my entrance before the age of twenty-one.

No one had thought about that opposition, the most invincible of all. However, without losing courage, I went myself with Papa and Céline to visit the priest, in order to try to touch him by showing him that I really did have the vocation for Carmel. He greeted us very coldly. In vain did my *incomparable* dear father join his pleas with mine: Nothing would change his mind. He told me that there was no peril remaining at home, that I could live the life of a Carmelite nun at home, that if I didn't take on the discipline everything wouldn't be wasted . . . etc., etc. Finally he ended by adding that he was only the *bishop's delegate*, and that if the bishop wanted to let me enter Carmel, he himself would have nothing more to say. . . .

I left the rectory filled with *tears*. Fortunately, my umbrella hid me, because the *rain* was falling in torrents. Papa didn't know how to comfort me. . . . He promised to take me to [see Bishop Hugonin in] Bayeux as soon as I showed the desire to do so, because I was resolved to *take this as far as necessary*. I even said that I would go to the *Holy Father* [Pope Leo XIII himself], if the bishop didn't want to allow me to enter Carmel at the age of fifteen. . . .

Many events happened before my trip to Bayeux. On the outside my life seemed the same. I studied, I took drawing lessons with Céline, and my capable teacher found me well suited to her art. Above all, I was growing in the love of God. In my heart I felt upward impulses that I had not known until then. Sometimes I was truly transported by love.

One night, not knowing how to tell Jesus that I loved Him and how much I desired that He be everywhere loved and glorified, I was thinking with sorrow that He could never receive in hell a single act of love. So I told God that to please Him I would willingly consent to find myself plunged into hell, so that He might be eternally loved in that place of blasphemy. . . . I knew that that couldn't glorify Him, since He desires only our happiness, but when one loves, one experiences the need to say a thousand foolish things. If I spoke that way, it wasn't because heaven excited my desire, but that my personal heaven was none other than Love, and I felt like St. Paul that nothing could separate me from the divine object that had stolen my heart! [Rom. 8:35–39] . . .

Before I left the world [that is, before I entered Carmel], God gave me the comfort of contemplating closely some *children's souls*. Since I was the youngest in the family, I had never had that pleasure. Here are the sad circumstances that brought this about: A poor woman, a relative of our maid, died in the flower of young age, leaving three very small children. During her illness we took into our home the two little girls, the elder of whom was not yet six years old. I took care of them all day long, and it was a great pleasure for me to see with what openness they believed everything that I told them. Holy Baptism must place into souls a very deep seed of the virtues of faith, hope, and charity, since from childhood they're already in evidence, and the hope of future good things is enough to cause them to accept sacrifices.

When I wanted to see my two little girls being considerate one to the other, instead of promising toys and candy to the one who would give in to her sister, I talked to them about the everlasting rewards that the little Jesus would give in heaven to good little children. The elder, whose reason was beginning to develop, looked at me with her eyes shining with joy, asking me a thousand charming questions about little Jesus and His beautiful heaven. She promised me enthusiastically that she would always prefer her sister, and said that never in her life would she forget "the great young lady," because that's what she called me. . . .

When I saw these innocent souls up close, I understood what an unfortunate thing it is not to teach them well as soon as their hearts awaken, while they are like soft wax on which virtues can be imprinted, but also vices. . . . I understood what Jesus said in the Gospel: "It would be better for you to be thrown into the sea . . . than for you to cause one of these little ones to stumble" [Lk. 17:2]. Oh! How many souls would reach holiness, if they were well directed! . . .

I know God doesn't need anyone to do His work, but just as He allows an able gardener to raise rare and delicate plants, and for that He gives him the knowledge he needs, but reserves for Himself the care to make the plants grow—this is how Jesus wants to be helped in His Divine cultivation of souls.

What would happen if a clumsy gardener didn't graft his bushes well? What if he didn't know how to recognize the nature of each one, and wanted to make roses bloom on a peach tree? . . . That would kill the tree, which even so was good and was capable of producing fruit.

That is how one must know how to recognize, beginning in childhood, what God asks of souls, and how to second the action of His grace, without ever speeding it up or slowing it down.

Just as little birds learn to *sing* by listening to their parents, in the same way children learn the knowledge of virtues, the sublime *song* of Divine Love, alongside souls that have been charged with forming them in life.

I remember that among my birds, I had a canary that sang delightfully. I also had a little linnet on which I poured out my *motherly* cares, having adopted it before it had been able to enjoy the happiness of its freedom. That poor little prisoner had no parents to teach it to sing, but hearing from morning to night its canary companion making joyful vocal flourishes, it wanted to imitate it. . . . This undertaking was difficult for a linnet, so its sweet voice had a great deal of trouble harmonizing with the vibrant voice of its music teacher. It was charming to see the efforts of the poor linnet, but they were at last crowned with success, for its song, while preserving a much greater sweetness, was absolutely the same as that of the canary.

Beloved Mother! You're the one who taught me to sing. . . . It was your voice that charmed me from childhood, and now I have the comfort of hearing that I'm like you! I know how far I am from being that, but I hope, in spite of my weakness, to repeat forever the same song as you! . . .

Before my entrance into Carmel, I had many more experiences with life and the wretchedness of the world, but those details would carry me too far away, so I'm going to go back to the story of my vocation.

———••———

October 31st [All Saints' Eve] was the day appointed for my trip to Bayeux. I left by myself with Papa, my heart full of hope, but also quite moved by the thought of presenting myself at the bishop's residence. For the first time in my life, I was going on a visit without being accompanied by my sisters, and that visit was to a *bishop*! I, who never needed to speak except to answer questions that were put to me, I was going to have to explain all by myself the purpose of my visit, and develop the reasons that caused me to petition for entry into Carmel— in a word, I needed to show how solid my vocation was.

Oh! What it cost me to make that trip! God had to grant me a very special grace in order for me to be able to overcome my great timidness.... It's also quite true that "Love never meets with impossibilities, because it believes that everything is possible and everything is permitted." It was truly love for Jesus alone that could have made me overcome these difficulties and those that followed it, because it pleased Him to make me gain my vocation through very great trials. . . .

Now that I enjoy the solitude of Carmel (resting in the shade of the One whom I so fervently desired) [Song 2:3], I find that I gained my vocation at very little cost, and I would be ready to endure much greater trials to acquire it if I still didn't have it!

It was *pouring* rain when we arrived in Bayeux. Papa didn't want to see his little queen enter the bishop's residence with her *beautiful outfit* all wet, so he had her climb into a carriage and drive to the cathedral. There my troubles began. His Excellency the bishop and all his clergy were attending a great funeral. The church was filled with ladies in mourning, all dressed in black, and everyone stared at me with my bright dress and my white hat. I would have wanted to leave the church but there was no thinking of it, because of the rain. And to humiliate me more, God allowed Papa with his patriarchal simplicity to bring me to the front of the cathedral. Not wanting to cause him pain, I carried myself with good grace and provided that distraction to the good citizens of Bayeux, whom I would have wished that I had never met. . . .

Finally I was able to breathe more easily in a chapel that stood behind the high altar, and I stayed there for a long time, praying fervently while waiting, that the rain would stop and let us leave. As we went back down, Papa had me admire the beauty of the building that seemed much bigger since it was deserted. But one single thought was on my mind, and I couldn't take pleasure in anything.

We went directly to see Fr. Révérony [the bishop's grand vicar, or representative], who had been instructed about our arrival, since he himself had set the date of the trip. But he wasn't home, so we had to wander in the streets, which seemed to me to be *quite sad*. Finally we arrived near the bishop's residence, and Papa had me enter into a beautiful hotel, where I didn't do honor to the capable cook. Poor dear Papa had an almost unbelievable tenderness toward me. He told me not to be vexed, that of course His Excellency was going to grant my request.

After resting, we returned to the home of Fr. Révérony. A gentleman arrived at the same time, but the grand vicar asked him politely to wait and had us enter first into his office. (The poor gentleman had the time to become bored, because the visit was long.) Fr. Révérony showed himself to be very pleasant, but I think that the purpose of this visit surprised him a great deal. After looking at me smilingly and asking a few questions, he told us, "I'm going to introduce you to His Excellency. Would you be so kind as to follow me." Seeing tears welling up in my eyes, he added, "Oh, I see some diamonds. . . . You mustn't show them to His Excellency! . . ."

He had us cross several very vast rooms, lined with bishops' portraits. Seeing myself in these great rooms had the effect on me of feeling like a poor little ant, and I wondered what I was going to dare to say to His Excellency. He [the bishop] was walking between two priests in a gallery. I saw Fr. Révérony say several words to him and come back with him. We were waiting for him in his office. There, three enormous armchairs were placed in front of the fireplace, in which a roaring fire was crackling.

Seeing His Excellency enter the room, Papa got down on his knees beside me to receive his blessing. Then His Excellency had Papa sit in one of the armchairs and sat across from him. Fr. Révérony tried to have me take the middle seat. I politely refused, but he insisted, telling me to show whether I was capable of being obedient. Immediately I sat down without thinking, and I was embarrassed to see him taking a chair while I was buried in an armchair in which four people like me would have been at ease (more at ease than I was, because I was far from being so! . . .).

I was hoping that Papa was going to speak, but he told me to explain to His Excellency myself the purpose of our visit. I did so, as *eloquently* as possible. His Excellency, who was used to *eloquence*, didn't seem very touched by my reasons. Instead of them one word from my parish priest would have served me well. Unfortunately, I didn't have it, and his opposition didn't plead in my favor at all. . . .

His Excellency asked me if I had wanted for a long time to enter Carmel. "Oh, yes! Your Excellency. . . ." "Let's see," began Fr. Révérony, laughing, "you can't say that you've had this desire for *fifteen years*." "That's true," I replied, smiling as well, "but there aren't many years to subtract, because I've wanted to become a nun beginning with my reaching the age of reason, and I desired to enter Carmel as soon as I got to know it well, because in that order I found that all the aspirations of my soul would be fulfilled." I don't know, Mother, if these are my exact words. I think I said them more poorly than that, but that's the gist of what I said.

His Excellency, thinking that he was being kind to Papa, tried to make me stay a few more years with him. So he was not a little *surprised* and *edified* to see him stand up for me, interceding for me to obtain the permission to leave the nest at the age of fifteen. However, it was all of no use. He said that before he made a decision a meeting with *the Superior of Carmel* was absolutely necessary. I couldn't have heard anything that would have given me greater suffering, because I knew about the total opposition of our rector. So without taking into account Fr. Révérony's admonition, I did more than *show diamonds* to His Excellency: I *gave* him some. . . . I saw clearly that he was touched by this. Grasping me by the neck, he leaned my head onto his shoulder and patted me, in a way, it would seem, that no one had ever been greeted by him.

He told me that everything was not lost, that he was quite happy for me to take the trip to Rome in order to affirm my vocation, and that instead of crying I ought to be joyful. He added that the next week, since he had to go to Lisieux, he would speak about me to the rector of St. James [our parish church], and that certainly I would receive his reply in Italy. I understood that it was useless to lodge more protests. Besides, I had nothing more to say, having exhausted all the resources of my *eloquence*.

His Excellency led us out as far as the garden. Papa *amused him a lot* by telling him that in order to look older I'd had my hair put up. (This wasn't wasted, because His Excellency never talks about "his little girl" without telling the story of her hair. . . .) Fr. Révérony wanted to go with us as far as the end of the bishop's garden. He told Papa that such a thing had never been seen before: "A father who was in as much a hurry to give his child to God as that child is to offer herself!"

Papa asked him for several explanations about the pilgrimage. Among them was how one should dress for an appearance before the Holy Father. I can still see him turn about in front of Fr. Révérony, asking him, "Do I look all right like this? . . ." He had also told His Excellency that if he didn't allow me to enter Carmel, I would ask that grace of the Supreme Pontiff [the Pope]. He was quite simple in his words and his manners, my beloved king, but he was so *handsome.* . . . He had a most natural distinction that must have pleased His Excellency a lot, accustomed as he was to being surrounded by persons who were acquainted with all the rules of etiquette of fine salons, but not the *king of France* and *Navarre* in *person* with his *little queen.* . . .

When I found myself in the street my tears began to flow again, not so much because of my disappointment, but rather on seeing my dear beloved father, who had just made a futile trip. . . . He, who had been imagining the joy of sending a dispatch to Carmel, announcing His Excellency's happy reply, was obliged to come back without having one. . . . Oh! What suffering I felt! . . . It seemed that my future was broken forever. The closer I came to the end, the more my affairs were becoming entangled. My soul was plunged into bitterness, but also into peace, because I was seeking only the will of God.

As soon as I arrived in Lisieux, I went to seek consolation at Carmel, and I found it at your side, beloved Mother. Oh, no! I will never forget all that you suffered because of me. If I wasn't afraid to profane them by using them, I could say the words that Jesus spoke to His apostles, on the night of His Passion: "*You* are those who have stood by me in my trials" [Lk. 22:28]. . . . My *beloved* sisters also offered me the *sweetest consolations.* . . .

⌢ 6
THE TRIP TO ROME
1887

Paris: Notre-Dame-des-Victoires [Our Lady of Victories]
Switzerland / Milan, Venice, Bologna, Loretto
The Coliseum and the catacombs / Audience with Leo XIII
Naples, Assisi, return to France / Three months of waiting

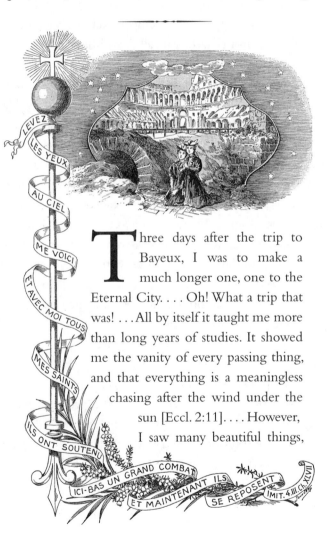

Three days after the trip to Bayeux, I was to make a much longer one, one to the Eternal City. . . . Oh! What a trip that was! . . . All by itself it taught me more than long years of studies. It showed me the vanity of every passing thing, and that everything is a meaningless chasing after the wind under the sun [Eccl. 2:11]. . . . However, I saw many beautiful things,

I contemplated all the marvels of art and religion, and above all I set foot on the same ground as the Holy Apostles, the ground drenched with the blood of the Martyrs, and my soul grew on contact with these holy things. . . .

I'm very happy to have been in Rome, but I understand the persons of the world who thought that Papa had me take that long trip in order to change my ideas about the religious life. There was in fact sufficient means to unsettle a vocation that wasn't quite firm.

Never having lived among the upper classes, Céline and I found ourselves among the nobility who almost exclusively comprised the pilgrimage. Oh! Far from dazzling us, all those titles and all those names with "de" in them [showing nobility] seemed to us only so much smoke. . . . Seen from afar, all that had sometimes thrown a bit of powder in my eyes, but up close, I saw that "all that glitters is not gold," and I understood this word from the *Imitation*: "Do not pursue that mirage that is called a great name; desire neither numerous entanglements, nor the particular friendship of any person."

I understood that true greatness is found in the *soul* and not in the *name*, since, as Isaiah said, ". . . you will be called by a new name that the mouth of the LORD will bestow" [Isa. 62:2], and St. John also said, "To those who are victorious, I will give some of the hidden manna. I will also give each of them a white stone with a *new name* written on it, known only to the one who receives it" [Rev. 2:17]. So it's in heaven that we will know what our titles of nobility are. Then each person will receive from God the praise that he merits, and the one who on earth attempted to be the poorest, the most forgotten for the love of Jesus, will be the first, the *noblest*, and the richest! . . .

The second experience that I had concerns the priests. Never having lived close to them, I couldn't understand the principal goal of the Carmelite reform [to pray for priests]. To pray for sinners delighted me, but to pray for the souls of priests, whom I thought of as purer than crystal, seemed astonishing to me. . . .

Oh! I understood *my vocation in Italy* was not to go looking too far for such a useful acquaintance. . . .

For a month I lived with many *holy priests*, and I saw that if their sublime dignity raises them above the Angels, they are nonetheless weak and fragile men. . . . If *holy priests* whom Jesus calls in the Gospel "the salt of the earth" show in their behavior that they have an extreme need of prayers, what can one say about the ones who are lukewarm? Didn't Jesus add, "But if the salt loses its saltiness, how can it be made salty again?" [Mt. 5:13].

Oh, Mother! How beautiful is the vocation that has as its object to *preserve the salt* that is destined for souls! That vocation is Carmel's, since the only objective of our prayers and our sacrifices is to be *the apostle of the apostles*, praying for them while they evangelize souls through their words and especially by their examples. . . . I have to stop; if I were to continue to talk about this subject I would never finish! . . .

—————

Beloved Mother, I'm going to tell you about my trip, giving some details. Forgive me if I give you too many of them. I don't reflect before writing, and I do it at so many different times, because of my having very little free time, that my tale will perhaps seem boring to you. . . . What comforts me is to think that in heaven I'll talk to you again about the graces that I received, and that I will be able to do so then in pleasant and charming terms. . . . Nothing more will come and interrupt our intimate outpourings, and in a single glance you will have understood everything. . . . Alas! Since I still have to use the language of the sad earth, I'm going to try to do so with the simplicity of a little child who knows the love of her Mother! . . .

It was the seventh of November that the pilgrimage left Paris, but Papa took us to that city several days beforehand in order to have us visit it.

One morning at 3:00 AM I passed through a still-sleeping Lisieux. Many impressions swirled through my soul at that time. I felt that I was going toward the unknown, and that great things were awaiting me there. . . . Papa was filled with joy; when the train got under way, he sang the old refrain, "Roll on, roll on, stagecoach, here we are on the big highway."

We arrived in Paris in the morning and immediately began to visit it. Poor dear Father got very tired in order to give us pleasure, so we had soon seen all the marvels of the capital. As for me, I found *only one* that delighted me, and that marvel was Notre-Dame-des-Victoires [Our Lady of Victories, a center of devotion to the Immaculate Heart of Mary]. Oh! What I felt at her feet I wouldn't be able to say. . . . The graces that she granted me moved me so deeply that only my tears betrayed my happiness, as on the day of my First Communion. . . .

The Blessed Virgin made me feel that it was *truly she who had smiled at me* and *had healed me.* I understood that she was watching over me, that I was *her* child, so that I could no longer call her anything but *Mama*, because that name seemed even more tender than that of Mother. . . . With what fervor I prayed to her to guard and keep me always, to soon realize my dream by hiding me *in the shadow of her virgin's mantle!* . . . Oh! That was one of my first desires as a child. . . . As I was growing up I had understood that it was at Carmel that it would be possible for me to truly find the mantle of the Blessed Virgin, and it was toward that fertile mountain that all my desires leaned. . . .

I once again pleaded with Our Lady of Victories to remove far away from me everything that might have been able to tarnish my purity. I was not unaware that on a trip like the one to Italy, I would encounter many things that were capable of troubling me. Especially because, not being acquainted with evil, I was afraid of uncovering it, not having experienced that for the pure, everything is pure [Titus 1:15], and that the simple and upright soul doesn't see evil in anything, because in fact evil exists only in impure souls and not in inanimate objects. . . .

I also prayed to St. Joseph to watch over me. Since childhood I had had for him a devotion that mingled with my love for the Blessed Virgin. Every day I used to recite the prayer "St. Joseph, Father and protector of virgins," so it was without fear that I undertook my trip to distant places. I was so well protected that it seemed impossible to me to be afraid.

After consecrating ourselves to the Sacred Heart of Jesus in the Sacré-Cœur [Sacred Heart] basilica in the Montmartre district—we left Paris on the morning of Monday the seventh. Soon we had met the persons who were going on the pilgrimage. I was so timid that ordinarily I hardly dared to speak, but I found myself completely rid of that troubling fault. To my great surprise I spoke freely with all the great ladies, the priests, and even His Excellency the Bishop of Coutances. It seemed to me that I had always lived in that world [of the privileged classes].

We were, I believe, well liked by everyone, and Papa was proud of his two daughters. But if he was proud of us, we were equally proud of him, because in all the pilgrimage there was no other gentleman who was more handsome or more distinguished than my dear king. He loved to be seen between Céline and me. Often when we were not in our carriage and I was some distance from him, he would call me so that I would give him my arm as in Lisieux. . . .

The Reverend Father Révérony was examining our actions carefully. I often saw him watching us from a distance. At mealtimes, when I wasn't facing him, he found the means to lean over me to see me and hear what I was saying. No doubt he wanted to get to know me to find out if I was truly capable of being a Carmelite nun. I think that he must have been satisfied with his examination, because at the end of *the trip* he seemed well disposed toward me. But in Rome he was far from being favorable to me, as I'm going to tell about later.

Before we arrived in the Eternal City, the objective of our pilgrimage, it was given to us to contemplate many marvels. First it was Switzerland, with its mountains with their summits lost in the clouds, its graceful waterfalls gushing in a thousand different ways, its deep valleys full of giant ferns and pink briars. Oh! Beloved Mother, how these beauties of nature, spread out in *profusion*, did good to my soul! How they lifted it up toward the One who was pleased to toss such masterpieces onto a land of exile that must last only a day. . . .

I didn't have eyes enough to look at it. Standing at the carriage door I almost lost my breath. I would have liked to be on both sides of the carriage at once, because as I turned from side to side, I saw countrysides of an enchanting aspect that were completely different from the ones that stretched out before me.

Sometimes we found ourselves on a mountain peak. At our feet there were sheer drops, whose aspect couldn't reveal their depth, that seemed ready to swallow us up. Or there was a delightful little village with its graceful chalets and its bell tower, above which softly hovered a few dazzling-white clouds. . . .

Farther on there was a vast lake that the last rays of the sun tinged with gold. The calm and pure waves, borrowing from the deep blue tint of the sky that mixed with the fires of the setting sun, presented to our marveling eyes the most poetic and most enchanting spectacle that could ever be seen. . . .

At the end of the vast horizon we could see the mountains, whose indistinct contours would have escaped our eyes if their snowy peaks made dazzling by the sun hadn't come to add one more charm to the beautiful lake that delighted us. . . .

As I looked at all these beauties, very deep thoughts arose in my soul. It seemed to me that I understood already the greatness of God and the marvels of heaven. . . . The religious life appeared to me *as it is* with its *obligations*, its little sacrifices accomplished in the shadows. I understood how easy it is to become fixated on oneself, to forget the sublime objective of one's vocation, and I said to myself, "Later, in the time of testing, when I'm a prisoner [a cloistered nun] in Carmel, I'll be able to contemplate only a little corner of the starry sky, and I'll remember what I'm seeing today. That thought will give me courage. I'll easily forget my petty little interests by seeing the grandeur and the power of God whom alone I want to love. I won't have the misfortune of becoming attached to *straw*, now that my *heart* has *seen* 'these things God has prepared for those who love him!' [1 Cor. 2:9] . . ."

———•——

After admiring God's power, I could still admire that which He has given to His creatures. The first city in Italy that we visited was Milan. Its cathedral all of white marble with its statues that were numerous enough to comprise a nearly countless people, we visited in all its smallest details. Céline and I were plucky, and were always the first to follow His Excellency directly in order to see everything concerning the relics of the Saints and to hear the explanations well. So while he was offering the Holy Sacrifice [saying Mass] on St. Charles's tomb, we were with Papa behind the altar, our heads leaning against the reliquary that houses the body of the Saint, dressed in its pontifical garments.

And that's how it was everywhere. . . . Except when it was a question of climbing up to where the dignity of a Bishop wouldn't allow, because then we knew quite well how to leave His Excellency behind. . . . Leaving the timid ladies hiding their faces in their hands after climbing up the first pinnacle turrets that ringed the cathedral, we followed the hardiest pilgrims and arrived at the peak of the last marble turret. There we had the pleasure to see at our feet the city of Milan, whose numerous inhabitants looked like a little *swarm of ants*. . . . Coming back down from our pedestal, we began our tours by carriage that were to last a month, and that would quench for good my desire to *keep moving indefatigably!*

The *campo santo*—the cemetery—delighted us even more than the cathedral, with all its white marble statues that a genius's chisel seemed to have brought to life. These statues are placed on the vast field of the dead in a sort of haphazard fashion that for me increases their charm. . . . One would be tempted to comfort the ideal personages who surround you. Their expression is so true, their sorrow so calm and so resigned, that one can't help recognizing the thoughts of immortality that must fill the hearts of the artists as they're executing these masterpieces. Here a child is tossing flowers on the tomb of its parents; the marble seems to have lost its weight, and the delicate petals seem to slide among the child's fingers. The wind seems already to disperse them, and it seems also to ruffle the light veils of the widows and the ribbons that adorn the girls' hair.

Papa was as delighted as we were. In Switzerland he'd been tired, but then his gaiety had reappeared, and I enjoyed the spectacle that we were contemplating. His artist's soul was revealed in the expressions of faith and admiration that appeared on his handsome countenance.

An elderly French gentleman, who no doubt didn't have as poetic a soul as we, was watching out of the corner of his eye, and he said, with ill humor, all the while looking as if he regretted not being able to share our admiration, "Oh! How enthusiastic the French are!" I think that this poor gentleman would have done better to stay at home, because he didn't seem to me to be happy with his trip. He was often near us, and always there were complaints coming out of his mouth. He was unhappy with the carriages, with the hotels, with the people, with the cities—in short, with everything. . . . Papa, with his customary greatness of soul, tried to comfort him, offered him his seat, and so on. In short, he was always at ease everywhere, being of a character that was diametrically opposed to that of his disagreeable neighbor. . . . Ah! How many different personalities we saw! How interesting it is to study the world when one is close to leaving it [in order to enter the religious life]! . . .

———•——

In Venice the scene changed completely. Instead of the noise of the great cities there was heard amidst the silence only the shouts of the gondoliers and the murmur of the waves stirred up by the oars. Venice is not without its charms, but I find that city sad. The Doges' palace is splendid; however it, too, is sad with its vast apartments in which are arranged gold, wood, the most precious marbles, and the paintings of the greatest masters. For a long time its resonant vaults have ceased to hear the voices of the governors who once pronounced judgments of life and death in the rooms that we crossed through. . . . They have ceased to suffer, those unfortunate prisoners who were locked up by the Doges in the cells and underground dungeons. . . .

When I visited those awful prisons, I thought I was back in the time of the Martyrs, and I would have liked to be able to stay there in order to imitate them! . . . But we had to leave promptly and pass over the Bridge of Sighs, so called because of the sighs of relief that the condemned prisoners heaved when they saw that they had been delivered from the horror of the dungeons, to which they preferred death. . . .

After Venice, we went to Padua, where we venerated the tongue of St. Anthony, then to Bologna where we saw St. Catherine, who retains the mark of the Child Jesus' kiss. There are many interesting details that I could give about each city and about the thousand little particular circumstances of our trip, but I would never finish, so I'm going to write down only the principal details.

It was with joy that I left Bologna [the site of a famous university]. That city had become intolerable for me because of the university students who filled it. They formed a hedge when we had the misfortune of setting out on foot, and especially because of the little adventure that happened to me with one of them, I was happy to take the road to Loretto.

I'm not surprised that the Blessed Virgin chose that place to transport her blessed home. [Loretto was the site of the *Santa Casa* (the "holy home"), thought to be Jesus' home in Nazareth, transported miraculously to Italy.] Peace, joy, and poverty reign supreme there. Everything is simple and primitive. The women have preserved their graceful Italian costume and have not, like the women of other cities, adopted *Paris fashion*. In short, Loretto charmed me!

What can I say about the blessed home? . . . Oh! My emotion was deep when I found myself under the same roof as the Holy Family, contemplating the walls on which Jesus had fixed His divine eyes, walking the ground that St. Joseph had watered with sweat, the place where Mary had carried Jesus in her arms, after carrying Him in her virgin's womb. . . . I saw the little room in which the Angel came down to the Blessed Virgin. . . . I placed my rosary beads into the Child Jesus' little bowl. . . . How delightful are those memories! . . .

But our greatest consolation was to receive *Jesus Himself* in His *home* and to be His living temple [1 Cor. 3:16] in the very place that He had honored with His presence. Following a custom in Italy, the Blessed Sacrament is preserved in each church only on an altar, and only there can one receive Holy Communion. That altar was in the very basilica in which the blessed home stood, enclosed like a precious diamond in a jewel case of white marble. That didn't make our happiness! It was in the *diamond* itself and not in the *jewel case* that we wanted to receive Communion. . . .

Papa, with his usual gentleness, did as everyone else did, but Céline and I went to find a priest who accompanied us everywhere and was in fact preparing to celebrate his mass in the *Santa Casa* by a special privilege. He asked for *two small hosts* that he placed on his paten [the gold or silver plate used to hold the host] with his large host, and you understand, my dear Mother, our delight that *both of us* were able to receive Holy Communion in that blessed house! . . . This was quite a heavenly happiness that words are powerless to describe.

So, what will it be like when we receive Communion in the everlasting dwelling of the King of heaven? . . . Then we will no longer see our joy come to an end, there will be no more sadness on leaving, and to carry away a souvenir it won't be necessary for us to *furtively scratch* the walls that have been hallowed by the Divine presence, since His *home* will be ours for eternity. . . . He doesn't want to give us an earthly home; He's content to show it [the humble home in Loretto] to us in order to make us love poverty and the hidden life. The home that's reserved for us is His Palace of glory where we'll no longer see Him hidden under the appearance of a Child or a white host, but as He is in the brightness of His infinite splendor (1 Jn. 3:2)!!! . . .

It now remains to me to talk about Rome—Rome, the objective of our trip, the place where I thought I would meet with consolation but where I found the Cross! . . . When we arrived it was nighttime, and since we had fallen asleep, we were awakened by the train station employees who were shouting, "Roma, Roma." It wasn't a dream: I was in Rome! . . .

The first day was spent outside the walls, and this was perhaps the most delicious day, because all the monuments have preserved their feel of antiquity, unlike at the center of Rome, where you could think you were in Paris when you saw the magnificence of the hotels and stores. This walk in the Roman countryside left me with a sweet memory.

I won't talk about the places that we visited—there are enough books that describe them in all their scope—but only about the *principal* impressions that I felt. One of the sweetest was the one that made me shudder when I saw the *Coliseum*. So I was finally seeing it, that arena in which so many Martyrs shed their blood for Jesus. I was preparing myself already to kiss the ground that they had made holy, but what a disappointment! The center is nothing but a pile of rubble that pilgrims have to be content to just look at, because a barricade prevents them from entering. Besides, no one is tempted to try to penetrate into the midst of those ruins. . . .

Must we have come to Rome without going down to the Coliseum? . . . That seemed impossible to me. I was no longer listening to the guide's explanations. One single thought was filling me: to go down into the arena. . . . Seeing a workman who was passing by with a ladder, I was on point of asking him. Fortunately I didn't put my idea into action, because he would have taken me for a madwoman. . . .

It's said in the Gospel that Mary Magdalene remained constantly near the tomb, and going down *several times* to look inside, ended up seeing two Angels [Jn. 20:11–12]. Like her, while recognizing the impossibility of seeing my desires become a reality, I continued to go down toward the ruins into which I wanted to enter. In the end, I didn't see Angels, but *what I was looking for*. I shouted with joy, saying to Céline, "Come quickly, we're going to be able to get in! . . ." Immediately we crossed the barrier that the rubble came up to at that spot, and there we were, climbing over the ruins, which crumbled under our footsteps.

Papa was watching us, completely surprised by our audacity. Soon he told us to come back, but the two fugitives were no longer hearing anything. In the same way as warriors who feel their courage increasing in the midst of peril, that's how our joy was growing in proportion to the trouble that we were having in reaching the object of our desires.

Céline, who was more farsighted than I was, had listened to the guide, and remembering that he had just indicated a certain paving stone in the form of a cross as being one on which the Martyrs had fought, started looking for it. Soon, finding it and kneeling on that sacred ground, our souls joined in one single prayer. . . . My heart was pounding when my lips approached the dust that was tinged with crimson by the blood of the first Christians. I asked for the grace also to be a Martyr for Jesus, and I felt in the depths of my heart that my prayer was being granted! . . .

All this was accomplished in a very short time. After taking a few stones, we went back toward the ruined walls to begin our perilous undertaking once again. Papa, who saw that we were so happy, couldn't scold us, and I saw clearly that he was proud of our courage. . . . God protected us visibly, because the pilgrims didn't catch sight of our undertaking, since they were farther along than we were. They were no doubt busy looking at the magnificent arcades, where the guide was showing us "the little *cornices* and the *cupids* that had been placed on them," so neither he nor "my lords the priests" knew about the joy that was filling our hearts. . . .

———————

The catacombs also left a sweet impression on me: They are just as I had imagined them to be when I read the description of them in the life of the Martyrs. After spending a part of the afternoon in them, it seemed to me that I had been there only a few moments, so much did the atmosphere that I was breathing there seem to have a lovely fragrance. . . .

I had to carry away some souvenir of the catacombs, so letting the procession go a little farther, Céline and Thérèse slipped away together into the bottom of the ancient tomb of St. Cecilia and took some of the earth that had been made holy by her presence. Before my trip to Rome I'd had no particular devotion for that Saint, but on visiting her home that had been changed into a church, the place of her martyrdom, and on learning that she had been proclaimed the queen of harmony, not because of her beautiful voice or her talent for music, but in memory of the *virgin's song* that she sang to her Heavenly Bridegroom who was hidden in the depths of her heart, I felt for her more than devotion: It was the true *tenderness of a friend.* . . . She became my favorite Saint, my intimate confidante. . . . Everything about her delighted me, especially her *abandon*, her boundless *trust* that rendered her capable of making virgins of souls who never desired any other joys than those of the present life. . . .

St. Cecilia is like the bride in the Song of Songs: In her I see "A *choir in an army camp!* . . ." Her life is none other than a melodious song in the very midst of the greatest of ordeals, and that doesn't surprise me, since "the holy Gospel *dwelt in her heart!" and in that heart dwelt* the Bridegroom of Virgins! . . .

The visit to the church of St. Agnes also was very sweet for me. She was a *childhood friend* whom I was going to visit in her home. I spoke to her for a long time about the one who bears her name so well [my sister Pauline, now Sr. Agnes of Jesus], and I made every effort to obtain one of the relics of the Angelical patron of my dear Mother in order to take it back to her. But it was impossible for us to have anything but a little red stone that came loose from a rich mosaic whose origin went back to the time of St. Agnes and that she must have often looked at. Wasn't it charming that the lovable Saint herself would give us what we were looking for and that was forbidden to us to take? . . . I've always regarded that as a nice touch, and a proof of the love with which sweet St. Agnes watches over and protects my dear Mother [Pauline]! . . .

———————

Six days went by as we visited the principal marvels of Rome, and it was on the *seventh* that I saw the greatest of them all: [Pope] "Leo XIII." . . . That was the day I desired to see and yet feared at the same time. That was the day on which my vocation depended, because the reply that I was to receive from the Bishop had not arrived, and I had learned through a letter from you, *Mother*, that he was no longer well disposed toward me. So my only life preserver was the permission of the Holy Father. . . . But to get it, I had to ask for it. I was required, in front of everyone, *to dare to speak*—*"to the Pope."* That thought made me tremble.

How much I suffered before the audience, God alone knows, along with my *dear Céline*. I'll never forget the part she took in all my ordeals. It seemed as if my vocation were hers. (Our love for each another had been remarked about by the priests on the pilgrimage. One night, since there were so many of us that we didn't have enough seats, Céline took me on her lap and we looked at each other so nicely that one priest exclaimed, "How they love each other! Oh! Those two sisters will never be able to be separated!" Yes, we loved each other, but our affection was so *pure* and so strong that the thought of separation didn't trouble us, because we felt that nothing, even the ocean, could make us distant one from the other. . . . Calmly, Céline was to see my little dinghy land on the shore of Carmel. She was to resign herself to remain as long as God would desire on the stormy sea of the world, sure that she would land in turn on the bank, the object of our desires. . . .)

Sunday, the twentieth of November, after dressing according to the ceremonial requirements of the Vatican (that is, in black, with a lace mantilla as a head covering), and having decorated ourselves with a large medal of Leo XIII hanging on a blue and white ribbon, we made our entrance into the Vatican in the Supreme Pontiff's chapel. At eight o'clock our emotion was deep when we saw him enter to celebrate Holy Mass. . . . After blessing the many pilgrims gathered around him, he climbed up the steps of the Holy Altar and showed us, through his piety that was worthy of the Vicar of Jesus, that he was truly *"the Holy Father."* My heart was beating strongly, and my prayers were most fervent, while Jesus came down into the hands of His Pontiff [as he celebrated Mass]. Nevertheless, I was full of confidence.

The Gospel for that day included these delightful words: "Do not be afraid, little flock, for your Father has been pleased to give you the kingdom" [Lk. 12:32]. No, I wasn't afraid, I was hoping that the kingdom of Carmel would belong to me soon. I wasn't thinking then about these other words of Jesus, "And I confer on you a kingdom, just as my Father conferred one on me ..." [Lk. 22:29]. That is to say, for you I'm reserving crosses and tribulation. That's how you'll be worthy of possessing that kingdom that you're longing for. Since it was necessary for Christ to suffer and through suffering enter into His glory, if you want to have a place beside Him, drink the cup that He Himself drank! . . . That cup was presented to me by the Holy Father, and my tears mingled with the bitter brew that was offered to me [Lk. 24:26; Mt. 20:21–23].

After the thanksgiving Mass that followed the one given by His Holiness, the audience began. Leo XIII was seated on a great chair. He was dressed simply in a white cassock and a cloak of the same color, and on his head he wore only a little skullcap. Around him stood cardinals, archbishops, and bishops, but I only saw them in general, since I was busy with the Holy Father. We passed before him in procession; each pilgrim knelt in turn, kissed Leo XIII's foot and hand, and received his blessing. Then two gentlemen of the Papal Guard touched the pilgrim ceremoniously, indicating by this that he should stand (the pilgrim, that is, because I'm explaining this so poorly that you might think I meant the Pope).

Before entering into the pontifical apartments I was quite resolved to *speak*, but I felt my courage weaken when I saw, at the Holy Father's right hand, Fr. *Révérony*! . . . Almost at the same moment we were told on *his behalf* that he *forbade us to speak* to Leo XIII, since the audience was going on too long. . . . I turned toward my beloved Céline, in order to learn her opinion. "Speak," she told me.

A moment later I was at the Holy Father's feet and had kissed his slipper, and he was extending his hand out to me. But instead of kissing it, I joined my hands together and, lifting toward his face my eyes bathed in tears, I cried out, "Most Holy Father, I have a great grace to ask of you! . . ." Then the Supreme Pontiff lowered his head toward me in such a way that my face almost touched his, and I saw his *dark* and *deep eyes* fix on me and seem to pierce me to the depths of my soul. "Most Holy Father," I said to him, "in honor of your jubilee, allow me to enter Carmel at the age of fifteen! . . ."

Thérèse at the Feet of Leo XIII

Most Holy Father, in honor of your jubilee,
allow me to enter Carmel at the age of fifteen!

Emotion had without a doubt made my voice tremble, so, turning around toward Fr. Révérony, who was looking at me with surprise and discontent, the Holy Father said, "I don't understand very well." If God had allowed it, it would have been easy for Fr. Révérony to obtain for me what I desired, but it was the cross and not consolation that He wanted to give me. "Most Holy Father," replied the Grand Vicar, "this is *a child* who wants to enter Carmel *at the age* of fifteen, but the superiors are examining the question right now." "Well, my child," the Holy Father continued as he looked at me kindly, "do what the superiors tell you." Then, placing my hands on his knees, I attempted one last effort, and I told him with a pleading voice, "Oh! Most Holy Father, if you were to say yes, everyone would be willing! . . ." He looked at me fixedly and pronounced these words, emphasizing each syllable: "All right. . . . All right. . . . *You will enter if it is God's will.*" (His tone of voice had something so penetrating and so convincing, that it seems to me that I can still hear it.)

The Holy Father's kindness was so encouraging that I wanted to speak to him some more, but the two gentlemen of the Papal Guard *touched me politely* to make me stand. Seeing that that wasn't sufficient, they took me by the arms, and Fr. Révérony helped them lift me up, because I was remaining there with my hands clasped together, leaning on Leo XIII's knees, and it was *by force* that they tore me away from his feet. . . . At the moment when I had been made to *stand up* in this way, the Holy Father put his hand over my lips, then raised it to bless me. Then my eyes filled with tears, and Fr. Révérony was able to contemplate at least as many *diamonds* as he had seen in Bayeux. . . . The two Papal Guards carried me so to speak as far as the door, and there, a third one gave me a Leo XIII medal.

Céline, who was following me, had witnessed the scene that had just taken place, and was almost as moved as I was. Nonetheless, she had the courage to ask the Holy Father for a blessing for Carmel. Fr. Révérony replied, in a displeased voice, "Carmel is already blessed." The good Holy Father repeated gently, "Oh, yes! It is already blessed."

Before us, Papa had come to Leo XIII's feet (with the gentlemen). Fr. Révérony had been charming to him, introducing him as the *father of two Carmelites.* The Supreme Pontiff, in a sign of particular benevolence, placed his hand on the venerable head of my beloved king, seeming in this way to mark him with a *mysterious seal,* in the name of the One whom he truly represents. . . .

Oh! Now that he's in heaven, this *father of four Carmelites,* it's no longer the hand of the Pontiff that rests on his forehead, prophesying martyrdom for him. . . . It's the *hand* of the Bridegroom of Virgins, the King of Glory, who makes the head of his Faithful Servant shine, and that adored hand will never again cease to rest on the forehead that it has glorified! . . .

My dear papa was very troubled to find me all in tears when I left the audience. He did everything he could to comfort me, but in vain. . . . In the depths of my heart I felt a great peace, since I had done absolutely everything that was in my power to do in order to respond to what God was asking of me. But that *peace* was in the *depths,* and bitterness *was filling* my soul, for Jesus was silent. He seemed to be absent; nothing was revealing His presence to me. . . . That day again the sun didn't dare to shine, and the beautiful blue sky of Italy, laden with dark clouds, didn't stop weeping with me. . . .

Oh! It was over. My trip no longer had any charm in my eyes, since its objective had been thwarted. However, the Holy Father's last words should have comforted me. Weren't they a veritable prophecy? Despite all the obstacles, what *God willed* had been accomplished. He did *not allow* creatures to do what they willed, but *His own will.* . . .

For some time I had offered myself to the Child Jesus to be His *little toy.* I had told Him not to use me like a valuable toy that children are happy to look at without daring to touch it, but like a little ball of no value that He could throw on the ground, kick around, *pierce,* leave in a corner or press to His heart if that pleased Him. In a word, I wanted to *entertain* the *little* Jesus and please Him. I wanted to give myself over to His *childish whims.* . . . He had granted my prayer. . . .

In Rome Jesus *pierced* His little toy. He wanted to see what was inside it, and then, having seen it, content with His discovery, He dropped His little ball and went to sleep. . . . What did He do during His sweet sleep, and what became of the little abandoned ball? . . . Jesus dreamed that He was still *entertaining Himself* with His toy, leaving it and taking it back up in turn, and then, after making it roll far away, He was pressing it to His heart, never letting it get far from His little hand again. . . .

You understand, beloved Mother, how sad the little ball was to see itself *on the ground*. . . . Nevertheless I didn't stop hoping against all hope [Rom. 4:18].

A few days after the audience with the Holy Father, Papa, who had gone to see the good Brother Simeon, met there none other than Fr. Révérony, who was very pleasant. Papa reproached him lightly for not having helped me in my *difficult undertaking*, and then he told the story of his *queen* to Brother Simeon. The venerable old man listened to his story with a great deal of interest, even taking notes on it, and said, with emotion, "We don't see that in Italy!" I think that this meeting made a very good impression on Fr. Révérony. Afterward he never stopped proving to me that he was *finally* convinced of my vocation.

The day after the memorable day, we had to leave in the morning for Naples and Pompeii. In our honor Vesuvius rumbled the whole day, letting off, with its *cannon blasts*, a thick column of smoke. The traces that it has left on the ruins of Pompeii are frightening. They show the power of God, ". . . who looks on the earth, and it trembles, who touches the mountains, and they smoke" [Ps. 104:32]. I would have liked to walk alone amidst the ruins, to dream about the fragility of human things, but the throngs of travelers took away a large part of the melancholic charm of the destroyed city. . . .

In Naples it was the opposite. The *great number* of two-horse carriages made our ride magnificent as we went to the monastery of San Martino, placed on a high hill dominating the whole city. Unfortunately, the horses that were pulling us were constantly taking the bit between their teeth, and more than once I thought I had reached the last hour of my life. In vain did the coachman constantly repeat the magic word used by Italian drivers, "*Appippo, appippo. . . .*" The poor horses tried to overturn our carriage, but finally, thanks to the help of our guardian angels, we arrived at our magnificent hotel.

During the whole trip, we had been placed in princely hotels. I had never been surrounded with so much luxury. It's quite the case that money doesn't buy happiness, because I would have been happier under a thatched roof with the hope of entering Carmel, than surrounded by gilded paneling, with white marble staircases, and silk carpets, with bitterness in my heart.

. . . Oh! I felt it so well: Joy isn't found in the objects that surround us; it's found in the innermost recesses of the soul. One can possess it as well in a prison as in a palace. The proof is that I'm happier at Carmel, even in the midst of inward and outward hardships, than in the world surrounded by the comfortable things of life and *above all* of the joys of my father's home! . . .

My soul was plunged into sadness. On the outside, however, I was the same, because I thought the request that I had made of the Holy Father was hidden. Soon I was able to convince myself to the contrary, when, having remained alone in the train with Céline (the other pilgrims having gotten off and gone to a buffet during the few minutes of the train stop), I saw Mr. Legoux, the vicar-general of Coutances, open the carriage door. Looking at me, smiling, he said, "Well, how is our little Carmelite nun doing? . . ." I understood then that the whole pilgrimage knew my secret. Fortunately, no one talked to me about it, but I saw by the sympathetic way in which they looked at me, that my request had not produced a bad effect—on the contrary. . . .

At the little city of Assisi, I had the opportunity to go into Fr. Révérony's carriage, a favor that was not granted *to any lady* during the whole trip. Here's how I obtained that privilege:

After visiting the places made fragrant by the virtues of St. Francis and St. Clare, we ended up at the convent of St. Agnes, St. Clare's sister. I had contemplated the Saint's head for as long as I liked, when, as I was among the last to leave, I noticed that I had lost my belt. I *looked for* it in the midst of the crowd. A priest took pity on me and helped me, but after finding it for me I saw him walk away, and I stayed alone *searching*, because I did have the belt, but it was impossible to put it on since the buckle was missing. . . . Finally I saw it shining in a corner and didn't take long to grab it and adjust its ribbon.

But the preceding work had taken a long time, so I was greatly surprised to find myself alone in the church. All the many coaches had disappeared, with the exception of that of Fr. Révérony. What course should I take? Should I run after the coaches, which I couldn't see any longer, expose myself to missing the train, and cause my dear papa to worry, or should I ask for a ride in Fr. Révérony's coach? . . . I decided to take the latter course. With my most gracious look, and the least *embarrassed* possible despite my extreme *embarrassment*, I exposed to him my critical situation and put him into an *embarrassing situation* himself, because his coach was filled with the most distinguished *gentlemen* of the pilgrimage, and there was no means of finding one more place. But a very gallant gentleman hastened to get off, had me climb into his place, and sat modestly next to the coachman.

I looked like a squirrel caught in a trap, and I was far from being at ease, surrounded as I was by all those great persons, and especially by the most *redoubtable* one [Fr. Révérony], across from whom I was seated. . . . However, he was very pleasant to me, from time to time interrupting his conversation with these gentlemen to talk to me about *Carmel*. Before arriving at the train station all these *great persons* took out their *big* wallets in order to give some money to the coachman (who had already been paid). I did as they did and took out my *very little* wallet. But Fr. Révérony wouldn't consent for me to take out some pretty *little* coins. He preferred to give one *big one* for us both.

Another time I found myself beside him on the trolley. He was even more pleasant, and promised to do everything he could in order for me to enter Carmel. . . . While putting a little salve on my wounds, these little encounters didn't keep the return trip from being much less pleasant than the original trip, because I no longer had the hope of "the Holy Father." I found no help on earth, which seemed to me to be a dry and parched desert [Ps. 63:1]. All my hope was in God *alone.* . . . I had just had the experience that it is better to have recourse to Him than to His Saints. . . .

The sadness of my soul didn't stop me from taking great interest in the holy places that we were visiting. In Florence I was happy to contemplate St. Magdalene di Pazzi in the midst of the choir of Carmelite nuns who opened their big grille for us. Since we didn't know how to take advantage of that privilege, many persons wanted to have their rosaries touch the Saint's tomb. I was the only one who could pass my hand through the grille that separated us, so everyone brought me their rosaries, and I was quite proud of my function. . . .

I always had to find the means to *touch everything*, so in the Church of the Holy Cross in Jerusalem (in Rome) we were able to venerate several pieces of the true Cross, two thorns and one of the sacred nails that were enclosed in a magnificent reliquary of wrought gold, but *without glass*. So I found a way, while venerating the precious relic, of slipping my *little finger* into one of the openings in the reliquary, and I *was able to touch* the nail that was bathed in the blood of Jesus. . . . I really was too daring! . . . Fortunately, God, who sees into the depths of the heart, knows that my intention was pure, and that for nothing in the world would I have wanted to displease Him. I acted toward Him like a *child* who thinks that everything is allowed her, and who regards her Father's treasures as her own [Lk. 15:31].

I still can't understand why women are so easily excommunicated in Italy. At every moment we were told, "Don't come in here. . . ." "Don't go in there, you would be excommunicated! . . ." Oh! Poor women, how they are disparaged! . . . However, they love God in much greater numbers than men, and during the Passion of Our Lord, the women had more courage than the apostles [Lk. 23:27] since they braved the insults of the soldiers and dared to wipe the adorable Face of Jesus. . . . It's no doubt for that reason that He allows scorn to be their lot on earth, since He chose that for Himself. . . . In heaven He'll know how to show that His thoughts are not man's thoughts [Isa. 55:8–9], because then the *last* will be the *first* [Mt. 20:16]. . . .

More than once during the trip, I didn't have the patience to wait for heaven in order to be the first. . . . One day when we were visiting a monastery of Carmelite monks, not content to follow the pilgrims in the *outer* galleries, I continued on walking into the *inner cloisters*. . . . Suddenly I saw a good elderly monk who from afar was signaling me to go away, but instead of leaving, I went up to him and, pointing to the paintings in the cloister, I made a sign to him that they were pretty. He recognized no doubt by my hair hanging down my back and my youthful look that I was a child, so he smiled at me kindly and went away, seeing that he didn't have an enemy in front of him. If I had been able to speak Italian to him, I would have told him that I was a future Carmelite nun, but because of the builders of the tower of Babel, that was impossible for me [Gen. 11:9].

After visits to Pisa and Genoa, we returned to France. On the trip the view was magnificent. At times we were traveling along the coast, and the train was so close to the sea that it seemed to me that the waves were going to come right up to us. (That spectacle was caused by a storm. It was nighttime, which made the scene even more imposing.) At other times we traveled through plains covered with orange trees bearing ripe fruit, green olive trees with light foliage, and graceful palm trees. . . . At nightfall we saw numerous little seaports lit up with a multitude of lights, while in the sky the first *stars* were shimmering. . . .

Oh! Such poetry was filling my soul at the sight of all those things that I was looking at for the first and last time in my life! . . . It was without regret that I saw them vanish into the distance; my heart was aspiring toward other marvels. It had had enough of contemplating *the beauties* of the *earth*; *the beauties* of *heaven* were the object of its desires, and in order to give them to *souls*, I wanted to become a *prisoner*! [That is, a cloistered nun.] . . . Before I saw opening before me the gates of the blessed prison after which I was longing, I still had to struggle and suffer. I felt that as I was returning to France. However, my confidence was so great that I didn't stop hoping that I would be allowed to enter on the twenty-fifth of December. . . .

———·—·———

Scarcely had we arrived in Lisieux, when our first visit was to the Carmelite convent. What a discussion that was! . . . We had so many things to tell each other, after a month of separation, a month that seemed longer to me and during which I learned more than during several years. . . .

Oh, my dear Mother! How sweet it was for me to see you again, to open up to you my poor wounded soul. To you who knew so well how to understand me, to whom one word, one glance were enough to guess everything! I gave myself up completely. I had done everything that depended on me, everything, even so far as speaking to the Holy Father, so I didn't know what I still should do.

You told me to write to His Excellency and to remind him about his promise. I did that immediately, as best as possible, but in terms that my uncle found a little too simple, so he redid my letter. At the moment when I was going to send it, I received one from you, telling me not to write, to wait for a few days. I obeyed immediately, because I was sure that this was the best way not to do the wrong thing. Finally, ten days before Christmas, my letter went on its way. Quite convinced that the reply wouldn't be long in coming, every morning after Mass I went to the post office with Papa, thinking that I would find the permission to fly away [to Carmel], but each morning brought a new disappointment that nonetheless didn't shake my faith. . . .

I asked Jesus to loose my bonds [Ps. 116:16]. He broke them, but in a very different way from the one I was expecting. . . . The beautiful celebration of Christmas came, and Jesus didn't wake up. . . . He left His little ball on the ground, without even glancing at it. . . .

My heart was broken as I went to the Midnight Mass. I had been counting so much on going to it behind the grille at the Carmelite convent! . . . This ordeal was very great for my faith, but the One whose heart is awake as He sleeps [Song 5:2], made me understand that to those whose faith is as *small as a mustard seed* [Lk. 17:6], He grants *miracles* and makes mountains move [Mt. 21:21], in order to strengthen that faith, which is so tiny. But for His *cherished* ones, for His *Mother*, He doesn't do miracles *until He has tested their faith*. Didn't He let Lazarus die, even though Martha and Mary had told Him that he was sick [Jn. 11:3]? . . . At the wedding at Cana, when the Blessed Virgin asked Jesus to help His hosts, didn't He answer her that His hour had not yet come [Jn. 2:1–11]? . . . But after that testing, what a reward! Water changes into wine . . . Lazarus is raised from the dead! . . . That's how Jesus acts toward His little Thérèse: after testing her for a *long time*, He fulfills all the desires of her heart. . . .

Having spent the afternoon of that dazzling celebration in tears, I went to see the Carmelites; great was my surprise to see, when they opened the grille, the delightful little Jesus holding in His hand a ball with my name written on it: the Carmelites, in place of Jesus, who was too little to talk, sang a hymn to me that was composed by my beloved Mother. Each word spread into my soul a most sweet consolation. Never will I forget that delicate mother's heart that always poured out upon me the most exquisite tenderness. . . .

After saying thank you as I shed sweet tears, I encountered the surprise that dear Céline had given me when we came back from Midnight Mass. I had found in my room, in the middle of a charming basin, a *little* boat that was carrying the *little* Jesus sleeping with a little ball next to Him. On the white sail Céline had written these words, "I'm sleeping, but my heart is awake" [see Song 5:2], and on the vessel this single word: "Abandonment!" Oh! If Jesus wasn't still speaking to His little bride, if His divine eyes were remaining closed, at least He was revealing Himself to me by means of souls who understood all the tenderness and love of His heart. . . .

——·——

The first day of the year 1888, Jesus made me another present of His Cross, but this time I was alone in carrying it, because it was all the more sorrowful since I couldn't understand it. . . . A *letter from Pauline* [now Sr. Agnes of Jesus] arrived, letting me know that His Excellency the bishop's reply had arrived on December 28th, the feast day of the

Holy *Innocents*, but that she hadn't let me know about it, having decided that my entrance would not take place *until after Lent*. I couldn't hold back my tears at the thought of such a long delay.

For me this trial had a most particular character. I was seeing my *bonds broken* from the point of view of the world, and this time it was the blessed ark that was refusing entrance to the poor little dove [Gen. 8:6–12]. . . . I'm willing to believe that I must have seemed unreasonable in not accepting joyfully my three months of exile, but I also believe that, without it appearing to be so, this was a *very great* hardship, and it made me *grow* a great deal in abandonment and in the other virtues.

How did these *three months* go by, these months that were so rich in graces for my soul? At first the thought came to me of not bothering to live as strict a life as I was used to doing. But soon I understood the value of the time that was being offered to me, and I resolved to give myself over more than ever to a *serious* and *mortified* life.

When I say mortified, this is not to make you believe that I was always doing penances. Alas! I *never did a single one*. Far from being like those beautiful souls who from childhood practiced every kind of mortification, I felt no attraction for them. Without a doubt this came from my cowardice, because I could, like Céline, have found a thousand little ways to make myself suffer. Instead of that I let myself always be coddled in cotton and fattened up like a little bird that has no need of doing penance. . . . My mortifications consisted in breaking my will, which was always ready to impose itself; in holding my tongue instead of answering back; in doing little things for others without hoping for a reward; in not slumping back when I was sitting down; etc., etc. . . .

It was through the practice of these *little nothings* that I prepared myself to become Jesus' bride, and I can't tell you how much that period of waiting left sweet memories for me. . . . Three months passed by very quickly, and finally the moment that I had so fervently longed for arrived.

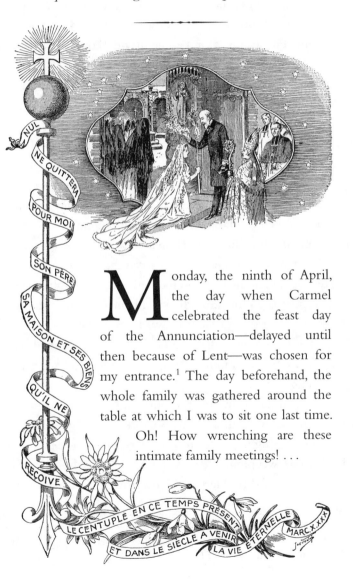

7
FIRST YEARS AT CARMEL
1888–1890

Confession to Fr. Pichon / Thérèse and her Superiors
The Holy Face / Taking the habit / Papa's illness / Small virtues

Monday, the ninth of April, the day when Carmel celebrated the feast day of the Annunciation—delayed until then because of Lent—was chosen for my entrance.[1] The day beforehand, the whole family was gathered around the table at which I was to sit one last time. Oh! How wrenching are these intimate family meetings! ...

Whereas you would wish to see yourself forgotten, the hugs, the tenderest of words are offered and make you feel the sacrifice of the separation. . . .

My dear king didn't say much of anything, but his gaze was fixed on me with love. . . . My aunt was crying from time to time, and my uncle gave me a thousand affectionate compliments. Jeanne and Marie [my cousins] were also full of tenderness toward me, especially Marie, who, taking me aside, asked my forgiveness for the troubles she thought she had caused me. Finally my dear Léonie, having come back from the Visitation convent a few months before, covered me even more with kisses and hugs. There remains only Céline that I haven't talked about, but you may guess, my dear Mother, how the last night was spent when we slept together in the same bed. . . .

The morning of the big day, after casting one last look about Les Buissonnets, that graceful nest of my childhood that I was not to see again, I left on the arm of my dear king to climb the mountain of Carmel. . . . As on the previous day, the whole family found itself gathered to attend Holy Mass and to receive Communion.

Immediately after Jesus had come down into the hearts of my beloved relatives, all I heard around me was sobs. I was the only one who wasn't shedding tears, but I felt my heart pound with *such violence* that it seemed impossible to me to go forward when someone came to beckon us to come to the convent door. I went forward nonetheless, wondering all the while if I wasn't going to die because the pounding of my heart was so strong. . . . Oh! What a moment that was; you would have had to go through it to know what it is. . . .

My emotions didn't show on the outside. After embracing all the members of my beloved family, I knelt before my incomparable father, asking for his blessing. In order to give it to me he *knelt as well* and blessed me while weeping. . . . This was a sight that ought make the Angels smile, that of this elderly man presenting his daughter to the

---

[1] The feast day of the Annunciation celebrates the angel Gabriel's announcement to the Virgin Mary that she would conceive a child by the Holy Spirit. Normally celebrated on the twenty-fifth of March, in 1888 this feast day was moved to the ninth of April so it could be commemorated outside of Lent.

Lord in the springtime of her life! . . . A few moments later, the doors of the blessed ark closed on me [Gen. 7:16], and there I received the welcoming embraces of the *dear sisters* [Marie and Pauline] who had served me as *mothers*, and whom I was henceforth going to take as the models for my actions. . . . Finally my desires had been accomplished, and my soul felt such sweet and such deep PEACE that it would be impossible for me to express it. And for seven and a half years that inner peace has remained my lot; it hasn't abandoned me amidst the greatest trials.

Like all postulants, I was led to the choir immediately after my entrance. It was dark because the Blessed Sacrament was exposed there. What struck my glance immediately were the eyes of our holy Mother Geneviève [the cofoundress of the convent] that were fixed on me. I remained for a moment on my knees at her feet, thanking God for the grace that He was granting me to meet a Saint, and then I followed Mother Marie de Gonzague [the Prioress of the convent] into the different places in the community. Everything seemed delightful to me—I thought I had been transported into a desert.[1] Our little cell was especially charming to me, but the joy that I felt there was *calm*; the slightest summer breeze didn't come to make ripples on the tranquil waters on which my little dinghy was sailing. Not a single cloud was covering my deep-blue sky. Oh! I was fully rewarded for all my trials! With what deep joy did I repeat these words, "It's forever, forever that I'm here!"

This happiness wasn't fleeting. It wasn't to fly away with "the illusions of the first days." As for the *illusions*, God gave me the grace *not to have* ANY as I entered Carmel. I found the religious life to be as I had conceived it. No sacrifice surprised me, despite the fact that, as you know, dear Mother, my first steps met with more thorns than roses! . . . Yes, suffering held out its arms to me, and I threw myself into those arms with love. . . .

What I was coming to do at Carmel, I declared at the feet of Jesus in the Host, in the examination that preceded my taking of vows: "I

[1] The desert was considered a place of calm meditation, as experienced by the Desert Fathers and Mothers in the early centuries of the Church.

came to save souls and above all in order to pray for priests." When you want to reach a goal, you must use every means to do so. Jesus made me understand that it was by the Cross that He wanted to give me souls, and my drawing toward suffering grew in proportion to the suffering that was increasing. For five years that path was mine, but outwardly, nothing betrayed my suffering, which was all the more sorrowful because I was the only one to be acquainted with it. Oh! What a surprise we will have at the end of the world when we read the story of souls! . . . How astounded people will be when they see the way by which mine has been led! . . .

It's true that, two months after my entrance, when Fr. Pichon [a Jesuit priest] came for the profession of Sr. Marie of the Sacred Heart [my sister Marie], he was surprised to see what God was doing in my soul. He told me that the previous day, as he had watched me praying in the choir, he had thought my fervor was quite childish and my path quite easy.

My meeting with the good Father was a very great comfort for me, but it was bathed in tears because of the difficulty I had in opening my soul. Nonetheless I made a general confession, as I had never done before. At the end Father spoke these words to me, the most comforting that had ever sounded in the ear of my soul: "In the presence of God, of the Blessed Virgin, and all the Saints, *I declare that you have never committed a single mortal sin.*" Then he added, "Thank God for what He's doing for you, because if He were to abandon you, instead of being a little angel, you would become a little demon."

Oh! I had no trouble believing him. I felt how weak and imperfect I was, but gratitude was filling my soul. I had such a great fear of soiling my baptismal robe, that such an assurance from the mouth of a spiritual director, as our Holy Mother Teresa [of Avila] desired, that is, joining *knowledge with virtue*, seemed to me to have issued from the very mouth of Jesus. . . .

The good Father continued on, saying these words that are sweetly engraved on my heart: "My child, may Our Lord always be your Superior and your Novice Master." In fact, He was, and He was also "my spiritual director." It's not that I mean by this that my soul was closed to my Superiors in the convent, oh! far from that. I have always tried to make my soul an *open book* to them. But our Superior [Mother Marie de Gonzague], who was often ill, had little time to be busy with me. I know that she loved me a great deal and said the best things possible about me, but nonetheless God permitted that, *without her knowing it*, she was VERY STRICT. I couldn't meet her without kissing the ground. It was the same in the rare meetings for spiritual direction that I had with her. . . . What an inestimable grace! . . . How *visibly* God was acting in the one who stood in His place! . . .

What would have become of me if, as persons of the world believed, I had been the "little doll" of the community? . . . Perhaps instead of seeing Our Lord in my Superiors I would have considered only the persons, and my heart, which had been so *well guarded* when I was in the outside world, would have become humanly attached when in the cloister. . . . Fortunately, I was preserved from that misfortune. Without a doubt *I loved* our Prioress *very much*, but with a pure affection that lifted me up toward the Bridegroom of my soul. . . .

Our Novice Mistress was a *real Saint*, the archetype of the first Carmelites. All day long I was with her, because she taught me to work. Her kindness toward me knew no bounds. And yet, my soul wasn't opening up. . . . It was only with effort that it was possible for me to participate in my spiritual direction. Not being used to talking about my soul, I didn't know how to express what was happening in it.

A kindly old nun understood what I was feeling: She told me one day during our recreation period, "Little girl, it seems to me that you must not have much to say to your superiors." "Why do you say that, Mother?" "Because your soul is extremely *simple*, but when you become perfect, you will be *even simpler*; the closer we come to God, the simpler we become." The good Sister was right. However, the difficulty that I was having in opening up my soul while coming out of my simpleness was a real ordeal. I recognize this now, because without ceasing to be simple, I express my thoughts with very great ease.

I said that Jesus had been "my spiritual Director." When I entered Carmel I met with the person [the priest assigned to be my spiritual director] who was to serve me in this capacity, but hardly had he admitted me among his spiritual children when he left for exile [in Canada]. . . . So I had met him only to have him immediately taken away. . . . I was reduced to receiving from him one letter per year compared to the twelve that I wrote to him, so my heart turned quite quickly toward the Director of directors: He it was who taught me in that knowledge that is hidden to the knowledgeable and the wise [Lk. 10:21], that He deigns to reveal to the *smallest ones*. . . .

The little flower that was transplanted onto the mountain of Carmel was destined to open in the shadow of the Cross. The tears and the blood of Jesus became the dew that watered it, and its Sun was His Adorable Face veiled with tears. . . . Until then I hadn't plumbed the depths of the treasures hidden in the Holy Face of Jesus [Isa. 53:3]. It was through you, dear Mother, that I learned to know them. Just as you had once gone before us all to Carmel, in the same way you were the first to penetrate the mysteries of love hidden in the Countenance of our Bridegroom. Then you called me, and I understood. . . . I understood what was the *real glory*. The one whose kingdom is not of this world [Jn. 18:36] showed me that true wisdom consists in "wanting to be unknown and counted as nothing, in placing one's joy in disdain for oneself." Oh! Like Jesus' face, I wanted "My face to be truly hidden, that on earth no one should recognize me" [see Isa. 52:14]. I was thirsty for suffering and for being forgotten. . . .

How merciful is the path along which God has always led me. He *never* made me desire anything without giving it to me, so His bitter cup seemed delicious to me. . . .

———

After the radiant celebrations of the month of May, celebrations of the taking of vows by Marie, *the eldest* of the family that *the youngest* had the happiness of crowning on the day of her becoming Jesus' bride, hardship had to come visit us. . . . The previous year in the month of May, Papa had been struck by an attack of paralysis in his legs. We were quite worried then, but the strong temperament of my dear king soon took the upper hand, and our fears disappeared. However, more than once during the trip to Rome, we had noticed that he would tire easily, and wasn't as jolly as usual. . . .

What I noticed the most was the progress that Papa was making in perfection. Following the example of St. Francis de Sales, he had reached the point of mastering his natural exuberance to the point where he seemed to have the gentlest nature in the world. . . . The things of earth seemed scarcely to graze him. He easily took the high road in the contrary things of this life. In short, God *flooded him with consolations*. During his daily visits to the Blessed Sacrament, his eyes would often fill with tears, and his face would breathe a heavenly bliss. . . . When Léonie left the Visitation convent [after a health crisis], he wasn't afflicted by this. He didn't reproach God for not having granted the prayers that he had prayed to Him to obtain a vocation for his dear daughter. It was even with a certain joy that he went to get her. . . .

With what faith Papa accepted his separation from his little queen: He announced it in these terms to his friends from Alençon: "My dear friends, Thérèse, my little queen, entered Carmel yesterday! . . . God alone can require such a sacrifice. . . . Do not feel sorry for me, because my heart is overflowing with joy."

It was time for such a faithful servant to receive the reward for his work [Mt. 25:21]. It was proper that his payment should be like the one that God gave to the King of heaven, His only Son. . . . Papa had just offered an *Altar* to God, and he was the victim chosen to be offered on it with the spotless Lamb. You know, my dear Mother, how bitter was the month of June, and especially the twenty-fourth in the year *1888*.[1] Those memories are too deeply engraved on the depths of our hearts for it to be necessary to write them. . . . Oh, Mother! How we suffered! . . . And this was only the *beginning* of our ordeal. . . .

---

[1] On the twenty-fourth of June, 1888, it was discovered that due to an attack of dementia, Louis Martin had disappeared the day before. He was found miles away at Le Havre on the twenty-seventh.

However, the time of my taking of the habit had arrived. I was welcomed by the chapter [the vowed community], but how could I think about celebrating? Already they were talking about giving me the blessed habit without making me come out, when they decided to wait. Against all hope, our dear father recovered from the second attack, and His Excellency fixed the date of the ceremony on the tenth of January. The wait was long, but also, what a beautiful celebration! . . . Nothing was missing, nothing, not even *snow*. . . .

I don't know if I've already talked to you about my love of snow. . . . When I was quite little, its whiteness used to delight me. One of my greatest pleasures was to go walking in the midst of falling snowflakes. Where did I get this liking of snow? . . . Perhaps from the fact that being a *little winter flower* [having been born in January], the first covering with which my child's eyes saw nature embellished must have been its white coat. . . . But then, I have always desired that on the day of my taking of the habit [wearing the white color of Novices], nature would be, like me, decked out in white. The day before that beautiful day I sadly watched the gray sky from which a fine rain was escaping from time to time, and the temperature was so warm that I was no longer hoping for snow.

The next morning the sky hadn't changed, but nonetheless, the celebration was delightful. And the most beautiful, the most delightful flower was my beloved king. Never had he been so handsome, so *dignified*. . . . He was the admiration of everyone.

"Ah," he cried out, "there she is, my little queen!" Then, offering me his arm, we made our way solemnly to the entrance to the chapel. This was his day of triumph, his last feast day here below! All his offerings had been made, and his family belonged to God. When Céline had confided in him that later she would also abandon the world to enter Carmel, this incomparable father had said, weeping in a transport of joy, "Come, let's go together before the Blessed Sacrament to thank the Lord for the graces that He is granting to our family, and for the honor that He is giving me to choose for Himself brides from my house. Yes, the good Lord is giving me a great honor by asking me for all my children. If I possessed anything better, I would hasten to offer it to Him." This *better thing* was himself! *Like gold in the furnace he tried them, and like a sacrificial burnt offering he accepted them* [Wis. 3:6 NRSV].

————·—·————

At the end of the ceremony, His Excellency intoned the *Te Deum.* A priest tried to point out that this hymn was chanted only at Professions, but the impulse had been given, and the hymn *of thanksgiving* continued to the end. Wasn't it necessary for the celebration to be *complete* since it joined all the others into one? . . .

After hugging my beloved king one last time, I went back into the enclosure. The first thing that I caught sight of under the cloister was "my little pink Jesus" smiling at me among the flowers and the lights, and then immediately my eyes fell on *snowflakes.* . . . The meadow was white, like me. What a tender touch from Jesus! Foreseeing the desires of His little bride, He was giving her snow. . . .

Snow! What mortal is so strong that he can cause snow to fall from heaven to charm his beloved? . . . Perhaps the persons of the world have asked themselves that question, but what is certain is that the snow at my taking of the habit seemed like a small miracle to them and the whole town was astonished at it. They thought that I had a curious taste in my love for snow. . . . Well and good, that brings out even more *the incomprehensible condescendence* of the Bridegroom of virgins . . . of the One who cherishes *lilies* that are *white* as SNOW! . . .

His Excellency entered after the ceremony. He had a most fatherly tenderness toward me. I quite think that he was proud to see that I'd succeeded. He told everyone that I was "*his* little girl." Each time he came back after that beautiful celebration, His Excellency was always most kind toward me. I especially remember his visit at the occasion of the commemoration of our father St. John of the Cross [the previous December 14th]. He took my face in his hands and gave me all kinds of signs of endearment. Never had I been so honored! At the same time God made me think about the signs of endearment that He wanted to shower on me before the Angels and the Saints, and of which He was giving me a pale image even on earth. So the comfort that I felt was very great. . . .

——·—··——

As I have just said, the day of the tenth of January was the triumph of my king. I compare it to Jesus' entrance into Jerusalem on Palm Sunday [Mt. 21:1–11]. Like that of Our Divine Master, Papa's glory for *one day* was followed by a sorrowful passion, and that passion wasn't for him alone. Just as Jesus' suffering pierced with a sword the heart of His Divine Mother [Lk. 2:35], our own hearts felt the sufferings of the one whom we cherished the most tenderly on earth. . . .

I remember that in the month of June 1888, at the moment of our first ordeals [when Papa disappeared for four days and turned up miles away], I said, "I'm suffering a lot, but I feel that I can endure even greater trials." I wasn't thinking then about the ones that were reserved for me. . . . I didn't know that on the twelfth of February, one month after my taking the habit, our beloved father would drink the *bitterest*, the *most humiliating* of all cups [by being obliged to enter the Bon Sauveur mental hospital in Caen]. . . .

Oh! That day I didn't say that I would be able to suffer more!!! . . . Words can't express our anguish, so I'm not going to try to describe it. One day in heaven we will love to talk to each other about our *glorious* times of trial—are we not already happy to have suffered them? . . . Yes, the three years of Papa's martyrdom seemed to me to be the most pleasant, the most fruitful of our entire life. I wouldn't give them in exchange for all the ecstasies and revelations of the Saints. My heart is overflowing with gratitude when I think about this inestimable *treasure* that must cause holy jealousy among the Angels of the heavenly court. . . .

My desire for suffering was gratified. However, my attraction for it didn't diminish, so my soul soon shared the sufferings of my heart. Dryness was my daily bread. Deprived of all consolation, I was nevertheless the happiest of creatures, since all my desires had been satisfied. . . .

Oh, my dear Mother! How sweet was our great time of trial, since from all our hearts there issued only sighs of love and gratitude! . . . We were no longer walking in the paths of perfection, all five of us were flying. The two poor little exiles in Caen [Céline and Léonie], though they were still in the world, were no longer of the world. . . . Oh! What marvelous things this ordeal did in the soul of my beloved Céline! . . . All the letters that she wrote at that time bear the imprint of acceptance and love. . . .

And what can we say about the meetings we used to have together? . . . Oh! Far from separating us, the grille of Carmel united our souls more strongly. We had the same thoughts, the same desires, the same *love for Jesus* and for *souls*. . . . When Céline and Thérèse talked together, never one word of the things of the earth came into their conversations, which were already completely in heaven [Phil. 3:20]. Just as once was the case in the *belvedere*, they dreamed about the things of *eternity*, and in order to enjoy right away that happiness without end, they chose here on earth, as their unique portion, "suffering and contempt."

That is how the time of my preparation for becoming Jesus' bride was spent. . . . It was very long for poor little Thérèse! At the end of my year [the usual length of the time as a Novice], our Mother [Marie de Gonzague] told me not to think about asking to make my Profession, that certainly the Reverend Father Superior would reject my request, so I had to wait another eight months. . . . At first it was very difficult for me to accept that great sacrifice, but soon light flooded my soul. I then meditated on *The Foundations of the Spiritual Life* by Fr. Surin.[1]

One day during prayers I understood that my keen desire to make my profession was tinged with great self-love. Since I had *given myself* to Jesus in order to please Him and comfort Him, I must not oblige Him to do *my will* instead of His. I understood further that a bride ought to be adorned for the day of her wedding, and I had done nothing toward that end. . . . Then I told Jesus, "Oh, my God! I'm not asking of You to take my blessed vows. *I'll wait as long as You wish*, only I don't

[1] Based on the *Imitation of Christ*, the Jesuit Jean-Joseph Surin's book *The Foundations of the Spiritual Life* was published in 1667.

want, due to my own fault, for my union with You to be put off. So I'm going to take every care to make myself a beautiful gown adorned with precious jewels. When You find it richly ornate enough, I'm sure that every creature will not keep You from coming down to me in order for me to unite myself to You for ever, my Beloved!"

Since my taking of the habit, I had received a great deal of illumination about religious perfection, principally on the subject of the vow of Poverty. During my postulancy, I was content to have nice things for my use and to find at hand everything that I needed. "*My Director*" suffered all that patiently, for He doesn't like to show everything to souls at the same time. Ordinarily He gives His light little by little. (At the beginning of my spiritual life, around the age of thirteen or fourteen, I used to wonder what I would have to gain later, because I thought that it was impossible for me to understand perfection any better. I very quickly recognized that the more one advances on this path, the farther one believes oneself from being near the end. So now I'm resigned to seeing myself as always imperfect, and in that I find my joy. . . .)

I'll come back now to the lessons that "*my Director*" was giving me. One night after Compline [the last office of the day, held in the evening] I looked in vain for our little lamp on the boards that were reserved for that use. It was the Great Silence [the time when no one in the convent speaks until morning], so it was impossible to ask for it. . . . I understood that one nun, thinking she was taking her lamp, had taken ours. I was in very great need of it, but instead of feeling annoyed at being deprived of it, I was quite happy, feeling that poverty consists in seeing oneself deprived not only of pleasant things but also of indispensable things. So in the *complete darkness* I was enlightened within. . . .

I was taken at that time with a real love of the ugliest and least fitting objects. So it was with joy that I saw myself deprived of our cell's pretty *little pitcher* and being given in its place a *large pitcher that was all cracked*. . . .

I also took great pains not to excuse myself, something that seemed quite difficult to me, especially with our Novice Mistress, from whom

I wouldn't have wanted to hide anything. Here's my first victory; it's not great, but it cost me dearly: A little vase placed behind a window was found broken. Our Mistress, thinking that I was the one who had left it behind, showed it to me, telling me to pay more attention in the future. Without saying anything I kissed the ground and then promised to be more orderly in the future. Because of my lack of virtue these little practices cost me a great deal, and I needed to think that at the Last Judgment everything will be revealed [Mt. 25:31–46], because I made this remark: When one has done her duty, never excusing herself, no one knows it. On the contrary, her imperfections appear immediately. . . .

I applied myself above all to practicing the little virtues, since I didn't have the facility for practicing the big ones. So I loved to fold the mantles that had been forgotten by the Sisters, and to do all the little services for them that I could.

The love of mortification was also given to me. It was even greater since nothing was permitted to me to satisfy it. . . . The only little mortification in the world that I used to do, consisting of not leaning back when I was sitting down, was forbidden to me because of my propensity for vaulting out of my chair. Alas! My fervor would no doubt not have lasted long if I had been assigned many penances to do. . . . The ones that were given to me without my asking for them consisted in mortifying my self-love, which did me much more good than bodily penances. . . .

The refectory [the dining room], which was my only job immediately after I took the habit, furnished me with more than one opportunity to put my self-love in its place, that is, under foot. . . . It's true that I took great consolation in being in the same job assignment as you, dear Mother, and to be able to contemplate your virtues up close, but being close to you was a subject of suffering. I didn't feel as *I used to*, free to tell you everything. There was the Rule to observe: I couldn't open up my soul to you. In short, I was at *Carmel* and no longer at *Les Buissonnets under Papa's roof!* . . .

However, the Blessed Virgin was helping prepare the garment of my soul. As soon as it was complete, the obstacles went away by themselves.

His Excellency sent me the permission that I had asked for: The Community was willing to receive me, and my Profession was set for the *eighth* of *September* [the Blessed Virgin Mary's birthday]. . . .

Everything I have just written in a few words would require many pages of details, but those pages will never be read on earth. Soon, dear Mother, I will talk to you about all the those things *in our Father's house*, in beautiful heaven, for which our hearts are longing! . . .

My wedding gown was ready. It was made rich with the *former* jewels that my Bridegroom had given me, but that was not enough for His generosity. He wanted to give me a new diamond with innumerable facets. Papa's ordeal was, with all its sorrowful circumstances, the *former* jewels, and the *new one* was an ordeal that was quite small in appearance, but that made me suffer a great deal: For some time, our poor dear father, since he was feeling a little better, had been allowed to go out in a carriage. There was even a question about letting him travel by train to come see us. Naturally, Céline thought right away that it would be necessary to choose the day of my taking the veil. "So as not to tire him out," she said, "I won't have him attend the whole ceremony. Only at the end I'll go get him and I'll lead him quite gently up to the grille so that Thérèse can receive his blessing."

Oh! In this I recognize quite well the heart of dear Céline. . . . It's quite true that "Never does love find a pretext of impossibility because it believes that everything is possible and that everything is allowed. . . ." *Human prudence*, on the contrary, trembles at every step and doesn't dare, so to speak, to put its foot down. So God, who wanted to test me, used human prudence as a passive instrument, and the day I took my bridal vows I was truly an orphan, no longer having a father on earth, but being able to look at heaven with confidence and to say in all truthfulness, "Our Father in heaven. . ." [Mt. 6:9].

8

FROM PROFESSION
TO THE OFFERING OF LOVE
1890–1895

Taking the veil / Mother Geneviève of St. Teresa
Epidemic of influenza / Retreat of Fr. Alexis
Priorship of Mother Agnes / Papa's death / Entrance of Céline
End of Manuscript A

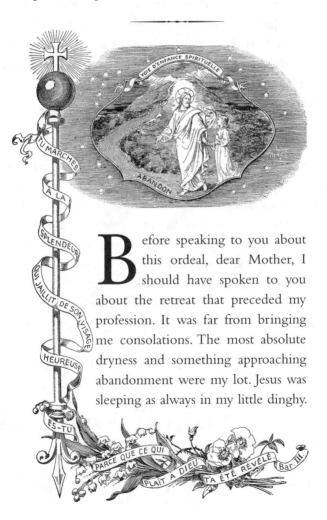

Before speaking to you about this ordeal, dear Mother, I should have spoken to you about the retreat that preceded my profession. It was far from bringing me consolations. The most absolute dryness and something approaching abandonment were my lot. Jesus was sleeping as always in my little dinghy.

Oh! I see clearly that souls rarely let Him sleep tranquilly within them. Jesus is so tired from always serving at others' expense and from their advances that He hurries to take advantage of the rest that I offer Him [Mk. 4:37–39]. No doubt He won't wake up before my great retreat of all eternity, but instead of causing me pain, that gives me extreme pleasure. . . .

I really am far from being a Saint. That alone is proof of it. Instead of rejoicing at my dryness, I should attribute it to the smallness of my fervor and faithfulness. I ought to be extremely sorry at sleeping (for seven years) during my prayers and my *times of thanksgiving*. Well, I'm not sorry. . . . I think that *little children* please their parents as much when they're asleep as when they're awake. I think that in order to perform operations, doctors put their patients to sleep. Finally, I think that the Lord "knows how we are formed, he remembers that we are dust" [Ps. 103:14].

So my retreat before my profession was, like all the ones that followed it, a retreat of great dryness. However, God showed me clearly, without my being aware of it, the way to please Him and to practice the most sublime of virtues. I've noticed many times that Jesus doesn't want to give me *food*. He's nourishing me at every moment with a completely new nourishment; I find it within me without knowing how it got there. . . . I believe quite simply that it's Jesus Himself, hidden in the depths of my poor little heart, who is giving me the grace within to act, and He causes me to think everything that He wants me to do in the present moment.

A few days before the day of my profession, I had the happiness of receiving the blessing of the Supreme Pontiff. I had asked for it through the good Brother Simeon for *Papa* and for me, and it was a great comfort to me to be able to give back to my dear father the grace that he had obtained for me by taking me to Rome.

Finally the *beautiful day* of my becoming a bride arrived. It was cloudless, but the day before there arose in my soul a storm like one that I had never seen before. . . . Not a single doubt about my vocation had yet come to my thoughts; it was necessary for me to become acquainted with that ordeal. That night, after visiting the Stations of the Cross after Matins [the early morning church service], my vocation appeared to me as a dream, a figment of my imagination. . . . I found life at Carmel to be quite beautiful, but the devil inspired in me the *assurance* that it wasn't made for me, that I'd be deceiving the Superiors by going forward along a path to which I wasn't called. . . . My darkness was so great that I could see or understand only one thing: I didn't have *the calling!* . . .

Oh! How can I depict the anguish of my soul? . . . It seemed to me (an absurdity that shows that this temptation came from the devil) that if I told all my fears to my Novice Mistress, she was going to prevent me from pronouncing my Holy Vows. However, I wanted to do God's will and return to the world rather than remain in Carmel doing my own will. So I asked my Mistress to come out, and, *full of embarrassment and shame,* I told her the state of my soul. . . .

Fortunately she saw more clearly than I did, and she reassured me completely. Besides, the act of humility that I had done had just put to flight the devil, who was perhaps thinking that I wasn't going to be daring enough to admit my temptation. Immediately after I finished speaking, my doubts left me. Nonetheless, in order to make my act of humility complete, I wanted to go on and confide my strange temptation to our Superior, who was content to laugh at me.

On the morning of the eighth of September, I felt myself *flooded* with a river of *peace* [Isa. 66:12], and it was in that peace, "which transcends all understanding" [Phil. 4:7], that I pronounced my Holy Vows. . . . My union with Jesus was made, not amidst thunder and lightning, that is, with extraordinary graces, but in the midst of a *gentle whisper* like the one that our father Elijah heard on the mountain [1 Kings 19:11–13]. . . . What graces I asked for that day! . . . I felt myself truly the QUEEN, so I took advantage of my title of nobility to deliver captives, to obtain the favors of the King toward His ungrateful subjects—in short, I wanted to deliver all souls from purgatory and convert sinners. . . . I prayed very much for my mother, my beloved sisters . . . for the whole family, but above all for my dear father who was so sorely tried and so holy. . . . I offered myself to Jesus so that He might accomplish His *will* perfectly in me without creatures ever placing any obstacle in its path. . . .

That beautiful day passed just as the saddest ones do, since the most radiant of days has a tomorrow. But it was without any sadness that I placed my crown at the feet of the Blessed Virgin. I felt that time wouldn't take away my happiness. . . . What a beautiful feast day was the birthday of *Mary* to become Jesus' bride! It was the *little* Blessed Virgin of one day who presented her *little* flower to the *little* Jesus. . . . That day everything was little except the graces and the peace that I received, except the *peaceful* joy that I felt that evening when I watched the stars twinkling in the heavens, as I was thinking that *soon*, beautiful heaven would open to my delighted eyes and I would be able to unite myself with my Bridegroom in the midst of everlasting joy and gladness. . . .

On the twenty-fourth the ceremony took place of my taking of the *veil*, but it was completely veiled with tears. . . . Papa wasn't there to bless his queen. . . . My director was in Canada. . . . His Excellency, who was to come and dine at my uncle's, fell sick and couldn't come, either. In short, everything was sadness and bitterness. . . . Nonetheless, *peace*, always *peace*, was found in the bottom of the cup. . . . That day Jesus allowed me to be unable to hold back my tears, and my tears weren't understood. . . . In fact, I'd gone through many greater trials without crying, but then I had been helped by a powerful grace. On the contrary, on the twenty-fourth, Jesus left me to my own strength, and I showed how small it was.

A week after my taking the veil Jeanne's marriage took place. To tell you, dear Mother, how much her example taught me about the tenderness that a bride should pour out on her bridegroom would be impossible for me. I listened eagerly to everything that I could learn, because I didn't want to do less for my beloved Jesus than Jeanne for

Francis, who was no doubt quite a perfect created being, but who was, after all, a *created* being! . . .

I even had fun composing a letter of invitation in order to compare it to hers. Here's how it read:

LETTER OF INVITATION TO THE WEDDING OF SISTER THÉRÈSE OF THE CHILD JESUS OF THE HOLY FACE.

Almighty God, Creator of heaven and earth, the Supreme Governor of the World, and the Very glorious Virgin Mary, Queen of the heavenly Court, request the honor of your presence at the Marriage of their August Son, Jesus, King of kings and Lord of lords, with Miss Thérèse Martin, now Lady and Princess of the kingdoms brought by dowry by her Divine Bridegroom, namely, the Childhood of Jesus and His Passion, her titles of nobility being: of the Child Jesus and of the Holy Face.

Mr. Louis Martin, Owner and Master of the Lordships of Suffering and Humiliation, and Mrs. Martin, Princess and Lady of Honor of the Heavenly Court, request the honor of your presence at the Marriage of their Daughter Thérèse, with Jesus, the Word of God [Jn. 1:1–3], second Person of the Adorable Trinity, who through the operation of the Holy Spirit was made Man and the Son of Mary, the Queen of Heaven.

Not having been able to invite you to the Nuptial blessing that was given them on the mountain of Carmel, the eighth of September, 1890 (only the heavenly court having been admitted), you are nonetheless requested to attend the Return from the Marriage Feast that will take place tomorrow, the Day of Eternity, on which day Jesus, Son of God, will come on the Clouds from heaven in the brightness of His Majesty, to judge the Living and the Dead [Mt. 25:31–40].

The time being still uncertain, you are invited to remain ready and to watch [Mt. 24:42–44].

Now, dear Mother, what is left for me to tell you? Oh! I thought I had finished, but I haven't told you anything yet about my happiness at having known our Holy Mother Geneviève. . . . That was an inestimable grace. Well, God, who had already given me so many graces, wanted me to live with a *Saint*, not one I couldn't imitate, but a Saint who was made holy through hidden and ordinary virtues. . . .

More than once I received great consolations from her, especially one Sunday. Heading to meet with her as usual in order make my little visit, I found two Sisters beside Mother Geneviève. I looked at her, smiling, and I was getting ready to leave since there can't be three persons at the bedside of a person who is ill, but she, looking at me with an inspired look, said to me, "Wait, my little daughter, I'm only going to tell you one little word. Each time that you come, you ask me to give you a spiritual bouquet. Well, today I'm going to give you this one: *Serve God with peace and with joy. Remember, my child, that our God is the God of peace*" [1 Cor. 14:33]. After thanking her simply, I left, moved to tears and convinced that God had revealed to her the state of my soul. That day I had been extremely tested, almost sad, and was in a night of soul such that I no longer knew if I was loved by God. But the joy and the comfort that I felt, you can well imagine, dear Mother! . . .

The following Sunday, I wanted to know what revelation Mother Geneviève had had. She assured me that she had not received *any*. Then my admiration was still greater, seeing to what an eminent degree Jesus was living in her and was making her act and speak. Oh! That *holiness* seemed to me the most *true*, the most holy, and that's what I desire, because in it there is no illusion. . . .

On the day of my Profession I was also quite comforted to learn from the mouth of Mother Geneviève that she had gone through the same ordeal as I before taking her own vows. . . . At the moment of our *great* sufferings, do you remember, dear Mother, the consolations that we found at her side? In short, the memory that Mother Geneviève left in my heart is a fragrant remembrance. . . .

The day she departed for heaven I felt that I was particularly touched. This was the first time that I was present at a death, and truly this was a delightful sight. . . . I was placed just at the foot of the bed of the dying Saint. I could see perfectly her slightest movements. It seemed to me during the two hours that I spent in that way that my soul ought to have felt full of fervor. On the contrary, a sort of insensitivity had taken hold of me, but at the *very moment* of the birth in heaven of our saintly Mother Geneviève, my inner disposition changed. In a twinkling of an eye I felt myself filled with an unutterable joy and fervor. It was as if Mother Geneviève had given me a part of the bliss that she enjoyed, because I'm quite persuaded that she went straight to heaven. . . . While she was living I told her one day, "Oh, Mother! You won't go to purgatory! . . ." "*I hope so*," she replied gently. . . . Oh! Of course God couldn't betray a hope so full of humility. All the favors that we received are proof of that. . . .

Each Sister hurried to claim some relic. You know, dear Mother, the one that I have the happiness of possessing. . . . During Mother Geneviève's agony, I noticed a *tear* shimmering on her eyelid, like a diamond. That *tear, the last one of all those* that she shed, didn't fall. I saw it still *shining* in the choir without anyone thinking of collecting it. Then, taking a piece of fine linen, I dared to approach her that evening without being seen and took as a *relic the last tear* of a Saint. . . . Since then I have always carried it in the little sachet that holds my vows.

I don't attach any importance to my dreams, and besides, I rarely have any symbolic ones. And I even wonder how it is that, thinking all day long about God, I'm not more concerned with Him during my sleep. . . . Usually I dream about the woods, flowers, streams, and the sea, and almost always, I see pretty little children, and I catch butterflies and birds like ones I've never seen. You see, Mother, that if my dreams have a poetic appearance, they are far from being mystical. . . .

One night after Mother Geneviève's death, I had a dream that was more comforting. I dreamed that she was making her testament, giving to each Sister one thing that had belonged to her. When my turn came, I thought I wouldn't receive anything, because she had nothing left. But standing up, she said three times with a penetrating accent, "To you, I leave my *heart*."

A month after our Holy Mother's departure, influenza was declared to be in the community. I was the only one left standing with two other Sisters. I'll never be able to tell all that I saw, and what life and everything that passes away seemed like to me. . . .

The day of my nineteenth birthday was celebrated by a death, followed soon by two others. At that time I was the only one in the sacristy. The head Sister for this duty being gravely ill, I was the one who had to prepare the burials, open the grilles of the choir at the time of Mass, and so on. God had given me many graces of strength at that time. I wonder now how I was able to do without fear all that I did. Death was the rule everywhere. The sickest ones were cared for by those who could hardly walk. As soon as one Sister had given up her last breath, we were obliged to leave her alone.

One morning as I got up, I had the feeling that Sr. Madeleine had died. The dormitory was in darkness, and no one was leaving the cells. Finally I decided to enter into Sr. Madaleine's cell, the door of which was open, and I saw her in fact dead, dressed and lying on her mattress, and I wasn't the least bit afraid. Seeing that she had no candle, I went to get one for her as well as a crown of roses.

The night of the death of the Sub-Prioress, I was alone with the infirmary Sister. It's impossible to describe the sad state of the community at that time. Those who were on their feet are the only ones who have any idea of it, but in the midst of all that abandonment, I felt that God was watching over us. It was without effort that the dying ones passed to a better life. Immediately after their death an expression of joy and peace spread over their features—one would have described it as a sweet sleep. It truly was one, since after the face of this world has passed away [1 Cor. 7:31], they will awaken to enjoy forever the delights reserved for the elect. . . .

The whole time that the community was tested in this way, I was able to have the indescribable consolation of receiving Holy Communion *every day*. . . . Oh! How sweet that was! . . . Jesus spoiled me for a long time, longer than His faithful brides, because He permitted me to *receive Him* without the others having the happiness of receiving Him. I was also quite happy to touch the sacred vessels, to prepare the little *linens* that were used to touch Jesus. I felt that I needed to be quite fervent, and I often remembered this word that was addressed to a holy deacon: "Be pure, you who carry the articles of the LORD's house" [Isa. 52:11].

I can't say that I often received consolations during my prayers of thanksgiving. This is perhaps the time when I usually have the least number of consolations. . . . I find that quite natural, since I offered myself to Jesus, not as a person who desires to receive His visit for her own consolation, but on the contrary for the pleasure of the One who gives Himself to me. I conceive of my soul as an *empty* field, and I pray to the Blessed Virgin to take away the *debris* that could prevent it from being *empty*. Then I implore her to raise up herself a vast tent worthy of *heaven*, to decorate it *with her own* finery, and then I invite all the Saints and Angels to come make a magnificent concert. It seems to me when Jesus comes down into my heart, that He is content to find Himself so well received there, and I am also happy. . . .

All that doesn't prevent distractions and sleepiness from coming to visit me, but when I leave the time of prayers of thanksgiving, seeing that I've done them so poorly, I make the resolution to spend all the rest of the day in thanksgiving. . . . You see, dear Mother, that I'm far from being led by the way of fear. I always know how to find the means to be happy and to profit from my wretchedness. . . . No doubt that isn't displeasing to Jesus, because He seems to encourage me on that road.

One day, contrary to my usual pattern, I was a little troubled when going to Communion. It seemed to me that God wasn't happy with me, and I told myself, "Oh! If today I receive only *one half of a host*, that's going to cause me pain. I'm going to believe that Jesus is coming regretfully into my heart." I approached. . . . Oh, happiness! For the first time in my life, I saw the priest take *two hosts* that were quite separated, and give them to me! . . . You understand my joy and the sweet tears that I shed when I saw such great mercy. . . .

The year after my profession, that is, two months before the death of Mother Geneviève, I received great graces during the retreat. Ordinarily, retreats that are preached are even more sorrowful for me than those that I do all alone, but that year it was otherwise. I had made a preparatory novena [nine days of prayer] with a great deal of fervor, in spite of the inner feeling that I had. That was because it

Sister Thérèse of the Child Jesus
Preparing the holy vessels when she was sacristan

seemed to me that the preacher wouldn't be able to understand me, since he was especially destined to do good to great sinners but not to religious souls. But since God wanted to show me that He alone was the director of my soul, He in fact used that priest, who was appreciated only by me. . . .

At that time I was having great inner trials of all kinds, going as far as wondering sometimes if there was a heaven. I felt myself disposed not to say anything about my inner dispositions, not knowing how to express them. Hardly had I entered into the confessional when I felt my soul expand. After saying a few words, I was understood in a marvelous way, as if *my thoughts were being read.* . . . My soul was like a book in which the priest was reading better than I was. . . . He launched me at full sail on the waves of *trust* and *love* that drew me so strongly but on which I didn't dare to advance. . . . He told me that *my faults did not grieve* God, and that *standing in God's place* he was telling me that *as far as he was concerned*, God was very happy with me. . . .

Oh! How happy I was at hearing those comforting words! . . . Never had I heard it said that faults could not grieve God. That assurance flooded me with joy and let me endure patiently the exile of life. . . . I felt clearly in the depths of my heart that it was true, because God is more tender than a mother. Well, you, dear Mother, aren't you always ready to forgive the little indelicate actions that I do to you involuntarily? . . . How many times have I had that sweet experience! . . . No reproach would have touched me as much as one of your tender gestures. I'm of a nature such that fear causes me to draw back; with *love* not only do I go forward, but I *fly.* . . .

Oh, Mother! It was especially after the blessed day of your election [as Prioress, in 1893] that I flew in the paths of love. . . . That day, Pauline became my living Jesus. . . . [Now *Mother* Agnes of Jesus,] she became, for the second time, "Mama! . . ."

For what will soon be three years I've had the happiness of contemplating *the marvelous things* that Jesus is operating by means of my beloved Mother. . . . I see that *suffering alone* can give birth to souls, and more than ever these sublime words of Jesus are unveiling their depth to me: "Very truly I tell you, unless a kernel of wheat falls to the ground and dies, it remains only a single seed. But if it dies, it produces many seeds" [Jn. 12:24].

What an abundant harvest you've gathered! . . . You've sown in tears, but soon you'll see the fruit of your work. You'll come back full of joy, bearing sheaves in your hands [Ps. 126:5–6]. . . . Oh, *Mother*, among those flowery sheaves, the *little white flower* is staying hidden, but in heaven she'll have a voice to sing of the *gentleness* and the *virtues* that she sees you practice every day in the shadow and the silence of the life of exile. . . .

Yes, for three years I've well understood mysteries that had been hidden for me until then. God showed me the same mercy that He showed to King Solomon [see 2 Chr. 1:7–11]. He didn't want me to have a single desire that wouldn't be fulfilled, not only my desires for perfection, but even those of which *I understood* the meaninglessness without having experienced it.

Having always regarded you, my dear Mother, as my *ideal*, I wanted to be like you in everything. When I saw you make beautiful paintings and delightful poems, I used to tell myself, "Oh! How happy I would be to be able to paint, to know how to express my thoughts in verse and also to do good to souls. . . ." I wouldn't have wanted to *ask for* those natural gifts, and my desires remained *hidden* in the depths of my *heart. Jesus*, who was also *hidden* in my poor little *heart*, was also pleased to show that all is meaningless and a chasing after wind under the sun [Eccl. 1:14]. . . .

To the great surprise of my Sisters, I was told to *paint*, and God allowed me to know how to take advantage of the lessons that my dear Mother gave me. . . . He also wanted me to be able to follow her example in writing poetry, composing poems that people found quite pretty. . . . Just as Solomon, *surveying all that his hands had done and what he had toiled to achieve, saw that everything was meaningless, a chasing after the wind* [Eccl. 2:11], in the same way I recognized through EXPERIENCE that happiness consists only in staying hidden, in remaining in ignorance of created things. I understood that without *love*, all works are only nothingness, even the most dazzling, such as raising the dead or converting entire peoples [1 Cor. 13:1–3]. . . .

Instead of doing me harm, leading me to meaninglessness, the gifts that God poured out on me (without my asking Him for them) led me to *Him*. I see that He alone is *unchanging*, that He alone can fulfill my immense desires. . . .

There are still other desires of another type that Jesus was pleased to fulfill, childish desires similar to those of the snow when I took the habit.

You know, dear Mother, how much I like flowers. By making myself a prisoner [a cloistered nun] at the age of fifteen, I renounced forever the happiness of running through fields decked with the treasures of springtime. Well! Never have I possessed more flowers than since my entrance into Carmel. . . . It is a custom for men who are engaged to be married to often offer bouquets to their fiancées. Jesus didn't forget. He sent me in profusion sheaves of cornflowers, big daisies, poppies, etc., all the flowers that delight me the most. There was even a little flower called the corn-cockle, which I haven't found since our stay at Lisieux. I wanted to see it again, that flower of *my childhood* gathered by me in the fields of Alençon. It was at Carmel that these flowers came to smile at me and show me that in the smallest things as well as in the biggest ones, God gives a hundred times as much in this present age to souls who have left everything for love of Him [Mk. 10:29–30].

But the most intimate of my desires, the greatest of all, that I thought I would never see come true, was the entrance of my beloved Céline into the same Carmel as us. . . . That *dream* seemed to me to be highly unlikely—to live under the same roof, to share the joys and the sorrows of the companion of my childhood. So I had completely made my sacrifice: I had entrusted to Jesus the future of my dear sister, being resolved to see her leave for the ends of the earth if necessary. The only thing that I couldn't accept was for her not to be the bride of Jesus, because, since she loved Him as much as I did, it was impossible for me to see her give her heart to a mortal. I'd already suffered by knowing that she'd been exposed in the world to dangers that I hadn't known. I can say that my affection for Céline was, since my entrance into Carmel, as much a motherly love as a sisterly one. . . .

One day when she was to go out to an evening ball, that gave me so much pain that I begged God to *prevent* her from *dancing* and even (contrary to my custom) I shed a torrent of tears. Jesus deigned to grant my request: He didn't allow His little bride *to be able to dance* that night (although she wasn't embarrassed to do so graciously when it was necessary). Though she'd been invited without being able to refuse, her escort found himself totally unable to get her to *dance*; to his great confusion, he was condemned to simply *walk* in order to take her back to her place. Then he slipped away and didn't reappear all evening. This adventure, unique in its kind, made me grow in trust and in love for the One who, having placed *His sign* on my forehead, had at the same time stamped it on the forehead of my beloved Céline. . . .

On the twenty-ninth of July last year, God, breaking the bonds of His incomparable servant [Papa], and calling him to his eternal reward, at the same time broke the bonds that held His beloved bride [Céline] to the world. She had fulfilled her first mission: Charged with *representing all of us* at the side of our father, who was so tenderly loved, she had accomplished that mission like an Angel. . . . And Angels don't stay on earth. When they've accomplished God's will, they immediately return to Him—that's why they have wings. . . .

Our angel as well shook her white wings. She was ready to fly *very far* in order to find Jesus, but Jesus made her fly *very near*. . . . She was content with accepting the great sacrifice that was very *sorrowful* for little Thérèse. . . . For *two years* her Céline had hidden a secret from her. . . . Oh! How she also had suffered! . . . Finally, from up above in heaven, my dear king, who on earth never liked to go slow, hurried to arrange the quite entangled affairs of his Céline, and the fourteenth of September [the Feast Day of the Exaltation of the Holy Cross], she joined us! . . .

One day when the difficulties seemed insurmountable, I told Jesus during my prayers of thanksgiving: "You know, my God, how much I desire to know if Papa went *straight to heaven*. I'm not asking You to speak to me, but give me a sign. If Sr. Aimée of Jesus consents to Céline's entrance or sets no obstacle to it, that will be the answer that Papa went *straight to You*." That Sister, as you know, dear Mother, found that three of us [in the same convent] were too many, and consequently didn't want to admit one more, but God, who holds in His hand the hearts of creatures and channels it as He wishes [Prov. 21:1], changed the attitude of that Sister. The first person that I met after my time of thanksgiving prayers was she, who called me with a kind attitude, told me to go up to see you, and spoke to me about *Céline* with tears in her eyes. . . .

Oh! How many subjects I have to thank Jesus for, Jesus who knew how to fulfill all my desires! . . .

Now I no longer have any desire, unless it's to *love* Jesus passionately. . . . My childish desires have all flown away. Undoubtedly, I still love to decorate with flowers the altar of the Little Jesus, but since He gave me the *Flower* that I desired, my *beloved Céline*, I no longer desire any other. It's she that I am offering as my most delightful bouquet. . . .

I don't desire suffering or death, either, and yet I love both of them. But it is *love* alone that draws me. . . . For a long time I desired them both. I possessed suffering, and I thought I was touching the shores of heaven. I thought that the little flower would be gathered in its springtime. . . . Now it's abandonment alone that guides me—I have no other compass! . . .

I can ask for nothing fervently any more except the perfect accomplishment of God's will in my soul [Mt. 6:10], without created things being able to place any obstacle in its path. I can say these words from the spiritual canticle of our father St. John of the Cross: "In the interior cell of my Beloved, I drank, and when I went out, in all that plain I no longer was familiar with anything, and I lost the flock that I had previously been following. . . . My soul was fully engaged with all its resources at its service. I no longer keep watch over a flock, I no

longer have any other office, because now my entire practice is *to Love*!
. . ." Or another passage: "Since I have experienced it, love is so powerful
in works that it knows how *to profit from everything*, from the good and
from the *bad* that it finds in me, and to transform my soul into LOVE
ITSELF."

Oh, beloved Mother! How sweet is the path of *love*. No doubt, one
can fall down, one can commit unfaithful acts, but love, knowing how to
profit from everything, quickly consumes *everything* that can be displeasing
to Jesus, leaving only a humble and profound peace in the depths of the
heart. . . .

Oh, how much enlightenment I have plumbed in the works of our
father St. John of the Cross! . . . At the age of seventeen and eighteen
I had no other spiritual nourishment, but later all books left me in
dryness, and I'm still in that state. If I open a book written by a spiritual
author (even the most beautiful, the most touching), right away I feel
my heart constrict, and I read, so to speak, without understanding, or
if I understand, my mind stops without being able to meditate. . . . In
that state of impotence, *Holy Scripture* and the *Imitation of Christ* come
to my aid. In them I find nourishment that is solid and completely
pure. But above all it is the *Gospels* that keep me fed during my times of
prayer. In them I find everything that is necessary to my poor little soul.
In them I always discover new illuminations, hidden and mysterious
meanings. . . .

I understand and I know by experience that "the kingdom of God
is in our midst" [Lk. 17:21]. Jesus has no need of books or teachers to
instruct souls. As the Teacher of teachers, He teaches without the noise
of words. . . . I have never heard Him speak, but I feel that He is with me.
At every moment, He guides me and inspires in me what I ought to say
or do. I discover, just at the moment when I need them, understandings
that I hadn't yet seen. Most often it's not during my times of prayer that
they're the most abundant, but rather in the midst of the occupations
of my day. . . .

Oh, beloved Mother! After so many graces can I not sing with the
psalmist, "For the LORD is good and his love endures forever" [Ps.

100:5]? It seems to me that if all creatures had the same graces as I, God would be feared by no one, but loved passionately, and that out of *love* and not out of trembling [in fear], no soul would ever consent to cause Him grief. . . .

I understand, however, that all souls can't look alike. There have to be some from different families in order to especially honor each of God's perfections. To me He's given His *infinite Mercy*, and it's *through it* that I contemplate and adore the other Divine perfections! . . . Then all of them appear to me radiant with love. Righteousness and Justice themselves (and perhaps even more than any other perfections) seem to me to be *clothed in love*. . . .

What sweet joy it is to think that God is *just*—that is, that He takes into account our weakness, He knows perfectly the fragility of our nature. What should I be afraid of? Oh! The infinitely just God who deigned to forgive with such kindness all the faults of the prodigal son [Lk. 15:21–24], should He not also be just toward me who am "always with him" [see Lk. 15:31]? . . .

————·—·————

That year on the ninth of June, the feast day of the Holy Trinity, I received the grace to understand more than ever how much Jesus desires to be loved.

I was thinking about the souls who offer themselves as victims to God's Justice in order to turn it aside and draw to themselves the chastisements reserved for the guilty. That offering seemed great and generous to me, but I was far from feeling myself brought to the point of doing it. "Oh, my God!" I cried in the depths of my heart, "will it only be Your Justice that will receive souls that offer themselves as sacrificial victims? . . . Doesn't Your Merciful *Love* need them as well? . . . Everywhere it is misunderstood, rejected. The hearts into which You desire to pour it are turned toward created things, asking them for happiness with their wretched affection, instead of throwing themselves into Your arms and accepting Your infinite *Love*. . . .

"Oh, my God! Meeting with such contempt, is Your Love going to remain in Your Heart? It seems to me that if You found souls that were offering themselves as sacrificial victims to Your Love, You would consume them rapidly. It seems to me that You would be happy not to dam up the waves of infinite tenderness that are within You. . . . If Your Justice, which extends only over the earth, likes to vent itself, how much more does Your Merciful Love desire to *set souls on fire*, since Your Mercy rises all the way to heaven [Ps. 36:5]. . . . Oh, my Jesus! Let *me* be that happy victim; consume Your sacrifice through the fire of Your Divine Love! . . ."

Beloved Mother, you who have allowed me to offer myself in this way to God, you know the rivers or rather the oceans of graces that have come to flood my soul. . . . Oh! Since that happy day, it seems to me that *Love* penetrates and surrounds me. It seems to me that at every moment that *Merciful Love* is renewing me, purifying my soul, and leaving there no trace of sin, so I cannot fear purgatory. . . . I know that in myself I wouldn't be worthy even to enter that place of expiation, since only holy souls can have access to it, but I also know that the Fire of Love is more sanctifying than that of purgatory. I know that Jesus can't desire useless sufferings for us, and that He wouldn't inspire in me the desires that I feel if He didn't want to fulfill them. . . .

Oh, how sweet is the path of Love! . . . How I want to apply myself to always doing, with the greatest abandonment, the will of God [Mt. 6:10]! . . .

There, beloved Mother, is all that I can tell you about the life of your little Thérèse. You know much better yourself what she is and what Jesus has done for her. So you will forgive me for having greatly abridged the story of her religious life. . . .

How will it end, this "story of a little white flower"? . . . Perhaps the little flower will be picked in its freshness or perhaps transplanted onto other shores. . . . I don't know, but what I am certain of is that God's Goodness and Love will always follow it [Ps. 23:6], and that she will never stop blessing the beloved Mother who gave her to Jesus. Forever she will rejoice at being one of the flowers in her crown. . . . Forever she will sing with that beloved Mother the ever-new hymn of Love [Rev. 14:3]. . . .

9

MY VOCATION, LOVE
1896

The secrets of Jesus / The venerable Mother Anne of Jesus
All vocations / Throwing flowers / The little bird
The divine Eagle / End of Manuscript B

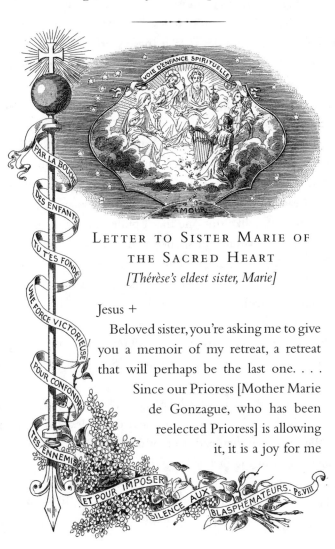

LETTER TO SISTER MARIE OF
THE SACRED HEART
[Thérèse's eldest sister, Marie]

Jesus +

Beloved sister, you're asking me to give
you a memoir of my retreat, a retreat
that will perhaps be the last one. . . .
Since our Prioress [Mother Marie
de Gonzague, who has been
reelected Prioress] is allowing
it, it is a joy for me

to come and speak with you, who are twice my sister, with you who lent me your voice, promising in my name [when you served as my sponsor at my baptism] that I wanted to serve only Jesus, when it was not possible for me to speak. . . .

Dear Godmother, it is the child whom you offered to the Lord who is going to talk to you this evening. She it is, who loves you as a child knows how to love its mother. . . . Only in heaven will you know all the gratitude that overflows from my heart. . . . Oh, beloved sister! You would like to hear the secrets that Jesus is confiding to "your little girl." I know that He confides in you these secrets, for it is you who taught me to gather the divine teachings. However, I am going to try to stammer out a few words, although I feel that it is impossible for the human voice to repeat things that the human heart can scarcely feel [1 Cor. 2:9]. . . .

Do not think that I am swimming in consolations. Oh, no! My consolation is in not having any consolations on earth. Without showing Himself, without making His voice heard, Jesus instructs me in secret. It is not by means of books, because I do not understand what I read, but sometimes a word like this one that I pulled out at the end of the prayer time (after remaining in silence and dryness) comes to comfort me: "Here is the teacher that I am giving you; He will teach you everything that you must do. I want to make you read in the book of life, in which is contained the knowledge of Love." The knowledge of Love, oh, yes! That word resounds sweetly in the ear of my soul. I desire only that knowledge; having given all my riches in exchange for it, I consider, as did the bride in the Song of Songs, that I have given nothing [8:7]. . . .

I understand so well that only love can make us pleasing to God, and that love is the only good thing that I covet. Jesus is pleased to show me the only way that leads to that divine furnace, and that way is the *abandonment* of the little child who falls asleep without fear in the arms of its Father. . . . "Let all who are *simple* come to my house," said the Holy Spirit through the mouth of Solomon [Prov. 9:4], and that same Spirit of Love said again that "to [one] that is little, mercy is granted" [Wis. 6:7 D-R]. In its name, the prophet Isaiah reveals to us that at the last day the Lord will tend "his flock like a shepherd: He gathers the lambs in his arms and carries them close to his heart" [Isa. 40:11]. And as if all these promises were not enough, the same prophet, whose inspired glance already plumbed into the eternal depths, cried out in the name of the Lord, ". . . you will nurse and be carried on her arm and dandled on her knees. As a mother comforts her child, so will I comfort you" [Isa. 66:12–13]. Oh, beloved Godmother! After such language, all we can do is keep silence and weep out of gratitude and love. . . .

Oh! If all weak and imperfect souls felt what the smallest of all souls feels, the soul of your little Thérèse, not a single one would despair of arriving at the top of the mountain of love, since Jesus does not ask for great actions, but only for abandonment and gratefulness. For He said, in Psalm 50[:9–13], "I have no need of a bull from your stall or of goats from your pens, for every animal of the forest is mine, and the cattle on a thousand hills. I know every bird in the mountains. . . . If I were hungry I would not tell you, for the world is mine, and all that is in it. Do I eat the flesh of bulls or drink the blood of goats?" . . .

"Offer to God a sacrifice of praise and thanksgiving" [see Ps. 50:14; Heb. 13:15]. This, then, is what Jesus requires of us. He has no need of our works, but only of our love, for this same God who declares that He has no need to tell us if He is hungry, was not afraid to *beg* for a little water from the Samaritan woman. He was thirsty. . . . But in saying, "Will you give me a drink?" [Jn. 4:7], it was the *love* of His poor creature that the Creator of the universe was asking for. He was thirsty for love. . . . Oh! I feel more than ever that Jesus is *thirsty*. He meets only ungrateful and indifferent people among the disciples of the world, and among His *own disciples*, He finds, alas! few hearts that give themselves to Him without reserve, who understand all the tenderness of His infinite Love.

Dear sister, how happy we are to understand the intimate secrets of our Bridegroom. Oh! If you wanted to write down all that you know about them, we would have beautiful pages to read; but I know, you prefer to keep in the depths of your heart "the secret of a King." To me you say, "how honorable to reveal and confess the works of God" [Tob. 12:7 D–R]. I find that you are right to keep silence, and it is only in order to please you that I write these lines, because I feel my powerlessness to use earthly words to tell about the secrets of heaven. And then, after having written pages and pages, I would find that I had not yet begun. . . . There are so many different horizons and so many infinitely varied nuances, that only the palette of the Heavenly Painter, after the night of this life, will be able to furnish me with the colors that are capable of painting the marvels that He is disclosing to the eye of my soul.

My dear sister, you have asked me to write to you about my dream and "my little doctrine," as you call it. . . . I have done so in the following pages, but so poorly that it seems impossible to me for you to understand. Perhaps you are going to find my expressions to be exaggerated. Oh, forgive me, that must come from my not-too-pleasant style. I assure you that there is no exaggeration in my *little soul*, and that there, all is calm and at rest.

(In writing, it is to Jesus that I speak. That makes it easier to express my thoughts. Alas! That does not stop them from being poorly expressed!)

SEPTEMBER 8TH, 1896
*[The celebration of the Nativity of the Blessed Virgin Mary,
and the sixth anniversary of my Profession]*

(To my dear Sister Marie of the Sacred Heart.)

Oh, Jesus, my Beloved! Who will be able to say with what tenderness, what sweetness, You are leading *my little soul*? How much it pleases You to make shine upon it the ray of Your grace even in the midst of the darkest storm. . . .

Jesus, the storm was roaring quite strongly in my soul after the beautiful celebration of Your triumph, the radiant feast day of Easter, when one Saturday in May, thinking about the mysterious dreams that are sometimes granted to certain souls, I was telling myself that this ought to be the sweetest comfort, but I was not asking for it. That night, considering the clouds that were darkening its sky, my *little soul* was saying again that beautiful dreams were not for it, and under that storm it went to sleep. . . . The next day was the tenth of May, the second Sunday of Mary's month, perhaps the anniversary of the day when the Blessed Virgin deigned to *smile at* her little flower. . . .

At the first light of day, I found myself (in a dream) in a sort of gallery. There were several other persons, but far away. Only our Mother was at my side, when suddenly, without my having seen how they had entered, I caught sight of three Carmelite nuns dressed in their mantles and large veils. It seemed to me that they were coming for our Mother, but what I understood clearly is that they were coming from heaven. From the depths of my heart, I cried out, "Oh! How happy I would be to see the face of one of these Carmelites."

Then, as if my prayer had been heard by her, the tallest of these holy ones advanced toward me. Immediately I fell to my knees. Oh! What happiness! The nun lifted her veil, or rather, raised it and covered me with it. . . . Without any hesitation I recognized the venerable Mother Anne of Jesus, foundress of the Carmelite order in France. Her face was beautiful, of an immaterial beauty. No ray of light was escaping it, and yet, in spite of the veil that was enveloping both of us, I saw that heavenly visage illuminated with an indescribably sweet light, a light that it was not receiving but that it was producing by itself. . . .

I would not know how to tell you the gladness that I felt in my soul. These things are felt and cannot be expressed. . . . Several months have passed since that sweet dream, yet the memory that it has left on my soul has lost nothing of its freshness, its heavenly charms. . . . I can still see the look and the smile *full of love* of the Venerable Mother. I think I can still feel the tender touches with which she flooded me. . . .

Seeing myself loved so tenderly, I dared to pronounce these words: "Oh, Mother! I implore you, tell me if God will leave me for a long time on earth? . . . Will He come soon to get me?" Smiling tenderly, the Saint murmured, "Yes, soon, soon. . . . I promise you." "Mother," I added, "tell me another thing, whether God is not asking me for something more than my poor little actions and my desires. Is He happy with me?" The Saint's face took on an expression that was *incomparably more tender* than the first time that she spoke to me. Her look and her caresses were the sweetest of replies. However, she told me, "God is not asking anything else from you, He is happy, very happy!" After she caressed me with more love than the most tender of mothers has ever done to her child, I saw her go away. . . . My heart was filled with joy, but I remembered my Sisters, and I wanted to ask for some graces for them, but alas! . . . I woke up!

Oh, Jesus! Now the storm was not roaring, the sky was calm and serene. . . . *I believed, I felt* that there is a heaven, and that heaven is peopled with souls who cherish me, who regard me as their child. . . . That impression remains in my heart, so much the better since, up till then, I had always been *absolutely indifferent* toward the Venerable Mother Anne of Jesus. I had never invoked her, and the thought of her never came to my mind except when I heard people talk about her, which was rare. So when I understood to what point *she loved me*, how little she was *indifferent* toward *me*, my heart melted in love and gratitude, not only for the Saint who had visited me, but also for all the blessed ones who dwell in heaven. . . .

Oh, my Beloved! This grace was only the prelude to greater graces that You wanted to shower on me. Let me, my only Love, remind You of them today. . . . Today, the sixth anniversary of *our union*. . . . Oh! Forgive me, Jesus, if I am talking nonsense by wanting to tell about my desires and my hopes that touch on the infinite. Forgive me and heal my soul by giving it what it hopes for!!! . . .

To be Your *Bride*, Jesus, to be a Carmelite nun, to be, through my union with You, the *mother* of souls, ought to be enough for me. . . . That is not the case. . . . No doubt, those three privileges are my vocation—

Carmelite, Bride, and Mother—but I feel within myself other vocations. I feel the vocation of Warrior, Priest, Apostle, Teacher, Martyr. In short, I feel the need and the desire to accomplish for You, Jesus, all the most heroic works. . . . I feel in my soul the courage of a Crusader, of a soldier in the papal army; I would like to die on a field of battle for the defense of the Church. . . .

I feel within me the vocation of *Priest*. With what love, Jesus, would I bear You in my hands when, at the sound of my voice, You would come down from heaven. . . . With what love would I give You to souls! . . . But alas! While desiring to be a Priest, I admire and I envy the humility of St. Francis of Assisi, and I feel in myself the vocation of being like him in refusing the sublime dignity of the priesthood.

Oh, Jesus! My love, my life. . . . How do I harmonize these contrasts? How can I realize the desires of my poor *little soul*? . . .

Oh! In spite of my littleness, I would like to shed light on souls like the Prophets, the Doctors. I have the vocation to be an Apostle. . . . I would like to travel across the world, preach Your name, and plant Your glorious Cross on the soil of unbelievers. But, my *Beloved*, a single mission wouldn't be enough for me. I would at the same time like to preach the gospel in the five parts of the world and as far as the remotest islands [Isa. 66:19]. . . . I would like to be a missionary, not only for a few years, but I would like to have been one since the creation of the world and be one until the end of the ages. . . . But above all, my Beloved Savior, I would like to shed my blood for You until the last drop. . . .

Martyrdom: That is the dream of my youth. That dream has grown within me under the cloisters of Carmel. . . . But there again I feel that my dream is foolishness, because I would not know how to limit myself to *one* type of martyrdom. . . . To satisfy me I would have to have *all of them*. . . .

Like You, my Beloved Bridegroom, I would like to be scourged and crucified. . . . I would like to die by being skinned alive like St. Bartholomew. . . . Like St. John, I would like to be plunged into boiling oil. I would like to undergo all the tortures inflicted on the Martyrs. . . .

With St. Agnes and St. Cecilia, I would like to present my neck to the sword, and like Joan of Arc, my dear sister, I would like to be burned at the stake, murmuring your name, *Jesus....*

When I think about all the torments that will be the lot of Christians at the time of the Antichrist, I feel my heart leap, and I would like for those torments to be reserved for me. . . . Jesus, Jesus, if I wanted to write down all my desires, I would have to borrow *Your book of life* [Rev. 20:12]. In it are the records of the actions of all the Saints, and those actions, I would like to have accomplished them for You. . . .

Oh, my Jesus! To all my foolishness, what are You going to reply? . . . Is there a soul that is *smaller* and more powerless than mine! . . . However, even because of my weakness, You were pleased, Lord, to fulfill my *little childish desires*, and You now want to fulfill other *desires that are bigger* than the universe. . . .

At prayer time my desires were making me suffer a true martyrdom, so I opened the letters of St. Paul in order to look for some sort of answer. Chapters 12 and 13 of the first letter to the Corinthians fell under my eyes. . . . I read in the first of those chapters, that *everyone cannot* be apostles, prophets, teachers, etc.; that the Church is composed of different members; and that the eye cannot at *the same time* be a hand [1 Cor. 12:29, 21]. . . . The answer was clear, but it did not fulfill my desires. It did not give me peace. . . .

Just as Mary Magdalene, who kept bending toward the empty tomb, ended up finding what she was looking for [Jn. 20:11–18], in the same way, abasing myself even as far as the depths of my nothingness, I raised myself so high that I was able to reach my goal. . . . Without becoming discouraged, I continued my reading, and this sentence gave me relief: "Now eagerly desire the greater gifts. And yet I will show you the most excellent way" [1 Cor. 12:31]. And the Apostle explains how the most *perfect gifts* are nothing without Love . . . and that Charity is the *excellent* way that leads surely to God. Finally I had found rest. . . .

Considering the mystical body of the Church, I had not recognized myself in any of the members described by St. Paul, or rather, I wanted

Cell of Sister Thérèse of the Child Jesus

The Inner Courtyard of the Carmel of Lisieux

The window marked by a cross is that of the cell where Sister Thérèse of the Child Jesus lived during the last years of her life. On the left is the Chapter room where she made her profession.

to recognize myself in *all of them*. . . . Charity gave me the key to my vocation. I understood that if the Church had a body composed of different members [1 Cor. 12:12], it was not missing the most necessary, the most noble of all: I understood that the Church had a heart, and that this heart was *burning with Love*. I understood that Love alone can cause the members of the Church to act. If Love were to be extinguished, the Apostles would no longer preach the gospel, the Martyrs would refuse to shed their blood. . . . I understood that *Love* contains all the Vocations, that Love is all, that it embraces all times and all places . . . in a word, that it is Everlasting!

Then in the excess of my delirious joy, I cried out, "Oh, Jesus, my Love . . . I have finally found my vocation: My vocation is Love! . . ."

Yes, I have found my place in the Church, and that place, my God, You have given me. . . . In the Heart of the Church, my Mother, I will be *Love*. . . . That way I will be everything . . . that way my dream will become a reality!!!

Why do I speak about a delirious joy? No, that expression is not accurate. It is rather the calm and serene peace of the navigator when he sees the beacon light that will lead him into port. . . . Oh, luminous Beacon Light of love, I know how to reach You, I have found the secret of appropriating Your flame to myself.

I am only a child, powerless and weak, but it is my very weakness that gives me the boldness to offer myself as a victim to Your Love, Jesus! In ancient times only pure and spotless hosts were accepted by the God of Power and Might. To satisfy Divine *Justice*, perfect victims were required [see Lev. 22:18–25]. But the law of fear was succeeded by the law of Love, and Love chose me to be a sacrifice, weak and imperfect creature that I am. . . . Is that choice not worthy of Love? . . . Yes, for Love to be fully satisfied, it is necessary for it to be abased, to be abased to nothingness, and for it to transform that nothingness into *fire*. . . .

Oh, Jesus, I know, love is repaid only by love, so I sought, I found, the means to relieve my heart by rendering to You, Love for Love. "Use worldly wealth to gain friends for yourselves, so that when it is gone, you will be welcomed into eternal dwellings" [Lk. 16:9]. That, Lord, is the advice that You gave to Your disciples after telling them that "the people of this world are more shrewd in dealing with their own kind than are the people of the light" [Lk. 16:8]. As a child of the light, I understood that my *desires to be all things*, to embrace every vocation, were riches that could well make me unrighteous, so I used them to make friends. . . .

Remembering the prayer of Elisha to his father Elijah when he dared to ask for a *double portion of his spirit* [2 Kings 2:9], I presented myself before the Angels and the Saints, and I told them, "I am the littlest of creatures, I know my wretchedness and my weakness, but I also know how much noble and generous hearts love to do good. I beg you, then, you Blessed inhabitants of heaven, I beg you to *adopt me as your child. To you alone will be the glory* that you will cause me to acquire, but deign to grant my prayer. It is foolhardy, I know, but nonetheless I dare to ask you to obtain this for me: *a double portion of your Love.*"

Jesus, I cannot make my request any deeper. I would be afraid to find myself crushed under the weight of my impudent desires. . . . My excuse is that I am only *a child*. Children do not think of the impact of their words, but their parents, when they are placed on the throne, though they possess immense treasures, do not hesitate to content the desires of the *little beings* that they cherish as much as themselves. To give them pleasure, they even do foolish things, they go as far as *weakness*. . . .

Well! I am THE CHILD of *the Church*, and the Church is Queen since she is Your Bride, O Divine King of kings. . . . It is not riches and glory (even the glory of heaven) that the heart of the little child clamors after. . . . The child understands that glory belongs by right to her brothers and sisters, the Angels, and the Saints. . . . The child's own glory will be the reflection of the one that springs from the brow of her mother. What she asks for is Love. . . . She knows only one thing, and that is to love You, Jesus. . . .

Dazzling works are forbidden to her; she cannot preach the gospel or shed her blood. . . . But what does it matter? Her brothers and sisters are working in place of her, and she, the *little child*, remains very close to the *throne* of the King and the Queen, and she loves in the place of her brothers and sisters who are going into combat. . . . But how will she bear witness to her Love, since Love is proved by works? Well, the little child will throw out *flowers*, she will use her *perfumes* to give a lovely fragrance to the royal throne, she will sing with her silvery voice the hymn of Love. . . .

Yes, my Beloved, that is how my life will be consumed. . . . I have no other means of proving my love for You than to throw flowers, that is, not to pass up any little sacrifice, any look, any word, to take advantage of all the little things and to do them out of love. . . . I want to suffer out of love and even rejoice out of love, so I will throw flowers before Your throne. I will not encounter a single one without *plucking off its leaves* for You [leaving only the pure beauty of the flower]. . . . Then, as I throw my flowers, I will sing (could a person weep while doing so joyful an action?). I will sing, even when I will have to gather my flowers among thorns, and my song will be all the more melodious as the thorns are long and piercing.

Jesus, what purpose will my flowers and my songs serve You? . . . Oh! I know well that this sweet-scented rain, these fragile petals that have no value, these songs of love of the littlest of hearts—these will charm You. Yes, these little nothings will give You pleasure. They will make the Triumphant Church [the Blessed ones in heaven] smile. That Church will gather up my flowers whose leaves have been plucked off *by Love*, and causing them to pass through Your Divine Hands, Jesus, that Church of heaven, wanting to play with its little child, will also throw *these flowers* that through Your divine touch have acquired an infinite value—that Church will throw them on the Suffering Church [the souls in purgatory] in order to put out its flames. It will throw them on the Church in Combat [Church Militant: the Christians still on earth] in order to make it win the victory! . . .

Oh, my Jesus! I love You, I love the Church, my Mother. I often remember that "The tiniest movement of *pure love* is more useful to it than all other works taken together." But is *pure love* at home in my heart? . . . Are not my immense desires just a foolish dream? Oh! If this is so, Jesus, let me know it: You know that I am seeking the truth. . . . If my desires are foolhardy, make them disappear, because these desires are for me the greatest of martyrdoms. . . . However, I know, Jesus, after aspiring toward the highest regions of Love, if it befalls to me not to attain them one day, I will have tasted more *sweetness in my martyrdom, in my folly*, than I will taste in the midst of the *joys of heaven*, unless by some miracle You take away the memory of my earthly hopes. So let me, during my exile, enjoy the delights of Love. Let me delight in the sweet bitterness of my martyrdom. . . .

Jesus, Jesus, if the *desire to love You* is delicious, what is it then to possess, to enjoy the fruits of Love? . . . How can a soul as imperfect as mine aspire to possess the fullness of Love? . . .

Jesus! My *first, my only Friend*, You whom ALONE *I love*, tell me, what is this mystery? Why do You not reserve these immense aspirations to great souls, to the eagles that soar in the heights? . . . I consider myself as a weak little bird covered only with light down. I am not an eagle, I simply have an eagle's *eyes* and *heart*. For, despite my extreme smallness, I dare to fix my eyes on the Divine Sun, the Sun of Love, and my heart feels in itself all the aspirations of the eagle. . . . The little bird would like to fly toward that brilliant Sun that charms its eyes. It would like to copy the eagles, its brothers, which it sees rising up to the Divine home of the Holy Trinity. . . . Alas! All that it can do is to *lift its little* wings. But to fly away, that is not in its *little* power! What is going to become of it? Die of disappointment when it sees how powerless it is? . . .

Oh, no! The little bird is not even going to be bothered by that. With daring abandon, it wants to stay fixed on its Divine Sun. Nothing could frighten it, neither wind nor rain, and if dark clouds come to hide the Star of Love, the little bird will not change its place. It knows that above the clouds its Sun is always shining, that its brilliance will not be able to be eclipsed for one single second.

Sometimes, it is true, the little bird's heart finds itself assailed by the storm. It seems to it that it cannot believe that anything else exists than the clouds that are enveloping it. This, then, is the moment of perfect joy for the weak little being. What happiness for it to *stay there* anyway, to remain fixed on the invisible light that reveals itself to its faith!!! . . .

Jesus, up till now I understand Your love for the little bird, because it does not go far from You. . . . But I know, and You know, too, often the imperfect little creature, while remaining in its place (that is, under the rays of the Sun), lets itself become a little distracted from its only duty [Lk. 10:41–42]. It takes a little seed from the right or the left, runs after a little worm. . . . Then, encountering a little puddle, it gets its feathers *wet*, feathers that have scarcely been formed. It sees a little flower that pleases it, so its little mind becomes busy with that flower. . . . Finally, not being able to soar like the eagles, the poor little bird becomes busy again with the worthless baubles of the earth.

However, after all its misadventures, instead of going to hide in a corner to weep over its misery and die out of repentance, the little bird turns toward its beloved Sun. It presents to Its kindhearted rays its little *wet* wings. It moans like a mourning dove [Isa. 38:14], and in its sweet song it confides, it tells in detail its unfaithfulness, thinking in its daring abandonment that in this way it will acquire more of a hold, attract more fully the love of the One who came not to call the righteous but sinners [Mt. 9:13]. . . . If the Adorable Star remains deaf to the plaintive chirpings of His little creature, if He remains veiled . . . Well! The little creature stays *wet*, it accepts to be chilled to the bone with cold, and it continues to rejoice at this suffering that, after all, it deserved. . . .

Jesus! How happy Your *little bird* is to be *weak and small*. What would happen to it if it were big and great? . . . Never would it dare to appear in Your presence, to *fall asleep* in Your sight. . . . Yes, there again is a weakness of the little bird, when it wants to fix its eyes on the Divine Sun and the clouds prevent it from seeing a single ray. In spite of itself, its little eyes close, its little head hides under its little wing, and the poor little being goes to sleep, thinking that it is still fixing its gaze on its Beloved Star.

When it wakes up, it does not become depressed. It begins its office of *love* once again. It invokes the Angels and the Saints, who rise like eagles toward the consuming Home, the object of its desire. And the eagles, taking pity on their little sister, protect it, defend it, and put to flight the vultures who would like to devour it. The vultures, images of the demons—the little bird does not fear them. It is destined not to become their *prey*, but that of *the Eagle* it contemplates at the center of the Sun of Love.

O Divine Word [Jn. 1:1–3], You are the adored Eagle whom I love and who *draws me*. You are the One who, launching out to this world of exile, was willing to suffer and die in order to *draw* souls to the midst of the Eternal Home of the Blessed Trinity. It is You, going back up toward the unapproachable Light that will henceforth be Your dwelling place [1 Tim. 6:16], it is You still remaining in the valley of tears, hidden under the appearance of a white host. . . . Everlasting Eagle, You want to feed me with Your divine Substance, I, poor little being, who would return back into nothingness if Your divine gaze were not giving me life at each moment. . . .

Oh, Jesus! Leave me in the excess of my gratitude; let me tell You that Your love goes so far as foolishness. . . . Faced with this Foolishness, how do You want my heart not to launch out toward You? How could my trust know any limits? . . . Ah! For You, I know, the Saints also did *foolish things*, and they did great things since they were *eagles*. . . .

Jesus, I am too little to do great things. . . . My own *foolishness* is to hope that Your Love might accept me as a sacrificial victim. . . . My foolishness consists in begging my brothers the eagles to obtain for me the favor of flying toward the Sun of Love with the very wings of the Divine Eagle [Deut. 32:10–11]. . . .

As long as You wish, my Beloved, Your little bird will remain without strength and without wings. Always it will remain with its eyes fixed on You. It wants to be *fascinated* by Your divine glance. It wants to become the *prey* of Your Love. . . . I have the hope that one day, my Adored Eagle, You will come to get Your little bird, and going back up with it to the Home of Love, You will plunge it for eternity into the burning Abyss of that Love to which it has offered itself as a sacrificial victim.

Jesus! If only I could tell all the *little souls* how indescribable is Your condescendence. . . . I feel that if by some impossibility, You were to find a weaker, smaller soul than mine, You would be pleased to pour out on it even greater favors if it abandoned itself with complete trust in Your infinite mercy [Lk. 10:21]. But why desire to communicate Your secrets of Love, Jesus? Is it not You alone who taught them to me, and can You not reveal them to others? . . . Yes, I know You can, and I entreat You to do this: I beg You to lower Your divine gaze on a great number of *little souls*. . . . I beg You to chose a legion of *little* sacrificial victims who are worthy of Your LOVE! . . .

The very little Sister Thérèse of the Child Jesus of the Holy Face, Carmelite Nun

THE TEST OF FAITH
1896–1897

Thérèse and her Prioress / The divine elevator
First hemoptysis [coughing of blood] / The table of sinners
The call of missions / What charity is

MANUSCRIPT ADDRESSED
TO SR. MARIE DE GONZAGUE
[my current Prioress]

June, 1897

Beloved Mother, you've shown me
the desire that I'm fulfilling with you to
sing the mercies of the Lord [Ps. 89:1].
I had begun that sweet song with your
dear daughter Agnes of Jesus [my sister
Pauline], who was the mother
charged by God to guide me

during the days of my childhood. So it was with her that I was to sing of the graces granted to the little flower of the Blessed Virgin, when she was in the springtime of her life.

But it's with you that I must sing of the happiness of that tiny little flower now that the timid rays of early morning have given way to the burning rays of midday. Yes, it's with you, beloved Mother; it's to respond to your desire that I'm going to repeat the feelings of my soul, my gratitude toward God, toward you who represent Him to me visibly. Wasn't it between your motherly hands that I gave myself entirely over to Him? Oh, Mother, do you remember that day [when I made my vows as a nun and you were Prioress]? . . . Yes, I feel that your heart wouldn't know how to forget it. . . . For me, I must await the beauties of heaven, since here below I can't find words that are capable of interpreting what happened in my heart on that blessed day.

Beloved Mother, there was another day when my soul became even more attached to yours, if that's possible. This was the day [in March, 1896] when Jesus imposed on you once again the burden of being Superior. On that day, dear Mother, you sowed in tears, but in heaven you'll be filled with joy when you see yourself bearing precious sheaves [Ps. 126:5–6].

Oh, Mother, forgive my childish simplicity. I feel that you're allowing me to speak to you without looking for what is allowed to a young nun to say to her Prioress. Perhaps I won't always remain within the boundaries prescribed to those who are under authority, but, Mother, I dare to say it, it's your fault. I'm behaving toward you as a child because you're acting toward me not as Prioress but as Mother. . . .

Oh! I feel it well, dear Mother. It's God who always speaks to me through you. Many of the Sisters think that you've spoiled me, and that since my entrance into the holy ark [of Carmel] [Gen. 7:13], I've received from you only strokes and compliments. However, that's not the way it is. You'll see, Mother, in the notebook that contains my childhood memories [chapters one through eight, written under obedience to Mother Agnes of Jesus (Pauline) when she was

Prioress], what I think about the *strong* and motherly upbringing that I received from you. From the deepest part of my heart I thank you for not having spared me. Jesus knew well that His little flower needed the life-giving water of humiliation. She was too weak to take root without that help, and it's through you, Mother, that that blessing was bestowed on her.

For a year and a half Jesus has wanted to change the way to make His little flower grow. No doubt He found her *watered* enough, for now it's the *sun* that's making her grow. Jesus no longer wants for her anything other than His smile, which He continues to give her through you, beloved Mother. That sun, rather than causing the little flower to wilt, is making it grow marvelously. In the bottom of her cup she's preserving the precious drops of dew that she has received [that is, the water of humiliation], and those drops always remind her that she's small and weak. . . . All creatures can bend toward her, admire her, overwhelm her with their praises—I don't know why, but all that wouldn't know how to add one single drop of false joy to the true joy that she savors in her heart, seeing herself as what she is in the eyes of God: a poor little nothing, nothing more. . . .

I say that I don't understand why, but isn't it because she was preserved from the water of praise the whole time that her little cup wasn't full enough of the dew of humiliation? Now [that she is so ill] there is no longer any danger. On the contrary, the little flower finds the dew with which she is filled to be so delicious that she would take great care not to exchange it for the tasteless water of compliments.

I don't want to talk, dear Mother, about the love and the confidence that you show me. Don't think that your child's heart is insensitive to them, only I feel strongly that I have nothing to fear now. On the contrary I can enjoy your love and trust, bringing back to God whatever good He has wanted to place within me. If it pleases Him to make me seem better than I am, that's not my responsibility. He's free to act as He wills. . . .

Oh, Mother, how different are the ways by which the Lord leads souls! In the lives of the Saints, we see that many are found who have wanted to leave nothing of themselves after their death—not the slightest memory, the least bit of writing. On the contrary, there are many, like our Mother St. Teresa of Avila, who have enriched the Church with their sublime revelations, not fearing to reveal the King's secrets [see Tob. 12:7 D-R], to the end that He may be better known and better loved by souls.

Which of these two types of Saints are the most pleasing to God? It seems to me, Mother, that they're equally pleasing to Him, since all have followed the movements of the Holy Spirit, and that the Lord has said: "Tell the righteous it will be well with them" [Isa. 3:10]. Yes, all is well, when we seek only the will of Jesus. It's for that reason that I, a poor little flower, obey Jesus by trying to give pleasure to my beloved Mother.

You know, Mother, that I've always desired to be a Saint, but alas! I've always stated, when I've compared myself to the Saints, that there is between them and me the same difference that exists between a mountain the summit of which is lost in the sky, and an obscure grain of sand that is trodden under foot by passersby. Instead of becoming discouraged, I've told myself: God wouldn't know how to inspire desires that can't be realized. So despite my littleness I can aspire to Sainthood. To make myself bigger is impossible; I have to put up with myself such as I am with all my imperfections. But I want to seek the means of going to heaven by a little way that is very straight, very short, a completely new little way.

We're in an age of inventions. Now there's no more need to climb the steps of a staircase. In rich homes there are elevators that replace stairs to great advantage. I would also like to find an elevator to lift me up to Jesus, because I'm too little to climb the rough staircase of perfection. So I sought in the holy books the indication of the elevator that is the object of my desire, and I read these words that come from the mouth of Eternal Wisdom: "Let all who are *simple* come to my house" [see Pr. 9:4]. So I came, suspecting that I had found what I was looking for, and wanting to know, God, what You would do with the simple little one who would respond to Your call.

I've continued my search, and here's what I've found: "As a mother comforts her child, so I will comfort you. . . . [Y]ou will nurse and be carried on her arm and dandled on her knees" [Isa. 66:13, 12]. Oh! Never have words more tender, more melodious, come to rejoice my soul. The elevator that must lift me up to heaven is Your arms, Jesus! For that I don't need to become big.

On the contrary, I have to stay little—may I become little, more and more.

God, You've surpassed my expectations, and I want to sing of Your mercies [Ps. 89:1]. "Since my youth, God, you have taught me, and to this day I declare your marvelous deeds. Even when I am old and gray, do not forsake me, my God" [Ps. 71:17–18]. When will be my time of being "old and gray"? It seems to me that it could be now, because two thousand years are not more in the Lord's eyes than twenty years . . . or than a single day [Ps. 90:4]. . . .

Oh! Don't think, beloved Mother, that your child desires to leave you. . . . Don't believe that she esteems it a greater grace to die at dawn rather than at sunset. What she esteems, the only thing that she desires, is to *give pleasure* to Jesus. . . . Now that He seems to be coming near to her to draw her to the dwelling of His glory, your child is rejoicing. For a long time she has understood that God doesn't need anyone (her even less than others) to do good on earth.

Mother, forgive me if I'm making you sad. . . . Oh! I would so much like to make you happy. . . . But do you believe that if your prayers are not granted on earth, if Jesus has separated the child from her Mother *for a few days*, those prayers won't be granted in heaven? . . .

Your desire is, I know, for me to accomplish near you a very light, very easy mission. Won't I be able to complete that mission from up in heaven? . . . Just as Jesus said one day to St. Peter, you said to your child, "Feed my lambs" [Jn. 21:15] [when you asked me to assist you in forming the Novices], and I was quite surprised at that. I told you that I was "too *little*.". . . I pleaded with you to feed your little lambs yourself, and to watch over me, to feed me by grace with them. And you, beloved Mother, responding *a little* to my just desire, you kept the little lambs with the sheep, but at the same time directing me to go often to feed them in the *shade*, to show them the best and most strengthening grasses, to take care to show them the brightest flowers that they must never touch so as not to crush them under their feet. . . .

You weren't afraid, dear Mother, that I would cause your little lambs to stray. My inexperience, my youth didn't frighten you. Perhaps you remembered that often the Lord is pleased to grant wisdom to those who are little, and that one day, transported with joy, He blessed His Father for having hidden His secrets from the wise and having revealed them to little children [Lk. 10:21]. Mother, as you know, rare are the souls who don't measure the divine power according to their diminutive thoughts. They are willing for there to be exceptions everywhere on earth, but only God has the right to do that.

For a very long time, I know, this approach to measuring experience by years has been the practice among humans, because, in his adolescence, the holy king David sang to the Lord, "I am very young and despised" [Ps. 118:141 d-r (Ps. 119)]. In the same psalm he wasn't afraid to say, however, "I have more understanding than the elders, for I obey your precepts" [v. 100]. . . . "Your word is a lamp to my feet and a light for my path" [v. 105]. . . . "I will hasten and not delay to obey your commands" [v. 60]. . . .

Beloved Mother, you weren't afraid to tell me one day that God was illuminating my soul, that He was even giving me the experience of *years*. . . . Oh, Mother! I'm *too little* to have vanity now, I'm *too little* still to turn beautiful phrases in order to make you believe that I have a great deal of humility. I prefer to concur quite simply that the Almighty has done great things in the soul of the child of His divine Mother [Lk. 1:49], and the greatest is to have shown her how *little*, how powerless she is.

Dear Mother, you know it well, God has consented to make my soul pass through many kinds of trials. I've suffered a great deal since I've been on earth, but if in my childhood I suffered with sadness, I no longer suffer that way now: It's in joy and peace. I'm truly happy to suffer. Oh, Mother, you have to know all the secrets of my soul in order not to smile when you read these lines, because is there a soul with fewer trials than mine if one were to judge by appearances? Oh! If the trial [my illness] that I've been suffering for a year were to be obvious, how surprised people would be! . . .

Beloved Mother, you're familiar with that trial. However, I'm going to talk to you about it some more, because I consider it to be a great grace that I received under your blessed Priorship.

Last year, God granted me the comfort of observing the fast of Lent in all its rigor. I had never felt as strong, and that strength stayed with me till Easter. However, on Good Friday, Jesus wanted to give me the hope of going soon to see Him in heaven. . . . Oh! How sweet that memory is to me! . . . After staying at the Tomb [the chapel where the reserved Sacrament is kept between Good Friday and the Easter Vigil on Holy Saturday evening] until midnight, I went into our cell, but hardly had I had the time to place my head on the pillow when I felt something like a wave that was rising, rising, boiling up to my lips. I didn't know what it was, but I thought that perhaps I was going to die, and my soul was flooded with joy. . . . However, since our lamp was out, I told myself that I would have to wait for morning to assure myself of my happiness, because it seemed to me that it was blood that I had vomited.

The morning wasn't long in coming. When I woke up, I thought right away that I had something joyful to learn. When I went to the window I was able to confirm that I hadn't been deceived. . . . Oh! My soul was filled with great comfort. I was thoroughly persuaded that Jesus, on the day of commemoration of His death, wanted to me to hear a first call. It was like a gentle, faraway murmur that was announcing to me the arrival of the Bridegroom [Mt. 25:6]. . . .

It was with very great fervor that I attended Prime [the second church service of the day] and the chapter of faults [the service of public confession of one's faults]. I was in a hurry to see my turn come in order to be able, while asking your forgiveness, to confide in you, beloved Mother, my hope and my happiness. But I added that I wasn't suffering at all (which was quite true), and I begged you, Mother, not to give me anything in particular. And in fact I had the consolation of spending the day on Good Friday as I desired.

Never had the austerities of Carmel seemed to me as delightful. The hope of going to heaven transported me with gladness. When the evening of that blessed day arrived, I had to rest, but just as happened the night before, the good Jesus gave me the same sign that my entrance into Everlasting life was not far off [because once again I coughed up blood]. . . . I rejoiced then with a faith that was so alive, so clear, that the thought of heaven became my whole happiness. I couldn't believe that there could be unbelievers who had no faith. I thought that they were speaking against their own thoughts by denying the existence of heaven, that beautiful heaven where God Himself would like to be their everlasting reward [Gen. 15:1].

During the most joyous days of Eastertide, Jesus made me feel that there truly are souls that don't have faith, who through the abuse of graces lose that precious treasure, the source of the only pure and true joys. He allowed my soul to be invaded by the thickest darkness, and for the thought of heaven, which was so sweet to me, to be only a subject of struggle and torment. . . . This trial was not to last for several days or weeks. It was to extend only until the time fixed by God, and . . . that time has not yet come. . . . I would like to be able to express what I feel, but, alas! I feel that it's impossible. You would have to travel in that dark tunnel to understand its darkness. Nonetheless, I'm going to try to explain it through a comparison.

In this comparison, I'm supposing that I was born in a country surrounded by a thick fog. I've never contemplated the laughing aspect of nature when it's flooded and transfigured by the brilliant sun. Since my childhood, it's true, I've heard about these marvels. I know that the country where I am is not my Homeland, that my home is another land toward which I must aspire without ceasing [Heb. 11:13–16]. It's not a story made up by an inhabitant of the sad country in which I find myself. It's a certain reality, because the King of the Homeland of the brilliant sun came to live for thirty-three years in the land of darkness. Alas! The darkness didn't understand that this Divine King was the light of the world [Jn. 1:5, 9–10]. . . .

Chapel of the Carmel of Lisieux

Choir of the Carmelites of Lisieux

The stall marked with a small cross was that of Sister Thérèse of the Child Jesus. On the right is the grille where the Sisters received Communion.

But Lord, Your child has understood Your divine light. She asks You for forgiveness for her brothers and sisters. She accepts to eat the bread of sorrow [Ps. 127:2] for as long as You wish, and doesn't want to rise from this table filled with bitterness, where poor sinners eat, before the day that You've appointed. . . . But also, can't she say in her name, in the name of her brothers and sisters, "Have mercy on us, Lord, for we are poor sinners. . . . Oh! Lord, send us away justified" [see Lk. 18:13–14]? . . .

May all those who haven't been lit with the gleaming torch of Faith finally see it glowing. . . . Oh, Jesus, if the table that has been soiled by them has to be purified by a soul who loves You, I'm willing to eat all alone the bread of trials until it pleases You to admit me into Your shining Kingdom. The only grace that I ask of You is never to give You any offense! . . .

Beloved Mother, what I'm writing you has no continuation. My little story that seemed like a fairy tale has suddenly changed into a prayer. I don't know what interest you'll be able to find in reading all these confusing and poorly expressed thoughts. After all, Mother, I'm writing, not to make a work of literature, but out of obedience. If I'm boring you, at least you will see that your child has given proof of her good will. So without becoming discouraged I'm going to continue my little comparison from the point where I left off.

I was saying that the certainty of going some day far away from the sad, dark country had been given to me beginning in my childhood. Not only did I believe according to what I heard people say, people who were more knowledgeable than I was, but even more I felt, in the depths of my heart, aspirations toward a more beautiful place. Just as the genius of Christopher Columbus caused him to feel that a new world existed, whereas no one had thought of it, in the same way I felt that another land would serve me some day as a stable dwelling place [Heb. 13:14].

But suddenly the fog that surrounds me becomes thicker. It penetrates into my soul and envelops it in such a way that it's no longer possible to find in my soul the sweet image of my Homeland. Everything has disappeared!

When I want to give rest to my heart, fatigued from the darkness that surrounds it, by remembering the luminous country toward which I aspire, my torment redoubles. It seems to me that the darkness, borrowing the voice of sinners, tells me mockingly, "You're dreaming up the light, this Homeland smelling of the sweetest perfume. You're dreaming up the *everlasting* possession of the Creator of all these marvelous things. You think that someday you're going to get out of all this fog that surrounds you. Go ahead, go ahead, rejoice in death, which will give you, not what you're hoping for, but a still deeper night, the night of nothingness."

Beloved Mother, the image that I tried to give you of the darkness that obscures my soul is as imperfect as a model compared to the real thing, but I don't want to write any longer, because I would be afraid of blaspheming. . . . I'm even afraid of having said too much already. . . .

Oh! May Jesus forgive me if I've caused Him pain, but He knows well that while I don't have the enjoyment of Faith, at least I try to do its works. I believe I've done more acts of faith in the past year than during my whole life. At each new opportunity to do battle, when my enemies come and provoke me, I conduct myself bravely. Knowing that it's cowardly to fight in a duel, I turn my back on my adversary without condescending to look him in the face. But I run toward my Jesus, I tell Him that I'm ready to shed my blood even to the last drop in order to confess that there is a heaven. I tell Him that I'm happy not to enjoy that beautiful heaven on earth in order that He might open it for eternity to the poor unbelievers.

So, despite this trial that's taking away *all enjoyment*, I can nonetheless cry out, "For you make me *glad* by your deeds, LORD" [Ps. 92:4]. For, is there a greater *gladness* than that of suffering out of love for You? . . . The more private the suffering is, the less evident it is to the eyes of created beings, the more it makes You glad, God. But if, against all possibility, You Yourself were not to know of my suffering, I would still be happy to possess it, if by it I could prevent or make reparation for a single fault committed against the Faith. . . .

Beloved Mother, I may perhaps seem to you to be exaggerating my trial. In fact, if you judge according to the sentiments that I express in the little poems that I've composed this year, I must seem to you to be a soul filled with consolations and for whom the veil of faith has almost torn open, and yet . . . it's no longer a veil for me, it's a wall that rises up to heaven and covers the starry sky. . . . When I sing of the happiness of heaven, the everlasting possession of God, I feel no joy because of it, because I simply sing of what *I want to believe*. Sometimes, it's true, a tiny little ray of sunshine comes in to illumine my darkness, and so the trial stops for *an instant*, but then the memory of that ray, instead of causing me joy, makes my darkness even thicker.

Oh, Mother, never have I felt so keenly how gentle and merciful the Lord is [Ps. 103:8]. He sent me this trial only at the moment when I had the strength to endure it. I really believe that if it had come earlier, it would have plunged me into discouragement. . . . Now it takes away everything that might have been found of natural satisfaction in the desire that I had for heaven. . . . Beloved Mother, it seems to me now that nothing is preventing me from flying away, for I no longer have any great desire, if it isn't that of loving to the point of dying from love. . . . (June 9th)

——·——

Dear Mother, I'm quite surprised when I see what I wrote you yesterday. What scribbling! My hand was trembling in such a way that it was impossible for me to continue, and now I'm sorry that I even tried to write. I hope that today I'm going to do it more legibly, because today I'm not in bed, but in a pretty little white armchair.

Oh, Mother, I'm quite aware that everything that I'm telling you has nothing to follow it, but I also feel the need, before writing you about the past, to tell you my present feelings. Later, perhaps, I will have lost the memory of them. I want to tell you first of all how touched I am by all your motherly tenderness. Oh! Believe it, beloved Mother, the heart of your child is full of gratitude—it will never forget all that it owes you. . . .

Mother, what touches me most of all is the novena [nine days of prayer] that you're making to Our Lady of Victories, and the Masses that you're having said in order to obtain my healing. I feel that all these spiritual treasures are doing great good to my soul. At the beginning of the novena, I was telling you, Mother, that the Blessed Virgin either must heal me or take me to heaven, because I found it quite sad for you and the community to have the care of a young, sick nun. Now I'm willing to be sick my whole life if that gives pleasure to God, and I consent even for my life to be very long. The only grace that I desire is for it to be broken by love.

Oh! No, I'm not afraid of living a long life. I'm not refusing the battle, because the Lord is the rock on whom I'm lifted up, who trains my hands for war, and my fingers for battle. He is my shield, I take refuge in Him [Ps. 144:1–2]. So I've never asked God to let me die young. It's true that I've always hoped that this is His will. Often the Lord is content with the desire to work for His glory, and you know, Mother, that my desires are very great. You also know that Jesus has presented me with more than one bitter cup that He's taken away from my lips before I drank it [Lk. 22:42], but not before making me taste its bitterness.

Beloved Mother, the holy king David was right when he sang, "How good and pleasant it is when God's people live together in unity!" [Ps. 133:1]. This is true, and I've felt it quite often, but it's in the midst of sacrifices that this unity must take place on earth. It was not to live with my natural sisters that I came to Carmel, it was only to respond to Jesus' call. Oh! I had a strong feeling that it must be a subject of continual suffering to live with one's sisters, when one doesn't want to make any concession to nature.

How can people say that it's more perfect to go far away from one's own family? . . . Has anyone ever reproached brothers for fighting on the same field of battle? Have they ever been reproached for hurrying together to wear the palm of martyrdom? . . . No doubt, people judged rightly that they were encouraging each other mutually, but also that the martyrdom of each one became that of all. So it is in the religious life, which theologians call a martyrdom. By giving oneself to God the heart doesn't lose its natural tenderness. On the contrary, that tenderness grows by becoming more pure and more divine.

Beloved Mother, it's out of that tenderness that I love you, that I love my sisters. I'm happy to fight *as a family* for the glory of the King of Heaven, but I'm also ready to fly to another field of battle if the Divine General were to express the desire for me to do so. An order wouldn't be needed, just a glance, a simple sign.

Since my entrance into the blessed ark [of Carmel], I've always thought that if Jesus didn't take me very quickly to heaven, the fate of Noah's little dove would be mine: One day the Lord would open the window of the ark and would tell me to fly very far, very far, toward the unfaithful shores, [to a foreign land as a missionary,] bearing with me the little olive leaf [Gen. 8:11–12].

Mother, this thought has made my soul grow. It has made me soar higher than all creation. I have understood that even at Carmel there could still be separations, that only in heaven will unity be complete and everlasting. Then I wanted my soul to live in heaven and to behold the things of earth only from afar. I accepted not only to be exiled in the midst of an unknown people, but what was *much more* bitter to me, I accepted the exile for my sisters.

I will never forget the second of August, 1896. That was the very day of the departure of the missionaries. There was a serious question about Mother Agnes of Jesus' leaving. Oh! I wouldn't have wanted to make a single movement to prevent her from leaving. Nonetheless I felt a great sadness in my heart. I found that her soul, which was so sensitive, so delicate, wasn't made to live among souls who would not know how to understand it.

A thousand other thoughts crowded into my mind, and Jesus fell silent and didn't rebuke the storm [Mk. 4:37–39]. . . . And I would tell Him, "My God, out of love for You I accept it all: If You so desire, I'm willing to suffer to the point of dying from sorrow." Jesus was content with the acceptance.

But several months later, there was talk about the departure of Sr. Geneviève and Sr. Marie of the Trinity. Then this was another type of suffering, extremely intimate, extremely deep. I pictured all the trials, the disappointments that they would have to suffer. In short, my sky was laden with clouds. . . . Only the depths of my heart remained in calm and peace.

Beloved Mother, your good sense knew how to discover God's will, and on His behalf you forbade your Novices to think now about leaving the cradle of their religious childhood. But you understood their aspirations, since you yourself, Mother, had asked in your younger days to go to Saigon [in French Indochina]. That's often the way—the desires of mothers find an echo in the souls of their children. Oh, dear Mother, your desire to be an apostle finds in my soul, as you know, a most faithful echo. Let me confide in you why I desired and still desire, if the Blessed Virgin heals me, to go to a foreign land and leave behind the delicious oasis where I live so happily under your motherly gaze.

To live in foreign Carmelite convents, one must have, Mother (you've told me this), a very special vocation. Many souls think they are called to it without being called in fact. You also told me that I had that vocation and that only my health was an obstacle. I know well that this obstacle would disappear if God were to call me far away. So I live without being worried.

If I were required someday to leave my dear Carmel, oh! that wouldn't be without hurt. Jesus didn't give me an insensitive heart, and it's precisely because it's capable of suffering that I desire for it to give to Jesus all that it can give. *Here*, beloved Mother, I live without any encumbrance of the cares of the wretched earth. I have only to fulfill the light and easy mission that you've entrusted to me. *Here* I'm showered with your motherly attentions. I don't feel poverty, since I have never lacked anything. But above all, *here* I'm loved, by you and all the Sisters, and this affection is most sweet to me. That's why I dream about a convent where I would be unknown, where I would have to suffer poverty, lack of affection, in short, the exile of the heart.

Oh! It's not with the intention of rendering service to the convent that would be willing to receive me, that I would leave everything that is dear to me. No doubt, I would do everything that would depend on me, but I know how incapable I am, and I know that while I was doing the best I could, I wouldn't end up doing well, not having, as I was saying a short time ago, any knowledge of the things of earth. So my only goal would be to accomplish the will of God, to sacrifice myself for Him in the manner that would be pleasing to Him [see Mt. 6:10].

I have the strong feeling that I wouldn't be at all disappointed, because when we expect a suffering that is pure and unalloyed, the slightest joy becomes an unhoped-for surprise. And then, as you know, Mother, suffering itself becomes the greatest of joys when we seek it as the most precious of treasures.

Oh, no! It's not with the intention of enjoying the fruit of my labors that I would like to go away. If that were my goal I wouldn't feel this sweet peace that floods me, and I would even suffer from not being able to realize my vocation for faraway missions. For a long time I've no longer belonged to myself. I'm totally given over to Jesus. He's therefore free to do with me as He pleases. He gave me the attraction toward a complete exile, He made me *understand all* the *sufferings* that I would encounter there, asking me if I wanted to drain this cup to the dregs [Mt. 20:21–23]. Immediately I attempted to grasp the cup that Jesus was presenting to me, but He, pulling back His hand, gave me to understand that He was content with my accepting it.

Oh, Mother, how many worries does one free oneself of by making the vow of obedience! How happy are simple nuns. Their only compass being the will of their Superiors, they are always assured of being on the right path. They have no fear of being wrong, even if it seems certain to them that their Superiors are wrong. But when one stops looking at the infallible compass, when, under the pretext of doing God's will, one steps away from the path that she says to follow and maintains that He isn't perfectly enlightening those who nonetheless stand in His place, immediately the soul goes astray into arid paths where it is soon lacking the water of grace.

Beloved Mother, you are the compass that Jesus gave me to lead me surely to the everlasting shore. How sweet it is for me to fix my gaze on you and then to accomplish the Lord's will. Since the time that

He began allowing me to suffer temptations against the faith, He has greatly increased in my heart the spirit of faith that makes me see in you, not only a Mother who loves me and whom I love, but especially that makes me see Jesus living in your soul and communicating His will through you.

I well know, Mother, that you treat me [gently,] as a weak soul, as a pampered child, so I have no trouble bearing the burden of obedience. But it seems to me, according to what I feel in the depths of my heart, that I wouldn't change my behavior and that my love for you wouldn't suffer any decrease, if it pleased you to treat me severely. For I would still see that it's the will of Jesus for you to act that way for the greater good of my soul.

This year, dear Mother, God has given me the grace to understand what charity is. It's true that I understood it before, but in an imperfect way. I hadn't gone to the core of this word of Jesus, "And the second [commandment] is like it, 'Love your neighbor as yourself'" [Mt. 22:39]. I applied myself especially to loving God, and it's in loving Him that I understood that it wasn't necessary for my love to be interpreted only by words, because, "Not everyone who says to me, 'Lord, Lord,' will enter the kingdom of heaven, but only those who do the will of my Father who is in heaven" [Mt. 7:21].

That will was revealed by Jesus many times—I ought to say, almost on every page of His Gospel. But at the Last Supper, when He knew that the heart of His disciples was burning with a more ardent love for Him, who had just given Himself to them in the ineffable mystery of His Eucharist, this gentle Savior wanted to give them a new commandment. He told them with inexpressible tenderness: "A new command I give you: Love one another. As I have loved you, so you must love one another. By this everyone will know that you are my disciples, if you love one another" [Jn. 13:34–35].

How did Jesus love His disciples, and why did He love them? Oh! It wasn't their natural qualities that could have attracted Him: Between them and Him there was an infinite distance. He was knowledge and Eternal Wisdom; they were poor fishermen, ignorant and full of earthly thoughts. However, Jesus called them His friends, His brothers. He wanted to see them reign with Him in His Father's kingdom [Lk. 22:30], and in order to open this kingdom to them, He was willing to die on a cross. For He said, "Greater love has no one than this: to lay down one's life for one's friends" [Jn. 15:13].

Beloved Mother, as I meditated on these words of Jesus, I understood how much my love for my Sisters was imperfect. I saw that I wasn't loving them as God loves them. Oh! Now I understand that perfect charity consists in bearing with others' faults, in not being surprised at their weakness, in being edified by the little acts of virtue that we see them practice. But above all I understood that charity ought not to stay enclosed in the depths of the heart. Jesus said, "Neither do people light a lamp and put it under a bowl. Instead they put it on its stand, and it gives light to *everyone* in the house" [Mt. 5:15]. It seems to me that this lamp represents charity, which ought to illumine and cause to rejoice, not only those who are the dearest to me, but everyone in the house, without any exception.

When the Lord had commanded His people to love their neighbor as themselves He hadn't yet come to earth, so, knowing well to what degree we love our own selves, He couldn't ask His creatures for a greater love than love for our neighbor [Lev. 19:18]. But when Jesus gave His apostles a new commandment, *His own commandment*, as He said later—He no longer talked about loving our neighbor as ourselves, but to love our neighbor as *Jesus loved him*, as He will love him until the end of the world. . . .

Ah! Lord, I know that You command nothing that is impossible, You know better than I my weakness, my imperfection. You know well that I would never be able to love my Sisters as You love them, if *You Yourself*, oh my Jesus, didn't continue to *love* them *in me*. It's because You wanted to grant me this grace that You gave a *new* commandment [Jn. 13:34]. Oh! How I love it because it gives me the assurance that Your will is to love *in me* all those whom You are commanding me to love! . . .

Yes, I feel it when I'm charitable: It's Jesus alone who is acting in me. The more I'm united with Him, the more also I love all my Sisters.

When I want to increase this love in me, especially when the devil is trying to put before the eyes of my soul the faults of such or such a Sister whom I find the least likable, I hasten to look for her virtues, her good desires. I tell myself that if I've seen her fall one time she could well have won a great number of victories that she hides out of humility, and that even what seems to me to be a fault could very well be, because of its intent, an act of virtue.

I have no problem persuading myself of this, because one day I did a little experiment that proved to me that we must never judge. It was during a recreation period. There were two knocks at the door. We had to open the big workmen's door in order to allow the trees to be brought in for the manger scene. The recreation period wasn't cheerful, because you weren't there, dear Mother, so I was thinking that if I were sent to serve as assistant, I would be very happy. In fact, the Sub-Prioress told me to go serve, or if not me, then the Sister who was beside me. Immediately I began to undo my apron, but rather slowly so that my companion might take hers off before me, because I thought I would be pleasing her by letting her be the assistant. The Sister who was replacing the depositary watched us, laughing, and, when she saw that I had stood up last, she told me, "Oh! I had thought that you weren't the one who was going to gain a pearl in your crown. You were going too slowly. . . ."

Most certainly the whole community thought that I had acted out of my nature [since at that point they didn't consider me to be a hard worker]. Yet I couldn't tell you how much such a little thing did good to my soul and made me nonjudgmental toward the weaknesses of others.

That also prevents me from having vanity when I'm judged favorably, because I tell myself this: Since they take my little acts of virtue for imperfections, they can just as well be wrong when they take as a virtue what is only imperfection. Then I say with St. Paul: "I care very little if I am judged by you or by any human court; indeed, I do not even judge myself. My conscience is clear, but that does not make me innocent. It is the Lord who judges me" [1 Cor. 4:3–4]. So, to make this judgment favorable, or rather in order not to be judged at all, I always want to have charitable thoughts, because Jesus said, "Do not judge, and you will not be judged" [Lk. 6:37].

Mother, in reading what I've just written, you could believe that the practice of charity isn't difficult for me. That's true. For several months I've no longer had to struggle to practice that beautiful virtue. I don't mean by this that it never happens that I commit faults. Oh! I'm too imperfect for that, but I don't have much trouble picking myself back up when I've fallen, because in a certain struggle I carried the victory. Therefore the heavenly Host now comes to my aid, not being able to suffer seeing me defeated after having been victorious in the glorious war that I'm going to try to describe.

There is in our community one Sister who has the talent of displeasing me in everything: Her manners, her words, her character seemed to me to be *very displeasing*. However, she's a holy nun who must be *very pleasing* to God. So, not wanting to give in to the natural dislike that I was experiencing, I told myself that charity doesn't consist in feelings but in works.

So I set about doing for this Sister what I would have done for the person that I love the most. Each time that I met her I prayed to God for her, offering Him all her virtues and her merits. I felt strongly that this was pleasing to Jesus, because there is no artist who doesn't like to receive praise for his works, and Jesus, the Artist of souls, is happy when one doesn't stop on the outside, but penetrating as far as the interior sanctuary that He has chosen for Himself as a dwelling, one admires its beauty.

I wasn't content just to pray a lot for the Sister who gave me so many struggles; I tried to render to her every possible service. And when I had the temptation to answer her in an unpleasant way, I contented myself with giving her my most pleasant smile, and I tried to turn the conversation in a different direction, because the *Imitation* says, "It is better to leave each one in his feeling than to stop to contest it."

Often, as well, when I wasn't at the recreation period (I mean during work times), having some work contact with this Sister, when my struggles were too violent, I fled away like a deserter. Since she absolutely didn't know what I was feeling toward her, she never suspected the motives of my conduct, and remains persuaded that her character is pleasing to me.

One day during the recreation period she told me something like these words, with a very happy appearance: "Would you please tell me, Sister Thérèse of the Child Jesus, what attracts you so much to me? Because every time you look at me, I see you smile." Oh! What attracted me was Jesus, hidden in the depths of her soul. . . . Jesus, who makes sweet what is the most bitter. . . . I answered her that I smiled because I was happy to see her (of course I didn't add that it was from a spiritual point of view).

Beloved Mother, as I told you, my *last means* of not being defeated in my struggles is desertion. I already used this means during my novitiate, and it has always worked perfectly for me. Mother, I want to cite you an example that I think will make you smile. During one of your bouts with bronchitis, I came one morning quite softly to put back in your room the keys to the Communion grille, since I was the sacristan. Inside, I wasn't upset at having this opportunity to see you. I was even very happy, but I was very careful not to let it show.

One Sister, who was enlivened by a holy zeal and who nonetheless liked me a lot, seeing me enter into your room, Mother, thought that I was going to wake you up. She tried to take the keys from me, but I was too clever to give them to her and give up *my rights*. I told her as politely as possible that I desired as much as she not to wake you up, and that it was *my* job to return the keys. . . .

I understand now that it would have been much more perfect to give in to this Sister, who was young, it is true, but after all older than I was. I didn't understand that then, so, absolutely wanting to follow her in, in spite of her pushing the door to prevent me from entering, soon the misfortune that we were dreading happened: The noise that we were making caused you to open your eyes. . . . Then, Mother, everything fell on my head. The poor Sister whom I had resisted launched into quite a speech, the gist of which was this: "Sister Thérèse of the Child Jesus is the one who made noise. God, how unpleasant she is. . . ." And so on. I, who was feeling quite the opposite, really felt like defending myself.

Fortunately a bright idea came to me. I told myself that certainly if I began to justify myself, I wasn't going to keep the peace of my soul. I also felt that I didn't have enough virtue to let myself be accused without saying anything. So my last escape hatch was flight. No sooner thought than done: I left without a drum roll or a trumpet, leaving the Sister to continue her speech, which was rather like the imprecations of Camillus against Rome.

My heart was beating so strongly that it was impossible for me to go far, and I sat down on the stairs to enjoy in peace the fruits of my victory. That's not much of an example of bravery, is it, dear Mother? But I think nonetheless that it's better not to expose oneself to battle when defeat is certain.

Alas! When I think back to the time of my novitiate, I see how imperfect I was. . . . I was bothered by such small things that I can laugh about them now. Ah! How good the Lord is to have made my soul grow, to have given it wings. . . . All the nets of the hunters couldn't frighten me, for, "a net is spread in vain before the eyes of them that have wings" [Prov. 1:17 D-R]. Later, no doubt, the time in which I now find myself will seem to me to be still filled with imperfections, but now I'm no longer surprised by anything. It doesn't trouble me to see that I'm *weakness* itself. On the contrary, it's in weakness that I glory [2 Cor. 12:5], and I expect every day to discover new imperfections in myself.

Remembering that charity "covers over a multitude of sins" [1 Pet. 4:8], I draw from that bountiful mine that Jesus has opened before me. In the Gospel, the Lord explains what His new commandment consists of [Jn. 13:34–35]: He says in St. Matthew, "You have heard that it was said, 'Love your neighbor and hate your enemy.' But I tell you, love your enemies and pray for those who persecute you" [Mt. 5:43–44].

No doubt, in Carmel you won't encounter enemies, but after all there are instinctive attractions: You feel attracted to one Sister, whereas in the case of another you would make a long detour to avoid meeting up with her. So even without knowing it, she becomes a subject of persecution. Well! Jesus told me that I must love this Sister, I must pray for her, even when her behavior would lead me to believe that she doesn't like me: "If you love those who love you, what credit is that to you? Even sinners love those who love them" [Lk. 6:32].

And it isn't enough to love; you have to prove it. We're naturally happy to give a present to a friend, we even love to give surprises, but that isn't charity, because sinners do that, too. Here's what Jesus goes on to teach me: "Give to everyone who asks you, and if anyone takes what belongs to you, do not demand it back" [Lk. 6:30]. To give to all those who *ask* is less sweet than to offer oneself through the movement of one's heart.

Again, when someone asks nicely, it doesn't cost me to give, but if unfortunately they don't use delicate enough words, instantly the soul revolts if it isn't set firmly on charity. It finds a thousand reasons to refuse what is asked of it, and it's only after having convinced the asker of her lack of refinement that it finally gives *by grace* what she's asking for, or that it gives her a light service that would have required twenty times less time to fulfill than it took to lay claim to imaginary rights.

If it's difficult to give to everyone who asks, it's even more so to let someone take what belongs to you without demanding it back [Lk. 6:30]. Oh, Mother, I say that it's difficult. I ought rather to say that it *seems* difficult, because the Lord's yoke is easy and His burden is light [Mt. 11:30]. When we accept it, we instantly feel its lightness, and we cry out with the Psalmist, "I have run the way of thy commandments, when thou didst enlarge my heart" [Ps. 118:32 D-R (Ps. 119)]. Only charity can enlarge my heart, Jesus. Since that gentle flame has consumed it, I'm running with You in the way of Your *new* commandment [Jn. 13:34–35]. I want to run in it until the blessed day when, joining with the train of virgins, I will be able to follow You in the infinite spaces, singing Your *new* song [Rev. 14:3–4], which must be the song of Love.

I was saying that Jesus doesn't want me to take back what belongs to me. That ought to seem easy and natural to me, since nothing is mine.

The goods of the earth—I renounced them through the vow of poverty, so I don't have the right to complain if someone takes away something that doesn't belong to me. On the contrary, I ought to rejoice, since it's my lot to feel poverty.

In the past it used to seem that I wasn't holding on to anything, but since I understood Jesus' words, I see that there are times when I'm quite imperfect. For example, when I sit down to paint, nothing belongs to me, I know that. But if, when I begin to work, I find brushes and paintings all in disorder, if a ruler or a knife has disappeared, patience is very close to abandoning me, and I have to take up my courage in both hands so as not to ask bitterly for the objects that I'm missing.

Sometimes it's necessary to ask for things we can't do without, but when we do so with humility, we're not missing out on Jesus' commandment. On the contrary, we're acting like the poor who hold out their hands in order to receive what is necessary to them. If they're refused, they're not surprised: No one owes them anything. Oh! What peace floods the soul when it rises above the responses of nature. . . .

No, there's no joy that can be compared to the one that's savored by one who is truly poor in spirit [Mt. 5:3]. If he asks with detachment for a needed thing, and not only is that thing refused to him, but an attempt is made to take what he does have, he follows Jesus' counsel: "And if any one wants to sue you and take your shirt, hand over your coat as well" [Mt. 5:40]. . . .

To give up my coat is, it seems to me, to give up my last rights, it's to consider myself as the servant, the slave of others. When I've left my coat behind, it's easier to walk, to run. So Jesus adds: "If anyone forces you to go one mile, go with them two miles" [Mt. 5:41]. Therefore it's not enough to give to whoever asks me for something [Lk. 6:30]. I have to go beyond my desires and give the impression of being very obliged and very honored to be of service. And if someone takes something that I use, I mustn't give the impression of regretting it, but on the contrary I must appear to be happy to *be rid of it*. . . .

Dear mother, I'm very far from practicing what I understand, but the very desire that I have to do so gives me peace.

More than on other days I feel that I've explained myself extremely poorly. I've made a *sort* of *speech* about charity that must have tired you out reading it. Forgive me, beloved Mother, and remember that right now the nurses are practicing on my behalf what I've just written. They're not afraid to go two miles when twenty steps would suffice. So I've been able to observe charity in action! Doubtless, my soul must find this to be a sweet perfume, but as far as my mind is concerned, I admit that it has become a bit paralyzed in the face of such devotion, and my pen has lost its lightness. In order for it to be possible for me to interpret my thoughts, I have to be like a bird alone on a roof [Ps. 102:7].

That's rarely my fate. When I begin to take up my pen, here's a good Sister who passes near me, a pitchfork over her shoulder. She thinks she's entertaining me by chatting with me a little. Hay, ducks, hens, a doctor's visit, everything's on the table. To tell you the truth, that doesn't last long, but there's *more* than one *good, charitable* Sister, and suddenly another hay cutter drops some flowers in my lap, thinking that perhaps she'll inspire some poetic ideas in me. Not seeking out flowers right then, I would prefer that they remain attached to their stems.

Finally, tired of opening and closing this notorious notebook [in which I'm writing], I open a book (that doesn't want to stay open) and I say resolutely that I'm copying sayings from the Psalms and the Gospels for our Prioress's birthday. That's quite true, because I'm not frugal with quotations. . . .

Dear Mother, I would amuse you, I think, by telling you all my adventures in the "thickets" at Carmel. I don't know if I've written ten lines without being disturbed. That shouldn't make me laugh or amuse me. However, for the love of God and for my Sisters (who are so charitable toward me), I try not only to give the impression of being happy, but also to *be* happy. . . .

Look, here's one hay cutter who's leaving after saying to me in a compassionate tone, "Dear little Sister, that must tire you out to write like that all day long." "Don't worry," I answered, "I look like I'm writing a lot, but in reality I don't write much of anything." "So much the better," she said to me, looking reassured, "but all the same, I'm sure happy that we're in the middle of cuttin' hay, 'cause that always distracts you a little." In fact, it's such a great distraction for me (without counting the nurses' visits) that I'm not lying when I say I don't write much of anything.

Fortunately, I'm not easy to discourage. To show you this, Mother, I'm going to finish explaining to you what Jesus has given me to understand on the subject of charity. So far I've talked to you only from the outside. Now I'd like to confide to you how I understand charity that is purely spiritual. I'm quite sure that it's not going to be long before I mix one with the other, but, Mother, since you're the one I'm talking to, I'm certain that it won't be difficult for you to catch my thought and to untangle your child's yarn.

It's not always possible, at Carmel, to practice to the letter the words of the Gospel. Sometimes because of duties we're obliged to refuse to do something for someone. But when charity has cast deep roots in the soul, it shows on the outside. There's a way to refuse what one can't give, that's so gracious that the refusal gives as much pleasure as the gift. It's true that it's less bothersome to ask for help from a Sister who's always disposed to oblige. But Jesus said, "Do not turn away from the one who wants to borrow from you" [Mt. 5:42]. So, under the pretext that one would be forced to refuse, one mustn't distance oneself from the Sisters who have the habit of always asking people to do things for them.

Neither must we be obliging in order to *give the appearance* of being obliging or in the hope that some other time the Sister that we're obliging will do something for us in turn. For Our Lord said again, "And if you lend to those from whom you expect repayment, what credit is that to you? Even sinners lend to sinners, expecting to be repaid in full. But . . . do good . . . and lend . . . without expecting to get anything back. Then your reward will be great" [Lk. 6:34–35]. Oh, yes! The reward is great even on earth. . . . When we follow that road it's only the first step that costs us.

To *lend without expecting to get anything back* seems hard to our nature. We would prefer to *give*, because something we give doesn't belong to us any more. When someone comes and tell us with a convincing look, "Sister, I need your help for a few hours. But don't worry, I have permission from our Superior, and I'll *pay back* the time that you're giving me, because I know how pressed for time you are." In truth, when we know quite well that the time we *lend* will never be paid back, we'd rather say, "I give it to you." That would make our self-love happy, because giving is a more generous act than lending, and then we make the Sister feel that we're not counting on her to do something for us. . . . Oh! How contrary Jesus' teachings are to the thoughts of nature. Without the help of His grace it would be impossible not only to put them into practice, but even more to understand them.

THOSE WHOM YOU HAVE GIVEN ME
1896–1897

Mother, Jesus gave this grace to your child to make her penetrate the mysterious depths of charity. If she could express what she understands, you'd hear a melody from heaven, but alas! I only have childish stammering to share with you....

If the very words of Jesus didn't serve me as a support, I'd be tempted to ask you for me to be excused and to set down my pen.... But no, I have to continue, out of obedience, what I began out of obedience.

Beloved Mother, I was writing yesterday that since the material things found here below are not mine, I shouldn't find it difficult to never get them back if sometimes they were taken from me. The things of heaven don't belong to me any more than those of earth. They've been *lent* to me by God, who can take them away from me without my having the right to complain about it. However, the good things that come directly from God—upward risings of the mind and the heart, deep thoughts—all those things form riches to which one can become attached as much as to a material thing that no one has the right to touch....

For example, if during a break someone says to a Sister some revelation received during the time of prayer, and then, a short time later, when speaking to another Sister, that Sister says the thing that had been confided in her as if she had thought of it herself, it seems as if she's taking something that isn't hers. Or if during a recreation period, someone says quietly to her neighbor an appropriate word that's full of spirit, and the second Sister repeats the word out loud without letting others know the source from which it comes, again, that seems to be stealing from the owner, who doesn't claim it but would really like to do so and seize on the first opportunity to delicately let it be known that someone has grabbed one of her thoughts.

Mother, I wouldn't be able to explain to you so well these sad reactions of nature, if I hadn't felt them in my heart. I would have liked to soothe myself with the sweet illusion that they've visited only my heart, if you hadn't asked me to listen to the temptations of your dear little Novices. I've learned a lot by fulfilling the mission that you entrusted to me. Especially, I've found myself forced to practice what I taught others. So now I can say it: Jesus has given me the grace not to be more attached to the things of the mind and the heart than to those of earth. If it happens to me to think and to say something that pleases my Sisters, I find it quite natural for them to take it over as belonging to themselves. That thought belongs to the Holy Spirit and not to me, since St. Paul said that without the Spirit of Love we can't give the name *Father* to our Father who is in heaven [Rom. 8:15]. So He's quite free to use me to give a good thought to a soul. If I believed that thought belongs to me, I would be like "the donkey bearing relics" who thought that the homage being paid to the Saints was addressed to him.

I don't spurn the deep thoughts that nourish the soul and unite it to God, but for a long time I've understood that I mustn't lean on them and make perfection consist in receiving many spiritual illuminations. The most beautiful thoughts are nothing without works. It's true that others can gain a lot of profit from them if they make themselves humble and show God their gratitude that He's allowing them to share in the feast of a soul that it pleases Him to enrich with His graces. But if this soul takes delight in her *beautiful thoughts* and prays the prayer of the Pharisee ("I thank you that I am not like other people" [Lk. 18:11]), it becomes like a person who's dying from hunger even though he's sitting in front of a table laden with food, all the while watching his guests taking an abundant meal from it and sometimes throwing a glance of envy at him, the one who has so many possessions. Oh! There's no good possession except God alone, who knows the depths of the heart. . . .

What stunted thoughts created beings have! . . . When they see one soul that's more enlightened than others, instantly they conclude from this that Jesus loves them less than that soul and that they can't be called to the same perfection. Since when does the Lord *no longer* have the *right* to use one of His creatures to distribute, to the souls that He loves, the food that is necessary to them? In the time of Pharaoh, the Lord still had *that right*, because in Scripture He said to that ruler, "But I have raised you up for this very purpose, that I might show you my power and that my name might be proclaimed in all the earth" [Ex. 9:16]. Centuries and centuries have passed since the Most High pronounced those words, and since then, His behavior hasn't changed: He has always used His creatures as instruments for doing His work in souls.

If the canvas on which an artist paints could think and speak, certainly it wouldn't complain about being constantly touched and retouched by a *brush*, and neither would it envy the role of that instrument, because it would know that it's not to the brush but to the artist who directs it that it owes the beauty that it bears. As for the brush, it couldn't take glory in the masterpiece that it has made. It knows that artists aren't inconvenienced: They make child's play of difficulties, taking pleasure in sometimes choosing instruments that are weak and defective. . . .

Beloved Mother, I'm a little brush that Jesus has chosen to paint His image on the souls that you've entrusted to me. An artist doesn't use just one brush, he needs at least two. The first one is the most useful—with it he gives the general colors, completely covering the canvas in a short time. The other, smaller one, he uses for the details.

Mother, you represent for me the precious brush that the hand of Jesus grasps with love when He wants to do a *big work* in the soul of your children. And I'm the *very little* one that He deigns to use afterward for the slightest details.

The first time that Jesus used His little brush was around the eighth of December, 1892 [the Feast Day of the Immaculate Conception]. I'll always remember that period as a time of graces. Dear Mother, I'm going to confide in you those sweet memories.

At the age of fifteen, when I had the happiness of entering Carmel, I found in the novitiate a classmate who had preceded me by a few months. She was eight years older than I was, but her childlike character made us forget the difference in years. Soon, you had the joy of seeing your two little postulants get along marvelously and become inseparable. In order to support that growing affection, which seemed to you would bear good fruit, you allowed us from time to time to have some little spiritual talks together. My dear classmate charmed me by her innocence and her expansive character. But on the other hand, I was surprised to see how much the affection that she had for you was different from mine. There were also many things in her behavior toward the Sisters that I would have wanted her to change. . . .

Since that period, God gave me to understand that there are souls for whom His mercy never tires of waiting, to whom He gives His light only by degrees. So I kept careful watch not to hurry His timetable, and I waited patiently for it to be pleasing to Jesus to make it come.

Reflecting one day on the permission that you had given us to talk together, as it is written in our holy constitutions: "In order to inflame in us greater love for our Bridegroom," I thought sadly that our conversations weren't attaining the desired result. Then God made me feel that the time had come, and that I mustn't be afraid to speak, or I should stop these talks that were like those of friends in the world. That day was a Saturday.

The next day during my time of thanksgiving prayers, I begged God to put into my mouth sweet and convincing words, or rather for Himself to speak through me. Jesus granted my prayer. He allowed the result to fulfill my hope entirely, for those who turn their eyes on Him will be enlightened [see Ps. 33:6 D-R]. And in the darkness the light dawned for the upright [Ps. 112:4]. The first of these verses was addressed to me, and the second one was for my classmate, who truly was upright. . . .

The time had come that we resolved to be together, and when the poor dear Sister cast her eyes on me, she saw right away that I was no longer the same. She sat down beside me, blushing, and I, pressing her head against my heart, told her with tears in my voice *everything I thought of her*, but with such tender expressions, showing her such great affection, that soon her tears mingled with mine. She agreed with great humility that everything I was saying was true. She promised me to begin a new life, and asked me as a grace to always alert her to her faults. Finally, at the moment when we parted, our affection had become quite spiritual; it no longer had anything human about it. In us was realized this passage from Scripture: "A brother that is helped by his brother, is like a strong city" [Prov. 18:19 D-R].

What Jesus did with His little brush would soon have been erased if He hadn't acted through you, Mother, in order to accomplish His work in the soul that He wanted to be completely His. The trial seemed quite bitter to my poor classmate, but your firmness triumphed, and it was then, as I tried to comfort this one whom you had given me as a sister among all of them, that I was able to explain to her what true love consists in.

Thérèse of the Child Jesus
After a painting by her sister—1912

I showed her that it was *herself* that she loved and not you. I told her how I loved you and the sacrifices that I was required to make at the beginning of my religious life in order not to attach myself to you in a material fashion, like a dog that becomes attached to its master. Love is fed with sacrifices. The more the soul refuses natural satisfactions, the more its tenderness becomes strong and impartial.

I remember that when I was a postulant, I sometimes had such violent temptations to enter your room in order to satisfy myself, to find a few drops of joy, that I was obliged to pass quickly in front of the storeroom and to hang on tightly to the stair rail. There came into my mind a large number of permissions to ask of you. In short, beloved Mother, I found a thousand reasons to make my nature happy. . . .

How happy I am now to have deprived myself of this from the very beginning of my religious life! I already enjoy the reward promised to those who fight courageously. I no longer feel that it's necessary to refuse all consolations of the heart, because my soul is strengthened by the only One whom I wanted to love. I see with happiness that by loving Him, the heart becomes enlarged. I see that it can give incomparably more tenderness to those who are dear to it, than if it were to concentrate on a self-centered and unfruitful love.

Dear Mother, I reminded you about the first work that Jesus and you deigned to accomplish in me; this was only the prelude to the ones that were to be entrusted to me. When it was given to me to penetrate into the sanctuary of souls, I saw right away that the task was beyond my strength, so I placed myself in God's arms, like a little child, and, hiding my face in His hair, I told Him, "Lord, I'm too little to feed Your children. If You want to give them through me what is proper for each one, fill my little hand, and without leaving Your arms, without turning my head, I'll give Your treasures to the soul who comes to me to ask for her food. If she finds it according to her taste, I'll know that it's not to me, but to You that she owes it. On the other hand, if she complains about what I present to her and finds it bitter, my peace won't be troubled. I'll try to persuade her that this food comes from You, and I'll take care not to look for any other food for her."

Mother, since I understood that it was impossible for me to do anything by myself, the task that you imposed on me no longer seemed difficult to me. I felt that the only thing needed was to unite myself more and more to Jesus, and that all the rest would be given to me as well [Mt. 6:33]. And in fact my hope never put me to shame [Rom. 5:5]: God deigned to fill my little hand as many times as it was necessary to nourish the souls of my Sisters.

I admit to you, beloved Mother, that if I had leaned in the slightest on my own strength, I would soon have turned my weapons back in to you. . . . *From afar* all that seems quite rosy, to do good to souls, to make them love God more, in order to shape them according to one's views and personal thoughts. *From up close* it's quite the opposite. The rosiness has disappeared. . . . You feel that doing good is something almost as impossible without God's help as making the sun shine at night. . . . You feel that you must absolutely forget your own desires and personal conceptions, and guide souls along the path that Jesus has traced for them, without trying to make them walk along your own path.

But this is still not the most difficult thing. What costs me above all is to observe the faults, the slightest imperfections, and to make war to the death against them. I was going to say, "unfortunately for me"! (but no, that would be cowardice), so I say, "fortunately for my Sisters." Since I've taken my place in Jesus' arms, I'm like the watchman observing the enemy from the highest tower of a castle. Nothing escapes my sight. Often I'm surprised to see so clearly, and I find the prophet Jonah to be quite excusable for running away instead of going to announce the ruin of Nineveh [Jon. 1:2–3].

I would a thousand times prefer to receive correction than to give it to others, but I feel that it's most necessary for that to be a suffering for me, because when you act according to nature, it's impossible for the soul to whom you want to reveal her faults to understand how wrong she is. All she sees is one thing: The Sister who's in charge of directing me is angry, and everything is falling on my head—and yet I'm full of the best of intentions.

I know well that your little lambs [the Novices] find me to be strict. If they were to read these lines, they'd say that it doesn't look as if it costs me the slightest thing in the world to run after them, to talk to them in a strict way when I show them that their beautiful fleece coat is dirty or to bring them some little scrap of wool that they've allowed to become torn by thorns on the path.

The little lambs can say all they want; in the end, they feel that I love them with a true love, that I'll never be like the hired hand who, when he sees the wolf coming, abandons the flock and runs away [Jn.10:11–13]. I'm ready to give my life for them, but my affection is so pure that I don't want them to know it. With Jesus' grace, I've never tried to draw their hearts to myself. I've understood that my mission was to draw them to God and to make them understand that here below, you were, Mother, the visible Jesus that they must love and respect.

I told you, dear Mother, that by teaching others I'd learned a great deal. I saw first of all that all souls have just about the same struggles, but they're so different from another point of view that I have no trouble understanding what Fr. Pichon said: "There's a much greater difference among souls than there is among faces." Therefore it's impossible to act with all of them in the same way. With certain souls, I feel that I have to make myself little, not being afraid to humble myself by admitting my struggles, my defeats. Seeing that I have the same weakness as they do, my dear Sisters in turn confess to me the faults that they reproach themselves for, and they rejoice that I understand them *through experience*. With others I've seen that on the contrary, in order to do them good I have to have a great deal of firmness and never take back anything once I've said it. In that case taking a low place wouldn't be humility, but weakness.

God has given me the grace not to be afraid of war; at all costs I have to do my duty. More than once I've heard this: "If you want to get anything out of me, you have to treat me gently. Come against me hard, and you'll get nothing." I know that no one is a good judge in his own case. A child that a doctor makes undergo a painful operation won't fail to cry loudly and to say that the cure is worse than the disease. However, if he finds himself cured a few days later, he's happy to be able to play and run. It's the same for souls. Soon they recognize that a little bitterness is sometimes preferable to sugar, and they're not afraid to admit it.

Sometimes I can't help smiling inside when I see what a change has taken place from one day to the next—it's enchanting. One comes and says to me, "You were right to be so strict yesterday. At first that revolted me, but afterward I remembered everything and I saw that you were very fair. . . . Listen, as I was walking away, I was thinking that it was all over. I was telling myself, 'I'm going to find our Superior and tell her that I'm not going to go anymore with Sister Thérèse of the Child Jesus.' But I felt that it was the devil who was inspiring that in me, and then it seemed to me that you were praying for me. So I stopped still, and the light began to shine. But now I need for you to explain it all to me, and that's why I'm coming." The conversation is quickly taken up, and I'm quite happy to be able to follow my heart's leading, without serving up any bitter food.

Yes, but . . . I quickly realize that you mustn't go too far, too fast. One word can tear down the beautiful structure that was built through tears. If I have the misfortune to say a word that seems to lessen the strength of what I said the day before, I see the dear Sister try to clutch hold of the branches again, so inside I say a little prayer, and the truth always wins out. Oh! It's prayer, it's sacrifice that are entirely my strength. These are the invincible weapons that Jesus has given me. Much more than words, they can touch souls—I've very often had that experience.

There is one experience among them all that made a gentle and deep impression on me. It was during Lent. At that time I was in charge of the one single Novice who was here and whose angel [advisor] I was. She came to find me one morning, all beaming. "Oh! If only you knew," she told me, "what I dreamed about last night. I was at my sister's side, and I wanted to disengage her from all the vain things that she loves so much. To do that I explained this couplet: 'Live in love. To love

You, Jesus, what a fruitful loss. All my sweet scents are Yours, no going back.' I could really feel that my words were penetrating her soul, and I was transported with joy. This morning as I was waking up, I thought that God perhaps wanted me to give Him that soul. How about if I write her after Lent to tell her my dream and tell her that Jesus wants her to be entirely His?"

Without thinking longer about it I told her that she might well try, but first, she needed to ask permission from our Superior. Since Lent was far from being over, you were, beloved Mother, quite surprised by a request that seemed too premature to you. And certainly, inspired by God, you answered that it wasn't through letters that Carmelites are to save souls, but through prayer.

When I learned about your decision I understood immediately that the words were from Jesus, and I told Sr. Marie of the Trinity, "We have to get to work, let's pray a lot. What a joy it would be if at *the end of Lent* our prayer were granted! . . ." Oh! Infinite mercy of the Lord, who's willing to listen to the prayer of His children. . . . At *the end of Lent*, one more soul was consecrating herself to Jesus. This was a true miracle of grace, a miracle obtained through the fervor of a humble Novice!

Therefore, how great is the power of prayer! It's like a queen's having constant free access to the king and being able to obtain all that she asks. It's not necessary in order for a prayer to be granted to read in a book a beautiful formula composed for the circumstance. If that were the case . . . alas! How I should be pitied! . . . Outside of the *Divine Office* [the services sung in Gregorian chant], which I'm *very unworthy* to recite, I don't have the courage to make a strict rule for myself to search in books for *beautiful* prayers. That gives me a headache, there are so many of them! . . . And then some are more *beautiful* than others. . . . I wouldn't know how to recite them all. Not knowing which one to choose, I do as children do who don't know how to read: I very simply tell God what I want to tell Him, without making beautiful phrases, and He always understands me. . . .

For me, prayer is an upward rising of the heart, it's a simple glance toward heaven, it's a cry of gratitude and love in the midst of trials as much as in the midst of joys. In short, it's something big, something great, something supernatural, that expands my heart and unites me to Jesus.

However, I wouldn't like you to think, beloved Mother, that the prayers we make in common in the nuns' choir, or in hermitages, I recite without devotion. On the contrary, I really love the prayers we say in common, because Jesus promised to be in the midst of those who gather together in His name [Mt. 18:19–20]. I feel then that the fervor of my Sisters adds to mine.

But when I'm all alone (I'm ashamed to admit), the recitation of the Rosary costs me more than one instrument of penance. . . . I feel that I say it so poorly. It's in vain that I attempt to meditate on the mysteries of the Rosary—I don't succeed in engaging my mind. . . . For a long time I was extremely sorry for this lack of devotion that surprised me, because *I love the Blessed Virgin* so much that it ought to be easy for me to pray in her honor prayers that are pleasing to her. Now I'm less sorry, because I think that since the Queen of Heaven is *my Mother*, she must see my good will and is happy with it.

Sometimes when my mind is in such dryness that it's impossible for me to pull a thought out of it to unite myself to God, I *very slowly* recite an "Our Father" [the Lord's Prayer, Mt. 6:9–13] and a "Hail Mary" [see Lk. 1:28]. Then those prayers delight me; they nourish my soul more than if I had recited them hurriedly a hundred times. . . .

The Blessed Virgin shows me that she's not angry with me; she never fails to protect me as soon as I invoke her. If some sort of worry, some difficulty, overtakes me, quickly I turn toward her and always, like the most tender of mothers, she shoulders my interests. . . . How many times, as I've been speaking to the Novices, has it happened to me to invoke her and to feel the blessings of her motherly protection! . . .

Often Novices tell me, "But you have an answer for everything. I thought this time I would stump you. . . . Where do you get what you say?" Some are even candid enough to think I read their soul because it's happened that I've caught them off guard by telling them what they were thinking. One night one of my Sisters had resolved to hide from me a painful thing that was making her suffer a lot. I met her in the morning, and she spoke to me with her face smiling, and I, without responding to what she was saying, told her with a convinced tone of voice, "Something is troubling you." If I had made the moon fall at her feet she wouldn't have looked at me with more astonishment. Her stupefaction was so great that it took me over, and for an instant I was seized with a supernatural fright. I was quite sure that I didn't have the gift of reading souls, and it surprised me that much more at having hit the mark so squarely. I knew that God was very near, and that, without my being aware of it, I had said, like a child, words that were not coming from me but from Him.

Beloved Mother, you understand that for Novices everything is allowed. They have to be able to say what they're thinking without any restriction, the good as well as the bad. That's so much easier for them with me since they don't owe me the respect that they would give to a teacher.

I can't say that Jesus makes me walk *externally* by the way of humiliations. He contents Himself to humble me *in the depths* of my soul. To the eyes of creatures everything is successful for me. I follow the path of honors, as much as that is possible in a religious order. I understand that it's not for me, but for others, that I have to walk along this path that seems so perilous. In fact, if in the eyes of the community I were to pass for a nun who is full of defects, incapable, without intelligence or good judgment, it would be impossible for you, Mother, to be helped by me. That's why God has thrown a veil over all my interior and exterior defects. That veil at times brings me a few compliments from Novices. I feel that they don't do this out of flattery but that it's the expression of their naïve feelings. Truly there would be no way for that to inspire vanity in me, because I have unceasingly present in my thoughts the memory of who I am.

However, sometimes the strong desire comes to me to hear something other than praise. You know, beloved Mother, that I prefer vinegar to sugar. My soul also gets tired of food that is overly sugary, and Jesus then allows it to be served a good little salad, topped with lots of vinegar and spices, with nothing lacking except oil, which gives it one more flavor. . . . That good little salad is served to me by the Novices at the moment when I expect it the least. God lifts the veil that hides my imperfections, and then my dear Sisters, seeing me as I am, no longer find me quite to their taste. With a simplicity that delights me, they tell me all the struggles that I give them, what they don't like about me. In short, they don't worry any more than they would if they were talking about somebody else, knowing that they give me great pleasure in behaving this way. Oh! Truly, it's more than a pleasure, it's a delicious banquet that floods my soul with joy. I can't explain how a thing that is so displeasing to nature can cause such great happiness. If I hadn't experienced it, I wouldn't be able to believe it. . . .

One day when I had particularly desired to be humiliated, it happened that a Novice took it on herself so well to satisfy my desire that I immediately thought about Shimei's cursing David [see 2 Sam. 16:5–13], and I told myself, "Yes, it's truly the Lord who has told her to say these things to me. . . ." And my soul savored deliciously the bitter food that was served it with such abundance.

This is how God reaches down to take care of me. He can't always give me the fortifying bread of outward humiliation, but from time to time, He allows me to feed on the crumbs that fall from the *children's* table [see Mt. 15:27]. Ah! How great is His mercy; I will be able to sing of it only in heaven.

Beloved Mother, since with you I'm starting to sing of this infinite mercy on earth, I must go on to tell you a great blessing that I got from the mission that you entrusted to me. It used to be when I saw a Sister who was doing something that I didn't like and that seemed irregular to me, I would tell myself, "Oh! If only I could tell her what I think, show her that she's wrong, that would do me good!" Since I've practiced the trade a bit, I assure you, mother, that I've completely changed my mind. When I happen to see a Sister doing an action that seems imperfect to me, I heave a sigh of relief and I tell myself, "What happiness! She isn't a Novice, so I'm not required to correct her." And then very quickly I try to excuse the Sister and to see in her the good intentions that she no doubt has.

Oh! Mother, since I've been sick, the care that you've lavished on me has taught me so much more about charity. No remedy seems too costly to you, and if it doesn't work, then, without becoming weary, you try something else. When I used to go to the recreation periods, what attention you gave to seeing that I was well sheltered from the wind. In short, if I were to say everything, I would never finish.

Thinking about all these things, I've told myself that I ought to be as compassionate toward the spiritual infirmities of my Sisters as you are, dear Mother, in caring for me with so much love.

I've noticed (and it's quite natural) that the holiest Sisters are the most loved. People seek out their conversation, and they render services to them without their asking for them. In short, these souls who are capable of enduring the lack of consideration and tact find themselves surrounded with the affection of everyone. One can apply to them this word from our father St. John of the Cross: "All good things were given to me when I no longer sought them out through self-love."

Imperfect souls, on the other hand, are not sought out. No doubt people remain on their behalf within the boundaries of religious politeness, but perhaps out of fear of saying some not-so-nice words to them, people avoid their company.

By saying "imperfect souls," I don't mean to speak only about spiritual imperfections, since the holiest of persons will be perfect only in heaven. I mean to speak about the lack of judgment, of manners, of susceptibility in certain characters—all the things that don't make life very pleasant. I know well that these moral infirmities are chronic. There's no hope of cure. But I also know full well that my Mother would not stop caring for me or trying to comfort me even if I were to remain ill for my whole life.

Here's the conclusion that I make from this: I must seek out during recreation periods, during free time, the company of the Sisters who are the least pleasant to me, and fulfill among those blessed souls the role of the good Samaritan. One word, one pleasant smile, are often enough to cause a sad soul to brighten up. But it's not absolutely to attain that goal that I want to practice charity, because I know that soon I would be discouraged: A word that I might have said with the best of intentions might perhaps be interpreted all wrong.

Therefore, so as not to waste my time, I want to be pleasant with everyone (and particularly with the least pleasant Sisters) in order to give joy to Jesus, and to respond to the counsel that He gave in the Gospel more or less in these terms: "When you give a feast, don't invite your family members and your friends out of fear that they won't invite you in turn, and thus you will have received your reward. But invite the poor, the lame, the crippled, and you will be happy that they won't be able to pay you back, because your Father who sees in secret will reward you" [see Lk. 14:12–14; Mt. 6:3–4].

What feast could a nun offer to her Sisters if it isn't a spiritual feast comprised of pleasant and joyful charity? For me, I don't know of any other, and I want to be like St. Paul, who rejoiced with those who rejoice [Rom. 12:15]: It's true that he also mourned with those who mourned, and tears must sometimes appear in the feast that I want to serve, but always I will endeavor that at the end those tears will change into joy [Jn. 16:20], since the Lord loves those who give cheerfully [2 Cor. 9:7].

I remember an act of charity that God inspired me to do when I was still a Novice. It was a small thing, but our Father who sees in secret, who looks at the intent rather than at the greatness of the action, has already rewarded me for it without waiting until the next life. It was at the time that Sister St. Peter was still going to the choir and the refectory. At evening prayers she was placed in front of me. Ten minutes before six o'clock, a Sister had to take the trouble to guide her to the refectory [the dining room], because at that time the nurses had too many other patients to come get her.

It cost me a lot to offer myself to render that little service, because I knew that it wasn't easy to make poor Sister St. Peter happy, she who was suffering so much that she didn't like to change guides. However, I didn't want to miss such a beautiful opportunity to practice charity, remembering that Jesus said, ". . . whatever you did for one of the least of these brothers and sisters of mine, you did for me" [Mt. 25:40]. So I offered myself quite humbly to guide her—and not without some difficulty, I managed to get my services accepted! Finally I set my hand to the work, and I did it with such good will that I succeeded perfectly.

Each evening when I would see Sister St. Peter shake her hourglass, I knew that that meant, "Let's go." It's unbelievable how much it cost me to take this trouble, especially in the beginning. Nonetheless I did it immediately, and then a whole ceremony would begin. I had to move and carry the bench in a certain way, and above all, never hurry. Then the walk would take place. It was a matter of following the poor invalid, supporting her by the waist. I did this with the greatest gentleness that was possible for me. But if, through some misfortune, she took a false step, instantly it seemed to her that I was supporting her poorly and that she was going to fall.

"Oh! Good Lord! You're going too fast. I'm going to break something." If I tried to go still more slowly, "Well, follow me, now, I can't feel your hand, you've let go of me, I'm going to fall. Oh! I was right that you're too young to guide me."

Finally we would arrive without accident in the refectory. There, other difficulties would crop up. It was a matter of taking Sister St. Peter to her seat and of acting nimbly so as not to hurt her. Then I had to roll back her sleeves (again in a certain way), and then I was free to go. With her poor crippled hands, she would arrange her bread in her bowl as best she could. I soon noticed this, and each evening, I left only after having rendered this one more little service to her. Since she hadn't asked me to do this, she was very touched by my attention, and it was through this means, which I hadn't sought out on purpose, that I gained her good graces completely, and especially (I found this out later) because after cutting her bread, before leaving her I would give her my most beautiful smile.

Beloved Mother, perhaps you were surprised that I'm writing you about this little act of charity that happened such a long time ago. Oh! If I did so, it's because I feel that because of it I have to sing of the mercies of the Lord: He reached down to leave me with this memory, like a perfume that leads me to practice charity.

I sometimes remember certain details that for my soul are like a spring breeze. Here's one that presents itself to my memory: One winter evening I was as usual fulfilling my little task [of guiding Sister St. Peter to the refectory]. It was cold, it was night. . . .

Suddenly [in a vision] I heard in the distance the harmonious sound of a musical instrument. Then I was able to make out a well-lit room, quite brilliant with gilding, with elegantly dressed girls giving each other compliments and worldly politeness. Then my glance fell on the poor invalid that I was holding up. Instead of a melody I heard from time to time her plaintive moaning; instead of gilding, I saw the bricks of our austere cloister, dimly lit by a weak glimmer.

I can't express what happened in my soul, but what I do know is that the Lord illuminated it with the rays of truth that so far surpassed the dark glitter of worldly feasts, that I couldn't believe my happiness. . . . Oh! In order to enjoy worldly feasts for a thousand years, I wouldn't have given up the ten minutes spent in fulfilling my humble office of charity. . . . If already when suffering, in the midst of battle, one can enjoy for an instant a happiness that surpasses all the happiness of earth, at the thought that God has taken us out of the world, what will it be in heaven when we will see, in the midst of gladness and eternal rest, the incomparable grace that the Lord has given us by choosing us to live in His house, the very gate of heaven [Gen. 28:17; Ps. 27:4]? . . .

It's not always with these transports of gladness that I've practiced charity. At the beginning of my religious life, Jesus wanted me to feel how sweet it is to see Him in the souls of His brides. Therefore when I was guiding Sister St. Peter, I would do it with so much love that it would have been impossible for me to do better if I'd had to guide Jesus Himself.

The practice of charity hasn't always seemed so sweet to me, as I was telling you just now, dear Mother. To prove this to you, I'm going to tell you about certain little battles that will certainly make you smile.

For a long time, at evening prayers, I was placed in front of a Sister who had a funny idiosyncrasy, and I think . . . a lot of inner illumination, because she rarely used a book. Here's how I noticed it: As soon as this Sister had arrived, she would begin making a strange little noise that sounded like one that would be made if you rubbed two shells against each other. I was the only one who noticed it, because I have extremely keen hearing (a little too keen sometimes).

To tell you, Mother, how much that little noise tired me out would be impossible. I really wanted to turn my head and look at the guilty one, who, of course, didn't notice her tic. That was the only way to let her know what was going on. But in the depths of my heart I felt that it was better to suffer that for the love of God and not to give the Sister any trouble.

So I kept quiet and tried to unite myself with God and to forget the little noise. . . . It was all of no use: I felt sweat pouring out of me, and I was obliged to simply pray a prayer of suffering. But as I was suffering, I was seeking the way to undergo it, not with agitation, but with joy and peace, at least in the innermost part of my soul. So I made every effort to love that little noise that was so unpleasant. Instead of trying not to hear it (which would be impossible) I placed all my attention on hearing it well, as if it had been a delightful concert, and my whole prayer (which was not the prayer of quietude) was spent in offering that concert to Jesus.

Another time I was doing laundry with a Sister who kept throwing dirty water in my face each time she picked up the handkerchiefs on her bench. My first movement was to draw back and dry my face, in order to show the Sister who was sprinkling me that she would do me a service if she would move gently, but immediately I thought that I was quite silly to refuse treasures that had been given to me so generously, and I took great care not to let my struggle show. I made every effort to desire to receive a lot of dirty water, so that in the end I had really taken a liking to this new form of sprinkling with holy water, and I promised myself to come back another time to that happy place where one received so many treasures.

Beloved Mother, you see that I am a *very little soul* who can offer to God only *very little things*. It still happens often that I miss out on doing these little sacrifices that give so much peace to the soul. That doesn't discourage me—I endure having a little less peace, and I try to be more vigilant another time.

Oh! The Lord is so good to me that it's impossible for me to be afraid of Him. He's always given me what I've desired, or rather, He's made me desire what He wanted to give me. So a short time before my trial against faith was to begin, I told myself, "I really don't have any great outward trials, and in order to have inward ones, the Good Lord would have to change my way. I don't think He'll do that, but I can't always live this way, at rest. . . . So what means will Jesus find to test me?" The answer wasn't long in coming, and it showed me that the One I loved isn't short on means. Without changing my way, God sent me the trial that was to mix a healthful bitterness with all my joys. It's not only when He wants to test me that Jesus makes me sense His presence and desire Him.

For a long time I had a desire that seemed quite unobtainable, namely to have a *priest brother*. I often thought that if my little brothers hadn't flown up to heaven I would have had the happiness of seeing them step up to the altar. But since God chose to make little angels out of them, I could no longer hope to see my dream come true. And yet, not only did Jesus give me the grace that I desired, but He also united me through ties of the soul to *two* of His apostles, who became my brothers. . . . Beloved Mother, I want to tell you in detail how Jesus granted my desire and even surpassed it, since I wanted only one priest brother who would think about me each day at the holy altar.

It was our Mother St. Teresa who sent me my first little brother as a birthday bouquet in 1895. I was in the laundry, quite immersed in my work, when Mother Agnes of Jesus [who was then Prioress] took me aside and read me a letter that she had just received. It came from a young seminarian [Maurice Bellière], inspired, he said, by St. Teresa, to ask for a Sister who would devote herself especially to the salvation of his soul and help him through her prayers and sacrifices when he became a missionary, to the end that he might be able to save many souls. He promised to always keep in remembrance this one who would become his sister, when he would in the future be able to offer the Holy Sacrifice. Mother Agnes of Jesus told me that she wanted me to be the one who would become the sister of this future missionary.

Mother, it would be impossible for me to tell you how happy I was. My desire, fulfilled in an unhoped-for way, gave birth in my heart to a joy that I would call childish, because I would have to go back to the days of my childhood to find the memory of those joys that were so lively that the soul is too little to contain them. For years I've never felt that type of happiness. I felt that because of it my soul was new. It was as if for the first time musical chords were played that had until then fallen into unconsciousness.

I understood the obligations that I was taking on, so I set to work trying to redouble my fervor. I have to admit that at first I had no consolations to stimulate my enthusiasm. After writing a charming letter full of heartfelt, noble sentiments to thank Mother Agnes of Jesus, my little brother showed no sign of life until the following July, except when he sent a letter in November to say that he was starting his required military service.

It was to you, Beloved Mother, that God had reserved the task of completing the work that had begun. No doubt it's through prayer and sacrifice that missionaries can be helped, but sometimes when it pleases Jesus to unite two souls for His glory, He permits that from time to time they may be able to communicate their thoughts to each other and excite one another to love God more. But that requires the *express desire* of authority, for it seems to me that otherwise that correspondence would do more harm than good, if not to the missionary, at least to the nun who is continually led through her lifestyle to withdraw within herself. Therefore, instead of uniting her to God, that correspondence (even at a distance) that she might have solicited would occupy her mind, making her imagine she's moving mountains and doing marvelous things. She would do nothing at all except to bring on herself, under the guise of zeal, a useless distraction.

For me it's the same with that as for everything else: I feel that for my letters to do good they have to be written out of obedience, and I feel repugnance rather than pleasure in writing them. So when I'm talking with a Novice, I try to mortify myself as I do so. I avoid asking her questions that would satisfy my curiosity. If she begins an interesting topic and then passes on to another that annoys me without finishing the first one, I take care not to remind her about the subject she has left aside, because it seems to me that you can't do any good when you're seeking yourself.

———·—·———

Beloved Mother, I notice that I'll never change and do better. Here I am, having wandered quite far from my subject, with all my dissertations. Forgive me, please, and let me start again at the first opportunity, since I can't do otherwise! . . . You behave as does God, who never gets tired of listening to me, when I tell Him quite simply my pains and my joys as if He weren't acquainted with them. . . . You also, Mother, have known for a long time what I think and all the little memorable events of my life. So I wouldn't know how to tell you anything new.

I can't help laughing when I think that I'm writing you scrupulously so many things that you know as well as I do. Well, dear Mother, I'm obeying you, and if now you don't find any interest in reading these pages, perhaps they will entertain you in your old age and will then serve as fuel for your fire, so I won't have wasted my time. . . . But I'm having fun talking like a child. Don't think, Mother, that I'm looking for what usefulness my little work can have. Since I'm doing it out of obedience, that's enough for me, and I wouldn't feel any distress if you were to burn it in front of me after reading it.

———·—·———

It's time for me to go back to the story of my priest brothers, who now hold such a big place in my life. Last year at the end of May, I remember that one day you sent for me before a mealtime. My heart was pounding when I entered your office, dear Mother. I was wondering what you could have to say to me, because this was the first time you had sent for me like that. After you told me to be seated, here's the proposal that you made: "Would you please take on the spiritual interests of a missionary who is to be ordained a priest and depart very soon?" And then, Mother, you read me the letter from that young priest [Fr. Adolphe Roulland] so that I might know just what he was asking for.

My first response was a feeling of joy that soon gave way to fear. I explained to you, beloved Mother, that since I had already offered my poor merits for a future apostle, I believed I wouldn't be able to do it again for the intentions of another one, and that, besides, there were many Sisters better than I who would be able to respond to his desire. All my objections were of no use; you replied that one could have several brothers. Then I asked you if obedience couldn't double my merits. You answered yes, and told me several things that made me see that I had to accept, without scruple, a new brother.

In my heart, Mother, I thought like you, and even, since "the zeal of a Carmelite nun should set the world on fire," I hope with the grace of God to be useful to more than *two* missionaries. And I would never be able to forget to pray for all of them, without setting aside simple priests whose mission is sometimes as difficult to fulfill as that of apostles preaching to the unconverted. In short, I want to be a daughter of the Church as was our Mother St. Teresa, and pray for the intentions of the Holy Father the Pope, knowing that his intentions embrace the whole world. There is the general goal of my life, but that wouldn't have prevented me from praying and uniting myself especially to the works of my dear little angels if they [my deceased brothers] had been priests.

Well! Here's how I've united myself spiritually to the apostles that Jesus gave me as brothers: Everything that belongs to me, belongs to each of them [Lk. 15:31]. I feel clearly how the *Good* Lord is too *good* to divide His inheritance. He's so rich that He gives without measure everything that I ask of Him. . . . But don't think, Mother, that I'm going to get lost in long enumerations.

Since I have two brothers and my little Sisters the Novices, if I wanted to ask for what each soul needs and set it out in detail, the days would be too short, and I would be very much afraid of forgetting something important. To simple souls, complicated means aren't required. As I'm among that number, one morning during my time of thanksgiving prayers, Jesus gave me a simple means of accomplishing my mission. He made me understand this word from the Song of Songs: "Draw me: we will run after thee to the odour of thy ointments" [1:3 D-R]. Jesus, therefore it's not even necessary to say, "By drawing me, draw the souls that I love." This simple word, "Draw me," is enough. Lord, I understand it. When a soul has let itself be captivated by the intoxicating fragrance of Your perfumes, it wouldn't know how to run all by itself. All the souls that it loves are brought along in its train. That's done without constraint, without effort. It's a natural consequence of its attraction toward You.

Just as a flooded stream, spilling impetuously into the ocean, carries along after it everything that it has encountered on its passage, in the same way, Jesus, the soul that plunges into the shoreless ocean of Your love draws with it all the treasures that it possesses. . . . Lord, You know that I have no other treasures than the souls that it has pleased You to unite with mine. Those treasures You've entrusted to me, so I dare to borrow the words that You addressed to the Heavenly Father on the last night that saw You still on our earth as a traveler and a mortal. Jesus, my Beloved, I don't know when my exile will end. . . . More than one night will see me still in exile singing of Your mercies [Ps. 89:1], but finally, for me as well, the last night will come. Then I would like to be able to say to You, my God: I have brought You glory on earth by finishing the work You gave me to do. . . . I have revealed You to those whom You gave me. . . . They were Yours; You gave them to me. . . . Now they know that everything You have given me comes from You. For I gave them the words You gave me and they accepted them . . . and they believed that You sent me. I pray for . . . those You have given me, for they are Yours. . . . I will remain in the world no longer, but they are still in the world, and I am coming to You. Holy Father, protect by the power of Your name those whom You have given me.... I am coming to You now, but I say these things while I am still in the world, so that they may have the full measure of my joy within them.... My prayer is not that You take them out of the world but that You protect them from the evil one. They are not of the world, even as I am not of it.... My prayer is not for them alone. I pray also for those who will believe in me through their message.... Father, I want those You have given me to be with me.... Then the world will know that You ... have loved them even as You have loved me. [see Jn. 17:4–26]

Yes, Lord, this is what I would like to repeat after You before flying away into Your arms. Is this perhaps impudence? No! For a long time You've allowed me to be audacious with You. Like the father of the prodigal son talking to his elder son, You've said to me, "Everything I have is yours" [Lk. 15:31]. So Your words, Jesus, are mine, and I can use them to draw the favors of the Heavenly Father upon the souls who are united with me. But, Lord, when I say that where I will be, I want those You have given me to be as well, I'm not claiming that they can't arrive at a higher glory than the one that it will please You to give me. I simply want to ask that one day we may all be reunited in Your beautiful heaven.

You know, God, I've never desired anything else than to love You. My ambition is for no other glory. Your love informed me beginning in my childhood. It grew with me, and now it's a chasm the depth of which I cannot fathom. Love attracts love, so, my Jesus, mine shoots up toward You. It would like to fill up the chasm that draws it, but alas! It's not even a drop of dew lost in the ocean! ...

To love You as You love me, I have to borrow Your own love; only then do I find rest. Oh my Jesus, it's perhaps an illusion, but it seems to me that You can't fill a soul with more love than You've filled mine. It's because of that, that I dare to ask You to love those whom You have given me as You have loved me [Jn. 17:23]. One day, in heaven, if I discover that You love them more than me, I'll rejoice at that, since I recognize even now that those souls merit Your love much more than

I do. But here below I cannot conceive of a greater immensity of love than the one that it has pleased You to pour out so lavishly on me, without any merit on my part [Rom. 3:23–24].

—————·—·—————

Dear Mother, I'm finally coming back to you. I'm quite surprised at what I've just written, because I had no intention to do so. Since it's written, it will have to remain, but before coming back to the story of my brothers, I want to tell you, Mother, that I don't apply to them, but rather to my little Sisters, the first words borrowed from the Gospel, "For I gave them the words you gave me" [Jn. 17:8], etc., because I don't think I'm capable of teaching missionaries. Fortunately I'm not yet proud enough for that! Nor would I have been capable of giving some counsel to my Sisters, if you, Mother, who represent God for me, hadn't given me leave to do so.

On the contrary, it's your dear spiritual sons who are my brothers that I was thinking about when I wrote those words of Jesus and the ones that followed, "My prayer is not that you take them out of the world. . . . I pray also for those who will believe in me through their message" [Jn. 17:15, 20]. How in fact could I not pray for the souls that they will save in their distant missions by means of suffering and preaching?

Mother, I think that it's necessary for me to give you a few more explanations about the passage from the Song of Songs, "Draw me, we will run" [Song 1:3 D-R], because what I tried to say about it doesn't seem to me to be very understandable. "No one," said Jesus, "can come to me unless the Father who sent me draws them" [Jn. 6:44]. Then, through inspiring parables, and often without even using that method that was so familiar to the common people, He taught us that it's enough to knock and the door will be opened, to seek and we will find, and to humbly hold out our hand and we will receive what we ask for [Lk. 11:9–13]. . . . He also said that everything that we ask of *His Father* in His name, He will grant it [Jn. 16:23]. It's for that purpose, no doubt, that the Holy Spirit, before the birth of Jesus, dictated that prophetic prayer, "Draw me, we will run."

What then does it mean to ask to be *drawn*, if not to unite ourselves in a personal way to the object that captivates our heart? If fire and iron had the faculty of reason, and the latter said to the former, "Draw me," wouldn't it prove that it desires to be identified with the fire in such a way that it penetrates and takes in its burning substance and seems to become only one with it?

Beloved Mother, this is my prayer: I ask Jesus to draw me into the flames of His love, to unite me so closely to Himself, that He may live and act in me [Gal. 2:20]. I feel that the more the fire of love will inflame my heart, the more I will say, "Draw me," the more also souls will come close to me (poor little useless dross of iron, if I were to move away from the divine clear glowing fire), and the more those souls will run quickly toward the fragrance of the perfumes of their Beloved.

For, a soul aflame with love can't remain inactive. Doubtless, like Mary Magdalene, it clings to Jesus' feet, it listens to His sweet and blazing word. Seeming to give nothing, it gives much more than Martha, who was upset about many things and would have liked for her sister to be like her. It's not Martha's works that Jesus blamed. Those works are the ones His divine Mother humbly accepted to do her whole life, since she had to prepare the meals for the Holy Family. It's only the anxiousness of His eager hostess that He wanted to amend [Lk. 10:39–42].

All the Saints understood this, and more particularly perhaps those who filled the world with enlightenment of the Gospel doctrines. Isn't it through prayer that Sts. Paul, Augustine, John of the Cross, Thomas Aquinas, Francis, Dominic, and so many other well-known Friends of God plumbed that Divine knowledge that delights the greatest minds? One scientist said, "Give me a lever, a point to support it, and I will lift the world." What Archimedes was unable to obtain because his request wasn't made to God and was made only from a material point of view, the Saints obtained in all its fullness. The Almighty gave them, as a point of support, *Himself*, and Himself *alone*. As a lever He gave prayer, which sets ablaze a fire of love, and that's how they lifted the world. That's how all the Saints who are still fighting the battle lift it, and that's how until the end of the world the Saints to come will lift it as well.

———————

Dear Mother, now I would like to tell you what I mean by the fragrance of the Beloved's perfumes [Song 1:3]. Since Jesus went back up into heaven, I can follow Him only by the prints that He left behind [Acts 1:9]. But those prints are so resplendent that they're perfumed! I have only to cast my eyes on the Holy Gospel, and immediately I breathe the perfumes of Jesus' life, and I know in which direction to run. . . . It's not to the first place, but to the last one, that I cast myself [Mk. 10:31]. Instead of pressing forward with the Pharisee, I repeat, full of confidence, the humble prayer of the tax collector [Lk. 18:10–14].

But above all I imitate Mary Magdalene's behavior, her surprising— or rather her loving—audaciousness that charmed Jesus' Heart and captivates mine [Lk. 7:36–38].

Yes, I feel it. Even when I might have on my conscience all the sins that can be committed, I would go with a heart broken with repentance to throw myself into Jesus' arms, because I know how much He cherishes the prodigal who comes back to Him [Lk. 15:20–24]. It's not because God, in His kind mercy, has preserved my soul from mortal sin that I rise and go to Him in confidence and love.

The Triumph

Let the little children come to me, and do not hinder them,
for the kingdom of God belongs to such as these. [Lk. 18:16]

Jesus!
Remember the divine tenderness
With which You flooded the tiny children;
I also want to receive Your tender touch;
Oh, give me Your delightful kisses;
To enjoy in heaven Your sweet presence
I will know how to practice the virtues of childhood;
You told us often:
Heaven is for children. . . .
Remember!

Thérèse of the Child Jesus

PART
TWO

Remembrances of Thérèse
by the Sisters of the Lisieux Carmel

In the years that followed Thérèse's death, the nuns of the Lisieux Carmel gathered firsthand stories of her final days as told by those who knew her intimately. In the 1920 edition of *The Story of a Soul*, these stories were published as chapter twelve of the book. The nuns also gathered memories of Thérèse's saintly counsel to them and, in an appendix to the 1920 edition, they published seventy-four personal recollections of the saint's words and the effect those words had on their lives.

Part two consists of this additional chapter twelve of *The Story of a Soul* and the Sisters' remembrances of Thérèse's words of advice and counsel, both of them translated in complete and unabridged form as they were published in 1920.

These stories, now available here for the first time in English translation, add a unique perspective to the saint's own writings.

THE STORY OF A SOUL, CHAPTER TWELVE
(WRITTEN BY THE SISTERS OF THE LISIEUX CARMEL)

CALVARY
SOARING UP TO HEAVEN

It is of the utmost importance for the soul to strongly practice LOVE, so that, becoming rapidly consumed, it will hardly stop here on earth, but will promptly arrive at seeing its God face to face.

—St. John of the Cross

"Many of the pages of this story will never be read on earth. . . ." St. Thérèse of the Child Jesus said this, and we are compelled to repeat this after her. There are some sufferings that it is not allowed to reveal here on earth. Only the Lord has jealously reserved to Himself to disclose their worthiness and glory in the clear vision that will rend every veil. . . .

And the sufferings that touched the sensitive heart of this angelic child are almost all of this type, so much so that for many people, perhaps, she seems to have spent her life on earth in the midst of smiles and warm tenderness, and to have known only the soft rays of the springtime sun, without enduring the melancholic rains of autumn and the blasts of the icy winter winds.

St. Thérèse of the Child Jesus suffered a great deal here on earth, and she recommended in her final days that her sufferings should be made known to souls after her death. She well knew that this seal of the cross, affixed on her life, would be for some the sign of the authenticity of her mission.

Nonetheless, it is not because of this martyrdom of the heart that she believed her desire was fulfilled, in her offering of herself as a sacrificial victim to the merciful Love of the Lord. Rather, she believed that it was fulfilled because she felt "overflowing in her heart the waves of infinite tenderness contained in the divine Heart." It is true that she said, in reply to the needs of certain souls who lacked flexibility with respect to the sometimes crucifying expressions of will of the heavenly Bridegroom, that "to offer oneself as a sacrificial victim to Love is to offer oneself up to every agony and distress." But she also said, to one soul who for her represented regenerate humankind thirsting for perfection and love, but still trembling before the cross, "Why are you afraid to offer yourself as a sacrificial victim to merciful Love? If you offered yourself to divine justice, you could be afraid, but merciful Love will have compassion on your weakness. He will treat you with gentleness, with mercy."

We saw how great was Thérèse's sacrifice when once and for all she left her father, who loved her so tenderly, and the family home where she had been so happy. But we might perhaps think that this sacrifice was made easier for her since at Carmel she rejoined her two older sisters, the dear confidants of her soul. Quite the contrary: For the young postulant this was the occasion for the most agonizing deprivation.

Solitude and silence were kept rigorously at Carmel. She saw her sisters only at the time of recreation. If she had been less dead to her self, she would often have been able to sit beside them. But "she preferred to seek out the company of the nuns she liked the least." Therefore it was said that no one knew whether she had the most particular affection for her sisters.

Some time after her entrance, she was assigned as an assistant to Sr. Agnes of Jesus, her "Pauline" whom she loved so much: This was a new source of sacrifices. Thérèse knew that useless words were forbidden, and she never allowed herself the slightest confidential remark. "Oh, my dear Mother!" she was to say later, "how I suffered then! . . . I couldn't open my heart to you, and I thought that you didn't know me any longer!"

After five years of this heroic silence, Sr. Agnes of Jesus was elected Prioress. On the evening of the election, the heart of "little Thérèse" must have pounded with joy at the thought that from now on she could speak to her "dear Mother" in complete freedom, and, as she had done in the past, pour out her heart to her "Pauline." However, God allowed Sr. Thérèse out of all the nuns to be the one who saw her Prioress the most rarely.

Several years later, her great supernatural spirit allowed her to say that she was "happy to die in the arms of another Prioress [Mother Marie de Gonzague], in order to be able to exercise all the more her spirit of faith in authority."

This Servant of God wanted to live life at Carmel with all the perfection asked for by the Reformer Saint [St. Teresa of Avila, author of *The Way of Perfection*]. When the type of work to which she was giving herself did not necessarily absorb her attention, thoughts of God came back to her naturally. One day a novice entering into her cell stopped, struck by the completely heavenly expression on her face. She was actively sewing, and yet she seemed to be lost in profound contemplation.

"What are you thinking about?" asked the young Sister. "I'm meditating on the Our Father," she replied. "It's so sweet to call God *our Father*!" And tears brimmed in her eyes.

"I don't see what I will have in heaven more than I have now," she said another time. "I'll see God, it's true. But as far as being with Him is concerned, I'm already completely there while I'm on earth."

A strong flame of love burned within her. Here is what she herself said:

> A few days after my offering to merciful Love, I was in the choir beginning the practice of the Way of the Cross, when I felt myself suddenly wounded by a shaft of flame that was so hot that I thought I would die. I don't know how to explain that transport; there is no comparison that could make another person understand the intensity of that flame. It seemed to me that an invisible force was plunging me completely and entirely into the fire. Oh, such fire! Such sweetness!

Since the Prioress was asking her if that experience of being carried away with strong and intensely pleasant emotion was the first one of her life, she replied simply:

> Mother, I have had several transports of love, particularly once, during my novitiate, when I remained for an entire week quite far from this world. I can't find words to express that. I was acting, it seemed to me, with a borrowed body. There was as if it were a veil thrown for me over all the things of the earth. But I wasn't burned by a real flame. I could undergo these delights without hoping to see my bonds break under their weight. Whereas, the day I'm talking about, one minute, one second more, and my soul would have separated from my body. . . . But alas! I found myself back on earth, and dryness immediately came back to live in my heart!

Only a little longer, sweet sacrificial victim of love! The divine hand withdrew its javelin of fire, but the wound was mortal. . . .

———·———

In this intimate union with God, Thérèse acquired a truly remarkable mastery over her actions. All the virtues outdid each other as they blossomed in the delightful garden of her soul.

But let no one think that this magnificent flowering of supernatural beauties grows without any effort.

> On this earth there is no fruitfulness without suffering, physical suffering, private anguish, trials known to God or to mortals. When, upon reading about the lives of the saints, reverent thoughts and generous resolutions begin to grow in us, we ought not to limit ourselves, as with ordinary books, to uttering some kind of admiring tribute to the genius of their authors. Rather, we ought much more to bear in mind the price that, without any doubt, they paid for the supernatural good they produce in each of us.
>
> —Dom Guéranger

And, if today "the little saint" brings about marvelous transformations in hearts, if the good that she does on earth is immense, we can believe in all truth that she bought it with the same price that Jesus paid to redeem our souls: suffering and the cross.

Not the least of her sufferings was the courageous struggle that she undertook against herself, refusing any satisfaction to the requirements of her proud and fiery nature. While still a child she had made it a habit never to make excuses for herself or to complain. At Carmel, she wanted to be the little servant of her sisters.

In that spirit of humility, she made every effort to obey all of them without distinction.

One day, during her illness, the community was to gather at the hermitage of the Sacred Heart to sing a hymn. Sr. Thérèse of the Child Jesus, already consumed with fever, had gone there painfully. She arrived, exhausted, and had to sit down immediately. A nun made a sign to her to stand up to sing the hymn. Without hesitation the humble child stood up, and, despite the fever and the oppression, remained standing right to the end.

The infirmary Sister had advised her to take a little walk every day for a quarter of an hour in the garden. That word of advice became an order for her. One afternoon, seeing her walking with great difficulty, a Sister said to her, "You would do much better to rest. Your walk can't be doing you any good under such conditions: You're wearing yourself out, I tell you." "It's true," replied this child of obedience, "but do you know what gives me strength? . . . Well, I'm walking for a missionary. I think that over there, so far away, one of them is perhaps worn out in his apostolic journeys. And, in order to lessen his fatigue, I offer mine to the Good Lord."

She gave to her novices sublime examples of detachment:

One day, for the birthday of the Prioress, our families and the monastery workmen had sent bouquets of flowers. Thérèse was arranging them with pleasure, when a lay Sister said to her with an unhappy tone, "It's plain to see that those big bouquets were given by your family. The ones that the poor people gave are going to be hidden behind them!" A sweet smile was the only response by the saintly nun. Immediately, despite the lack of harmony that would result from the change, she put the poor people's bouquets out in front.

Full of admiration in the sight of such great virtue, that lay Sister went to see the Prioress and confessed her fault, highly praising the patience and humility of Sr. Thérèse of the Child Jesus.

Later, when the "Little Queen" had left her earthly exile for the kingdom of her Bridegroom, that same lay Sister, filled with faith in her power, placed her forehead on the ice-cold feet of the virginal child, asking her forgiveness for the fault she had committed. At that same instant, she felt herself healed from cerebral anemia that, for many long years, had kept her from reading and from mental prayer.

Far from fleeing her humiliations, Thérèse sought them eagerly. This is how she offered herself to help a Sister that everyone knew was difficult to satisfy; her generous proposal was accepted. One day when she had just been heaped with many expressions of disapproval, a novice asked her why she seemed so happy. How surprised this novice was when she heard this reply: "It's because Sister has just said unpleasant things to me. Oh! What pleasure she gave me! I would like to meet up with her right now in order to be able to smile at her." At that very moment that same Sister knocked at the door, and the amazed novice was able to see how Saints forgive.

"I soared so high over all things," she said one day, "that I went away strengthened by humiliations."

To all these virtues she joined extraordinary courage. As soon as she entered the convent at age fifteen, except for fasts she was allowed to follow all the practices of our austere rule. Sometimes her fellow novices noticed how pale she was and tried to have her excused either from the evening office or from rising very early. The Prioress [Mother Marie de Gonzague] did not agree to their requests: "A soul of this kind," she said, "must not be treated like a child. Excused absences are not made for her. Leave her alone; God sustains her. Besides, if she is sick, she ought to come say so herself."

But Thérèse had this principle that she had to push to the very end of her strength before complaining. How many times did she go to Matins with dizzy spells or violent headaches! "I can still walk," she told herself, "so I must attend to my duty!" And, thanks to that energy, she accomplished heroic acts quite simply.

Her delicate stomach adjusted with difficulty to the frugal diet at Carmel. Certain foods made her ill, but she knew so well how to hide this that no one ever suspected it. One nun who sat at her table said she tried in vain to find out what foods Thérèse liked. So the kitchen Sisters, seeing that she was so agreeable, invariably served her the leftovers.

It was only during her final illness, when she was ordered to say what was hurting her, that her mortification was unveiled.

"When Jesus wants a person to suffer," she used to say at that time, "we must absolutely pass that way. So, while Sister Marie of the Sacred Heart [her sister Marie] was the provisional, she made every effort to take care of me with the tenderness of a mother, and I seemed to be quite spoiled! Nonetheless, how many mortifications did she cause me to undergo, because she served me food according to her tastes, which were absolutely the opposite of mine!"

Her spirit of sacrifice was universal. Everything that was the hardest and the least pleasant, she hurried to undertake it as the part that was her due. Everything that God asked of her, she gave Him, without regard to herself.

"During my postulancy," she said, "it cost me a great deal to do certain outward mortifications that are the custom in our convents. But never did I give in to my dislikes: It seemed to me that the crucifix in the courtyard was looking at me with pleading eyes and begging me for these sacrifices."

Her vigilance was such that she never left unobserved any of the recommendations of the Prioress, none of those little rules that make the religious life so deserving of esteem. One elderly Sister, who noticed her extraordinary faithfulness on this point, considered her already to be a Saint.

She gave herself over very little to bodily penances beyond the Rule. The Holy Spirit had given her to understand that mortification of the mind and heart is incomparably more sanctifying. Nonetheless, it happened that she became sick because of having worn for too long a little iron cross whose sharp points had penetrated her flesh. "That wouldn't have happened to me for such a small thing," she said later, "if the Good Lord had not wanted me to understand that the mortification of the flesh by the Saints wasn't made for me, nor for the little souls who will walk on the same path of becoming little children."

Being deprived of heat, during the winter, was the hardest of her physical sufferings at the Carmel. One can easily guess what that delicate child must have endured through the long Normandy winters, in the humid climate of Lisieux.

When the temperature was the most rigorous, after being chilled to the bone the entire day, the Servant of God used to go in the evening, after Matins, to warm up for a few minutes in the community's great hall. However, in order to go to her cell, she had to walk outdoors for fifty meters [over 150 feet], under the cloister. The rest of the way, up the stairs and down the long, icy corridor, ended up taking from her the little warmth that had been so sparingly granted her.

Therefore, when she stretched out on her straw mat, wrapping herself in her two small blankets, she found rest that was shortened by frequent insomnia. Sometimes she even spent the whole night trembling with cold without being able to sleep. If, beginning in those first years, she had told the Novice Mistress, she would have immediately obtained some relief. But she wanted to accept that harsh mortification without complaining, and revealed it only on her deathbed by these expressive words: "What I suffered physically the most, during my religious life, was the cold. I suffered from it to the point of dying from it!"

If, in her generosity, she had nonetheless joyfully embraced that austere penance, in her saintly wisdom and discretion, she also knew also how to make it understood with obedience and respect that this excess that God had allowed was not His desire, and that it would be good, in the future, to soften the extremes. She believed that not to take account, while enforcing the Rule, of the differences in latitude and diversity of temperaments, was to tempt God and to sin against good judgment.

We are familiar with the call on Good Friday, April 3rd, 1896, when, as she expressed it, Sr. Thérèse heard "as it were a faraway murmur that was announcing the arrival of the Bridegroom." Long, extremely painful months were still to pass before that blessed hour of deliverance.

On the morning of that Good Friday she knew so well how to make others believe that her spitting up blood would be without consequence, that the Prioress, blind to her condition, allowed her to accomplish all the penances prescribed by the Rule that day. That afternoon a novice caught sight of her cleaning some windows. Her face was ashen, and, despite her energy, she seemed at the end of her strength. Seeing her so worn out, that novice, who loved her dearly, burst into tears and begged Sr. Thérèse to give her permission to ask for some kind of relief for her. But her young mistress expressly forbade her to do so, saying that she could quite well stand up to a slight fatigue on the day when Jesus had suffered so much for her. Her Sisters found out about that first incident only in May of 1897. And as Mother Agnes of Jesus scolded her gently for having hidden it, she exclaimed, "Oh, my dear Mother, thank God for it! If you had known my condition and had seen me so little cared for, you would have been too upset!"

Soon her persistent cough worried the Prioress. She placed Sr. Thérèse of the Child Jesus on a fortifying diet, and the cough disappeared for several months.

"Really," the dear Sister said at that time, "sickness is too slow a driver. I'm counting only on love."

Strongly tempted to respond to the appeal by the Carmel in Hanoi [in French Indochina], which was urgently asking for her to go there, she began a novena to the venerable Théophane Vénard [one of the missionary Martyrs of Vietnam], with the goal of obtaining her complete healing. But alas, that novena became the starting point for the gravest of conditions.

————

After passing, like Jesus, through the world doing good, and after being forgotten and misunderstood as He was, our little Saint followed in His footsteps by climbing a painful Calvary.

Accustomed to seeing her constant suffering, and her continuing nonetheless to remain ever courageous, her Prioress allowed her to follow the community practices, some of which made her extremely fatigued.

When evening came, the heroic child had to climb the stairs to the dormitory by herself. Stopping on each stair step to catch her breath, she painfully reached her cell, arriving there so exhausted that she sometimes needed—as she later admitted—an hour to undress. And, after such fatigue, it was on her hard straw mattress that she had to spend her time of rest.

Therefore the nights were very bad. And, as people asked her if she did not need some kind of help during those hours of suffering, she replied, "Oh, no! I consider myself quite happy, on the contrary, to find myself in a cell that is far enough away from the others that my Sisters do not hear me. I'm content to suffer alone. The moment that people feel sorry for me and heap me with niceties, I no longer have any enjoyment."

She often underwent hot needles in her side. One day, when she had particularly suffered from this, she was resting in her cell during the recreation period. It was then that she heard one of the Sisters in the kitchen talking about her in these terms: "Sister Thérèse of the Child Jesus is going to die soon. And I really wonder what our Prioress will be able to say about that after her death. She will be quite embarrassed and troubled, because that little Sister, as likeable as she is, for sure has done nothing that's worth talking about."

The infirmary Sister, who had heard all this, told that Sister,

> If you had relied on the opinion of created beings, you would be quite disillusioned today! People's opinion! Ah! Fortunately the Good Lord has always graced me to be absolutely indifferent to it. Listen to a little story that ended up showing me what she's worth. This is what she told me:
>
> "A few days after taking the habit, I went to see our Prioress. A lay Sister who was there saw me and said, 'Mother, there you've received a novice that's an honor to you! She looks so good! I hope that she will follow the Rule for a long time!' I was quite happy with this compliment, when another Sister who was wearing a white veil arrived in turn and said, 'My, my, poor little Sister Thérèse of the Child Jesus, how tired you look! You have a look on your face that makes me tremble. If that keeps up you won't follow the Rule for a long time!' I was only sixteen then, but that

little anecdote gave me such an experience that ever afterward I no longer counted as anything the opinion of others, which varies so much."

I said to her, "People say that you have never suffered much."

Smiling then, and showing me a glass containing a bright-red potion, she said,

"Do you see this little glass? People might think it contains a delicious liqueur. In reality, I don't drink anything that is more bitter. Well, that is the image of my life: In the eyes of others, it has always been decked out with smiling colors. It has seemed to them that I was drinking an exquisite liqueur; and it was bitterness! Bitterness, I say, and yet my life has not been bitter, because I have found out how to make every bitterness into my joy and my sweetness."

"You're suffering a lot right now, aren't you?"

"Yes, but I've desired it so much!"

"How painful it is to us to see you suffering so much, and to think that perhaps you will still suffer more," her novices used to say to her.

"Oh! Don't trouble yourselves for me, I've come to the point of not being able to suffer any longer, because every suffering is sweet to me. Besides, you are quite wrong to think about what painful thing might happen in the future. That's like getting involved in creating! We who run on the path of life, we must never torment ourselves about anything. If I weren't suffering from minute to minute, it would be impossible for me to keep my patience. But I see only the present moment, I forget the past, and I keep myself from having a mental picture of the future. If we become discouraged, if sometimes we lose hope, it's because we are thinking about the past and the future. However, pray for me: Often, when I implore heaven to come to my help, it is then that I am the most forsaken!"

"How do you keep from becoming discouraged in those moments of forsakenness?"

"I turn to the Good Lord, to all the Saints, and I thank them anyway. I believe that they want to see how far I will pursue my hope. . . . But it is not in vain that the word of Job entered into my heart: 'Though he slay me, yet will I hope in him; I will surely defend my ways to his face'

[Job 13:15]. I admit it, I spent a long time before reaching that degree of self-abandonment. But now I'm there: The Lord took me and put me there!

"My heart is full of the will of Jesus," she continued. "Therefore, when someone spills something on it, it doesn't penetrate to the depths. It's a little nothing that slides easily, like oil on the surface of calm water. Oh, if my soul wasn't filled in advance, if it had to be filled with feelings of joy or sadness that came so quickly one after the other, that would be a very bitter wave of anguish! But all those alternatives do is brush my soul lightly. So I always stay in a deep peace that nothing can trouble."

Nevertheless, her soul was enveloped in thick darkness: Her temptations against faith, always defeated and always coming back, were there to take away from her any feeling of happiness at the thought of her impending death.

"If I didn't have an ordeal that is impossible to understand," she used to say, "I think that I would die for joy at the thought of leaving this earth soon."

The divine Master wanted, through this ordeal, to achieve her purification and to allow her not only to walk with rapid steps, but also to fly on her little way of trust and self-abandonment. Her words prove this at every moment:

"I don't want to die more than I want to live. If the Lord offered me a choice, I wouldn't choose anything. I want only what He wants. It's what He does that I love!

"I have no fear at all of the last battles, or of the sufferings of illness, as great as they may be. The Good Lord has always come to my aid: He has helped me and led me by the hand beginning with my earliest childhood. . . . I'm counting on Him. The suffering will be able to reach its extreme limits, but I'm sure that He will never abandon me."

Such trust must have aroused the fury of the devil, who, in the last moments, puts into action all his infernal ruses in order to try to sow despair in human hearts. Thérèse once told Mother Agnes of Jesus,

Last night I was gripped with a real anguish, and my darkness increased. I don't know what cursed voice was saying to me, "Are you sure you are loved of God? Has He come to tell you so? It's not the opinion of a handful of people that will justify you before Him?"

I had been suffering with these thoughts for a long time when someone came to bring me your providential note. You were reminding me, Mother, of all the privileges of Jesus on my soul. And, as if all my anguish had been revealed to you, you were telling me that I was greatly cherished by God, and was on the eve of receiving the everlasting crown from his hand. Already, calm and joy were being reborn in my heart. Nonetheless, I told myself, "It's my Mother's affection for me that made her write these words." Immediately then I was inspired to pick up the holy Gospel, and as I opened it by chance, my eyes fell on this passage that I had never noticed: "For the one whom God has sent speaks the words of God, for God gives the Spirit without limit" [Jn. 3:34].

Then I fell asleep completely comforted. It was you, Mother, that the Good Lord sent for me, and I must believe you, since you say the same things as God.

During the month of August Thérèse remained for several days as if she were outside of herself, entreating us to have prayers said for her. We had never seen her like that. In that state of inexpressible anguish, we often heard her repeat, "Oh! How much we must pray for those who are in the agony of death! If only we knew!"

One night she pleaded with the infirmary Sister to sprinkle holy water on her bed, saying, "The devil is around me. I can't see him, but I feel him. . . . He's tormenting me, he's holding me as if with an iron hand to keep me from taking the slightest relief. He's making my illness worse so that I'll lose all hope. . . . And I can't pray! All I can do is look on the Blessed Virgin and say, 'Jesus!' How necessary is that prayer from Compline, 'Deliver us from the terrors of the night.'

"I'm experiencing something mysterious. I'm not suffering for myself, but for another soul . . . and the devil doesn't want me to."

The infirmary Sister, strongly touched by this, lit a blessed candle, and the spirit of darkness fled away, never to return. However, our little Sister remained right up to the end in extreme pain.

One day, as she was looking at the sky, someone said to her, "Soon you will live beyond the blue sky; and with what love you are thinking of that day!"

She was content to smile and then said to Mother Agnes of Jesus, "Mother, our Sisters don't know about my suffering! While I was looking at the blue sky, I was thinking only about finding the sky pretty; heaven beyond it is more and more closed to me. At first I was distressed by this remark that had been made, but then an inner voice answered me, 'Yes, you were looking at the sky out of love. Since your soul is entirely given over to love, all your actions, even the most neutral ones, are marked with this divine stamp.' Instantly I was comforted."

Despite the darkness that enveloped her completely, from time to time the divine Jailer cracked open the door of her dark prison; at those moments she experienced transports of exuberance, trust, and love.

One day as she was walking in the garden, held up by one of her Sisters, she stopped in front of a charming painting of a little white hen sheltering her sweet family under her wings. Soon Thérèse's eyes filled with tears, and, turning toward her dear guide, she said, "I can't stay any longer, let's go back in quickly."

And, in her cell, she wept for a long time without being able to utter a single word. Finally, looking at the Sister with a heavenly expression, she added,

> I was thinking about Our Lord, about the lovely comparison that He made to bring us to belief in His tenderness. All my life, that's what He has done for me: He has completely hidden me under His wings! I can't express what has happened in my heart. Oh! The Good Lord does well to hide Himself from my sight, to show me on rare occasions and, as it were, "peering through the lattice" [Song 2:9], the effects of His mercy. I feel that I wouldn't be able to bear its sweetness.

On June 5th, 1897, we began a fervent novena to Our Lady of Victories, not being able to resign ourselves to losing this treasure

General View of the Carmel of Lisieux

As seen from the convent garden.
The infirmary and the cell of Sister Thérèse of the Child Jesus are marked with a cross.
The first is on the ground floor, the second on the floor above.
The Servant of God, on the day when she wept on seeing the little white hen,
was on the courtyard at the left, in the foreground.

The Child Jesus in the Cloister

The statue is shown here in the same place where Sister Thérèse of the Child Jesus
used to decorate it with flowers.

of virtues. We were hoping that one more time the most holy Virgin would raise back up by a miracle the little flower of her love. But she did not give us the same reply as the blessed martyr Théophane, and we had to accept the bitter prospect of an impending separation.

At the beginning of July, her condition became more serious, and she was finally taken to the infirmary.

Seeing her cell empty, and knowing that she would never go back up to it, Mother Agnes of Jesus told her, "When you are no longer with us, I'll feel such grief at the sight of this cell!" "To comfort yourself, my dear Mother," Thérèse replied, "you will think about how I'm very happy up above, and that a great part of my happiness was acquired in that little cell; because," she added while lifting her eyes toward heaven with her beautiful, deep gaze, "I suffered very much there. I would have been happy to die there."

Upon entering the infirmary, Thérèse's eyes turned first toward the statue of the miraculous Virgin that we had placed there. It would be impossible to interpret the expression of that look: "What do you see?" asked her sister Marie, the very same one who, during her childhood, was witness to her ecstasy and also served as mother to her. She replied, "She has never seemed so beautiful to me! . . . but today it's the statue. That other time, you know well that it wasn't the statue. . . ."

Often afterward, the angelic child was comforted in the same way. One night she exclaimed:

How I love the Virgin Mary! If I had been a priest, how well I would have spoken about her! People portray her as inapproachable, but she must be shown to be imitable. She is more mother than queen! I've heard it said that her brightness eclipses all the Saints, as the sun at its rising makes the stars disappear. Dear Lord! How strange that is! A mother who makes the glory of her children disappear! I think it's just the opposite: I think she will greatly increase the splendor of the elect. . . . The Virgin Mary! How simple it seems to me that her life was!

And, continuing to speak, she made us a painting of the interior of the Holy Family that was so sweet, so delightful, that we remained in utter admiration.

———·——

A very painful trial awaited her. From August 16th to September 30th, the blessed day of her eternal communion, because of the vomiting that she underwent constantly, it was not possible for her receive the holy Eucharist. The bread of Angels! Who had loved it more than this angel on earth? How many times, even in the cold of winter during that last year, after her nights of cruel suffering, did the courageous child rise as soon as morning came to go to the holy Table! She never thought it was too high a price to pay to gain the happiness of uniting with her God.

Before she was deprived of that heavenly food, Our Lord often visited her on her bed of pain. The Communion of July 16th, the feast day of Our Lady of Mount Carmel, was particularly touching. During the night, she composed the following poem, which was to be sung before Communion:

> You who know my extreme littleness,
> You do not fear to bend down toward me!
> Come into my heart, O Sacrament that I love;
> Come into my heart . . . it reaches out to You.
> I want, Lord, for Your goodness to let me
> Die for love after that favor;
> Jesus! hear the cry of my tenderness,
>   Come into my heart!

———·——

In the morning, at the passing of the Blessed Sacrament, the pavement of our cloisters used to disappear under a shower of field flowers and rose petals. A young priest, whose turn it was to celebrate that very day his first Mass in our chapel, brought the sacred viaticum to our sweet invalid. And Sr. Marie of the Eucharist, whose melodious voice had heavenly tones, sang of her desire:

> To die of love is a most sweet martyrdom,
> And that is the one that I would like to suffer.
> O Cherubim! tune your lyre,
> For, I feel it, my exile is going to end. . . .
> Divine Jesus, make my dream come true:
> To die of love!

A few days later, Jesus' little sacrificial victim found herself sicker. So, on July 30th, she received Extreme Unction [the anointing of the sick]. Radiant, she then said, "The door of my somber prison is opening. I'm full of joy, especially since our Father Superior assured me that my soul today is like that of a little child after its baptism."

Without a doubt, she thought that she would very soon fly upward to heaven. She did not know that two months of martyrdom still separated her from her deliverance!

One day, she told the Prioress, "Mother, please, give me permission to die. Let me offer my life to such an intention."

And, since that permission was refused, she replied:

Well, I know that right now the Good Lord desires so much to have a little cluster of grapes that no one wants to offer Him, that He's going to find Himself obliged to come and steal it. . . . I'm not asking for anything— that would be to leave my path of self-abandonment—but I only pray to the Virgin Mary to remind her Jesus of the title of *Thief* that He gave Himself in the Holy Bible [2 Thess. 5:2], so that He will not forget to come and *steal me*.

One day someone brought her a sheaf of wheat. She picked one up that was so full of kernels that it was bending over on its stem, and she considered it for quite a while. Then she said to the Prioress, "Mother, this sheaf is the image of my soul: The Good Lord has filled me with graces for myself and for many others! Oh! I want to always bend over under the abundance of heavenly gifts, recognizing that everything comes from above."

She was right: Yes, her soul was filled with graces . . . and how easy it seemed to recognize the Spirit of God praising Himself through that innocent mouth!

Did not that Spirit of truth cause the great Teresa of Avila to write this?

> With a humble and holy presumption, let souls that have arrived at divine union hold themselves in high esteem, let them have unceasingly before their eyes the remembrance of the blessings they have received, and let them take great care not to believe they are doing acts of humility in not recognizing God's graces. Is it not clear that a faithful remembrance of blessings increases love toward the one who blesses? How can those who are not aware of the riches that they possess, share them and distribute them liberally?

———·+·———

This is not the only time that little Thérèse of Lisieux pronounced words that were truly inspired.

In April 1895, when she was in very good health, she confided in an elderly nun who was worthy of faith: "I will die soon. I'm not telling you that it will be in a few months, but in two or three years at the most. I sense this by what is happening in my soul."

The novices expressed their surprise when they saw her guessing their most intimate thoughts. "Here's my secret," she told them: "I never make any observations to you without invoking the Blessed Virgin. I ask her to inspire within me what ought to do you the most good. And I myself am often astounded by the things that I teach you. I simply feel, as I say them to you, that I am not mistaken, and that Jesus is speaking to you through my mouth."

During her illness, one of the Sisters had just had a moment of painful anguish, almost of discouragement, at the thought of an inevitable and forthcoming separation. Immediately afterward she went into the infirmary, without letting any of her troubles show, when she was quite surprised to hear our holy invalid say to her with a serious and sad tone, "You mustn't cry like those who have no hope!"

One of our nuns who had come to visit her did a little something nice for her. "How happy I would be," she thought, "if this angel said to me, 'In heaven I will repay you for this!' " At that very instant, Sr. Thérèse of the Child Jesus turned toward her and said, "Mother, in heaven I will repay you for this!"

But the most surprising thing is that she seemed to be conscious of the mission for which the Lord had sent her on earth. The veil of the future seemed to have fallen before her, and more than once, she revealed secrets in prophecies that have already come true: "I have never given anything to the Good Lord than love," she used to say. "He will give me back love. AFTER MY DEATH I WILL SEND DOWN A SHOWER OF ROSES."

A Sister was talking to her about the bliss of heaven. She interrupted, saying, "That's not what attracts me." "What then?" "Oh, it's Love! To love, to be loved, and to come back to earth to cause Love to be loved."

One night she greeted Mother Agnes of Jesus with an expression of particularly serene joy:

> Mother, some notes from a faraway concert have just reached me, and I thought that soon I will hear incomparable melodies. But that hope was able to give me joy for only an instant. Only one thing I am waiting for makes my heart beat: It's the love that I will receive and that I will be able to give!
>
> I feel that my mission is going to begin, my mission to cause the Good Lord to be loved as I love Him . . . to give my little way to souls. I WANT TO SPEND MY HEAVEN DOING GOOD ON EARTH. This is not impossible, because even in the very bosom of the beatific vision, the Angels watch over us. No, I will not be able to take any rest until the end of the world! But when the Angel says, "Time is no more!" then I'll rest, I'll rejoice, because the number of the elect will be complete.

"What little way do you want to teach souls, then?" asked Mother Agnes of Jesus.

> Mother, it's the way of spiritual childhood, it's the path of trust and total abandonment of self. I want to show them the little means that have

so perfectly succeeded for me. I want to tell them that there is only one thing to do here on earth: to throw to Jesus the flowers of little sacrifices, to take Him by caresses! That's how I took Him, and it's for this that I will be so well received!

"If I'm leading you into error with my little way of love," she used to say to her novices, "don't be afraid that I'm leaving you to follow it for a long time. I would appear to you soon to tell you to take another road. But, if I don't come back, believe in the truth of my words: We never have too much trust in the Good Lord, who is so powerful and so merciful! We obtain everything from Him according to the measure with which we hope for it!"

The day before the feast day of Our Lady of Mount Carmel (July 16th), a novice told her, "If you were going to die tomorrow, after Communion, that would be such a beautiful death that it would comfort me from all my sorrow, it seems to me."

And Thérèse replied strongly, "Die after Communion! On an important feast day! No, that's not how it will be: Little souls wouldn't be able to imitate that. In my little way, there are only very ordinary things. It has to be that everything I do, little souls can do it."

Often people brought her roses, and she would pluck off their petals and place them on her crucifix, caressing it with each petal. One day those precious relics fell on the ground. "Pick up all those petals," she said, "they will serve to bring you pleasure later. Don't lose a single one." (They served, not only to bring pleasure, but to work miracles.)

Another thing she said to her "little Mother" [Mother Agnes of Jesus] was this: "In heaven I will obtain many graces for those who have done good things to me. For you, Mother, everything will not be enough for you. There will be many of them to bring you joy."

———·—·———

One of the Sisters doubted her patience. One day, while visiting her, this Sister saw on her face an expression of heavenly joy and wanted to know the cause of it.

"It's because I'm feeling very sharp pain," she replied. "I have always forced myself to love suffering and to greet it warmly."

"When I suffer a great deal," the Servant of God used to say, "when painful and unpleasant things happen to me, instead of looking sad, I respond with a smile. At first I didn't always succeed. But now it's a habit that I'm very happy to have cultivated."

"Why are you so lighthearted this morning?" asked Mother Agnes of Jesus. "It's because I have had two little pains; nothing gives me little joys like little pains."

And another time she was asked, "Have you had many trials today?" "Yes, but . . . since I love them! . . . I love everything that the Good Lord gives me."

"Is it horrible, what you are suffering?" "No, it's not horrible. Could a little sacrificial offering of love find it horrible what her Bridegroom sends her? At every moment He gives me what I can bear, no more. And if, the next moment, He increases my suffering, He also increases my strength. However, I could never ask Him for greater suffering, because I'm too little. Then they would become my own sufferings, and I would have to bear them all alone. And I have never been able to do anything all alone."

This is how on her deathbed this wise and prudent virgin, whose lamp, always filled with the oil of virtues, shone right up to the end.

If the Holy Spirit tells us in Proverbs 19:11, "A person's wisdom yields patience," those who heard her can believe in her wisdom, now that she has proved it by her unconquerable patience.

At each visit, the doctor expressed his admiration: "Oh, if you knew what she endures! I've never seen anyone suffer so much, with that expression of supernatural joy. She's an angel!" And as we were expressing our distress at the thought of losing such a treasure, he replied, "I won't be able to heal her: she's a soul that is not made for this world."

Seeing her extreme weakness, he ordered strengthening potions. Thérèse was sad about this at first, because of their high price. Then she told us, "Now I'm no longer troubled at taking expensive remedies, because I read that Saint Gertrude was glad for them, thinking that everything would be an advantage to those who do good to us, since Our Lord said, 'Whatever you did for one of the least of these brothers and sisters of mine, you did for me' [Mt. 25:40].

"I'm convinced that medicines are useless to heal me," she added, "but I've arranged things with the Good Lord so that He will bring benefit from them to poor missionaries who have neither the time nor the means to care for themselves."

Touched by the attention of His little bride, the Lord, who never lets Himself be outdone in generosity, also surrounded her with His divine attention, whether by means of bunches of flowers sent by her family, or by a little robin that came hopping on her bed, giving her a knowing look and showering her with niceties.

"Mother," she said at that time, "I'm deeply moved by God's delicacy toward me. On the outside, I'm flooded with them . . . and yet I live in the deepest darkness! . . . I'm suffering a lot—yes, a great deal! But along with that, I find myself in an amazing peace. All my desires have come true . . . I'm full of trust."

A short time afterward, she told the story of a touching deed:

One night, at the hour of grand silence, the infirmary Sister came to put a bottle of hot water at my feet and tincture of iodine on my chest.

I was consumed with fever, and a burning thirst was devouring me. While undergoing these remedies, I couldn't stop myself from complaining to Our Lord: "My Jesus," I told him, "you are my witness: I'm burning up and they're bringing me yet more heat and fire! Oh, if I had, instead of all that, a half-glass of water, how relieved I would be! . . . My Jesus! Your little daughter is very thirsty! But she is happy nonetheless to find the opportunity to lack what is necessary, in order to be more like You and to save souls."

Soon the infirmary Sister left me, and I wasn't counting on seeing her again until the next morning, when, to my great surprise, she came back a few minutes later, bringing a refreshing drink: "I just had the thought that you might be thirsty," she told me. "From now on I'll make it a habit to offer you this relief every night." I looked at her, unable to speak, and when I was alone I burst into tears. Oh! How good our Jesus is! How sweet and tender He is! How easily touched is His heart!

———·◦·———

One of the delicate touches from Jesus' heart that caused her the most joy was the one on September 6th, the day when, through an entirely providential happening, we received a relic of the blessed Théophane Vénard. Several times already, she had expressed the desire to possess something having belonged to her holy friend. But, seeing that no one pursued this, she stopped speaking about it. Therefore her emotion was great when the Prioress placed that precious object in her hands. She covered it with kisses and did not want to be separated from it.

So why did she cherish the angelic missionary to such an extent? She confided the reason to her beloved sisters in a touching meeting with them: "Théophane Vénard is a little Saint; his life is quite ordinary. He loved the Immaculate Virgin very much, and he loved his family very much."

Then, underscoring these last words, she said, "I also love my family very much! I don't understand Saints who don't love their families! . . . As a farewell remembrance, I've copied for you certain passages of the last letters that he wrote to his parents. These are my thoughts—my soul is like his."

Here is this letter, which came from the pen and the heart of our angel:

I find nothing on earth that makes me happy. My heart is too big: Nothing that is called happiness in this world can satisfy it. My thoughts fly toward eternity; time is going to end! My heart is peaceful like a tranquil lake or a serene sky. I do not miss the life of this world: I thirst for the waters of eternal life. . . .

Yet a little while and my soul will leave the earth, will finish its exile, will end its combat. I'm going up to heaven! I'm going to enter into the dwelling of the elect, see beauties that the human eye has never seen, hear harmonies that the ear has never heard, delight in joys that the heart has never known. . . . See, I have been brought to this time that each of us has desired so much! It's really true that the Lord chooses *little ones* to confound the great in this world. I don't lean on my own strength, but on the strength of the One who, on the cross, defeated the powers of hell.

I am a springtime flower that the Master of the garden picks for his pleasure. We are all flowers planted on this earth and that God picks in his time: a little sooner, a little later. . . . I, a little short-lived one, am going away the first of all! One day we will meet each other again in paradise, and we will enjoy true happiness.

—Sr. Thérèse of the Child Jesus,
borrowing the words of the angelic martyr Théophane Vénard

———·•·———

Toward the end of September, as a Sister was telling her about something that had been said at the recreation period, touching on the responsibility of those who have the care of souls, she revived her strength for a moment and pronounced these beautiful words:

" 'For to him that is little, mercy is granted!' [Wis. 6:7 D–R]. It's possible to stay little, even in the midst of the most formidable duties. And isn't it written that at the end, God will arise in judgment, to save all the meek and humble of the earth? He doesn't say that He will judge, but rather *save!*"

However, the waves of pain became stronger and stronger. Her weakness became so excessive that soon the holy little invalid was reduced to not being able to make the slightest movement without help. To hear voices speaking near her, even quietly, became a painful suffering. The fever and the oppression did not allow her to articulate a single word without feeling the most extreme fatigue. Nevertheless, in that state her smile did not leave her lips. Did a cloud pass over her forehead? It was fear of giving the Sisters an excess of pain. Until two days before her death she wanted to be alone at night. Nonetheless, her nurse went to see her several times, despite her protests. On one of these visits, she found her with her hands clasped and her eyes raised to heaven.

"What are you doing like that?" asked the nurse. "You ought to try to sleep."

"I can't, Sister, I'm suffering too much! So I pray. . . ."

"And what do you say to Jesus?"

"I don't say anything. *I love Him!*"

———·+·———

"Oh, how good the Good Lord is!" she used to cry out at times. "Yes, He has to be good in order to give me the strength to bear all that I'm suffering."

One day she told the Prioress, "Mother, I would like to tell you the state of my soul, but I can't; I'm too moved right now."

And, that night, she penciled these lines, with a trembling hand: "Oh dearest God, how good You are to the little sacrificial victim of Your merciful love! Even now that You are joining outward suffering to the trials of my soul, I cannot say, 'The sorrows of death surrounded me' [Ps. 17:5 D-R]. But I cry out, in my gratefulness, 'For though I should walk in the midst of the shadow of death, I will fear no evils, for thou art with me, Lord' " [Ps. 22:4 D-R].

"Some Sisters think that you're afraid of death," said Mother Agnes of Jesus.

"That might well happen," she replied. "I never lean on my own thoughts—I know how weak I am. But I want to enjoy the feeling that the Good Lord is giving me now. There will always be time to suffer the opposite.

"The chaplain asked me, 'Are you resigned to dying?' I answered, 'Oh, Father, I find that I need resignation only for living . . . for dying, it's joy that I feel.'

"Don't be troubled, Mother, if I suffer a lot, and if I don't show any sign of happiness at the last moment. Didn't Our Lord die the Victim of love, and see what agony He had!"

———··———

On September 29th, the day before her death, at nine o'clock in the evening, the Servant of God and her youngest sister, Céline (Sr. Geneviève of the Holy Face), both heard very distinctly the sound of wings in the garden. Soon a turtledove—coming from no one knows where—landed, cooing, on the edge of the window. A few moments later it flew back up into the sky.

The two sisters were gently impressed by this visit, remembering the word from Song of Songs, "Rise up, my love, my fair one, and come away. For, lo, the winter is past, the rain is over and gone; the flowers appear on the earth; the time of the singing of birds is come" [2:10–12 KJV].

———··———

Finally, the dawn of the eternal day came! It was Thursday, September 30th. In the morning, our sweet sacrificial victim, speaking about her last night in exile, looked at the statue of Mary, saying, "Oh! I prayed to her with fervor! . . . But it's the purest agony, without any mixture of consolation. . . . I miss the air of earth—when will I have the air of heaven?"

At 2:30 she sat up in bed, something that she had not been able to do for several weeks, and cried out, "Mother, the cup is full to the brim! No, I would never have believed that it would be possible to suffer so much. I can explain that to myself only through my extreme desire to save souls. . . ."

And a short time afterward: "All that I wrote about my desires for suffering, oh! It's really true! I'm not sorry for having given myself over to love."

She repeated those last words several times.

And a little later: "Mother, prepare me to die well."

Her esteemed Prioress encouraged her with these words: "My child, you are completely ready to appear before God, because you have always understood the virtue of humility."

She then bore this beautiful witness to herself: "Yes, I feel it, my soul has never looked for anything but the truth. . . . Yes, I have understood humility of the heart!"

At 4:30, the symptoms of her final agony began to show. As soon as the angelic dying one saw the community enter, she thanked them with the most gracious smile. Then, grasping the crucifix in her dying hands, she gathered herself for the supreme combat. Profuse sweat covered her face; she was trembling. . . . But, just as in the midst of a furious storm the pilot who is bearing down on the port does not lose courage, in the same way this soul of faith, catching sight of the shining lighthouse of the eternal shore, valiantly gave the final strokes of the oar to reach the port.

When the convent bell sounded the evening Angelus, she fixed an inexpressible gaze on the Star of the Sea, the immaculate Virgin. Was this not the moment to sing:

> You, who came to smile at me on the morning of my life,
> Come smile at me again, Mother, this very night!

At a few minutes past seven, our little martyr, turning toward her Prioress, said, "Mother, isn't this the agony? . . . Am I not going to die? . . ."

"Yes, my child, this is the agony, but Jesus wants perhaps to prolong it for a few hours."

Then, with a resigned tone: "All right . . . let's go . . . let's go . . . oh! I wouldn't like to suffer less!"

Then, looking at her crucifix:

"OH! . . . I LOVE HIM! . . . MY GOD, I . . . LOVE . . . YOU!!!"

These were her last words. She had hardly pronounced them when to our great surprise she sank back suddenly, her head inclined to the right, in the attitude of those virgin martyrs offering themselves up to the stroke of the sword; or rather, as a sacrificial victim of love, awaiting from the divine Archer the flaming arrow from which she desires to die. . . .

Suddenly she raised her head back up, as if called by a mysterious voice. She opened her eyes and fixed them, shining with heavenly peace and with an ineffable happiness, a little above the image of Mary.

That gaze was prolonged for the space of a *Credo*, and her blessed soul, having become the prey of the *divine Eagle*, flew up to heaven.

———·+·———

This angel had told us several days before leaving this world, "The death from love that I wish for is that of Jesus on the cross." Her desire was fully granted: Darkness and anguish accompanied her agony. However, can we not also apply to her the sublime prophecy of St. John of the Cross, concerning souls that are consumed in divine love:

> They die in admirable transports and delicious assaults that love gives them, like the swan whose song is more melodious when it is on the point of death. This is what made David say that "precious in the sight of the Lord is the death of his saints." For it is then that the rivers of love escape from the soul and go lose themselves in the ocean of divine love.

———·+·———

Immediately after her blessed death, the joy of the last instant was imprinted on her forehead; an inexpressible smile lightened her face. We put a palm branch in her hand, the palm that, thirteen years later, at the time of her exhumation, was found intact in her coffin.

At the same time, certain extraordinary events began to happen in the community. Here are some examples of them: The first one, mentioned earlier, is that of the lay Sister who, upon kissing the feet of the angelic virgin and pressing her forehead against them with faith and confidence, was instantly healed of cerebral anemia.

Another Sister smelled a very strong scent of violets in her cell, where there were no flowers. Another had a gentle and fresh impression of a kiss on her cheek given by an invisible being. One Sister saw a distinct ray in the sky, and another Sister saw a shining crown that rose from the earth and disappeared into the sky.

On Saturday and Sunday a large, hushed crowd kept coming before the grille in the choir, contemplating in the majesty of death the "little queen," who was still gracious, and having her body touched by hundreds of rosaries, medals, and even jewelry.

In that crowd, a ten-year-old child smelled a very strong scent of lilies—a scent that was unexplainable, since all the lilies that surrounded the virginal remains were artificial. It was only recently that we found out about this favor, whose beneficiary is still deeply moved by the memory of it.

On October 4th, the day of her burial, the Servant of God was surrounded by a beautiful circle of priests. This honor was due to her: She had prayed so much for priestly souls!

Finally, after being solemnly blessed, the precious grain of wheat was placed into the ground by the motherly hands of the holy Church.

Ever since, she has magnificently made the word of the divine Harvester come true: "Unless a grain of wheat falls into the earth and dies, it remains just a single grain; but if it dies, IT BEARS MUCH FRUIT" [John 12:24 NRSV].

Most often, here on earth, these fruits remain hidden, but the Lord, this time, anticipating the time of the eternal revelations, desires for us to contemplate the divine harvest that all around us is whitening the face of the earth.

May divine mercy be praised forever! It is the Author of all these marvelous things.

This painting by Céline faithfully represents the expression on the face and the inclination of the head of Sister Thérèse of the Child Jesus immediately after her death.

From the world her fleeting image passed. . . . Heaven is mine!

2
REMEMBRANCES OF THÉRÈSE
AND HER WORDS OF COUNSEL

In Thérèse's conversations with her novices we find the most precious teachings.

1.

"I was quite discouraged at the sign of my imperfections," recalled one of the novices, "when Sister Thérèse of the Child Jesus said this to me:"

You make me think of the tiny child who is learning to stand up, but doesn't know how to walk yet. Absolutely wanting to reach the top of the stairs to find his mother, he lifts his little foot in order to climb the first step. But his trouble is of no use! He falls back down without being able to advance. Well, you be that little child. Through the practice of all the virtues, lift your little foot in order to climb the stairway of saintliness, and don't imagine that you will be able even to climb the first step! No. But all the Good Lord asks of you is good will. From the top of those stairs, He looks at you with love. Soon, won over by your useless efforts, He will come down Himself, and, taking you in His arms, He will carry you for all time to His kingdom, where you will never leave Him anymore. But if you stop lifting your little foot, He will leave you on earth for a long time.

The only way to make rapid progress in the way of love is that of always remaining very little. That is what I have done. Therefore now I can sing with our father Saint John of the Cross:

> And humbling myself so low, so low,
> I raised myself so high, so high,
> That I was able to reach my goal!

2.

"In the midst of a temptation that seemed insurmountable to me, I told Thérèse, 'This time I'm not able to rise above it—it's impossible.' She replied:"

Why are you looking to rise above it? *Pass underneath it*, quite simply. It's good for great souls to fly over the clouds when the thunderstorm is crashing. As for us, all we have to do is to patiently endure the rainstorms. Too bad if we get a little wet! Afterward we will dry off under the sun of love.

On that subject I remember a little story from my childhood: A horse was blocking the entrance to our garden. Around me people were talking about how to make him back up. But I let them go on discussing, and I quietly passed under his legs. . . . That's what we gain when we keep ourselves little!

3.

"Our Lord once replied to the mother of the sons of Zebedee," said Thérèse, " 'To sit at my right or left is not for me to grant. These places belong to those for whom they have been prepared by my Father' [Mt. 20:23]. I figure that these choice places, which have been refused to great saints and martyrs, will be the portion of little children.

"Didn't David predict this when he said, 'There is the little tribe of Benjamin, leading them' [Ps. 68:27]?"

4.

"You are wrong," said Thérèse, "to find yourself repeating to this person or that person to seek for everyone to submit to your way of seeing things. Since we want to be *little children*, little children don't know what is best; they find everything to be good. Let's pattern ourselves after them. Besides, there's no spiritual credit to be earned by doing what is rational and reasonable."

5.

"My protectors in heaven and my privileged ones," Thérèse said, "are those who have stolen it, such as the Holy Innocents [the children killed by royal decree when king Herod learned of the Messiah's birth in Bethlehem] and the good thief [who hung on a cross beside Jesus and asked Him to remember him when He came into His kingdom]. The great Saints gained heaven through their works. As for me, I want to follow the example of the thieves: I want to gain it through ruse, a subterfuge of love that will open its entrance, to me and to the poor sinners. The Holy Spirit is encouraging me, since He says in Proverbs that the proverbs are 'for giving prudence to those who are simple, knowledge and discretion to the young' [1:4]."

6.

"What would you do if you could begin your religious life again?" asked a Sister.

"It seems to me that I would do what I have done," Thérèse replied.

"So you don't experience the feeling of that hermit who said, 'Even though I may have lived long years in penance, as long as I have a quarter of an hour left, a breath of life, I would be afraid of being damned'?"

"No, I cannot share that fear. I'm too little to be damned: *little children are not damned.*"

"You always seek to be like the little children, but tell us what we need to do in order to possess the spirit of childhood. What does it mean to remain little?"

"To remain little is to recognize our nothingness, to expect everything from the Good Lord, not to be to distressed at our faults. Finally, it's not to gain or earn fortune, luck, or wealth, not to be worried about anything. Even among the poor, as long as a child is very little, he is given what is necessary. But when he has grown up, his father no longer wants to feed him and tells him, 'Work now! You can get along by yourself.' Well, it's so as not to hear that, that I have never wanted or tried to grow up, feeling myself incapable of earning *my living, eternal life!*

"To stay little is again not to attribute to ourselves the virtues that we practice, but to recognize that the Good Lord places that treasure in the hand of His little child, in order to use it when He needs it."

7.

"In order to follow the example of our angelic Novice Mistress [Thérèse]," wrote one of the Sisters, "I didn't want to grow up—so she called me 'the little child.' During one retreat she addressed these words to me:"

Don't be afraid of telling Jesus that you love Him, even without feeling it. That's the way to force Him to give you help, to carry you like a little child who is too weak to walk.

It's a great hardship to see everything as black, but that doesn't depend completely on you. Do what you can to detach and withdraw your heart from the cares of the earth, and especially of created things. But you can be sure that Jesus will do the rest. He won't allow you to fall into a bottomless pit. Take comfort, little child: In heaven you won't see *everything as black*, but *everything as white*. Yes, everything will be clothed with the divine whiteness of our Bridegroom, the Lily of the valley. Together, we will follow Him everywhere He goes. . . . Oh! Let's take advantage of the short instant that is life! Let's give pleasure to Jesus, let's save souls for Him through our sacrifices. Above all, let's be little, so little that everyone can tread us under foot, without our even looking as if we feel it and suffer from it.

I'm not surprised at the failures of the little child. He forgets that being both a missionary and a warrior, he must deprive himself of all-too-childish consolations. But it's unseemly to spend our time moping around, instead of falling asleep on the Heart of Jesus!

If the night makes the little child afraid, if he complains about not seeing the One who is carrying him, *let him close his eyes*: This is the only sacrifice that Jesus asks of him. By keeping himself peaceful in this way, the night won't make him afraid, since he won't see it any more. And soon calm, if not joy, will be reborn in his heart.

8.

"In order to help me accept a humiliation," wrote a Sister, "she told me this in confidence:"

"If I hadn't been accepted into Carmel, I would have entered an asylum for reformed prostitutes, in order to live there unknown and despised in the midst of those poor 'penitents.' My happiness would have been to pass for one of them in the eyes of all. And I would have made myself the apostle of my companions, telling them what I think of the Good Lord's mercy. . . ."

"But how would you have managed to hide your innocence from your confessor?"

"I would have told him that when I was out in the world I had made a general confession, and that I was forbidden to tell it again."

9.

"Oh!" said a Sister, "when I think about all that I have to achieve!"

"Say rather *to lose!*" replied Thérèse. "It's Jesus who takes on Himself to fill your soul, in the measure that you empty it of its imperfections. I see clearly that you're on the wrong road; you'll never come to the end of your journey. You want to climb a mountain, and the Good Lord wants you to go down it: He's waiting for you at the bottom of the fertile valley of humility."

10.

"It seems to me that humility is truth," said Thérèse. "I don't know if I'm humble, but I do know that I see the truth in all things."

11.

"Truly," said a Sister, "you're a Saint!"

"No," replied Thérèse, "I'm not a Saint. I've never done the actions of the Saints. *I'm a very little soul that the Good Lord has flooded with grace. . . .* You'll see in heaven that I'm telling the truth."

"But you've always been faithful to the divine graces, haven't you?"

"Yes, *since the age of thirteen,* I have refused nothing to the Good Lord. Nevertheless, I can't glorify myself because of that. Look at how this evening the setting sun is touching the treetops with gold. In the same way my soul appears to you to be shining and golden, because it is exposed to the rays of love. If the divine Sun were no longer to send me its fires, I would immediately become dark and full of shadows."

"We would also like to become all golden. How can we do that?"

"You must practice the little virtues. That's difficult sometimes, but the Good Lord never refuses the first grace that gives us the courage to conquer ourselves. If the soul agrees to that and conforms to it, it finds itself immediately bathed in light. I have always been struck by the word of praise addressed to Judith: 'For thou hast done manfully, and thy heart has been strengthened' [15:11 D-R]. First, you have to act with courage. Then your heart is strengthened, and you march from victory to victory."

12.

"Sister Thérèse of the Child Jesus never used to lift her eyes in the refectory [the dining room]," wrote a Sister, "as is called for in our Rule. Since I had a lot of trouble keeping myself from doing that, she composed this prayer that for me was a revelation of her humility, because in it she asks for herself a grace that I alone needed:"

Jesus, Your two little brides make a resolution to keep their eyes bowed during meals, in order to honor and follow the example that You gave them in Herod's palace. When that irreverent prince was mocking You, O infinite Beauty, not a single complaint escaped Your lips. You did not even stoop to fix Your adorable eyes on him. Oh! Without a doubt, divine Jesus, Herod was not worthy to be looked at by You. But we, who are your brides, we desire to draw to ourselves Your divine gaze. We ask you to repay us by that glance of love, each time that we deprive ourselves of lifting our eyes. And even, we ask You not to refuse us that gentle glance when we have fallen, since we will humble ourselves sincerely before You because of having done so.

13.

"I told her in confidence that I wasn't getting anywhere," wrote a Sister, "and that I was discouraged by that."

She replied: "Until the age of fourteen, I practiced virtue without feeling its sweetness or tenderness. I desired suffering, but I didn't think about making it my joy. That is a grace that was granted to me later. My soul was like a beautiful tree whose flowers fell off as soon as they had opened.

"Give to the Good Lord the sacrifice of never picking fruit. If He wants you, your whole life, to feel dislike at suffering, at being humiliated; if He allows all the flowers of your desires and your good will to fall to earth without producing anything, don't be troubled by this. In the blink of an eye, at the moment of your death, He will know quite well how to make the beautiful fruits of the tree of your soul come to ripeness.

"We read in Sirach, 'There are others who are slow and need help, who lack strength and abound in poverty; but the eyes of the Lord look kindly upon them; he lifts them out of their lowly condition and raises up their heads to the amazement of the many. . . . Trust in the Lord and keep at your job; for it is easy in the sight of the Lord to make the poor rich suddenly, in an instant. The blessing of the Lord is the reward of the pious, and quickly God causes his blessing to flourish' [11:11–13, 21–22 NRSV]. "

"But," replied the Sister, "if I fall, people will find me to be still imperfect, whereas in you people recognize virtue."

"Perhaps that's because I have never desired it. . . . But if you are found to be still imperfect, that's what is needed; that's your gain. To believe ourselves to be imperfect and to find others to be perfect, that is happiness. Let created beings recognize you as being without virtue: That doesn't take anything away from you and it doesn't make you poorer. They're the ones who lose inner joy! For there is nothing sweeter than to think about the good of our neighbor.

"As for me, I experience great joy, not only when people find me to be imperfect, but above all when I feel that I am imperfect. On the contrary, compliments only cause me grief and distress."

*Sister Thérèse of the Child Jesus
in the Convent Garden*

Oh! Already in the present I recognize Him; yes, all my hopes will be fulfilled . . . yes, the Lord will do for me marvelous things that will infinitely surpass my *immense desires*!

14.

"The Good Lord has a particular love for you," said one Sister to Thérèse, "since He entrusts other souls to you." Thérèse replied:

That doesn't give me anything, and I am really only what I am in the sight of God. . . . It's not because He wants me to be His interpreter to you that He loves me more: Rather, He's making me your little servant. It's for you and not for me that He gives me the charms and the virtues that appear before your eyes.

I often compare myself to a little bucket that the Good Lord fills with all sorts of good things. All *the little cats* come to take their part in it. Sometimes they argue among themselves about which one will get more. But the Child Jesus is there, lying in wait! "I really want you to drink from my little bucket," He says, "but take care not to tip it over and break it!"

In truth, there is no great danger, because I'm sitting on the ground. For Prioresses, it's not the same thing: Since they're placed on tables, they run the risk of a lot more perils. Being honored is always dangerous.

Oh! What poison in the form of praise is served daily to those who hold the first places! What deadly incense! And how much must a soul be detached from itself not to experience harm from it!

15.

"For you it's a comfort to do good, to bring about the glory of God," said a Sister. "How I would like to see myself so privileged!"

What does it do for me for the Good Lord to use me, rather than another, to bring about His glory? Provided that His kingdom is established in souls, the instrument matters little. Besides, He doesn't need anyone.

A little while ago I was looking at the wick of a little votive candle that had almost gone out. One of our Sisters touched her tall taper to it, and through that taper, everyone in the community was given light. Then I had this thought: "Who then can take glory from her works? In this way, by means of the feeble glow of that lamp, it would be possible to set the universe aglow. We often think we receive graces and divine lights through the means of brilliant tall tapers. But where do those tapers get their flame? Perhaps from the prayers of a humble, quite hidden soul, without any apparent brilliance, without any recognized virtue, lowly in its own eyes, ready to burn out."

Oh! How many mysteries will we see later! How many times have I thought I perhaps owed all the graces with which I have been flooded to the earnest entreaties of a little soul that I will meet only in heaven!

It's the Good Lord's will that in this world souls should communicate among themselves the heavenly gifts through prayer, so that, having returned to their Homeland, they may be able to love each other with a grateful love, and affection that is so much greater than that of the most ideal family on earth.

There, we won't encounter indifferent looks, because all the saints will owe each other something.

We won't see envious glances anymore. In addition, the happiness of each of the elect will be the happiness of them all. With the martyrs, we will resemble martyrs; with the doctors [of the Church], we will be like the doctors; with the virgins, like the virgins; and just as the members of the same family are proud of one another, so will we be proud of our brothers, without the slightest jealousy.

Who even knows if the joy that we experience when we see the glory of the great Saints, knowing that, through a secret working of Providence, we have contributed to it—who knows if that joy will not be as intense, and perhaps sweeter, than the happiness that they themselves possess?

And, in turn, do you think that the great Saints, seeing what they owe to all the little souls, won't love them with an incomparable love? There, there will be, I am sure, delightful and surprising instinctive attractions. The privileged one of an apostle, of a great doctor, will perhaps be a simple shepherd. And the intimate friend of a patriarch may be a simple little child. Oh! How I would like to be in that kingdom of love!

16.

"Believe me, writing pious books, composing the most sublime poetry—all that is not worth the smallest act of self-renunciation. However, when we suffer from our powerlessness to do good, our only resource is to offer the works of others. That is the blessing of the communion of the saints. Remember that beautiful verse from the spiritual canticle of our father Saint John of the Cross:

> *Come back, my dove,*
> *For the wounded deer*
> *Appears on the top of the hill,*
> *Drawn by the air of your flight, and he enjoys its coolness.*

"You see, the Bridegroom, *the wounded Deer*, is not attracted by *the height* of the hilltop, but by the *air* of the flight, and a simple flap of the wing is enough to produce that breeze of love."

17.

"The only thing that is not subject to envy is the last place. So the last place is the only thing that is not vanity and affliction of spirit. Therefore 'I know that people's lives are not their own; it is not for them to direct their steps' [Jer. 10:23]. And, sometimes, we surprise ourselves by desiring what dazzles. Then, let us rank ourselves humbly among those who are imperfect. Let us consider ourselves to be souls that the Good Lord must hold up every moment. As soon as He sees us to be convinced of our nothingness, as soon as we say to Him, ' "My foot is slipping," your unfailing love, LORD, supported me' [Ps. 94:18], then He holds out His hand to us. But if we want to try to do something great, even under the pretext of godly fervor, He leaves us alone. So it's enough to humble ourselves, to gently bear our imperfections: That is true saintliness for us."

18.

"I was complaining one day about being more tired than my Sisters," wrote one nun, "because in addition to the common work I had another job that no one knew about." Thérèse replied:

"I would always like to see you as a valiant soldier who does not complain about his troubles, who finds the wounds of his friends to be very grave, and who holds his own wounds to be only scratches. Why do you feel this fatigue to such an extent? It's because no one knows about it. . . .

"Blessed Margaret-Mary, who had two whitlows [inflammations of the fingers], said that she had truly suffered only from the first one, because it was impossible for her to hide the second one, which then became the object of the compassion of her Sisters.

"That feeling is natural to us. But we behave as common people when we want for others to know when we are hurting."

19.

"We must never believe, when we commit a fault, that it is due to a physical cause, such as sickness or the weather. Rather, we must attribute our fall to our imperfection without ever becoming discouraged. 'Occasions of adversity best show the measure of virtue or strength each one has. For such occasions do not make us weak, but they reveal what we already are' [*Imitation of Christ* I.16.4]."

20.

"The Good Lord has not permitted our Prioress to tell me to write down my poems as soon as I composed them, and I would not have wanted to ask her for this, for fear of committing a fault against poverty. Therefore I would wait for the period when we had free time, and it was not without extreme difficulty that I would remember, at eight o'clock in the evening, what I had composed in the morning.

"These small things are a martyrdom, it is true, but we must take great care not to diminish it by allowing ourselves, or causing ourselves to be allowed, a thousand things that would make the religious life pleasant and comfortable for us."

21.

"One day when I was crying," wrote a Sister, "Sister Thérèse of the Child Jesus told me to get used to not letting my little sufferings be seen in this way, adding that nothing makes community life sadder than inequality in temperament.

" 'You're right,' I replied to her, 'I had thought of that myself. And from now on I will never cry anymore except with the Good Lord. To Him alone I will confide my sufferings. He will understand me and will always comfort me.' She replied sharply:"

"To cry before the Good Lord! Watch out that you do not act that way. You ought to appear sad even much less before Him than before created beings. What! All the good Master has to bring joy to His heart is our monasteries and convents. He comes among us to rest, to forget the continual complaints of His friends in the world. For most often in the world, instead of being grateful for the prize of the Cross, people weep and moan. Are you going to do like common mortals? . . . Frankly, that is not disinterested love. *It's up to us to comfort Jesus, it's not up to Him to comfort us.*

"I know, *He is so good-hearted* that if you cry, He will wipe away your tears. But then He will go away quite sad, since He was unable to find rest in you. Jesus loves joyful hearts. He loves a soul that is always smiling. So when will you find out how to *hide your sufferings from Him,* or tell Him while singing that you are happy to suffer for Him?

"The face is the reflection of the soul," Thérèse added. "You ought unceasingly to have a calm and serene face, like a little child who is always happy. When you are alone, continue to act in the same way, because you are continually in the sight of the Angels."

22.

"I wanted her to congratulate me for having practiced an act of heroic virtue, as I saw it," wrote one Sister about Thérèse, "but she told me:"

"What is this little act of virtue, in comparison to what Jesus has the right to expect from your faithfulness? You ought rather to humble yourself for letting get away from you so many opportunities from Him to prove your love."

"Not at all satisfied with this reply, I waited for a difficult opportunity, in order to see how Sister Thérèse of the Child Jesus would conduct herself. That opportunity was not long in coming. Since our Reverend Mother Prioress had asked us to do a fatiguing job that was subject to a thousand contradictions, I allowed myself maliciously to increase [Thérèse's] burden. But I could not for a single instant find fault in her. I saw her always gracious, loving, not taking her fatigue into account. Was it a question of taking the trouble to serve others? She offered herself with good spirits. In the end, not being able to hold it in any longer, I threw myself into her arms and confided in her the feelings that had agitated my soul.

" 'How do you manage' I asked her, 'to practice virtue in this way, to be constantly joyful, calm, and ever like yourself?' "

"I haven't always done this," she replied, "*but since I began never to look out for myself, I have led the happiest life that can be seen.*"

23.

"At the recreation period more than elsewhere," our angelic Novice Mistress used to say, "you will find the opportunity to exercise your virtue. If you want to take great advantage of it, do not go with the thought of taking recreation for yourself, but with the thought of seeing that others take recreation. There, practice a complete detachment from yourself. For example, if you are telling one of your Sisters a story that seems interesting to you, and that Sister interrupts you to tell you something else, listen to her with interest, even though it doesn't interest you at all, and do not seek to pick your original conversation back up. By behaving in this way, you will leave the recreation period with a great inner peace, and clothed with a new strength to practice virtue—because you have not gone in search of satisfying yourself, but of giving pleasure to others. If people only knew what we gain when we renounce ourselves in all things . . . !"

"You know this well," I replied. "Is this what you have always done?"

"Yes, I have forgotten myself; I have attempted not to seek myself in anything."

24.

"We must subdue ourselves when someone rings for us or when someone knocks at our door, to the point of not sewing a single extra stitch before replying. I have practiced that, and I assure you that it is a source of peace."

"After that advice," wrote one Sister, "when the opportunity presented itself, I stirred myself promptly. One day, during her illness, she was witness to this, and she told me:"

"At the moment of death, you will be very happy to find yourself doing that! You have just done an action that is more glorious than if, through clever proceedings, you had obtained the good will of the government toward religious communities, and all of France acclaimed you as if you were Judith [whose story is told in the biblical book of that name]!"

25.

A Sister wrote, "When Thérèse was asked about her manner of making meals holy, she replied:"

In the refectory, we have only one thing to do: accomplish this lowly activity with elevated thought. I will admit that it is often in the refectory that the sweetest aspirations of love come to me. Sometimes I'm forced to stop myself, remembering that if Our Lord were in my place, in front of the foods that are served to me, He would certainly eat them. . . . It's probable that, during His mortal life, He ate the same foods: *He ate bread and fruit.*

Here are my little childish musings:

I think of myself as being in Nazareth in the home of the Holy Family. If I'm served, for example, *salad, cold fish, wine, or some other thing that has a strong flavor, I offer it to the good Saint Joseph. To the Holy Virgin, I give the hot portions, well-ripened fruit, etc.; and the foods served on feast days, particularly porridge, rice, jam, I offer them to the Child Jesus.* Finally, when I have been served a bad dinner, I tell myself gaily, *"Today, my little girl, all that is for you!"*

"In this way she hid from us the subjection and denial of her bodily appetites by abstinence, under a gracious outward appearance. However, one fast day when our Reverend Mother Prioress had imposed her a relaxation of the fast, I surprised her seasoning with absinthe [a somewhat bitter-tasting beverage], that delightful food that was all too much suited to her taste.

"Another time, I saw her slowly drinking a horrible-tasting remedy.

" 'Well, hurry up now,' I told her, 'drink that in one big gulp!' "

"Oh, no!" she replied. "Must I not take advantage of the little opportunities that we encounter in order to subdue my bodily appetites a little, since I'm forbidden to seek out great ones?"

"This is how," continued the Sister, "during her novitiate—I found this out during the final months of her life—one of our Sisters, having attempted to reattach Thérèse's scapular, pierced her shoulder with her big pin, a suffering that Thérèse endured for several hours with joy.

"Another time, she gave me proof of her inner subjection of her body through discomfort. I had received a very interesting letter that had been read at the recreation period during her absence. That evening, she manifested the desire to read it in turn, and I gave it to her. Some time later, as she was returning that letter to me, I asked her to tell me her thoughts about something that would have particularly charmed her. She seemed embarrassed, and she finally replied,"

"The Good Lord asked me for this sacrifice, because of the big hurry that I was in the other day; I didn't read it. . . ."

26.

"I was talking to her about the denial of the bodily passions and appetites by abstinence or self-inflicted discomfort by the saints. She replied:"

"Our Lord did well to let us know in advance *that there are many dwelling-places in His Father's house! If it were not so, He would have told us* [see Jn. 14:2]. . . . Yes, if all the souls that have been called to perfection had been obliged, in order to enter heaven, to waste away by excessive fasting, He would have told us, and we would have imposed this on ourselves with all our heart. But He announced to us *that there are many dwelling-places in His house.* If there is the one for great souls, the one for the desert Fathers and for martyrs of penance, there must also be the one for little children. Our place is kept there, if we love Him a lot, Him and our heavenly Father and the Spirit of love."

27.

"Once, when I was in the world [before entering Carmel]," said Thérèse, "when I woke up in the morning I used to think about what happy or troublesome thing was probably going to happen to me during that day. And if I could foresee only troubles, I would get up sad. Now, it's quite the opposite: I think about the troubles, the sufferings that await me; and I get up even more joyful and full of courage because I foresee more opportunities to bear witness to my love of Jesus *and to win the lives of my children,* since I am a mother of souls. Then I kiss my crucifix, I place it delicately on the pillow the whole time I am getting dressed, and I say to him:

" 'My Jesus, You worked enough and wept enough during the thirty-three years of Your life on this poor earth! Today, rest. . . . It's my turn to battle and to suffer.' "

28.

"One washday," wrote a Sister, "I was heading toward the laundry room without hurrying, looking at the flowers as I was passing through the garden. Sister Thérèse of the Child Jesus was going there too, walking rapidly. She encountered me and said:"

"Is this how people hurry when they have children to feed and they are obliged to work in order to earn a living for them?"

29.

Thérèse said, "Do you know what are my Sundays and my feast days? . . . It's the days when the Good Lord puts me all the more to the test."

30.

"I was very sorry for my lack of courage," wrote a Sister, "when dear little Sister Thérèse said to me:"

"You are complaining about what ought to cause your greatest happiness. Where would your merit be if you had to engage in combat only when you feel courage? What does it matter if you don't have any, provided that you act as if you did! If you find yourself too cowardly to pick up a bit of string, and nevertheless you do it for the love of Jesus, you have more merit than if you were to accomplish a much more considerable action in a moment of fervor. So instead of being sad, rejoice to see that by letting you feel your weakness, our good Jesus is providing you the opportunity to save a greater number of souls for Him!"

31.

"I asked her if Our Lord was not unhappy with me when he saw how wretched I was," wrote a Sister. "She replied:"

Be reassured that the One that you have taken for your Bridegroom has all the desirable perfections. But, if I dare say so, at the same time He has a great infirmity: *It's to be blind!* And there is one area of knowledge that He does not know: *It's how to count.* These two great defects, which would be extremely regrettable gaps in a mortal bridegroom, make ours infinitely worthy of love.

If He had to see clearly and if He knew how to count, do you believe that in the presence of all our sins He wouldn't cause us to be reduced to nothingness? No, His love for us makes Him positively blind!

See, rather: If the greatest sinner on earth, repenting of his offenses at the moment of his death, expires in an act of love, immediately, without adding up on one hand the many graces that the wretch abused, and on the other all his crimes, He doesn't see them. He no longer counts anything than his last prayer, and He receives him without delay in the arms of His mercy.

But, in order to make Him blind like that and to prevent Him from making the slightest addition, we have to know how to take Him by the heart; that is His weak side. . . .

32.

"I had given her trouble," wrote a Sister, "and I went to ask her forgiveness. She seemed quite moved, and said,"

"If only you knew what I am experiencing! I have never understood so well with what love Jesus receives us when we ask Him for forgiveness after committing a fault! If I, His poor little creature, have felt so much tenderness for you, at the moment that you came back to me, what must be going on in the heart of the Good Lord when we come back to Him! . . . Yes, certainly, even more quickly than I have just done, He will forget all our iniquities and will never remember them again. . . . He will even do more than that: He will love us even more than before our fault! . . ."

33.

"I was extremely afraid of God's judgments," wrote a Sister, "and, in spite of all that [Thérèse] could tell me, nothing took away that fear. One day I told her this objection: 'We are told over and over that God finds tarnish even in His angels. How do you think that I could not tremble?' She replied:"

"There is only one way to force the Good Lord not to judge us for everything, and that is to present ourselves to Him with empty hands."

"How do we do that?"

"It's quite simple: Don't hold anything back. Give your good deeds up to Him as soon as you do them. As for me, if I live to the age of twenty-four, I will still be as poor; I don't know how to spend sparingly: Everything I have, I spend it immediately to buy souls.

"If I waited till the moment of my death in order to present my little coins and have them appraised for their just value, Our Lord would not fail to discover in them some kind of alloy that I would certainly have to have removed in purgatory.

"Isn't it said that great Saints, when they arrive at God's tribunal with their hands overflowing with merits, sometimes go to that place of expiation, because every good thing is soiled in the eyes of the Lord?"

"But," I replied, "if God doesn't judge our good actions, He will judge our bad ones, and then what?"

"What are you saying? Our Lord is Justice itself. If He doesn't judge our good actions, He won't judge our bad ones. For the sacrificial victims of love, it seems to me that there will be no judgment. Rather, the Good Lord will hurry to repay, with eternal delights, His own love that He will see burning in their hearts."

"In order to enjoy that privilege, do you think that it's sufficient to do the act of offering that you composed?"

"Oh, no! Words are not enough. . . . In order to truly be a sacrificial victim of love, we have to give ourselves over totally. *We are consumed by love only insomuch as we give ourselves over to love.*"

34.

"I was repenting bitterly for a fault that I had committed," wrote a Sister. "She told me:

" 'Take your crucifix and kiss it.'

"I kissed its feet.

" 'Is that how a child kisses its Father? Quick, kiss His face. . . .'

"I obeyed.

" 'That's not all. You have to receive His strokes of affection.'

"And I was obliged to place the crucifix on each of my cheeks. Then she said,

" 'That's good. Now, all is forgiven!' "

35.

"When I'm reproached for something," I told her, "I prefer to have been worthy of it than to be accused wrongly." She replied:

As for me, I prefer to be accused unjustly, because I have nothing to reproach myself for, and I offer that to the Good Lord with joy. Then I humble myself at the thought that I would be quite capable of doing what I'm accused of.

The more you advance, the fewer battles you will have. Or rather, you will conquer them with greater ease, because you will have seen the good side of things. Then your soul will rise above created things. Everything that people can say to me now leaves me absolutely indifferent, because I have understood how little solidity there is in human judgments.

When we are misunderstood and judged unfavorably, what good is it to defend ourselves? Let's set that aside; let's not say anything. How sweet it is to allow ourselves to be judged no matter how! It is not said in the Gospel that Saint Mary Magdalene explained herself when her sister accused her of being at Jesus' feet without doing anything to help her. She didn't say, "Martha! If you only knew the happiness that I'm experiencing, if you only understood the words that I'm hearing, you also would leave everything in order to share my joy and my repose." No, she preferred to keep quiet. . . . O blessed silence that gives such peace to the soul!

36.

"In a moment of temptation and struggle," wrote a Sister, "I received this note from her:"

"The just shall correct me in mercy, and shall reprove me: but let not the oil of the sinner fatten my head" [Ps. 140:5 D-R]. I can be rebuked and corrected only by the righteous, since all my Sisters are pleasing to God. It's less bitter to be rebuked by a sinner than by a righteous person. But, *out of compassion for sinners*, in order to obtain their conversion, I ask You, O God, to be rebuked by the righteous souls who surround me. I ask You further that *the oil of praise*, which is so sweet to human nature, *not fatten my head*, that is, my mind, by making me believe that I possess virtues that I have hardly practiced several times.

O my Jesus! "Your name is like perfume poured out" [Song 1:3]; it is into that divine perfume that I want to plunge myself completely, far from the gaze of created beings.

37.

Thérèse said: "To want to persuade our Sisters that they are in the wrong, even when it's perfectly true, is not waging a good war, since we are not responsible for their behavior. We must not be *judges of peace*, but rather *angels of peace*."

38.

"You give yourselves over too much to what you are doing," she used to say to us. "You torment yourselves too much with your work, as if you alone were responsible for it. Are you thinking, right now, about what is happening in the other Carmels? Whether the nuns there are in a hurry or not? Does their work prevent you from praying, from saying prayers? Well, you must exile yourself even from your personal needs, and spend conscientiously the time you are assigned, but with detachment of heart.

"I've read that in the olden days the Israelites built the walls of Jerusalem, working with one hand and holding a sword in the other [Neh. 4:17]. This is just the image of what we ought to do: Work with only one hand, as it were, and with the other defend our souls from the self-indulgence that prevents them from uniting with the Good Lord."

39.

"One Sunday," Thérèse described, "I was walking quite joyfully along the chestnut tree lane. It was spring, and I wanted to enjoy the beauties of nature. What a pity! What a cruel disappointment! My beloved chestnut trees had been pruned. The branches, already laden with green-colored buds, were there, lying on the ground! When I saw that disaster and thought that I would have to wait three more years before seeing it repaired, my heart was broken. However, my anguish lasted only a short while: *If I were in another convent*, I thought, *what would it matter to me if the chestnut trees at the Carmel of Lisieux were entirely cut down?* I no longer want to be troubled about passing things. My Beloved will occupy the place of everything else. I want to walk unceasingly in the groves of His love, which no one can touch."

40.

A novice asked several Sisters to help her shake out some blankets, and was urging the Sisters a bit strongly to be careful not to rip them because they were somewhat worn. Sister Thérèse of the Child Jesus said this:

Lane of Chestnut Trees in the Garden of the Carmel of Lisieux

The little wheelchair, after having served the father
of Sister Thérèse of the Child Jesus, was given to the Carmel.
It was in this wheelchair that the Servant of God,
now suffering from illness, wrote, in this very spot,
the last pages of *The Story of a Soul*.

"What would you do if you hadn't been given the responsibility of mending these blankets? With what freedom of mind would you be acting! And, if you called attention to the fact that they're easy to rip, with what lack of self-interest would you say this! In the same way, in all your actions never let the slightest shadow of personal interest slip in."

41.

"Seeing that one of our Sisters was quite tired," wrote a Sister, "I said to Sister Thérèse of the Child Jesus, 'I don't like to see people suffer, especially holy souls.' Immediately, she answered:"

"Oh, I'm not like you. Holy persons who suffer never make me feel sorry for them! I know that they have the strength to endure their sufferings, and that in this way they give great glory to God. But those who are not holy, who don't know how to profit from their sufferings, oh! How I feel sorry for them! I pity them! I would use every possible means to comfort and relieve them."

42.

Thérèse said: "If I were to live longer, the duty of nurse would be the one I would like more. I would not like to ask for it, but if it came directly to me out of obedience, I would think of myself as being quite privileged. It seems to me that I would fulfill it with a tender love, always thinking about what Our Lord said, 'I was sick and you looked after me' [Mt. 25:36]. The bell of the infirmary [rung by a patient] ought to be for you a heavenly melody. You ought to pass on purpose by the windows of the sick, in order to make it easy for them to call you and to ask you for assistance. Shouldn't you consider yourself to be like a little slave that everyone has the right to order around? If only you saw the Angels who, from heaven above, are watching you fight in the arena! They are awaiting the end of the battle in order to cover you with flowers and crowns. You know quite well that we claim to be *little martyrs*: It's up to us to win our victory palms!

"The Good Lord doesn't despise these battles that are unknown and therefore much more worthy. 'Better a patient person than a warrior, those with self-control than those who take a city' [Prov. 16:32].

"By our little acts of charity practiced in obscurity, we convert souls from afar, we help the missionaries, we attract abundant alms to them; and, in that way we build true spiritual and material dwellings for Jesus-in-the-Host."

43.

"I had seen our Prioress speaking preferentially to one of our Sisters and showing her, it seemed to me, more trust and affection than she showed toward me," wrote a Sister. "I was telling my troubles to Sister Thérèse of the Child Jesus, thinking that I would receive sympathetic condolences, when to my great surprise she said to me,"

"Do you think that you love our Prioress a great deal?"

"Certainly! If I didn't love her, it wouldn't matter to me to see her prefer others to me."

"Well, I'm going to prove to you that you are absolutely wrong: It's not our Prioress that you love—it's yourself.

"When we really love, we rejoice in the happiness of the person we love; we make every sacrifice to bring happiness to them. Therefore, if you had that true and disinterested love, if you loved our Prioress for herself, you would rejoice to see her finding pleasure at your expense. And, since you think that she has less satisfaction in talking with you than with someone else, you ought not to be troubled when you find yourself forsaken."

44.

"I was quite upset about my numerous distractions in my prayers," a Sister wrote.

"I also have many of them," Thérèse told me, "but immediately when I become aware of them, I pray for the persons who occupy my imagination, and in that way they benefit from my distractions.

"...I accept everything for the love of the Good Lord, even the most extravagant thoughts that come to my mind."

45.

"Someone asked me for a pin that was very comfortable for me, and I missed it," a Sister wrote. "Then she told me,"

"Oh, how rich you are! You cannot be happy!"

46.

"Being in charge of decorating the Child Jesus statue, and knowing that certain scents bothered one of our nuns, she always deprived herself of placing scented flowers in it, even a little violet, which was a matter of real sacrifice.

"One day when she had just placed a beautiful artificial rose at the foot of the statue, our good Prioress called for her. Sister Thérèse of the Child Jesus, guessing correctly that it was to have her remove the rose, and not wanting to humiliate her, took the flower and, forestalling any reflection, she said,

" 'You see, Mother, how they imitate nature nowadays. Wouldn't you say that this rose had just been picked from the garden?' "

47.

One day she said, "There are moments when we're so uncomfortable *within ourselves*, inside, that we must hurry to get out of ourselves. The Good Lord does not oblige us to remain in our own company then. Often He even allows us to be disagreeable and unpleasant, so that we will leave our own company. And I don't see any other means of leaving *our inner selves* than to visit Jesus and Mary, by running to do acts of charity."

48.

Thérèse said, "The principal plenary indulgence is the one that everybody can earn without the ordinary conditions, namely the indulgence of *love that covers over all wrongs* [Prov. 10:12]."

49.

"What does me good," said Thérèse, "when I picture the interior of the Holy Family, is to think about a quite ordinary life.

"The Holy Virgin and Saint Joseph knew quite well that Jesus was God, but great mysteries nevertheless remained hidden from them, and, like us, they lived by faith. Haven't you noticed that word from the sacred text, 'They did not understand what he was saying to them' [Lk. 2:50], and that other one that is no less mysterious, 'The child's father and mother marveled at what was said about him' [Lk. 2:33]? Wouldn't you think that they were learning something? Because that admiration supposes a certain amazement."

50.

"At Sext [the noon office]," said Thérèse, "there is a verse that I pronounce every day reluctantly. It's this: *Inclinavi cor meum ad faciendas justificationes tuas in æternum, propter retributionem* ["I have inclined my heart toward doing Your righteous deeds for ever, because of the reward," based on Ps. 119:11 in the Vulgate].

"Inwardly I hasten to say, 'O my Jesus, You know well that it is not for a reward that I serve You, but only because I love You and in order to save souls.' "

51.

"Only in heaven," said Thérèse, "will we see the absolute truth in all things. On the earth, even in the holy Scriptures, that is the obscure and mysterious side. I'm upset at seeing the differences among translations. If I had been a priest, I would have learned Hebrew in order to be able to read the word of God as He deigned to express it in human speech."

52.

"She often would speak to me," wrote a Sister, "about a well-known game with which she used to amuse herself during her childhood. It was a kaleidoscope, a sort of telescope at the far end of which can be seen pretty designs of various colors; if the instrument is turned, these designs vary infinitely. She told me,"

This object excited my admiration. I wondered what could produce such a charming phenomenon. One day, after a serious examination, I saw that it was simply a few bits of paper and wool tossed here and there, and cut up at random. I pursued my research and I caught sight of three lenses in the interior of the tube. I had the key to the problem.

This was for me the image of a great mystery: As long as our actions, even the smallest ones, do not leave the focus of love, the Holy Trinity—figured by those three lenses—gives them an admirable reflection and beauty. Jesus, looking at us through the little viewing lens, that is, as it were through Himself, finds our proceedings to be always beautiful. But, if we leave the indescribable center of love, what will He see? Bits of straw . . . actions that are soiled and of no value.

53.

"One day," wrote a Sister, "I was telling Sister Thérèse of the Child Jesus about the strange phenomena produced by mesmerism on persons who are willing to give their will over to the mesmerizer. Those details seemed to interest her greatly, and the next day she told me,"

"Your conversation of yesterday did me good! *Oh! How I would like to be mesmerized by Our Lord!* That's the first thought that came to me when I woke up. With what sweet gentleness I have given Him my will! Yes, I want Him to take possession of my faculties, in such a way that I will no longer do human and personal actions, but rather actions that are wholly divine, inspired and directed by the Spirit of love."

54.

"Before my profession," wrote a Sister, "I received a very personal grace through my saintly Novice Mistress. We had been cleaning the whole day, and I was overcome with fatigue, burdened down by inner troubles. That evening, before the time of prayer, I wanted to say a few words to her about this, but she replied,"

"The bell is ringing for the time of prayer; I don't have time to comfort you. Besides, I see clearly that I would be taking useless trouble to do that: The Good Lord wants you to suffer alone for the moment."

"I followed her to the prayer time, in such a state of discouragement that, for the first time, I doubted my vocation. *Never will I have the strength to be a Carmelite*, I said to myself. *This life is too hard for me!*

"I had been on my knees for a few minutes, in this struggle and in these sad thoughts, when suddenly, without having prayed, without even having desired peace, I felt in my soul a sudden, extraordinary change; I no longer recognized myself. My vocation seemed beautiful, pleasant to me; I saw its charms, the price of suffering. All the deprivations and fatigues of the religious life seemed to me to be infinitely preferable to the satisfactions of the world. In the end, I left the time of prayer absolutely transformed.

"The next day, I recounted to Sister Thérèse of the Child Jesus what had happened the evening before; and since she seemed quite moved by this, I wanted to know the cause.

" 'Oh, how good God is!' she told me then. 'Last night, you were causing me to have such deep sympathy for you that I didn't stop, at the beginning of the prayers, to pray for you, asking Our Lord to comfort you, to change your soul and to show you the price of suffering. He granted my request!' "

55.

"Since I am a child in character," wrote a Sister, "the little Jesus inspired in me, in order to help me practice virtue, *to play a game with Him*. I chose the game of *ninepins*. I imagined them in all sizes and all colors, in order to personify the souls that I wanted to reach. The bowling ball was *my love*.

"In December 1896, the novices received, for the benefit of the missions, different trinkets for a Christmas tree. And so it was that, by chance, in the bottom of the enchanting box there was an object that was quite rare at Carmel: *a top*. My companions said, 'That's so ugly! What good could that be?' I, who knew the game very well, snatched up the top, shouting, 'But it's a lot of fun! It could go a whole day without stopping, as long as you hit it right with a whip!' And then and there I took upon myself the duty of giving them a representation that completely amazed them.

"Sister Thérèse of the Child Jesus observed me without saying anything, and, on Christmas Day, after the Midnight Mass, I found in our cell *the wonderful top* with this little letter whose envelope bore as address:"

To my little beloved spouse,
THE ONE WHO PLAYS NINEPINS *on the Mountain of Carmel*

Christmas Night 1896

MY LITTLE BELOVED SPOUSE,

Oh! How happy I am with you! The whole year long you have amused me so much *by playing ninepins.* I've had so much pleasure that the Angels' court was surprised and charmed by this. Several little cherubim asked me why I hadn't made them into children. Others wanted to know if the melody of their instruments wasn't more pleasing to me than your joyful laugh, when you made *a pin* fall down with your *ball of love.* I replied to them all that they mustn't be upset at not being children, since one day they would be able to play with you on the meadows of heaven. I told them that, certainly, your smile was sweeter to me than their melodies, because you could play and smile only by suffering and forgetting yourself.

My little beloved spouse, I have something to ask of you in turn. Are you going to refuse me? . . . Oh! No, you love me too much for that. Well, I would like to change games: *Ninepins are great fun for me, but now I would like to play "top."* And, if you are willing, you will be my top. I'm giving you one as a model; you see that it doesn't have any outward charms. Anyone who doesn't know how to use it will kick it away. But a child who catches sight of it will jump for joy and will say, "Oh! that's so much fun! It can go the whole day long without stopping!"

I, the little Jesus, I love you, although you are without charm, and I beg you to always spin to amuse me. But, to make the top spin, it needs *to be hit with a whip*! Well, let your Sisters render this service to you, and be grateful to those who are the most persistent at making you spin faster. . . . Once I have had great fun with you, I will take you on high and we will be able to play without suffering.

Your little brother,
JESUS

56.

"I was in the habit of crying continually and over nothing, something that caused her great grief," wrote a Sister about Thérèse.

"One day, a brilliant idea came to her: Taking a mussel shell off her painting table, and holding my hands to oblige me not to wipe my eyes, she began gathering my tears into that shell. Instead of continuing to cry, I couldn't stop myself from laughing.

" 'All right,' she told me, 'from now on I will allow you to cry as much as you want, as long as it's into the shell.'

"Now, a week before her death, I had cried all evening long at the thought of her impending departure. She noticed this and said to me,

" 'You've been crying. *Was it into the shell?*'

"I couldn't lie . . . and my confession made her sad. She began again:

" 'I'm going to die, and I'm not going to be free of agitation on your behalf if you don't promise me faithfully to follow my recommendation. I'm attaching the utmost importance to this for your soul.'

"I gave my word, asking nonetheless, as a grace, for permission to cry freely at her death.

" 'Why cry at my death? Now, those are useless tears. You'll be crying over my happiness! All right, I have pity for your weakness and I'll allow you to cry for the first days. But after that, you have to go back to the shell.'

"I have to say that I was faithful to this, although it cost me heroic efforts.

"When I wanted to cry, I armed myself courageously with this pitiless instrument. But, however pains I took, the care that it required to move the shell from one eye to the other distracted my thoughts from the subject of my troubles, and that ingenious means wasn't long in curing me entirely from my all-too-great sensitiveness."

57.

"I wanted to deprive myself of holy Communion," wrote a Sister, "for an unfaithfulness that had caused her much grief, but for which I bitterly repented. I wrote her of my resolve, and here is the note that she sent me:"

"Beloved little flower of Jesus, it's quite enough that, for the humbling of your soul, *your roots should eat the dirt*. . . . You must open up, or rather, raise your petals, so that the Bread of Angels may come, like a divine dew, to strengthen you and give you all that you are lacking.

"Good night, poor little flower, ask Jesus that all the prayers that are made for my healing may serve to increase the fire that must consume me."

58.

"At the moment of receiving Communion," said Thérèse, "I sometimes imagine my soul in the form of a little baby of three or four years old who, because of its playing, has its hair and its clothing all dirty and disordered—those misfortunes have happened to me while battling with souls—but soon the Virgin Mary hastens around me. She has quickly undertaken to remove *my very soiled apron*, to comb my hair, and to adorn it with a pretty ribbon or simply a little flower . . . and that's enough to make me graceful and to cause me to sit without embarrassment at the Angels' banquet."

59.

"In the infirmary, we had hardly waited for her prayers of thanksgiving to be completed in order to talk with her and ask her advice. She was sad about this at first, and reproached us gently for it. Then soon she allowed us to continue, saying,

" 'I thought that I shouldn't desire more rest than Our Lord. When He withdrew into the desert after His preaching, the people came immediately to trouble His solitude. Approach me as much as you want. I must die with my weapons in my hands, having in my mouth "the sword of the Spirit, which is the word of God" [Eph. 6:17].' "

60.

"Give us some advice for our spiritual directions," some Sisters asked. "How must we do them?"

"With great simplicity, without counting too much on help that you may lack at first. You will be quickly forced to say with the bride in the Song of Songs, 'The watchmen took away my cloak, they bruised me; and it was only by PASSING them a little that I found the One my heart loves!' [see Song 5:7, 3:4]. If you ask humbly and unslavishly where your Beloved is, *the watchmen* will show it to you. Nonetheless, the most often, you will find Jesus only after having *passed by* every created being. How many times, for my part, have I not repeated this stanza of the spiritual Canticle [of Saint John of the Cross]:

From now on
Do not send me messengers
Who do not know how to tell me what I want.
. . . .
All those who concern themselves with You, without exception,
Talk to me continually about Your myriad graces
And all of them wound me still more;
And above all what makes me die
IS AN I-DON'T-KNOW-WHAT THAT ALL THEY DO IS STAMMER OUT.

61.

"If, though it's impossible, the Good Lord Himself didn't see my good actions," said Thérèse, "that wouldn't bother me. I love Him so much that I would like to be able to bring Him pleasure, without His knowing that it's I who am doing it. Knowing what I do and seeing it, He is as it were obliged to repay it to me . . . I would not like to give Him that trouble."

62.

"If I had been rich," said Thérèse, "I wouldn't have been able to see a poor person going hungry without giving him something to eat. I do the same thing in my spiritual life: As I gain something, I know that some souls are on the point of falling into hell. Then I give them my treasures and I have not yet found a moment to tell myself, 'Now I'm going to work for myself.' "

63.

"There are some people who take everything," Thérèse said, "in such a way that they bring themselves the most grief. For me it's the opposite: I always see the good side of things. If I have only pure suffering, without any enlightenment, well, all right, I make this into my joy."

64.

"I have always liked what the Good Lord has given me," said Thérèse, "even the things that seem to me to be less good and less beautiful than those that belong to others."

65.

"When I was very little," said Thérèse, "when I was at my aunt's house someone put a beautiful book into my hands. As I was reading a story, I saw that people highly praised a boarding house owner because she knew how to cleverly extricate herself from a difficult situation without causing hurt to anyone. I especially noticed this sentence: 'She said to this one, "You aren't wrong," and to that one, "You're right." ' And as I was reading along, I was thinking, 'Oh, I wouldn't have done that; one must always tell the truth.'

"And now I always tell the truth. I have more grief, it's true, because it would be so easy, when someone comes to tell you about a problem, to place the wrong on those who are absent; soon the one who is complaining would be appeased. Yes, but . . . I do exactly the opposite. If I'm not loved, too bad! People shouldn't come find me if they don't want to know the truth.

"For a reprimand to bear fruit, it has to cost to give it. And it must be given without any shadow of passion in the heart.

"Goodness must not degenerate into weakness. When we have rightly scolded someone, we have to stop there and not let ourselves be moved to pity to the point of becoming tormented for having caused someone grief. To run after the afflicted one in order to comfort her is to do her more harm than good. To leave her to herself is to force her to expect nothing from the human side, to have recourse to the Good Lord, to see her wrongs, to humble herself. Otherwise she would become accustomed to being consoled after a reproach that she deserved, and she would act like a spoiled child who stomps her feet and shouts, knowing quite well that she will make her mother come back to dry her tears.

" 'Let the sword of the spirit, which is the word of God, dwell perpetually in your mouth and in your hearts' [see Eph. 6:17]. If we find a disagreeable soul, let's not be disgusted or lose heart or abandon it. Let's always have *the sword of the spirit* in order to point out her faults. Let's not let things go along in order to preserve the peace. Let's fight without stopping, even when there is no hope of winning the battle. What does success matter! Let's keep on going, no matter how tiring the struggle may be. Let's not say, 'I'm not going to obtain anything from that soul; she doesn't understand; let's give up on her!' Oh, that would be despicable slackness! We have to do our duty right to the end."

66.

"It used to be," said Thérèse, "that if someone in my family were having trouble, and in the parlor I hadn't been able to succeed at bringing that one comfort, I would go away heartbroken. But soon, Jesus gave me to understand that I was incapable of comforting a soul. From that day on, I was no longer troubled when someone went away sad: I turned over to the Good Lord the sufferings of those who were dear to me, and I knew that my prayers had indeed been answered. Since that experience, when I have involuntarily been the cause of grief, I haven't tormented myself: I simply ask Jesus to repair what I've done."

67.

"What do you think about all the graces with which you have been flooded?" asked a Sister. Thérèse replied,

"I think that 'The wind blows wherever it pleases' [Jn. 3:8]."

68.

Thérèse said to her Prioress:

"Mother, if I were unfaithful, if I committed only the slightest unfaithfulness, I feel that it would be followed by the most frightful troubles, and I would no longer be able to accept death."

And since the Prioress showed her surprise at hearing her speak that way, she continued:

I'm talking about an unfaithfulness of pride. For example, if I said, "I have acquired such or such a virtue, so I can practice it"; or, "Dear God, I love You too much, You know it well, to stop with a single thought against the faith"; immediately, I feel it, I would be assailed by the most dangerous temptations, and I would certainly succumb to them.

To avoid that disaster, all I have to do is humbly say from the bottom of my heart, "Dear God, please, do not allow me to be unfaithful!"

I understand quite well how Saint Peter fell. He counted too much on the strength of his feelings instead of leaning solely on divine strength. I'm quite sure that if he had said to Jesus, "Lord, give me the courage to follow You all the way to death," that courage would not have been refused him.

Mother, how is it that Our Lord, knowing what was going to happen, did not say to Him, "Give me the strength to accomplish what You desire"? I believe that it is to show us two things: The first is that He taught no-thing to His apostles by His physical presence than He teaches us through the good inspirations of His grace. The second is that, destining Saint Peter to govern the whole church in which there are so many sinners, He wanted him to experience for himself what humanity is capable of without God's help. It's for that reason that, before Peter's fall, Jesus told him, "When you have turned back, strengthen your brothers" [Lk. 22:32]; in other words, tell them the story of your sin; show them by your own experience how much it is necessary, for salvation, to lean only on Me.

69.

"I was very grieved to see her sick," wrote a Sister, "and I often used to repeat to her, 'Oh, how sad life is!' But she scolded me immediately, saying,

" 'Life isn't sad! On the contrary, it's quite exciting. If you were to say, "Exile is sad," I would understand you. People are mistaken when they give the name of *life* to what is going to end. It is only to the things of heaven, to what is never going to die, that we ought to give that beautiful name. And, since we enjoy it already in this world, life isn't sad, but keenly exuberant, and happily exciting!'

"She was herself full of wonderful exuberance: For several days she had been feeling much better, and we said to her, 'We don't yet know the sickness that you're going to die from.'

" 'But I will die *of death*! Didn't the Good Lord tell Adam what he would die from? He told him, "You will die the death!" [Gen. 2:17 D-R].'

" 'Well, so it's death that will come looking for you!'

" 'No, it's not death that will come looking for me, it's the Good Lord. Death isn't a ghost, a horrible specter as it's represented in pictures. It's written in the catechism that *death is the separation of the soul from the body*, and that's all it is! Well, I'm not afraid of a separation that will reunite me forever to God.'

" 'Will *the divine Thief* come soon to steal away His little grape cluster?'

" 'I perceive Him from afar and I take great care not to shout, "Stop, thief!" On the contrary, I call out to Him, saying, "Over here! Over here!" ' "

70.

"I was telling her," wrote a Sister, "that the beautiful Angels, dressed in white robes, their faces joyful and resplendent, would carry her soul up to heaven. She replied,"

"All those images don't do me any good. I can feed only on the truth. God and the Angels are pure spirits; no one can see them with the eyes of the body as they are in reality. That's why I have never desired extraordinary graces. I prefer to await the eternal vision."

The Sister replied, "I've asked God to send me a beautiful dream to comfort me after your departure."

"Oh, that's something that I would never have done! To ask for consolations! . . . Since you want to be like me, you know quite well that I say:

Oh, don't be afraid, Lord, that I will wake You up:
I'm waiting peacefully for the shore of heaven. . . .

"It's so sweet to serve the Good Lord in the night and in the midst of trials. We only have this life to live by faith."

71.

"I'm quite happy to go away to heaven," said Thérèse, "but when I think about this word of the Lord, 'Look, I am coming soon! My reward is with me, and I will give to everyone according to what they have done,' I tell myself that He will be quite perplexed for me: I don't have any works. . . . Well! He will give to me ACCORDING TO HIS OWN WORKS!"

72.

"Certainly," a Sister said to Thérèse, "you won't spend a single minute in purgatory, or no one is ever going to go straight to heaven!"

"Oh," replied, Thérèse, "I'm hardly concerned about that; I'll always be happy with the Good Lord's decision. If I go to purgatory, well, I'll walk in the midst of the flames, like the three Hebrews in the fiery furnace [Dan. 3:8–29], singing the song of love."

73.

"You'll be placed in heaven among the seraphim," said a Sister.

"If that's the way it will be, I won't imitate them. *They will all cover their wings* at the sight of God; *I'll take great care not to cover my wings!*"

74.

"I was showing her a photograph representing Joan of Arc being comforted in prison by her voices [the voices of Saints and Angels that only Joan of Arc could hear]. She told me,

" 'I am also comforted by an interior voice. From on high, the Saints are encouraging me; they tell me, "As long as you are in chains, you cannot fulfill your mission; but later, after your death, that will be the time of your conquests." ' "

75.

"The Good Lord will do all that is my will in heaven," said Thérèse, "because I have never done my will on earth."

76.

People were asking her what name they should use to pray to her once she was in heaven.

"You will call me *little Thérèse*," she replied humbly.

77.

"You'll be watching us from above in heaven, won't you?" asked a Sister.

"No," she replied, "*I will come down.*"

78.

Let us once again tell this touching story:

A few months before the death of Sister Thérèse of the Child Jesus, we were reading in the refectory about the life of Saint Louis de Gonzague, and one of our good nuns was struck by the touching and reciprocal affection between the young saint and a venerable religious of the Society of Jesus, Father Corbinelli.

"You are little Louis," said this nun to our saintly little Thérèse, "and I am the old Father Corbinelli. When you are in heaven, remember me."

"Would you like, Mother, for me to come soon to get you?"

"No, I haven't suffered enough yet."

"Oh, Mother, I tell you myself that you really have suffered enough."

And Mother Hermance of the Heart of Jesus replied:

"I don't dare say yes to you yet.... For such a serious matter, I need the sanction of authority."

In fact, the request was addressed to the Prioress; and, without attaching any importance to it, she gave an affirmative response.

Now, on one of the last days of her life, Sister Thérèse of the Child Jesus, who was hardly able to speak because of her great weakness, received, at the hands of the nurse, a bouquet of flowers picked by our dear Mother Hermance of the Heart of Jesus, with the urgent request of Thérèse to give her subsequently, by way of thanks, a single word of affection. And here is the word that Thérèse gave:

"Tell Mother Heart of Jesus that this morning, during Mass, I saw the grave of Father Corbinelli very near the grave of the little Louis."

"Very well," replied the good nun, quite moved. "Tell Sister Thérèse of the Child Jesus that I have understood...."

From that moment on, she remained persuaded of her imminent death, which in fact occurred one year later.

And, following the prediction of *the little Louis, the grave of Father Corbinelli was found quite near hers.*

I'm strongly counting on not remaining inactive in heaven.
My desire is to still work for the Church and for souls. I'm asking God for
this, and I'm certain that He will grant my prayer.

PART
THREE
Prayers

1

ACT OF OFFERING OF MYSELF AS A SACRIFICIAL VICTIM TO THE MERCIFUL LOVE OF THE GOOD GOD

This prayer was found, after the death of Sister Thérèse of the Child Jesus, in the book of the holy Gospels that she carried day and night on her heart.

O God, blessed Trinity, I desire to love You and to make You loved, to work for the glorification of the holy Church, by saving souls that are on earth and by delivering those that suffer in Purgatory. I desire to accomplish perfectly Your will and arrive at the degree of glory that You have prepared for me in Your kingdom. In a word, I desire to be holy, but I feel my powerlessness and my inability, and I ask You, O God, to be my holiness Yourself.

Since You have loved me to the point of giving me Your only Son to be my Savior and my Bridegroom, the infinite treasures of His merits are mine. I offer them to You with happiness, imploring You to look on me only through the Face of Jesus and in His Heart that is burning with love.

I offer You still more all the merits of the Saints who are in heaven and on the earth, their acts of love and those of the holy Angels. Finally, I offer You, O blessed Trinity, the love and the merits of the holy Virgin, my beloved Mother. It is to her that I abandon my offering, asking her in prayer to present it to You.

Her divine Son, my beloved Spouse, during the days of His mortal life, told us, "My Father will give you whatever you ask in my name" [Jn. 16:23]. I am therefore certain that You will grant my desires. . . . I know, O God, that *the more You want to give, the more You make us desire Your gifts.*

I feel within my heart immense desires, and it is with confidence and trust that I ask You to come and take possession of my soul. Oh, I cannot receive holy Communion as often as I desire it; but, Lord, are You not All-powerful? Remain in me as in the Tabernacle; never withdraw from your little Communion host.

I would like to comfort You for the ingratitude of the wicked, and I implore You to take away from me the freedom to displease You. If through weakness I sometimes fall, may Your divine gaze immediately purify my soul, consuming all my imperfections, like the fire that transforms all things into itself.

I thank You, O God, for all the graces that You have granted to me: in particular for having made me pass through the crucible of suffering. It is with joy that I will contemplate You at the Last Day, bearing the scepter of the cross. Since You have deigned to give me to share in that most precious cross, I hope in heaven to look like You, and to see shining on my glorified body the sacred stigmata of Your passion.

After the exile of earth, I hope to go on to enjoy You in the Homeland. But I do not want to collect for myself merits for heaven; I want to work for Your love alone, to the sole end of pleasing You, of comforting Your sacred Heart, and of saving souls who will love You forever.

On the evening of this life, I will appear before You with empty hands. For I do not ask You, Lord, to take my words into account. . . . All our righteous acts are like filthy rags [Is. 64:6]! Therefore I want to clothe myself with Your own Righteousness, and to receive from Your love the eternal possession of Yourself. I want no other throne and no other crown than You, O my Beloved.

In Your eyes, time is nothing; *a thousand years in your sight are like a day that has just gone by* [Ps. 90:4]. Therefore You can in an instant prepare me to appear before You.

In order to live in an act of perfect love, I OFFER MYSELF AS A SACRIFICIAL VICTIM TO YOUR MERCIFUL LOVE, entreating You to consume me without ceasing, letting overflow in my soul the waves of infinite tenderness that are enclosed in You, and in this way may I become a martyr of Your love, O God!

May this martyrdom, after having prepared me to appear before You, make me die at last, and may my soul rush forward without delay into the eternal embrace of Your merciful love!

I desire, O my Beloved, at each beat of my heart, to renew this offering an infinite number of times, until, *the shadows having fled* [Song 4:6], I may keep repeating to You my love in an eternal face-to-face!!!

MARIE-FRANÇOISE-THÉRÈSE OF THE CHILD JESUS
AND OF THE HOLY FACE

Discalced Carmelite Nun

Feast of the Most Holy Trinity, June 9th,
of the year of grace 1895

⮑ 2
CONSECRATION TO THE HOLY FACE
(Composed for the Novitiate)

O adorable Face of Jesus! Since You have deigned to choose particularly our souls in order to give Yourself to them, we come to consecrate them to You.

It seems to us, O Jesus, that we hear You saying to us, "*Open to me, my sisters, my darlings, my doves, my flawless ones. My head is drenched with dew, my hair with the dampness of the night*" [Song 5:2]. Our souls understand Your language of love; we will and desire to wipe Your sweet Face and comfort You for the forgetfulness of the wicked. In their eyes, You are still *as it were hidden . . . they consider you as an object of scorn!* [see Is. 53:3].

O Countenance more beautiful than the lilies and the roses of springtime, You are not hidden to our eyes! The tears that veil Your divine gaze appear to us like precious diamonds that we want to gather up, in order to buy, with their infinite value, the souls of our brothers and sisters.

From Your mouth that we adore, we have heard the loving groan. Understanding that the thirst that consumes You is a thirst for love, we would like, in order to quench Your thirst, to possess an infinite love!

Beloved Bridegroom of our souls! If we had the love of every heart, that love would be Yours. . . . So then, give us that love, and come to quench Your thirst in Your little brides.

Souls, Lord, we need souls! Especially the souls of apostles and martyrs; so that, through them, we may set aflame with Your love the multitude of poor sinners.

O adorable Face, we will know how to obtain this grace from You! Forgetting our exile, *by the rivers of Babylon,* we will sing in Your ears the sweetest melodies. Since You are the true, the only Homeland of our souls, *our songs will not be sung while in a foreign land* [see Ps. 137:4].

O dearest Face of Jesus! While awaiting the eternal day when we will contemplate Your infinite glory, our only desire is to charm Your divine eyes, while also hiding our face, so that here below no one may be able to recognize You. . . . Your veiled gaze—there is our heaven, O Jesus!

3
CONSECRATION TO THE DIVINE BRIDEGROOM
(Composed for the Making of Her Vows)

O Jesus, my divine Bridegroom, make it so that my baptismal robe will never be soiled! Take me, rather than leave me here below to soil my soul by committing the slightest voluntary fault. May I never seek and never find anything but You alone! May all created beings be nothing for me, and I, nothing for them! May none of the things of the earth trouble my peace.

O Jesus, I ask You only for peace! . . . Peace, and above all LOVE that knows no boundaries, no limits! Jesus! For You may I die a martyr: Give me the martyrdom of the heart or that of the body. No, rather, give me both of them!

Make it so that I will fulfill my promises in all their perfection. Let no one be troubled for me, let me be trodden under foot, forgotten like a little grain of sand. I offer myself to You, my Beloved, so that You may accomplish perfectly in me Your holy will, without created beings ever being able to place any obstacle before this.

⮑ 4
VARIOUS PRAYERS
OF THÉRÈSE OF LISIEUX

PRAYERS FOR SOULS

Whatever you ask in my name the Father will give you.
—John 15:16

Eternal Father, Your only Son, the sweet Child Jesus, is mine, since You have given Him to me. I offer You the infinite merits of His divine Childhood, and I ask You, in His Name, to call to the joys of heaven innumerable hosts of little children who will eternally follow this divine Lamb.

> *Just as, in a kingdom, one procures all that one desires with the effigy of the prince, in the same way, with the precious coin of My holy humanity, which is My adorable Face, you will obtain all that you will desire.*
> —Our Lord to Sr. Marie of St. Peter

Eternal Father, since You have given me as my heritage the adorable Face of Your divine Son, I offer it to You and I ask You, in exchange for that infinitely precious Coin, to forget the ingratitude of the souls who are consecrated to You and to forgive poor sinners.

PRAYER TO THE CHILD JESUS

O little Child Jesus! My only treasure, I abandon myself to Your divine whims. I want no other joy than that of making You smile. Imprint on me Your graces and Your childish virtues, so that on the day of my birth in heaven, the angels and the saints may recognize in Your little bride: THÉRÈSE OF THE CHILD JESUS.

PRAYER TO THE HOLY FACE

O adorable Face of Jesus, the only beauty that delights my heart, deign to imprint in me Your divine likeness, so that You may not look on the soul of Your little bride without contemplating Yourself. O my Beloved, for love of You, I accept not to see here below the sweetness of Your gaze, not to feel the inexpressible kiss of Your mouth; but I implore You to inflame me with Your love, so that it may consume me rapidly and may soon cause to appear before You: THÉRÈSE OF THE CHILD JESUS.

PRAYER INSPIRED BY A PICTURE REPRESENTING THE BLESSED JOAN OF ARC

Lord, God of the hosts of armies, You who told us in your Gospel, *I did not come to bring peace, but a sword* [Mt. 10:34], arm me for the battle. I am burning to fight for Your glory. But, I implore You, strengthen my courage. . . . Then, with the holy king David, I will be able to cry out, *You alone are my shield; you, Lord, teach my hands to fight, and my fingers to war* [see Ps. 143:1 D-R].

O my Beloved! I understand to what combats You have destined me; it is not on the fields of battle that I will fight. . . . I am the prisoner of Your love; I have freely riveted the chain that unites me to You and separates me forever from the world. My sword is LOVE! With it *I will chase the foreigner from the kingdom, I will make You proclaimed King* in souls.

There is no doubt, Lord, that such a weak instrument as I am is not necessary to You. But Joan, your virginal and valorous bride, said it: *We must do battle so that God will give the victory.* O my Jesus, I will therefore do battle for Your love right up to the evening of my life. Since You did not will to enjoy rest on earth, I want to follow Your example; then this promise that issued from Your divine lips will become a reality in me: *Whoever serves me must follow me; and where I am, my servant also will be. My Father will honor the one who serves me* [Jn. 12:26]. To be with You, to be in You, that is my only desire; the assurance that You give me of its becoming a reality helps me to endure exile, while awaiting the radiant day of the eternal face-to-face.

PRAYER TO OBTAIN HUMILITY
(Composed for a Novice)

O Jesus, when You were a traveler on earth, You said, *Learn from me, for I am gentle and humble in heart, and you will find rest for your souls* [Mt. 11:29]. Powerful Monarch of the Heavens, yes, my soul finds rest by seeing You, clothed in the form and nature of a slave, stooping so low as to wash the feet of Your apostles. I then remember these words that You pronounced, in order to teach me to practice humility: *I have set you an example that you should do as I have done for you. Very truly I tell you, servants are not greater than their master. . . . Now that you know these things, you will be blessed if you do them* [Jn. 13:15–17]. Lord, I understand these words that issued from Your gentle and humble Heart. I want to practice them, with the help of Your grace.

I want humbly to bring myself low and submit my will to that of my Sisters, without contradicting them in anything, and without seeking to find out if they have, or not, the right to give me orders. No one, O my Beloved, had that right toward You, and nevertheless You obeyed, not only the Holy Virgin and Saint Joseph, but even those who tortured You and put You to death. Now it is in the Host that I see You carrying the bringing of Yourself down to nothing to its fullest extent. With what humility, O divine King of glory, do You submit Yourself to all Your priests, without making any distinction between those who love You and those who are, alas! lukewarm or cold in Your service. They can advance or retard the time of the holy Sacrifice, and always You are ready to descend from heaven at their call.

O my Beloved, under the veil of the white Host, how gentle and humble in heart You appear to me! To teach me humility, You cannot bring Yourself any lower; therefore I want, in order to respond to Your love, to place myself in the lowest rank, to share Your humiliations, in order to *have a part with You* [Jn. 13:8] in the kingdom of heaven.

I implore You, my divine Jesus, to send me a humiliation each time that I try to raise myself up higher than others.

But, Lord, my weakness is known to You. Each morning I make the resolution to practice humility, and, in the evening, I recognize that yet again I have committed many faults of pride. Seeing that, I am tempted to become discouraged. But, I know it well, discouragement is also pride. Therefore I want, O God, to found and build my hope on You alone: Since You are capable of everything, reach down and cause to be born in my soul the virtue that I desire. In order to obtain this grace from Your infinite mercy, I will repeat often to You:

Jesus, gentle and humble in heart, make my heart like Yours.

PRAYER IN VENERATION
OF THE HOLY FACE OF JESUS
AS SEEN IN THE SHROUD OF TURIN

O Jesus, who in Your cruel Passion became "despised and rejected, a man of suffering," I venerate Your divine Face, on which the beauty and sweetness of divinity shone, now become for me "like the face of a leper"! But under those disfigured features, I recognize Your infinite love, and I am consumed with the desire to love You and to make You loved by all people. The tears that flowed so abundantly from Your eyes appear to me like precious pearls that I want to gather, in order to buy, with their infinite value, the souls of poor sinners.

O Jesus, whose Face is the only beauty that delights my heart, I accept not to see here below the sweetness of Your gaze, not to experience the inexpressible kiss of Your mouth: But I implore You to imprint in me Your divine likeness and to set me aflame with Your love, so that it may consume me rapidly, and that I may soon come to see Your glorious Face in Heaven!

Amen.

(Prayer of the servant of God, Thérèse of the Child Jesus of the Holy Face)

PART
FOUR
Letters

1
LETTERS TO CÉLINE

MAY 8TH, 1888

There are moments when I wonder if it's really true that I'm at Carmel; sometimes I can't believe it! What have I done to the Good Lord to make Him flood me with so many graces?

Already a month since we have been separated! But why should I say "separated"? Even if the ocean were between us, our souls would remain united. However, I know it, you are suffering from not having me, and if I were to listen to myself, I would ask Jesus not to give me any occasions for sadness. But, you see, I don't listen to myself. I would be afraid of being self-centered, wanting the best part for myself, that is, suffering.

You're right, life is often burdensome and bitter. It's hard to begin a day's work, especially when Jesus hides Himself from our love. What is this gentle Friend doing? Does He not see our anguish, the weight that oppresses us? Where is He? Why doesn't He come and comfort us?

Céline, don't be afraid of anything: He's there, quite near us! He's watching us. He's the One who is begging us for this trouble, these tears . . . He needs them for souls, for our soul; He wants to give us such a beautiful reward! Oh, I assure you that it costs Him a great deal to give us bitterness to drink, but He knows that it's the only means of preparing us to *know Him as He knows Himself, to become gods ourselves*! Oh! What a destiny! How great is our soul! Let's rise above what is happening; let's keep ourselves at a distance from the earth. Up higher, the air is so pure! Jesus can hide, but we can tell He's there. . . .

OCTOBER 20TH, 1888

May your powerlessness not cause you any sorrow. When in the morning we don't feel any courage, any strength to practice virtue, that's a grace. That's the moment to *lay the ax to the root of the tree* [Mt. 3:10], counting on Jesus alone. If we fall, everything is restored in an act of love, and Jesus smiles! He helps us without looking as if He's doing so; and the tears that the wicked make Him shed are wiped dry by our poor and weak love. Love can do everything; the most impossible things seem easy and sweet to Him. You know well that Our Lord doesn't look so much at the greatness of our actions, nor even at their difficulty, as He does at the love with which we accomplish them. What do we have to fear?

You would like to become a saint, and you're asking me if that's too much to dare. Céline, I won't tell you not to aim at the angelic holiness of the most privileged souls, but rather to *be perfect, as your heavenly Father is perfect* [Mt. 3:10]. So you see that your dream, that our dreams and our desires are not illusions of the mind, since Jesus Himself has made them *a commandment*.

JANUARY 1889

Jesus is presenting you with the cross, a very heavy cross! And you're afraid of not being able to bear that cross without becoming weak; why? Our Beloved, on the way to Calvary, fell a full three times: Why wouldn't we imitate our Bridegroom?

What a privilege from Jesus! How He loves us to send us such great suffering! Oh, eternity will not be long enough to bless Him for that. He floods us with His favors, just as He used to flood the great Saints with them. So what are His designs of love on our souls? There is a secret that will be unveiled to us only in our Homeland, on the day when *the Lord will wipe every tear from our eyes* [Rev. 22:4].

Now, we have nothing more to hope for on earth; *the cool mornings have passed away* [St. John of the Cross], and only suffering remains for us! Oh, what a fate worthy of envy! The seraphim in heaven are jealous of our happiness.

In recent days I've found this admirable word: *Resignation is still distinct from the will of God; there is the same difference that exists between union and unity: in union there are still two; in unity there is no longer anything but one* [Madame Swetchine].

Oh, yes! Let's be only one with God, even in this world; and for that, let's be more than resigned: Let's embrace our cross with joy.

FEBRUARY 28TH, 1889

My dear little sister,

. . . You're right, it costs a great deal to give to Jesus what He's asking. And what joy it is that it costs so much! What happiness it is to bear our cross *weakly!*

Céline, far from complaining to Our Lord about this cross that He's sending us, I can't understand the infinite love that has brought Him to treat us this way. Our father must be very much loved by God, because he has so much to suffer! What a delight it is to be humiliated with him! Humiliation is the only way that makes Saints, I know. I also know that our trying time is a gold mine to be exploited. I, a little grain of wheat, I want to put myself to work, without courage, without strength. And that powerlessness itself will make the undertaking easier; I want to work out of love. This is martyrdom that's beginning. Together, my dear sister, let's have a go at it; let's offer our sufferings to Jesus to save souls. . . .

MARCH 12TH, 1889

. . . Céline, I need to forget the earth; here below everything tires me out. I find only one joy, that of suffering . . . and this joy that is not felt is above every joy. Life is passing, eternity is advancing; soon we will live on the very life of God. After having drunk from the spring of bitterness, we will find our thirst quenched by the very fountain of all sweetness.

Yes, *the world in its present form is passing away* [1 Cor. 7:31]; soon we will see new heavens. "A more radiant sun will shine with its splendors on ethereal seas and infinite horizons. . . ." We will no longer be prisoners on an earth of exile; everything will have passed away! With our heavenly Bridegroom, we'll row on lakes that have no shores. *By the rivers of Babylon . . . there on the poplars we hung our harps*; but on the day of our deliverance, what harmonies will we not hear! With what joy will we make all the strings of our instruments vibrate! Today, *we will weep when we remember Zion; how can we sing the songs of the LORD in a foreign land?* [see Ps. 137:1–4].

Our refrain is the hymn of suffering. Jesus is presenting us a most bitter chalice. Let's not withhold our lips from it; let's suffer in peace! When we say *peace* we aren't saying *joy*, or at least a joy we can feel. In order to suffer in peace, it's enough to be willing to do all that Our Lord wants.

Let's not believe that we can find love without suffering. Our nature is there, and it's not there for nothing; but what treasures it causes us to acquire! It's our livelihood; it's so precious that Jesus descended to earth on purpose in order to possess it. We would like to suffer generously, grandly; we would like never to fall: such illusion! And what does it matter to me if I fall every instant! In this I feel my weakness, and I find it to be a source of great profit. Dear God, You see what I can do if You don't carry me in Your arms. And if You leave me alone, well! It's because it pleases You to see me *on the ground*; why then should I be troubled by this?

If you want to peacefully undergo the trial of not pleasing yourself, you will give the divine Master a sweet place of retreat. It is true that you will suffer, since you will be at the gate of your home, but don't be afraid: The poorer you will be, the more Jesus will love you. I know that He prefers to see you run into the stones on the road at night, than to walk in full daylight on a road that is spangled with flowers, because those flowers would be able to slow down your progress.

July 14th, 1889

My dear sister,

My soul isn't leaving you. Oh, yes, it's quite hard to live on this earth! But tomorrow, in one hour, we will be at the port! Dear God, what will we see then? What then is that life that will have no end? . . . The Lord will be the soul of our soul. What an unfathomable mystery! *The human eye has not seen the uncreated light, the eye has not heard the incomparable melodies of the heavens, and the heart cannot understand what is reserved for it in the future* [see Isa. 4:4]. And all that will come soon! Yes, soon, if we love Jesus with passion.

It seems to me that the Good Lord doesn't need years to do His work of love in a soul. A ray from His Heart can, in an instant, cause its flower to blossom for eternity. . . . Céline, during the short moments that we have left, let's save souls. I feel that our Bridegroom is asking us for souls, the souls of priests, above all. . . . He is the One who wants me to tell you that.

There's only one thing to do here below: Love Jesus, save souls for Him so that He may be loved. Let's be jealous to find the slightest opportunities to bring Him joy; let's not refuse Him anything. He has such need for love!

We are the lilies that He prefers. He resides in the midst of us, He resides there as King, and He makes us share the honors of His royalty: His divine blood waters our blossoms; and His thorns, by tearing us, allow the perfume of our love to be given out.

October 22nd, 1889

I'm sending you an image of the Holy Face. I find that this divine subject is so perfectly fitting to the true little sister of my soul. . . . Oh! May she be another Veronica! May she wipe away all the blood and tears of Jesus, her only Beloved! May she give Him souls! May she open a way through the midst of the soldiers, that is, the world, to arrive at His side! . . . Oh! may she be happy when she shall see one day, in glory, the worth of that mysterious drink with which she will have quenched the thirst of her heavenly Espoused Husband; when she will see His lips, once parched by a burning thirst, tell her the only and eternal word of Love! the *thank-you* that will have no end. . . .

Until soon, dear *little Veronica.*[1] Tomorrow, no doubt, the Beloved will ask you for a new sacrifice, a new slaking of His thirst. But *Let us also go, that we may die with him* [Jn. 11:16].

July 18th, 1890

I'm sending you a passage from Isaiah that will comfort you. See, this was written such a long time ago! And already the soul of the prophet plunged like ours into the hidden beauties of the divine Face. . . . Centuries ago! Ah! I wonder what time is. Time is only a mirage, a dream. Already God sees us in glory; He enjoys our everlasting bliss. How this thought does good to my soul! I understand then why He lets us suffer. . . .

Well, since our Beloved *has trodden the winepress alone* [Isa. 63:3], to make the wine that He gives us to drink, in turn, let's not refuse to wear the garments spattered with blood. Let's tread for Jesus a new wine that will quench His thirst, and *looking around Him, He'll no longer be able to say that He's alone* [see Isa. 63:5]: We'll be there to come to His aid.

His face was hidden, alas! It still is today; no one understands His tears. . . . *Open to me, my sister, my darling, my dove, my flawless one. My head is drenched with dew, my hair with the dampness of the night* [Song 5:2]. Yes, that is what Jesus says to our soul when He's abandoned, forgotten. . . . To be *forgotten*—it seems to me that this is what still gives Him the most pain.

And our dear father! Ah! My heart is broken. But how can we complain, since Our Lord Himself was considered as *punished by God,*

---

[1] *Veronica* means *true portrait.* It is remarkable that Sr. Thérèse of the Child Jesus should have called her sister Céline by this name, for later, under her inspiration, Céline was to reproduce so faithfully the *true portrait* of Our Lord Jesus Christ, according to the Shroud of Turin. (A photograph of Céline's portrait of the Holy Face is found on page 377).

stricken by Him, and afflicted [Isa. 53:4]? In this great suffering, let's forget ourselves and *let's pray for priests*; let our lives be consecrated to them. The divine Master is making me feel more and more that this is what He wants from the two of us. . . .

SEPTEMBER 23RD, 1890

Oh, Céline, how can I tell you what is happening in my soul? . . . What a wound! But I feel that it is being made by a friendly hand, but a hand that is *divinely jealous*! . . .

Everything was already ready for my wedding [my taking the veil tomorrow]; however, don't you find that something was missing at the celebration? It's true that Jesus had already put many jewels in my basket, but one more was needed, without any doubt, one of incomparable beauty, and that precious diamond, Jesus gave it to me today. . . . Papa won't come tomorrow! Céline, I'll admit it to you, my tears flowed. . . . They're flowing now while I'm writing you—I can hardly hold my pen.

You know how much I wanted to see our dear father again. Well! Now I feel that it's the will of the Good Lord that he won't be at my celebration. He has allowed that simply to test our love. . . . Jesus wants me to be an *orphan*; He wants me to be alone with Him alone, in order to unite Himself more intimately to me. And He also wants to give back to me, in the Homeland, the so legitimate joys that He has refused me while in exile.

Today's test is a difficult suffering to understand: A joy was offered to us, it was possible and natural, we reach out our hands . . . and we cannot grasp that consolation that we have so desired! But it's not a human hand that is doing that, it's Jesus! Céline, understand your Thérèse! And, both of us, let's accept with a good heart the thorn that is presented to us. Tomorrow's celebration will be a celebration of tears for us, but I feel that Jesus will be so comforted!

OCTOBER 14TH, 1890

I understand all that you are suffering; I understand your heartbreak and I share it. Oh, if only I could communicate to you the peace that Jesus put into my soul when I was in the deepest shedding of tears. . . . Take comfort! Everything passes! The life we once had has passed away. Death will pass away as well, and then we will enjoy life, true life, for millions of centuries, forever!

While we're waiting, let's make our hearts into a garden of delights where our sweet Savior can come to rest. . . . There, let's plant only lilies, and then let's sing, with Saint John of the Cross:

> With my face inclined over my Beloved,
> I remained there and forgot myself;
> Everything disappeared for me and I abandoned myself,
> Leaving behind all my anxious cares,
> Lost in the midst of the lilies.

APRIL 26TH, 1891

Three years ago, our souls had not yet been shattered, and happiness smiled on us here below. But Jesus *looked upon us*, and that look became for us an ocean of tears, but also an ocean of graces and love. The Good Lord snatched away the one that we loved with such tenderness. Isn't this so that we might be able to truly say, *Our Father who art in heaven?* How comforting is that divine word! What horizons it opens to our eyes!

My dear Céline, you who used to ask me so many questions when you were little, I wonder how you never asked me this one: "Why did God not create me as an angel?" Well, I'm going to answer you anyway: The Lord wants to have His court here below just as in heaven above. He wants martyr angels, apostle angels; and if He didn't create you as an angel in heaven, it's because He wanted you as an angel on earth, so that you might be able to suffer for His love.

Céline, my dear sister! The shadows soon will flee away, the hard winter frosts will be followed by the rays of the eternal sun. . . . Soon we will be in our native country; soon the joys of our childhood, the Sunday evenings, the intimate outpourings of our hearts—these will be given back to us forever and ever!

AUGUST 15TH, 1892

In order to write you today I'm obliged to steal a few moments from Our Lord. He won't be cross with me for that, because it's about Him that we're going to speak together.

Céline, the vast solitudes, the enchanting horizons that are opening before you, in the beautiful countryside where you live—these things must greatly lift your soul. I don't see all that; I content myself with saying with Saint John of the Cross in his Spiritual Canticle:

> In my Beloved I have the mountains,
> The solitary, wooded valleys. . . .

Recently I was thinking about all that it's possible for me to undertake to save souls. And this simple word from the Gospel shed some light on this for me. Once, Jesus was saying to His disciples, as He was showing them the fields of ripening wheat,

Open your eyes and look at the fields! They are ripe for harvest [Jn. 4:35]. And a little later He said, *The harvest is plentiful but the workers are few. Ask the Lord of the harvest, therefore, to send out workers into his harvest field* [Mt. 9:37–38].

What a mystery! Isn't Jesus all-powerful! Don't created beings belong to the One who created them? *Ask the Lord of the harvest to send out workers* . . . ? Ah, it's because He has for us a love that is so incomprehensible, so delicate, that He doesn't want to do anything without making us partners in it. The Creator of the universe awaits the prayer of a poor little soul in order by it to save a multitude of others, redeemed by that soul at the price of her blood.

Our vocation is not to go and harvest in the fields of the Father of the family. Jesus is not saying to us, "Lower your eyes, harvest the fields"; our mission is even more sublime. Here are the words of the divine Master: "*Open your eyes and look*. . . . See how in heaven there are empty places; it's up to you to fill them. . . . All of you are my Moses praying on the mountain. Ask me for workers and I'll send them. I'm waiting only for a prayer, a sigh from your heart!"

Isn't the apostolate of prayer, so to speak, higher than that of the word? It's up to us to form Gospel workers who will save thousands of souls for whom we will become the mothers. So what do we have to envy in the Lord's priests?

[UNDATED]

Our tenderness as children has changed into a very large union of thoughts and feelings. Jesus drew us both together, because aren't you His already? He has put the world under our feet. Like Zacchaeus, we have climbed into a tree in order to see Him—a mysterious tree that lifts us high above all things. Then we are able to say, *Everything belongs to me, everything is for me: the earth is mine, the heavens are mine, God is mine, and the Mother of my God is mine* [Saint John of the Cross].

Speaking of the holy Virgin, I have to confide in you one of my simplicities: Sometimes I surprise myself saying to her, "Do you know, my dear Mother, that *I'm happier than you*? I have you for my Mother, and *you don't have the holy Virgin to love like I do*! . . . It's true that you are the Mother of Jesus, but you have given Him to me. And He, on the cross, gave you to us as our Mother. So we're richer than you! Once, in your humility, you wished to become the little servant of the Mother of God. And I, a poor little creature, I am, not your servant, but *your child*! You are the Mother of Jesus and you are *my Mother*!

Céline, how admirable therefore is our greatness in Jesus! How many mysteries has He unveiled to us by causing us to climb up the symbolic tree that I was talking about just now! And now, what knowledge is He going to teach us? Hasn't He taught us everything? Let's listen:

Come down immediately. I must stay at your house today [Lk. 19:5].

What? Jesus asks us to come down! So where must we go? Once, the Jews asked Him,

Master, where are you staying? [Jn. 1:38], and He replied, *Foxes have holes and birds have nests, but the Son of Man has no place to lay his head* [Lk. 9:58]. That's how far down we must come in order to be able to serve as a place where Jesus may dwell: *We must be so poor that we have no place to lay our heads.*

That illumination was given to me during my retreat. Our Lord desires us to receive Him in our hearts. No doubt they're empty of created things, but, alas, mine isn't empty of myself, and it's for this that I'm commanded to come down. Oh! I want to come down very low, in order that in my heart Jesus might lay His divine head, and that there He will feel Himself loved and understood. . . .

APRIL 25TH, 1893

I want to share with you the desires of Jesus on your soul. Remember that He didn't say, "I am the flower of the gardens, the cultivated rose," but, *I am a rose of Sharon, a lily of the valleys* [Song 2:1]. Well then, you must always remain *a drop of dew* hidden in the divine petals of the beautiful Lily of the valleys.

A drop of dew: What is there more simple and more pure? It's not the clouds that formed it; it's born under the starry sky. Dew exists only at night. When the sun shoots forth its warm rays, the charming pearls that shimmer at the ends of the blades of grass soon change into a light vapor. There is the portrait of my little Céline. . . . Celine is a drop of dew come down from the beautiful sky, the beautiful heaven, her Homeland. During the night of this life, she must hide in the bright red blossom of *the Flower of the fields*; no glance must discover her there.

Blessed and happy little drop of dew, known to God alone, don't stop considering the resounding course of the rivers of this world; don't even envy the clear stream that snakes across the prairie. No doubt its murmur is quite gentle and sweet, but creatures can hear it, and then the blossom of *the Flower of the fields* wouldn't know how to contain it. To approach Jesus, we must be so little! Oh, how few souls there are that aspire to be little and unknown! "But," they say, "aren't the river and the stream more useful than the drop of dew? What does it do? We judge it to be good for nothing, except to refresh for an instant the fragile petals of a flower of the field."

Ah, you aren't familiar with the true *Flower of the fields*! If you were familiar with it, you would better understand Our Lord's reproach to Martha. The Beloved doesn't need our dazzling works or our beautiful thoughts. If He wants sublime concepts, doesn't He have His Angels, whose knowledge infinitely surpasses that of the greatest minds of this world? It's neither our minds nor our talents that He comes in search of here below. . . . He made Himself *the Flower of the fields* only to show us how much He treasures simplicity.

The Lily of the valleys asks only for *a drop of dew*, which, during only one night, will remain hidden from human sight. But when the shadows begin to fall, when *the Flower of the fields* has become *the Sun of Righteousness* [Mal. 4:2], the humble companion of His exile will rise up to Him like a vapor of love. He will fix on it one of His rays, and, before the whole heavenly court, it will shine eternally, like a precious pearl, the shining mirror of the divine Sun.

August 2nd, 1893

What you have written me fills me with joy; you are walking along a royal road. The bride of the Song of Songs, not having been able to find her Beloved resting, rose, she says, to search for him in the city, but in vain. . . . She was able to find him only outside the gates [Song 3:2–4]. Jesus doesn't want us to find His adorable presence in rest; He hides, He wraps Himself with darkness. . . . This is not how He behaves with respect to the crowds, for we read in the holy Gospel that *All the people hung on his words* [Luke 19:48] as soon as He began speaking.

Jesus charmed the weak souls through His divine words. He endeavored to make them strong for the day of temptation and trial. But small was the number of His friends when He remained silent before His judges! Oh, what a melody for my heart is this silence of the divine Master!

He wants us to do charity to Him as to a poor person. He places Himself, so to speak, at our mercy. He doesn't want to take anything without our giving it to Him with all our heart, and the smallest farthing is precious in His divine eyes. He holds out His hand to us to receive a little love, so that at the shining day of Judgment, this gentle Savior may be able to address to us these inexpressible words:

Come, you who are blessed by my Father; take your inheritance, the kingdom prepared for you since the creation of the world. For I was hungry and you gave me something to eat, I was thirsty and you gave me something to drink, I was a stranger and you invited me in, I needed clothes and you clothed me, I was sick and you looked after me, I was in prison and you came to visit me [Mt. 25:34–36].

My dearest Céline, let's rejoice on our behalf. Let us give, let us give to the Beloved. Let's be extremely generous toward Him, but let's never forget that He is a hidden Treasure: few souls know how to find Him. To find something hidden, we must hide ourselves; let our life be a mystery. *Do you want to learn something that will serve you well?* said the author of *The Imitation of Christ*; *love to be unknown and considered as nothing. . . . After leaving everything, you must go on to leave yourself. Let this one glorify himself for one thing, and that one for another; as for you, place your joy only on distaste for yourself.*

[UNDATED]

You tell me, dear Céline, that my letters do you good. I'm happy for that, but I assure you that I'm making no mistake about myself. *Unless the LORD builds the house, the builders labor in vain* [Ps. 127:1]. All the most beautiful words would be incapable of making one act of love come out, without the grace that touches the heart.

Here is a beautiful peach, so pink and so sweet that all the candy confectioners wouldn't know how to make up anything that tastes like it. Tell me, Céline, is it for the peach that the Good Lord created that pretty color and that velvety skin that is so pleasant? Again, is it for the peach that He has dispensed so much sugar? No, it's for us. What belongs to it uniquely, that which makes the essence of its being, is its seed; it only owns that.

In this way Jesus takes pleasure in pouring out His gifts on some of His creatures, with the goal of attracting other souls to Himself. But inwardly, He humbles them in His mercy; He forces them gently to recognize their nothingness and His all-powerfulness. These feelings form in them as a seed of grace that He hastens to develop for the blessed day when, clothed with an immortal and imperishable beauty, they will be served without danger on the table of heaven.

Dear little sister, sweet echo of my soul, your Thérèse doesn't find herself in the heights right now. But you see, when I'm in the midst of dryness, incapable of praying or of practicing virtue, I seek out little opportunities, little nothings, to bring pleasure to my Jesus. For example, a smile, a kind word; then I would like to fall silent and show listlessness. If I don't have opportunities, I want at least to repeat often to Him that I love Him. That's not difficult, and that maintains the fire in my heart. Even when it may seem to me that this fire of love has gone out, I would still throw little blades of straw on the embers, and I'm sure that it would light back up again.

It's true that I'm not always faithful, but I never become discouraged; I abandon myself in the arms of the Lord. He teaches me to *gain profit from everything, from the good and the bad that He finds in me* [Saint John of the Cross]. He teaches me to play the bank of cards of love, or rather, He's the One who plays for me, without telling me how He's doing it. That's His business, and not mine. What does concern me is for me to give myself entirely, without reserving anything for myself, not even the enjoyment of knowing how much the bank is bringing me. . . . After all, I'm not the prodigal son; there's no reason for Jesus to hold a feast for me, because *I am always with Him* [Lk. 15:31].

I've read in the holy Gospel that the divine Shepherd leaves behind all the faithful sheep in the desert to run after the lost sheep. How touched I am by this trust! How sure He is of them! How could they run away? They're captives of love. In this way the beloved Shepherd of our souls strips away from us His perceptible presence, in order to give His comfort to sinners. Or to put it another way, if He leads us to Mount Tabor, the Mount of Transfiguration, it's only for an instant. . . . The valleys are almost always the place of pasture; it's there *where you rest your sheep at midday* [Song 1:7].

OCTOBER 20TH, 1893

I find in the holy Song of Songs this passage that suits you perfectly: *What do you see in the bride, except a choir of music in an army camp?* [Song 7:1, after the Vulgate]. Through suffering, your life is in fact a battlefield. A choir of music is needed there; well! You will be Jesus' little lyre. But is a concert complete when no one sings? Since Jesus is playing, mustn't Céline sing? When the tune is sad, she will sing the songs of exile; when the tune is joyful, she will modulate a few refrains from on high. . . .

All that may happen, whether happy or burdensome, all the happenings on earth will be only distant noises, incapable of making Jesus' lyre vibrate. Alone, He reserves to Himself the right to gently pluck its strings.

I can't think about the dear little Saint Cecilia without being delighted; what a model! In the midst of a pagan world, in the height of danger, at the moment of being united to a mortal who breathed only profane love, it seems to me that she ought to have trembled and wept. But no, *while the instruments of joy were celebrating her marriage, Cecilia was singing in her heart.* What abandonment! She was no doubt hearing other melodies than those of earth; her divine Bridegroom was also singing, and the choir of Angels was repeating this refrain from a blessed night, *Glory to God in the highest heaven, and on earth peace to those on whom his favor rests* [Lk. 2:14].

The glory of God! Oh! Cecilia understood it, she called it with her deepest wishes, she discovered that her Jesus was thirsty for souls. . . . That's why her whole desire was to bring Him soon the soul of that young Roman who was thinking only about human glory. That wise virgin was to become a martyr because of that, and multitudes were to follow in her footsteps. She was not afraid of anything: The angels promised and sang of peace. She knew that the Prince of Peace was obliged to protect her, to guard her virginity and to give her reward to her. *O how beautiful is the chaste generation with glory!* [Wis. 4:1].

My dear sister, I don't know too much about what I'm telling you; I let myself follow the current of my heart. You write me that you feel your weakness. That's a grace. Our Lord is the One who is imprinting on your soul these feelings of mistrust of yourself. Don't be afraid; if you remain faithful to giving Him pleasure in the smallest opportunities, He will find Himself obliged to help you in the big ones.

The apostles, without Him, worked for a long time, a whole night, without catching a single fish. Their work was nonetheless pleasant to Him, but He wanted to prove that He alone can give us something. He asked only one act of humility: *Friends, haven't you any fish?* [Jn. 21:5]. And the good Saint Peter admitted his powerlessness: *Lord, we have fished all night without catching anything!* That's enough! The Heart of Jesus was touched; He was moved. . . . Perhaps if the apostle had caught a few small fish, the divine Master might not have done a miracle. But he had *nothing*, and therefore through divine power and goodness his nets were soon filled with large fish!

Now that's the character of Our Lord: As God He gives, but He desires the humility of our hearts.

JULY 7TH, 1894

I don't know if you still find yourself in the same disposition of mind that you manifested in your last letter. I suppose so, and I'm replying using this passage from the Song of Songs that perfectly explains the state of a soul that is steeped in dryness, a soul that nothing can gladden or comfort:

I went down into the garden of nuts, to see the fruits of the valleys, and to look if the vineyard had flourished, and the pomegranates budded. I knew not: my soul troubled me for the chariots of Aminadab [6:10–11 D-R].

There is the image of our souls. Often we go down in to the fertile valleys where our hearts love to feed. Yet the vast field of the Holy Scriptures, which so often has opened to lavish in our favor its richest treasure, that field itself looks to us like an arid, waterless desert. We don't even know where we are any more: Instead of peace and light, trouble and darkness are our portion. . . .

But, like the bride in the Song of Songs, we know the cause of this time of trial: "Our soul is troubled because of the chariots of Aminadab." We are not yet in our Homeland, and temptation must purify us like gold when it is acted on by fire. We sometimes believe we're abandoned, alas! *The chariots*, that is, the vain noises that assail and afflict us—are they inside us or outside us? We don't know! But Jesus knows; He is the witness of our sadness, and in the night, suddenly, His voice makes itself heard: *Return, return, O Sulamitess: return, return that we may behold thee* [6:12].

What a call! What! We didn't dare even to look at ourselves; we were horrified by our condition—and Jesus calls us to look upon us at His leisure. He wants to see us, He comes, and the two other adorable Persons of the Holy Trinity come with Him to take possession of our souls.

Our Lord had once promised this when He said with inexpressible tenderness, *Anyone who loves me will obey my teaching. My Father will love them, and we will come to them and make our home with them* [Jn. 14:23]. To keep Jesus' word is the only condition for our happiness, the proof of our love for Him. And it seems to me that *that word* is Himself, since He names himself as the uncreated *Word* of the Father.

In the same Gospel of Saint John, He makes this sublime prayer: *Sanctify them by the truth; your word is truth* [Jn. 17:17]. In another place, Jesus teaches us that He is *the way and the truth and the life* [Jn. 14:6]. Therefore we know what is the *word* that we must keep. We cannot say, as Pilate did, *What is truth?* [Jn. 18:38]—we own *the truth* since the Beloved lives in our hearts.

Often *my beloved is to me a sachet of myrrh* [Song 1:12]; we partake of the chalice of His suffering. But how sweet it will be one day to hear this pleasant word: *You are those who have stood by me in my trials. And I confer on you a kingdom, just as my Father conferred one on me* [Lk. 22:28–29].

AUGUST 19TH, 1894

This is perhaps the last time, my dear little sister, that I will be using a pen to talk with you. The Good Lord has granted my dearest wish! Come, we will suffer together . . . and then *Jesus will take one of us*, and the others will remain for a short time in exile. Listen carefully to what I'm going to tell you: *Never, never will the Good Lord separate us; if I die before you, don't think that I will go far away from your soul: never will we be more united.* Above all don't be troubled by my prophecy—it's just a childish saying! I'm not sick, I have a constitution of iron; but *the Lord can break iron like clay.* . . .

Our dear father makes his presence felt in a way that touches me deeply. After a death of five long years [due to his dementia], what a joy to find him again as he once was, and even more fatherly! Oh, how he is going to repay you for the care that you have lavished on him! You were his angel, and he will be your angel in turn. See now, it has been less than a month that he's been in heaven, and already, through his powerful intervention, all the steps you're taking are succeeding. Now it's easy for him to take care of our affairs, so he has less concern for his Céline than for his little queen [as he used to call me]!

For a long time you've been asking me for news about the novitiate, especially news about my assignment. I'm going to satisfy your request:

I'm *a little hunting dog*, and that title gives me many causes of anxiety and care, because of the functions it requires, as I'll let you judge: All day long, from morning to night, I run after the prey. The hunters—the Reverend Mother Prioress and the Novice Mistress—are too big to run through the bushes, whereas a little dog can nip in and out everywhere . . . and does it have a fine nose! Therefore I watch my little rabbits closely. I don't want to hurt them, but I lick them by telling them at times that their fur isn't smooth enough, and at other times that they're looking too much like wild rabbits. . . . Finally I try to make them into such as the Hunter desires them: simple little rabbits, busy only with the lawn grass on which they ought to graze.

I'm laughing, but in the end I think quite sincerely that one of those little rabbits—the one that you know—is worth a hundred times as much as the little dog: He has run through many dangers. . . . I swear to you that if I were in his place, a long time ago I would have become lost forever in the vast forest of the world.

[UNDATED]

I'm happy, my little Céline, that you don't feel any conscious attraction in coming to Carmel. This is a delicate touch by Jesus, who wants to receive a present from you. He knows that it's much better to give than to receive. What happiness to suffer for the One who loves us madly, and to pass for fools in the eyes of the world! We judge others according to ourselves, and since the world is crazy, naturally it calls us by that name.

Let's take comfort: We're not the first to experience this! The only crime with which Herod reproached Our Lord was that of being crazy . . . and frankly, it was true! Yes, it was madness to come seeking the poor little hearts of mortals in order to make them into His thrones, He, the King of glory who is above the cherubim! Wasn't He perfectly happy in the company of His Father and the Spirit of love? Why should He come here below to seek out sinners to make them into His intimate friends?

We will never be able to accomplish for our Bridegroom the foolishness that He has accomplished for us. Our acts are quite reasonable in comparison with His. Let the world leave us alone! I'll say it again: The world is the one that's crazy, since it doesn't know what Jesus did and suffered to save it from damnation.

Neither are we do-nothings, prodigals: The divine Master has taken our defense upon Himself. Listen: He was at table with Lazarus and His disciples, Martha was serving. As for Mary, she wasn't thinking about eating, but about giving pleasure to her Beloved, *therefore she poured over the Savior's head a jarful of very expensive perfume, and, when she broke the jar* [Mark 14:3], *the whole house was filled with the fragrance of that perfume* [Jn. 12:3].

The apostles mumbled their discontent with Mary Magdalene. That's what is still happening to us: The most fervent Christians find that we're doing way too much, that we ought with Martha to serve Jesus instead of consecrating to Him the jars of our lives with the perfumes enclosed within them. Yet, nonetheless, what does it matter if these jars are broken, since Our Lord is comforted, and since, in spite of itself, the world is constrained to smell the perfumes that are emanating from them! Oh! Those perfumes are quite necessary to purify the unhealthy atmosphere that the world breathes.

Until soon, my dearest sister. See, your boat is near the port; the wind that is pushing it is a wind of love, and that love is faster than lightning! Good-bye! In a few days we'll be reunited at Carmel, then in heaven! Didn't Jesus say, during His Passion, SOON *you will see the Son of Man sitting at the right hand of the Mighty One and coming on the clouds of heaven?*

We'll be there!!!

Your Thérèse

[Note: Céline Martin entered the Carmel of Lisieux after her father's death in 1894.]

*Thérèse and Céline
at Les Buissonnets*

Then our voices mingled,
Our hands linked one to another;
Together, singing the sacred wedding song,
Already we were dreaming of Carmel,
Heaven!

2
LETTERS TO THE REVEREND MOTHER AGNES OF JESUS
(Thérèse's Sister Pauline)

1887, A FEW MONTHS BEFORE THÉRÈSE'S
ENTRANCE INTO CARMEL

My dearest Mother,

You're right to say that that the drop of bitter gall must be mixed with every chalice, but I find that trials are a great help for becoming detached from the earth. They make us look up higher than this world. Here below nothing can satisfy us; we enjoy a little rest only when we're ready to do the will of the Good Lord.

My little dinghy is having a lot of trouble reaching the port. For a long time I've been catching sight of it, but I still find myself far away. But Jesus is guiding that little dinghy, and I am sure that on the day chosen by Him, it will be happily beached on the blessed shore of Carmel. Oh, Pauline! When Jesus has given me this grace, I want to give myself entirely to Him, always suffer for Him, and no longer live but for Him. Oh, no, I won't be afraid of His blows, for, even in the bitterest of sufferings, we can feel that it's His sweet hand that strikes.

And when I think that, for a suffering we undergo with joy, we'll love the Good Lord all the more, forever! Oh, if at the time of my death I could have a soul to offer to Jesus, how happy I would be! There would be one less soul in hell, one more to bless the Good Lord for all of eternity!

JANUARY 1889,
DURING HER RETREAT BEFORE TAKING THE HABIT

. . . In my relationship with Jesus: dryness! Sleep! Since my Beloved wants to sleep, I won't stop Him; I'm too happy to see that He isn't treating me at all like a stranger, that He isn't worried about me. He's peppering *His little ball* with the most painful pinpricks. When it is that gentle Friend who Himself is piercing His ball, suffering is only sweetness, His hand is so gentle, so sweet! What a difference from the hand of His created beings!

Nevertheless, I'm happy, yes, quite happy to suffer! If Jesus doesn't directly pierce His little ball, then He's the one who is guiding the hand that is wounding it! Oh, Mother, if only you knew to what extent I want to be indifferent to the things of the earth! What do all these created beauties matter to me? I would be quite unhappy if I possessed them! Oh, how my heart seems big, when I consider it with respect to the things of this world, since all of them taken together couldn't make it happy. But when I consider it with respect to Jesus, how little it seems to me!

How good to me is the One who will soon be my Bridegroom! How divinely kind He is in not allowing me to become captivated by anything here below! He knows that, if He were to send me only a shadow of happiness, I would attach myself to it with all my energy, all the strength of my heart; and that shadow He refuses me! . . . He prefers to leave me in darkness rather than to give me a false glimmer that would not be Himself.

I do not want created things to have a single atom of my love. I want to give all to Jesus, since He is making me understand that He alone is perfect happiness. Everything will be for Him, everything! And even when I have nothing to offer Him, like this evening, I will give Him that nothing. . . .

1889

Yes, I desire these wounds of the heart, these needle pricks that cause so much suffering! . . . I prefer sacrifice over every kind of ecstasy. That's where happiness lies for me; I find it nowhere else. *The little reed* has no fear of being broken, since it is planted beside the waters of love. Therefore, when it bends, that wholesome water strengthens it and makes it want another storm to come again and bend its head. *It's my weakness that makes all my strength.* I cannot be broken, since whatever happens to me, I see only Jesus' sweet, gentle hand.

There is nothing too great to suffer in order to win the palm of victory!

SEPTEMBER 1890,
DURING HER RETREAT BEFORE MAKING HER PROFESSION
[her vows as a nun]

Your little solitary one must give you the itinerary for her journey.

Before leaving, my Betrothed asked me in what country I wanted to travel, what road I wanted to follow. I answered Him that I had only one desire, that of arriving *at the peak of the Mountain of* LOVE.

Immediately, a multitude of roads offered themselves to my sight. But there were so many perfect ones that I saw myself incapable of choosing any of them with my complete will. Then I said to my divine Guide: You know where I want to go, You know for Whom I want to climb the mountain, You know the One Whom I love and Who is the only One I want to make happy. It's for Him alone that I'm undertaking this journey. So take me along the paths of His choosing. As long as He is content, I will be overflowing with happiness.

And Our Lord took me by the hand and made me enter into an underground passage where it was neither cold nor hot, where the sun does not shine, where the rain and the wind have no access—an underground passage where I see nothing but a half-veiled light, the light that the lowered eyes of the Face of Jesus spread around them.

My Betrothed says nothing to me, and I say nothing to Him, either, except that I love Him more than myself, and I feel in the depths of my heart that this is true, since I am more His than mine.

I don't see that we are advancing toward the goal of our journey, since it is being carried out underground. And nonetheless it seems to me, without knowing how, that we are approaching the peak of the mountain.

I thank my Jesus for making me walk in darkness; there, I am in profound peace. Willingly I consent to remain for my whole religious life in that dark underground passage into which He has made me enter. I desire only that my darkness will obtain light for sinners.

I am happy, yes, quite happy to not have any comfort. I would be ashamed if my love were like that of earthly brides who are always looking at their grooms' hands to see if they aren't bringing them some kind of present, or at their faces to surprise them in a smile of love that brings them delight.

Thérèse, the little bride of Christ, loves Jesus for Himself. She wants to look on the face of her Beloved only to surprise Him in tears that delight her through their hidden charms. Those tears she can wipe away; she wants to gather them, like diamonds of inestimable value, in order to use them to embroider her wedding gown.

Jesus! I want to love Him so much! To love Him as He has never been loved!

At all cost, I want to win the crown of Saint Agnes [a martyr for her love of God after refusing to marry, and the patron saint of virgins]; *if it's not through blood, it must be through* LOVE.

1890

Love can take the place of a long life. Jesus does not look at time, since He is eternal. *He looks only at love.* Oh, my dear Mother, ask Him to give me an abundance of it! I don't want love I can feel consciously; provided that Jesus can feel it consciously, that is enough for me. Oh!

To love Him and to make Him loved, how sweet that is! Tell Him to take me on the day of my profession if I were to offend Him any more, because I would like to carry up to heaven the white robe of my second baptism, without any stain or spot. Jesus can grant me the grace of not offending Him anymore or rather to commit only faults *that do not offend Him*, that do not cause Him grief, but serve only to humble me and to make my love stronger.

There is no support to be sought or asked for outside of Jesus. He alone is unchangeable. What happiness to think that He cannot change!

1891

Oh, how much good your letter did me! This passage was enlightening for my soul: *Let us hold back any word that could elevate us in the sight of others.* Yes, we must save everything for Jesus with a jealous zeal; it is good to work for Him all alone! Then, how the heart is filled with joy! How light the soul is! . . .

Ask Jesus that *His grain of sand* may save many souls in a short time, in order to fly more promptly up to His adored Face.

1892

Here is the dream of *a grain of sand*: Jesus only! . . . Nothing but Him! The grain of sand is so little that, if it wanted to open its heart to another besides Jesus, there would no longer be any place for its Beloved.

What happiness to be so hidden that no one thinks about us, to be unknown, even to the persons who live with us! Oh, my dear Mother! How I desire to be unknown by all creatures! I never desired human glory; my heart had been attracted to being scorned. But, having recognized that even that was too glorious for me, I became impassioned about being forgotten.

The glory of my Jesus, that is my entire ambition. As for mine, I abandon it to Him. And if He seems to forget me, well! He is free to do so, since I am no longer mine, but His. He will become tired more quickly of making me wait than I am of waiting for Him!

MAY 28TH, 1897

That day, while Sister Thérèse of the Child Jesus was suffering from a strong bout of fever, a Sister came to ask her immediate assistance for a work of painting that was difficult to execute. For an instant, her face betrayed the inner struggle she was going through. Mother Agnes of Jesus [Pauline], who was present, noticed this. That evening, Thérèse wrote her this letter:

My beloved Mother,

A short while ago your child shed sweet tears, tears of repentance, but still more of gratitude and love. Today I showed you my virtue, my treasures of patience! And I who preach so well to others! I am happy that you saw my imperfection. You did not scold me . . . but nevertheless I deserved it. But in every circumstance, your gentleness tells me much more than harsh words; you are for me the image of divine mercy.

Yes, but Sister [name omitted], on the contrary, is ordinarily the image of the harshness of the Good Lord. Well, I have just encountered her. Instead of passing coldly near me, she embraced me, saying, "Poor little Sister, I felt so sorry for you! I don't want to make you tired; leave the work that I asked of you. I was wrong."

I, who felt perfect contrition in my heart, was quite surprised not to receive any words of correction. I know well that deep down she must find me to be imperfect; it's because she thinks I'm going to die soon that she spoke to me that way. But no matter, I heard only gentle, tender words coming from her mouth. Then I found her to be quite good, and as for myself, I found myself quite bad!

Upon returning to our cell, I asked myself what Jesus was thinking of me. Instantly, I remembered that He said one day to the woman taken in adultery, "Has no one condemned you?" [Jn. 8:10]. And I, with tears in my eyes, answered Him, "No one, Lord . . . neither my dear Mother Agnes of Jesus, nor that Sister, who is the image of Your justice and righteousness. And I feel clearly that I can go in peace, because You will not condemn me either!"

Oh, my beloved Mother, I declare it frankly to you, I am much happier that I was imperfect than if, sustained by grace, I had been a model of patience. It does me so much good to see that Jesus is always as gentle, as tender toward me. Truly, that is enough to make me die for gratitude and love.

My dear Mother, you will understand that, this evening, the jar of divine mercy has overflowed for Your child. *Oh, even right now, I recognize Him: Yes, all my hopes will be filled to overflowing. . . . Yes, the Lord will do for me great marvels that will infinitely surpass my immense desires.*

LETTERS TO THE TWO MISSIONARIES
WHO WERE HER SPIRITUAL BROTHERS

In chapter 11 of The Story of a Soul *Thérèse wrote about two missionary priests, Fr. Maurice Bellière and Fr. Adolphe Roulland, whom she took for her spiritual brothers. The following are letters she wrote to them.*

DECEMBER 26TH, 1895

Our Lord never asks us for sacrifices above our strength. Sometimes, it is true, this divine Savior makes us feel all the bitterness of the chalice that He presents to our souls. When He asks for the sacrifice of all that is the dearest in the world, it is impossible, unless we have a quite particular grace, not to cry out, as He did in the garden of His agony, *Abba, Father . . . take this cup from me.* But let us hasten to add as well, *Yet not what I will, but what you will* [Mk. 14:36]. It is very comforting to think that Jesus, the divine Strong One, was acquainted with all our weaknesses, and that He trembled at the sight of the bitter chalice, that chalice that He had once so ardently desired.

Reverend Father, your portion is truly beautiful, since Our Lord chose you and since, first, He placed His lips on the cup that He is presenting to you. A Saint said this: *The greatest honor that God can give to a soul is not to give much to it; it is to ask much from it.* Jesus is treating you as a privileged one. He wants you to begin your mission already and, through suffering, for you to save souls. Is it not by suffering, by dying, that He Himself redeemed the world? I know that you are aspiring to the happiness of sacrificing your life for Him. But the martyrdom of the heart is no less fruitful than the shedding of blood. And, even now, that martyrdom is yours. Therefore I am right to say that your portion is beautiful, that it is worthy of an apostle of Christ.

1896

Let us work together for the salvation of souls. We have only the single day of this life to save them, and in this way to give to the Lord the proofs of our love. The day following this day will be eternity: Then Jesus will return to you a hundredfold the sweetest joys that you are sacrificing for Him. He knows the extent of your sacrifice. He knows the suffering of those who are dear to you increases yours all the more; but He Himself suffered that martyrdom in order to save our souls. He left His mother; He saw the Immaculate Virgin standing at the foot of the cross, her heart pierced by a sword of suffering. Therefore I hope that our divine Savior will comfort your dear mother, and I am earnestly asking Him to do that.

Oh, if the divine Master let those that you are going to leave behind out of love for Him catch sight of the glory He is reserving for you, and the multitude of souls who will follow behind your train in heaven, they would already be rewarded for the great sacrifice your going far away will cause them.

1896

I am asking you to pray every day for me this little prayer that contains all my desires:

Merciful Father, in the name of Your sweet Jesus, of the holy Virgin, and the saints, I ask you to set my Sister on fire with Your Spirit of love, and to grant her the grace of making You to be greatly loved.

If the Lord takes me soon to be with Him, I implore you to continue that same prayer every day, because I will desire in heaven the same thing as on earth: TO LOVE JESUS AND TO MAKE HIM TO BE GREATLY LOVED.

JUNE 21ST, 1897

This letter was written three months before her death.

You are able to sing of the divine mercies! They shine in you in all their splendor. You love Saint Augustine, Saint Magdalene, those souls to whom many sins were remitted because they loved much. I also love them: I love their repentance and above all their loving audaciousness. When I see Magdalene go forward in front of Simon's many guests and bathe with her tears the feet of the Master whom she adores, feet that she is touching for the first time, I feel that her heart understood the depths of love and mercy of the Heart of Jesus, and that, not only was He disposed to forgive her, but also to pour out on her the blessings of His divine intimacy, to raise her up to the highest peaks of contemplation.

Oh, my brother, since it has been given to me, as well, to understand the love of the Heart of Jesus, I acknowledge that it has chased away all fear from my heart. The remembrance of my faults humbles me and causes me never to lean on my own strength, which is nothing but weakness. But, still more, that remembrance speaks to me of mercy and love. How, when we throw our faults, with the confidence and trust of a child, into the burning fire of love—how could they not be consumed without anything coming back to us in turn?

I know that a great number of Saints spent their lives doing astounding mortifications to expiate their sins, but what are we going to do! *In my Father's house there are many mansions* [Jn. 14:2 D-R], Jesus said, and it's for that reason that I follow the path that He is tracing for me: I endeavor not to be considering myself in anything. And what Jesus stoops down to perform in my life, I abandon it to Him without holding anything back.

1897

On this earth where everything changes, only one thing remains stable: the behavior of the King of heaven with respect to His friends.

Since He raised the standard of the Cross, it's in the shadow of the Cross that all must fight and bring about the victory. *Every missionary's life is filled with crosses*, said Théophane Vénard [one of the martyrs of Vietnam]; and again, *True happiness is to suffer, and to live, we have to die.*

My brother, the beginnings of your apostolate are marked with the seal of the cross: Rejoice! It's truly more through suffering and persecution than by brilliant preaching that Jesus wants to confirm His kingdom in souls.

You say: "I'm still a little child who doesn't know how to talk." Father Mazel, who was ordained a priest the same day as you, didn't know how to talk, either. However, he has already earned the palm of victory. . . . Oh, how the thoughts of God are higher than ours! . . . On learning that this young missionary had died, even before setting foot on the soil of his mission, I felt myself brought to invoke him. It seemed to me that I saw him in heaven in the glorious choir of martyrs. No doubt, in the eyes of mortals, he was not worthy of the title of martyr. But in the sight of the Good Lord, that sacrifice is no less fruitful than those of the confessors of the faith [those who have been persecuted and tortured for the faith].

If we must be quite pure in order to appear before the God of all holiness, I know, myself, that He is infinitely just. And that justice that causes fear in so many souls is the subject of my joy and my trust. To be just is not only to exercise severity toward the guilty, but also to recognize right intentions and to recompense virtue. I hope for as much from the justice of the Good Lord as from His mercy. It's because He is just that He is *compassionate and gracious, slow to anger, abounding in love. For he knows how we are formed, he remembers that we are dust. As a father has compassion on his children, so the LORD has compassion on those who fear him* [Ps. 103:8, 14, 13].

Oh, my brother! When we hear these beautiful and comforting words from the Prophet-King, how can we doubt that the Good Lord wants to open the doors of His kingdom to His children who loved Him to the point of sacrificing all for Him, and who not only left their family and their country in order to make Him known and loved, but also desire to give their lives for Him! . . . Jesus was quite right to say that there is no greater love than that! So how would He let Himself be surpassed in generosity? How would He purify, in the flames of Purgatory, souls that are consumed by the fires of divine love?

These are many sentences to explain my thought, or rather not to be able to do it. I wanted simply to tell you that, in my view, all missionaries are martyrs though desire and will, and that, as a result, not one of them should go to Purgatory.

There, my brother, is what I think about the Good Lord's divine justice. My way is wholly that of confidence and love. I don't understand souls who are afraid of so tender a Friend. Sometimes, when I read certain books in which perfection is shown through a thousand obstacles, my poor little mind becomes tired quite quickly. I close the lofty book that is giving me a headache and drying out my heart, and I pick up the Holy Scriptures. Then everything seems clear, a single word discloses infinite horizons to my soul, and perfection seems easy to me. Then I see that it's enough to recognize our nothingness and to abandon ourselves, like a child, into the arms of the Good Lord. Leaving to great souls, to sublime spirits, the beautiful books that I cannot understand, and even less can put into practice, I rejoice at being little, since *only children and those who are like them will be admitted to the heavenly banquet* [see Mt. 19:14]. Happily, the Kingdom of Heaven is made of many mansions! For, if it were composed only of the ones whose description and path seem incomprehensible to me, certainly I would never enter it.

JULY 13TH, 1897

This letter was written two and a half months before her death.

Your soul is too big to attach itself to comforts here below! It's in heaven that you ought to live in advance, because it is written, *For where your treasure is, there your heart will be also* [Lk. 12:34]. Isn't Jesus your only treasure? Since He is in heaven, it's there that your heart should dwell.

That gentle Savior has, for a long time, forgotten your unfaithfulnesses. Only your desires for perfection are present to Him to rejoice His Heart.

I entreat you, do not stay at His feet any longer. Follow that first impulse that carries you into His arms. That is your place, and I remark, even more than in your letters, that it is forbidden to you to go to heaven by any other way than that of your little Sister.

I agree completely with you: The Heart of Jesus is much more saddened by the multitude of imperfections of His friends than by the faults, even the serious ones, that His enemies commit. But, my brother, it seems to me that it is only when those who are His make a habit of their offensive behaviors and do not ask His forgiveness for them, that *If someone asks, "What are these wounds on your body?"* He can say, *The wounds I was given at the house of my friends* [Zech. 12:6].

For those who love Him and then, after each little fault, come and throw themselves into His arms, asking His forgiveness, Jesus jumps for joy. He tells His angels what the prodigal son's father told his servants: *Put a ring on his finger and let us celebrate* [see Lk. 15:22]. Oh, my brother, how little known are the goodness and merciful love of the Heart of Jesus! It is true that, in order to enjoy these treasures, we have to humble ourselves and own up to our nothingness, and that is what many souls do not want to do.

1897

What draws me to the Homeland in heaven is the Lord's call, the hope of finally loving Him as I have desired so much, and the thought that I will be able to make Him loved by a multitude of souls who will bless Him throughout eternity.

I have never asked the good Lord to die young: That would have seemed to me to be laxness or cowardice. But He, from my childhood, has reached down to give me the intimate persuasion that my course here below would be short.

I feel it, we must go to heaven by the same path: suffering united to love. When I have arrived at port, I will teach you how you must navigate on the stormy sea of the world: with the abandon and the love of a child who knows that his father loves him, and would not know how to leave him alone at the hour of danger.

Oh, how I would like to make you understand the tenderness of the Heart of Jesus, what He awaits from you! Your last letter made my heart leap gently. I understood to what extent your soul is the sister to mine, since it is called to go up to God by *the elevator of love*, and not to climb the rough stairs of fear. I am not surprised to see that familiarity with Jesus seems difficult to you: We cannot get there in one day. But I am sure that I will help you much more to walk on that delicious path when I have been delivered from my mortal outer covering. And soon you will say, like Saint Augustine, *Love is the weight that is carrying me.*

JULY 26TH, 1897

This letter was written eight weeks before her death.

When you read this little note, perhaps I will no longer be on earth. I do not know the future, but I can nevertheless tell you with assurance that *the Bridegroom is at the door.* It would take a miracle to keep me here in exile, and I do not think that Jesus will do that, because He does nothing that does not serve a purpose.

Oh, my brother, how happy I am to die! Yes, I am happy, not because I will be delivered from suffering here below: Suffering united with love is, on the contrary, the thing that seems desirable to me in the valley of tears. I am happy to die because, much more than here below, I will be useful to the souls who are dear to me.

Jesus has always treated me as a spoiled child. . . . It is true that His cross has accompanied me right from the cradle; but He has made me love that cross with a passion.

AUGUST 14TH, 1897

This letter was written six weeks before her death.

At the moment of appearing before the Good Lord, I understand more than ever that there is only one thing that is necessary: to work only for Him, and to do nothing for ourselves or for created beings. Jesus wants to possess your heart completely. For that to happen, you must suffer a great deal . . . but also what joy will flood your soul when you have arrived at the happy moment of your entrance into heaven!

I am not dying, I am entering into life . . . and all that I cannot tell you here below, I will make you understand from up above in heaven.

PART
FIVE
Poems

INTRODUCTION TO THE POEMS

The beauty of Thérèse's prose is matched by that of her poems. Thérèse's poetry cannot be rendered perfectly from French to English, because her poems contain meter and rhyme that it is not possible to replicate in translation. Here is the first stanza in French of "Mon chant d'aujourd'hui," the first of the poems given below:

> *Ma vie est un instant, une heure passagère,*
> *Ma vie est un moment qui m'échappe et qui fuit.*
> *Tu le sais, ô mon Dieu, pour t'aimer sur la terre,*
> *Je n'ai rien qu'aujourd'hui!*

The meter is 12-12-12-6, meaning that there are twelve syllables in each of the first three lines and six in the fourth. The rhyme scheme is a-b-a-b, meaning that the first and third syllables rhyme, as do the second and fourth.

This short technical explanation is sufficient to show that Thérèse's poetry demonstrates considerable skill as well as a high level of education. Many of the poems were composed to be sung to hymn tunes that were familiar to late nineteenth-century French worshipers. Because Thérèse wrote her poems only for her personal edification, never intending that they would be published, they are given here unpolished and unedited. In English translation, it is clear that they nonetheless continue the theme that runs like a steady heartbeat throughout Thérèse's writing: *I will sing of the mercies of the Lord forever.*

My Song of Today
June 1894

My life is an instant, a fleeting hour,
My life is a moment that escapes me and flees away.
You know, O God, that to love You on earth,
    I only have today.

Oh, how I love You, Jesus! . . . toward You my soul aspires. . . .
For one day only my sweet support remains!
Come reign in my heart, give me Your smile
    Only for today!

What does it matter, Lord, if the future is dark!
To pray to You for tomorrow, oh! No, I cannot. . . .
Preserve my heart pure, cover me with Your shadow
    Only for today!

If I think about tomorrow, I fear my inconstancy,
I feel rising in my heart sadness and ennui;
But I am willing, dear God, to undergo trials and suffering,
    Only for today!

I must see You soon on the eternal shore,
O divine Pilot, whose hand is guiding me!
Over the stormy waves guide my dinghy in peace,
    Only for today!

Oh! Let me, Lord, hide myself in Your Face;
There I will no longer hear the vain noise of the world.
Give me Your love, preserve in me Your grace
    Only for today!

Near Your divine Heart, forgetting what is happening,
I no longer fear the wiles of the enemy.
Ah! Give me, Jesus, a place in Your heart,
    Only for today!

Living Bread, Bread of heaven, divine Eucharist,
O touching mystery that love has produced!
Come live in my heart, Jesus, my white Host,
Only for today!

Bend down and unite me to you, holy and sacred Vine,
And my feeble branch will give You its fruit,
And I will be able to offer you a golden cluster,
Lord, starting with today.

That cluster of love whose seeds are souls,
I have only this fleeting day to form it. . . .
Oh, give me, Jesus, the flames of an apostle,
Only for today!

O Immaculate Virgin! O you, the sweet star
That shines on Jesus and unites me to Him,
O Mother! Let me hide myself under your veil,
Only for today!

O my guardian Angel! Cover me with your wing,
Light my path with your fires, O gentle friend!
Come direct my steps, help me, I call upon you,
Only for today!

I want to see my Jesus, without veil, without cloud;
Even though here below I am very near Him. . . .
His loving Countenance will be hidden
Only for today!

I will fly up soon to tell His praises,
When the day that knows no sunset on my soul will have Him;
Then I will sing on the Angels' lyre,
THE ETERNAL TODAY!

To Live on Love!
February 25th, 1895

Anyone who loves me will obey my teaching. My Father will love them, and
we will come to them and make our home with them. . . .
Peace I leave with you. Now remain in my love.
—John 14:23, 27; 15:9

On the evening of love, speaking without parable,
Jesus said, *If anyone wants to love Me,*
Faithfully let them keep My word,
My Father and I will come visit them;
And in their hearts, making Our dwelling place,
Our palace, Our living home,
Filled with peace, We desire them to dwell
                    In Our love.

To live on love is to guard and keep You,
Uncreated Word! Word of my God!
Ah, you know it, divine Jesus, I love You!
The Spirit of love will set me aflame with His fire.
It is in loving You that I will draw the Father,
My feeble heart keeps Him without expecting a return;
O Trinity! You are the prisoner
                    Of my love.

To live on love is to live on Your life,
Glorious King, delight of the elect!
You live for me hidden in a host. . . .
I want to hide myself for You, O Jesus!
Lovers need solitude,
A heart-to-heart that lasts day and night;
Your glance alone makes my blessedness,
                    I live on love!

To live on love is not on earth
To fix our tent at the peak of Tabor;
With Jesus, it is to climb Calvary,
It is to look at the cross as a treasure!
In heaven, I will live on joy;
Then the time of trial will have flown away, never to return:
But, here below, I want in the midst of suffering
                    To live on love!

To live on love is to banish all fear,
All memory of the faults of the past.
Of my sins I see no imprint,
In the divine fire each one has been erased.
Sacred flame, O most sweet furnace,
On Your hearth I fix my dwelling;
Jesus, there it is that I sing to my heart's content:
                    I live on love!

To live on love is to guard within oneself
A great treasure in a mortal jar.
My Beloved! My weakness is extreme!
Oh, I am far from being an Angel from heaven.
But, if I fall at each passing moment,
And get up, clasping myself from turn to turn,
You come to me, You give me Your grace,
                    I live on love!

To live on love is to navigate without ceasing,
Sowing joy and peace in hearts;
Beloved Pilot! Charity is pressing me,
For I see You in other souls, my sisters.
Charity, that is my only star;
By its light, I sail without detour
I have my motto written on my sail:
                    To live for love!

To live for love, when Jesus is sleeping,
Is to rest on stormy seas.
Oh! Do not be afraid, Lord, that I will wake You up;
I wait in peace on the shore of heaven. . . .
Faith soon will tear its sail,
And my Hope will count only one day;
Charity inflates and pushes my sail,

I live on love!

To live on love is, O my divine Master!
To entreat You to spread Your fires
In the elect and saintly soul of Your priest;
May he be purer than the seraphim of heaven!
Protect Your immortal Church,
I entreat You at each moment of the day.
I, its child, set myself aflame for it,

I live on love!

To live on love is to wipe Your Face,
It is to obtain forgiveness for sinners.
O God of love! Let them enter into Your grace,
And forever may they bless Your Name!
All the way to my heart the blasphemy blares forth;
To erase it I say again every day:
O sacred Name! I adore You and I love You,

I live on love!

To live on love is to imitate Mary
Bathing with tears, with precious perfumes,
Your divine feet, which she kisses in delight,
Wiping them with her long hair;
Then, rising, with a holy audacity,
She embalms Your Face with the perfume in turn:
As for me, the perfume with which I embalm Your Face

Is my love!

"To live on love, what strange folly!"
The world tells me; "Oh, cease your song;
Do not waste your perfumes, your life;
Know how to employ them usefully!"
—To love You, Jesus, what a fruitful loss!
All my perfumes are Yours without my expecting any return.
I want to sing, as I leave this world:
I am dying of love!

To die of love is a most sweet martyrdom,
And that is the one that I desire to suffer.
O Cherubim! Tune your lyres,
For, I feel it, my exile is coming to an end. . . .
Burning dart, consume me without truce,
Wound my heart in this sad dwelling place.
Divine Jesus, make my dream a reality:
To die of love!

To die of love, that is my hope—
When I shall see my bonds break,
My God will be my great reward;
I do not want to possess anything else at all.
For His love I am impassioned,
Let Him come at last to set me aflame without any going back!
There is my heaven, there is my destiny:
To LIVE ON LOVE!

HYMN TO THE HOLY FACE
AUGUST 12TH, 1895

Jesus, Your ineffable image
Is the star that guides my steps;
You know well that Your sweet Face
For me is heaven on earth!
My love reveals the charms
Of Your eyes made beautiful by weeping.
I smile through my tears,
When I contemplate Your sufferings.

Oh! I want to comfort You,
To live unknown and alone;
Your beauty, which You know how to veil,
Reveals to me all its mystery,
And toward You I would like to fly!

Your Face is my only Homeland,
It is my kingdom of love;
It is my smiling prairie,
My gentle sun of each day;
It is the lily of the valleys
Whose mysterious perfume
Comforts my exiled soul—
Makes it taste the peace of heaven.

It is my rest, my sweetness,
And my melodious lyre. . . .
Your Face, O my sweet Savior,
Is the divine bouquet of myrrh
That I wish to guard and keep on my heart!

Your Face is my only richness;
I ask for nothing more.
In it, unceasingly hiding myself,

I will look like You, Jesus!
Leave within me the divine imprint
Of Your features so full of sweetness,
And soon I will become holy;
Toward You I will draw hearts!

So that I may be able to store up
A beautiful golden harvest,
Reach down and set me afire with Your flames!
Soon, with Your adored mouth,
Give me the kiss that endures forever!

The Holy Face of Our Lord Jesus Christ
According to the Shroud of Turin
Painting by Céline

THE ETERNAL SONG
SUNG WHILE YET IN EXILE
MARCH 10TH, 1896

Your bride, O my God, on the foreign shore
Can sing of the love of the eternal song;
Since in the midst of exile You stoop down, on earth, and
With the fire of Your love set her aflame as in heaven!

My Beloved, supreme beauty!
To me You give Yourself;
But in return, Jesus, I love You:
Make of my life a single act of love!

Forgetting my great wretchedness,
You come to live in my heart.
My feeble love, oh, what a mystery!
Is enough to hold You fast, Lord.

Love that sets me aflame,
Penetrate my soul!
Come, I call out to You,
Come, consume me!

Your ardor presses me
And I desire unceasingly,
Divine furnace,
To plunge myself in the immeasurable gulf of You.

Lord, suffering
Becomes joy,
When love bursts forth
Toward You without expecting a reward.

Heavenly Homeland,
Infinite sweetness,
My delighted soul
Has You every day. . . .
Heavenly Homeland,
O infinite joy,
All You are is LOVE!

To the Venerable Théophane Vénard
February 2nd, 1897

Théophane Vénard was a French missionary priest to Indochina.
Though he had not yet reached sainthood in Thérèse's lifetime, in 1988 he
was declared a saint, along with nineteen other "Martyrs of Vietnam."

All the elect celebrate your praises,
O Théophane, angelic martyr!
And I know it, in the saintly armies,
The seraphim aspire to serve you.
Not being able, on the foreign shore,
To mingle my voice with those of the elect,
I wish at least, on this poor earth,
To take up my lyre and sing your virtues.

Your short exile was like a sweet hymn
Whose accents knew how to touch hearts,
And, for Jesus, your poetic soul,
At every moment, made flowers bloom. . . .
As you rose up to the heavenly sphere,
Your good-bye song breathed the air of springtime;
You murmured, *I, the little ephemeral one,*
Into beautiful heaven I am the first to go!

Blessed martyr, at the hour of your torture,
You savored the happiness of suffering!
To suffer for God seemed a delight to you;
Smiling, you knew how to live and die.
To your executioner you hastened to say,
When he offered to you to shorten your torment:
The longer my painful martyrdom lasts,
The more it will be of value, and the happier I will be!

Virginal lily, in the springtime of your life,
The King of heaven heard your desire;
I see in you *the opened flower*
That the Lord picks for His pleasure.
And now you are no longer in exile,
The blessed ones admire your splendor;
The rose of love, the immaculate Virgin
Breathes the freshness of your perfume.

Soldier of Christ, oh, lend me your weapons;
For sinners, I would like here below
To struggle, suffer, give my blood, my tears;
Protect me, come and hold up my arms.
I desire for them, not ceasing to war,
To take the kingdom of God by force;
For the Lord brought to earth,
Not peace, but the sword and fire.

I love it, that unbelieving shore
That was the object of your ardent love;
With happiness I would fly toward it,
If my Jesus were to require it one day. . . .
But in His sight distances are wiped away;
It is but a single point, this entire vast universe!
My actions, my little sufferings
Are making God loved even across the seas.

Oh, if I were only a springtime flower
That the Lord would want to pick soon!
Come down from heaven at my last hour,
I entreat you, O blessed martyr!
With your love, in virginal flames,
Come and set me on fire in this mortal dwelling place,
And I will be able to fly up with the souls
That will form your everlasting train.

HYMN OF SAINT AGNES
JANUARY 21ST, 1896

*Saint Agnes was a third-century martyr who was executed for refusing to
marry because she felt called by God to be a virgin dedicated to Him.
She is the patron saint of virgins, and is often symbolized by a lamb,
since her Latin name is similar to the word for "lamb."*

Christ is my life, He is all my life,
He is the Bridegroom who alone delights my eyes;
Already I hear vibrating, with His sweet harmony,
  The melodious sounds.

My hair is adorned with precious stones;
Already on my finger the wedding band shines;
He has bent down and covered with shining stars
  My virginal mantle.

He has adorned my hand with matchless pearls,
He has placed on my neck necklaces of great price;
On this blessed day, there shine on my ears, earrings
  Of heavenly rubies.

Yes, I am betrothed to the One whom the Angels
Will serve, trembling for all of eternity;
The moon and the sun tell of His praises,
  And admire His beauty.

His empire is heaven, His nature is divine;
A Virgin here below for mother, He chooses for Himself;
His Father is the true God who knows no origin;
  He is a pure spirit.

When I love Christ and when I touch Him,
My heart becomes purer, I am yet more chaste;
Of virginity, the kiss of His mouth
  Has given me the treasure.

He has already placed His sign on my face,
So that no lover may dare approach me;
My heart is sustained by the divine grace
  Of my beloved King.

With His precious blood I am turned purple,
I feel that I already enjoy the delights of heaven!
And I can gather on His sacred mouth
  The milk with the honey.

Therefore I fear nothing, neither iron, nor flame,
No, nothing can trouble my inexpressible peace;
And the fire of love that consumes my soul
  Will never go out.

My Heaven
June 7th, 1896

To endure the exile of the land of tears,
I must have the glance of my divine Savior;
That glance full of love has unveiled to me His charms,
He has made me feel in advance the happiness of heaven.
My Jesus smiles at me, when I sigh toward Him;
Then I no longer feel the trial of faith.
The gaze of my God, His delightful smile,
> *There is my heaven!*

My heaven is to draw toward the blessed Church,
On guilty France and on each sinner,
The grace spread out by this fair stream of life
Whose source I find, O Jesus, in Your Heart.
I can obtain everything when, in the mystery,
I speak heart-to-heart with my divine King.
That sweet prayer, close to the sanctuary,
> *There is my heaven!*

My heaven is to feel within me the resemblance
Of the God who created me with His powerful breath;
My heaven is to remain always in His presence,
To call Him my Father and to be His child;
In His divine arms I do not fear the storm. . . .
Total abandonment, there is my only law!
To slumber on His Heart, so close to His Face,
> *There is my heaven!*

My heaven, I have found it in the holy Trinity
That resides in my heart, prisoner that it is of love.
There, contemplating my God, I repeat to Him without fear
That I wish to serve Him and love Him without reward.
My heaven is to smile at this God whom I adore,
When He wishes to hide to test my faith;
To smile, while waiting for Him to look at me again,
> *There is my heaven!*

I THIRST FOR LOVE!
APRIL 30TH, 1896

In Your love, exiling Yourself on earth,
Divine Jesus, You sacrificed Yourself for me.
My Beloved, receive my whole life;
I want to suffer, I want to die for You.

Lord, You told me this Yourself:
We can do nothing greater
Than to die for those we love.
And my supreme love
Is You, Jesus!

It is growing late, already the day is ending:
Stay with me, heavenly Pilgrim.
With Your cross I climb the hill;
Come and guide me, Lord, on the road!

Your voice finds an echo in my soul:
I want to look like You, Lord;
Suffering, I call out for it. . . .
Your word of flame
Burns my heart!

Before entering into eternal glory
It was necessary for the God-Man to suffer.
It is by His cross that He gained the victory;
O gentle Savior, did You not tell us so?

For me, on the foreign shore,
What scorn did You not receive! . . .
I want to hide myself on earth,
To be in all things the last,
For You, Jesus.

My Beloved, Your example invites me
To bring myself low, to shun honor:
To delight You, I want to remain little;
Forgetting myself, I will charm Your Heart.

> My peace is in solitude,
> I ask nothing more.
> To please You is my only study,
>> And my blessedness
>>> Is You, Jesus!

You, the great God that the universe adores,
You live in me, a prisoner night and day;
Your gentle voice at every moment implores me,
You say continually to me, *I thirst! I thirst for love!*

> I am also Your prisoner,
> And I want to repeat in turn
> Your tender and divine prayer,
>> My Beloved, my Brother:
>>> *I thirst for love!*

I thirst for love! Fulfill my hope to overflowing:
Increase in me, Lord, Your divine fire!
I thirst for love! Very great is my suffering.
Oh, I would like to fly toward you, my God!

> Your love is my only martyrdom;
> The more I feel it burning in me,
> The More my soul desires You.
>> *Jesus, make me expire*
>>> *Out of love for You!*

Sister Thérèse of the Child Jesus
After a painting by her sister—1901

What draws me to the Homeland in heaven is the Lord's call,
the hope of finally loving Him as I have desired so much,
and the thought that I will be able to make Him loved
by a multitude of souls who will bless Him throughout eternity.

Appendices

1

"THE DIVINE PRISONER'S LITTLE FLOWER"

St. Thérèse of Lisieux's Favorite Childhood Poem

In chapter four of *The Story of a Soul*, Thérèse wrote, "'The Divine Prisoner's Little Flower' told me so many things that I was completely immersed in it. . . . I used to offer myself to Jesus to be His little flower. . . ." Here, in French and English, is the text of that poem.

LA PETITE FLEUR DU DIVIN PRISONNIER

THE DIVINE PRISONER'S LITTLE FLOWER

Entre deux froids barreaux, croissait une humble plante
Qui charmait les ennuis d'un pauvre prisonnier;
C'était le seul bonheur de son âme souffrante,
L'unique passe-temps de son triste foyer! . . .
Sous les murs ténébreux de sa sombre retraite,
Sa main l'avait plantée . . . il l'arrosait de pleurs! . . .
Et pour prix de ses soins, il voyait la pauvrette
Lui donner à l'envi ses parfums et ses fleurs. . . .

Between two cold prison bars, there grew a humble plant
That charmed away the weariness of a poor prisoner;
It was the only happiness of his suffering soul,
The only pastime of his sorrowful home! . . .
Beneath the gloomy walls of his dismal dwelling place,
His hand had planted it . . . he watered it with tears! . . .
And as a reward for his care, he saw the poor little thing
Give him unceasingly its perfumes and its flowers. . . .

Ah! mon divin Maître, au fond du tabernacle,
Depuis 1800 ans prisonnier par amour,

Oh! My divine Master, in the depths of the tabernacle,
For 1800 years a prisoner out of love,

Malgré notre froideur, par un constant miracle,

Vous avez près de nous fixé votre séjour;

Et là, plus délaissé, plus solitaire encore,

Que le pauvre captif dont je plains l'abandon,

De vos enfants pervers, votre tendresse implore

Ces cœurs dont les ingrats vous refusent le don. . . .

Hélas! Puisqu'à vous fuir, ils s'obstinent sans cesse,

Puisqu'ils vous laissent seul, ô le Dieu de mon cœur!

Abaissez par pitié les yeux sur ma bassesse,

Je serai, mon JESUS, votre petite fleur. . . .

De mon âme écoutez l'incessante prière,

C'est Vous qui l'inspirez, Seigneur, exaucez-la.

Ah! dites-moi comment, humble fleur, pour vous plaire,

Mon âme entre vos mains, sans retour s'oubliera.

Jésus

Eh! bien, c'est dans la FOI . . . c'est dans une FOI NUE . . .

Que ma main planterait cette petite fleur,

Despite our coldness, through a constant miracle,

Near us You have fixed Your dwelling place;

And there, more abandoned, even more alone

Than the poor prisoner whose neglected state I pity,

Your tenderness implores, yea, begs for the hearts

Of Your perverse children, those ingrates who refuse You this gift....

Alas! Since they never cease to flee obstinately from You,

Since they leave You all alone, O God of my heart!

Out of pity, lower Your eyes to look on my lowliness—

I will be, my JESUS, Your little flower....

Hear the unceasing prayer of my soul:

It is You who are inspiring it, Lord; grant my request.

Oh! Tell me how, humble flower that I am, in order to please You,

My soul, placed in Your hands, will forget itself, expecting nothing in return.

Jesus:

So! It is into FAITH ... it is into UNDISGUISED FAITH ...

That My hand would plant that little flower,

Qui vivant pour MOI SEUL . . . des
  hommes inconnue,
N'aurait d'autre Soleil qu'un regard
  de mon cœur.

A cette tendre fleur, je voudrais pour
  Racine,
Cette espérance en moi qui jamais ne
  faiblit;
Espérance infinie en ma Bonté
  divine . . .
Abandon de l'enfant qui sait qu'on le
  chérit. . . .

Pour Tige, il lui faudrait, sans désir et
  sans crainte
Un tranquille, un joyeux, un prompt
  acquiescement
Au plus léger appel de ma volonté
  sainte . . .
Sans hésitation . . . sans nul raisonne-
  ment.

Elle me ravirait, si, prenant pour
  Feuillage
Le mépris de l'estime et des regards
  humains,
Elle savait voiler à l'œil qui l'envisage,
Les dons qu'elle a reçus de mes divines
  mains.

Je lui voudrais pour Fleur une con-
  stante joie,
Que ne pourraient troubler ni revers
  . . . ni douleur . . .

Who, living for ME ALONE ...
  unknown and unrecognized by
  mortals,
Would have no other Sun than a
  glance from My heart.

For this tender flower, I would like
  as Root,
That hope in Me that never
  weakens;
Infinite hope in My divine
  Goodness ...
Abandonment of a child who knows
  that it is cherished....

For its Stem, it would need, without
  desire and without fear
A tranquil, a joyful, a prompt
  acquiescence
To the slightest call of My holy
  will ...
Without hesitation, without any
  reasoning.

It would delight me if, taking for its
  Leaves
Complete disregard for the esteem
  and consideration of others,
It knew how to veil, to the eye that
  beholds it,
The gifts that it has received from
  My divine hands.

I would want it to have as its Flower
  a constant joy,
That could be troubled neither by
  setbacks ... nor sorrow ...

Qui même à la souffrance, à
l'amertume en proie,
Saurait se réjouir encor de mon
bonheur.

Son Fruit enfin serait cette
vertu si pure
Qui ne voit que DIEU SEUL ... ici-
bas, comme aux cieux ...
Qui n'a plus de regard pour nulle
créature,
Qui ne cherche qu'en MOI le terme
de ses vœux. . . .

Par là de mes desseins réalisant
l'attente,
Elle aura mérité la plus douce
faveur;
Et sur mon cœur sacré, greffant mon
humble plante
En l'unissant à MOI, je ferai son
bonheur.

That even racked by suffering and
bitterness,
Would still know how to delight in
my joy.

Finally, its Fruit would be that virtue
that is so pure
That it sees GOD ALONE ... here
below, as in heaven ...
That no longer has regard for any
created thing,
That seeks in ME alone the end and
goal of its desires....

In this way, achieving the expecta-
tion of my plans,
It will have been made worthy of the
sweetest favor;
And into My sacred heart, grafting
my humble plant
By uniting it to MYSELF, I will
make its true joy.

2
IMPORTANT DATES

1873, January 2:	Birth of Marie-Françoise-Thérèse Martin
1873, January 4:	Baptism
1877, August 28:	Death of Zélie Martin, Thérèse's mother, of breast cancer
1882, October 2:	Thérèse's "second mother," her sister Pauline, enters the Carmelite convent at Lisieux.
1883, March 25:	Thérèse becomes seriously ill.
1883, May 13:	The Blessed Virgin's smile; Thérèse recovers from illness.
1884, May 8:	First Communion
1884, June 14:	Confirmation
1886, October 15:	Marie, Thérèse's eldest sister and godmother, enters Carmel.
1886, December 25:	Conversion on the Feast of the Nativity
1887, November 20:	Audience with Leo XIII
1888, April 9:	Thérèse enters Carmel.
1889, January 10:	Thérèse takes the Carmelite habit.
1890, September:	Thérèse receives a Blessing from Pope Leo XIII.
1890, September 8:	Thérèse makes her Profession (takes her vows as a nun).
1890, September 24:	Thérèse takes the veil.
1890, December:	Influenza breaks out at Carmel.
1893, February 20:	Sr. Agnes of Jesus (Thérèse's sister Pauline) is elected Prioress; the outgoing Prioress, Mother Marie de Gonzague, takes over responsibility for the Novitiate; Thérèse is assigned as her assistant in the spiritual formation of the Novices.
1894, July 29:	Death of Louis Martin, Thérèse's father
1894, September 14:	Thérèse's sister Céline enters Carmel.

1894–95, Winter: Out of obedience, Thérèse begins writing the memoirs of her childhood (Manuscript A, chapters one–eight of this edition).

1895, June 9: Thérèse offers herself to Love.

1896, March 21: Mother Marie de Gonzague is reelected Prioress; she retains oversight of the Novitiate and asks Thérèse to devote herself totally to the Novices.

1896, April 2–3: Thérèse has her first episode of hemoptysis (coughing up blood, a symptom of tuberculosis).

1896, September: Various writings (Manuscript B, chapter nine of this edition) for Sr. Marie of the Sacred Heart

1897, June: Out of obedience, Thérèse writes Manuscript C (chapters ten–eleven of this edition).

1897, September 30: Death of Sr. Thérèse of the Child Jesus of the Holy Face

1898, September 30: Publication of two thousand copies of *The Story of a Soul*

1914, June 9: Cause of Beatification introduced in Rome

1923, April 29: Beatification (Thérèse is now called "Blessed")

1925, May 17: Canonization (Thérèse is declared a Saint)

1927, December 14: Pope Pius XI proclaims Thérèse joint Patron of the Missions with St. Francis Xavier.

1956: A facsimile edition of Thérèse's manuscripts including the original, unedited version of *The Story of a Soul* is published.

1988: The Centenary Edition is published (a critical edition of Thérèse's complete works).

1992: The New Centenary Edition is published (presented to Pope John Paul II on February 18, 1993).

1997, October 19: Pope John Paul II declares St. Thérèse of Lisieux a Doctor of the Church.

ABOUT PARACLETE PRESS

WHO WE ARE

Paraclete Press is an ecumenical publisher of books and recordings on Christian spirituality. Our publishing represents a full expression of Christian belief and practice—from Catholic to Evangelical, from Protestant to Orthodox.

Paraclete Press is the publishing arm of the Community of Jesus, an ecumenical monastic community in the Benedictine tradition. As such, we are uniquely positioned in the marketplace without connection to a large corporation and with informal relationships to many branches and denominations of faith.

We like it best when people buy our books from booksellers, our partners in successfully reaching as wide an audience as possible.

WHAT WE ARE DOING
BOOKS

Paraclete Press publishes books that show the richness and depth of what it means to be Christian. Although Benedictine spirituality is at the heart of all that we do, we publish books that reflect the Christian experience across many cultures, time periods, and houses of worship.

We publish books that nourish the vibrant life of the church and its people—books about spiritual practice, formation, history, ideas, and customs.

We have several different series of books within Paraclete Press, including the best-selling Living Library series of modernized classic texts; A Voice from the Monastery—giving voice to men and women monastics about what it means to live a spiritual life today; award-winning literary faith fiction; and books that explore Judaism and Islam and discover how these faiths inform Christian thought and practice.

RECORDINGS

From Gregorian chant to contemporary American choral works, our music recordings celebrate the richness of sacred choral music through the centuries. Paraclete is proud to distribute the recordings of the internationally acclaimed choir Gloriæ Dei Cantores, who have been praised for their "rapt and fathomless spiritual intensity" by *American Record Guide,* and the Gloriæ Dei Cantores Schola, which specializes in the study and performance of Gregorian chant. Paraclete is also the exclusive North American distributor of the recordings of the Monastic Choir of St. Peter's Abbey in Solesmes, France, long considered to be a leading authority on Gregorian chant performance.

Learn more about us at our Web site:
www.paracletepress.com,
or call us toll-free at 1-800-451-5006